Crowning Glory

AMERICAN WIVES OF PRINCES AND DUKES

by Richard Jay Hutto

Henchard Press, LTD.

Publisher   Henry S. Beers
Associate Publisher   Richard J. Hutto
Executive Vice President   Robert G. Aldrich
Operations Manager   Gary G. Pulliam
Editor-in-Chief   Joni Woolf
Art Director/Designer   Julianne Gleaton
Designer   Daniel Emerson
Director of Marketing   Mary D. Robinson
   and Public Relations

Printed in the U.S.A.
Second printing

Library of Congress Control Number: 2007921747

ISBN: (10 Digit) 0972595177
       (13 Digit) 9780972595179

Henchard Press books are available at quantity discounts with bulk purchase for educational, business, or sales promotional use.
For information, please write to: Henchard Press, SunTrust Bank Building, 435 Second Street, Suite 320, Macon, GA 31201
or call 866-311-9578.

www.henchardpress.com
www.americanprincesses.com

Crowning Glory

AMERICAN WIVES OF PRINCES AND DUKES

for Katherine

"Lily's preference would have been for an English nobleman with political ambitions and vast estates; or, second choice, an Italian prince with a castle in the Apennines and an hereditary office in the Vatican. Lost causes had a romantic charm for her."

EDITH WHARTON, *THE HOUSE OF MIRTH*, 1905

"She was not fast, nor emancipated, nor crude, nor loud, and there wasn't in her, of necessity at least, a grain of the stuff of which the adventuress is made. She was simply very successful, and her success was entirely personal. She hadn't been born with the silver spoon of social opportunity; she had grasped it by honest exertion."

HENRY JAMES, *PANDORA*, 1884

I am uniquely suited to appreciate *Crowning Glory: American Wives of Princes and Dukes,* written by Richard Jay Hutto, as my father appears as one of the most notable examples of such a marriage. In essence, starting at the second half of the 19th century and extending even until today, rich American girls married impoverished titled Europeans. One imagines innocent virgins on the other side of the Atlantic sacrificed to the snobbery of their mother's newly-made millions coupled with the greed of destitute young European aristocrats and then supposes that all these unions were inevitably unhappy. Such a view is both simplistic and false.

There were happy endings such as Consuelo Vanderbilt who waited decades but finally found happiness after separating from the husband imposed by her mother and then she married the love of her life. There were also happy marriages like that of my father to Nancy Stewart. No one forced them to marry. They knew each other and deeply loved one another. My father's family cordially welcomed his wife, as she deserved, and one only has to read the pages my father devoted to his first wife in his memoirs to be convinced of the sincerity and depth of his feelings.

I have read with great interest of the other marriages chronicled here by Richard Jay Hutto. Initially I discovered there were more of these American-European unions than I had imagined and that they included many of the aristocratic families of all the European countries. The book is ablaze with riveting photographs, new characters, and interesting anecdotes. Ultimately we are able to share in an entertaining chapter of social history. The stories of how the couples met and what eventually happened to their lives is enthralling.

Despite protestations to the contrary, Americans have always been fascinated with titles of royalty and nobility. The best colonial families were only too happy to offer their daughters as ladies-in-waiting to the wives of royal governors. One early governor of New York was Lord Cornbury, eldest son of the Earl of Clarendon, who was so proud of his resemblance to his first cousin, Queen Anne, that he called attention to it by sometimes dressing in his wife's clothes. At the end of his term he was so deeply in debt that he languished in prison until coming into his father's title. Perhaps it was a harbinger of the role that money was to play in Anglo-American relations and how liberating was the elusive title.

General George Washington's third-in-command was Major General William Alexander. Although a Scottish court ruled him the nearest heir to the titles of the Earl of Stirling, the House of Lords refused to give him a seat in the chamber. That did not prevent, however, his being called "Lord Stirling" by everyone in the colonies, including his commanding general. He married Sarah Livingston, whose family owned more land than any other family in the colony and their daughter, "Lady Kitty," was given away at her marriage by

Washington, whose personal chaplain performed the ceremony.

Nor did a yearning for democracy preclude an affection for titles. In 1798 Sally McKean, daughter of the governor of Pennsylvania (and also a signer of the Declaration of Independence) and a close friend of eventual First Lady Dolley Madison, married the Marquess de Casa Irujo, Spain's minister to the United States. Their son would serve as prime minister of Spain and succeed as the Duke of Sotomayor.

John Jay, the first U.S. Chief Justice (his wife was another member of the celebrated Livingston family), had two granddaughters who successively married the 6th Viscount Exmouth, who was a naturalized U.S. citizen. The eldest son was born and educated in the United States, and fought in the Spanish-American War before reclaiming British nationality and succeeding as the 7th Viscount Exmouth.

The last-living signer of the Declaration of Independence was Charles Carroll of Carrollton, Maryland, whose three Caton granddaughters married the 7th Duke of Leeds, the 8th Baron Stafford, and the 1st Marquess Wellesley, brother of the Great Duke of Wellington. Mary Caton, the daughter who married Wellesley, had first been married to Robert Patterson, brother of the famous beauty Betsey Patterson who

The American reading public kept abreast of which heiress was rumored for which titles and popular cartoonists made great fun of the exchange.

was to become so celebrated for marrying Jerome Bonaparte, brother of Napoleon I and the future king of Westphalia. Mary, Dowager Marchioness Wellesley, would end her days in a grace-and-favor apartment at Hampton Court, a gift to her from Queen Victoria, whose reign would witness the apex of American and British marriages.

The opening of the floodgates came in the 1870s. Oscar Wilde (whose brother married an American heiress) declared that "the American invasion has done English society a great deal of good. American women are bright, clever, and wonderfully cosmopolitan." It was Jennie Jerome's marriage in 1874 to Lord Randolph

Left: Sir Winston Churchill with his son, Randolph, and grandson, Winston.

Right: Winston's American mother, Lady Randolph Churchill, was one of the three Jerome sisters known as "the Beautiful [Jennie], the Good [Clara], and the Witty [Leonie]." Leonie would marry Sir John Leslie, 2nd Baronet.

Churchill, brother of the 8th Duke of Marlborough, that really began the onslaught of trans-continental alliances. Although there had been others before her, she was the first to be widely accepted into society and to earn the approval of the popular Prince of Wales (later Edward VII). Her famous son, Winston Churchill, would be taunted years later for being a "half-blood."

Consuelo Yznaga's marriage two years later to the future 8th Duke of Manchester confirmed the trend. In 1895 nine American heiresses married titled Brits including a duke, an earl, and three barons.

But the marriage market soon became glutted with heiresses. The British system allowed only the eldest son to inherit a title (other than a "Lord" in front of the first name of sons of dukes and marquesses) while the European system was much more liberal in sharing titles with sons. For Catholic American girls (or those who were willing to become Catholic), and those who wanted an immediate title without waiting for a father-in-law to die, the hunting was better on the continent. But if the British system did not proffer titles to younger sons, primogeniture did at least concentrate family money on the eldest. As Honore' de Balzac wrote in *The Ball at Sceaux*, "The wealthiest member of our peerage has not half the income of the least rich lord in the English Upper Chamber. Thus all the French peers are on the lookout for great heiresses for their sons, wherever they may meet with them. The necessity in which they find themselves of marrying for money will certainly exist for at least two centuries."

For the truly adventurous, there was always Russia, although it was a much higher mountain to scale. One American divorcee, Harriet Blackford (who took the nom de plume Fanny Lear), lived with and expected to become the wife of Grand Duke Nicholas, nephew of Tsar Alexander II and grandson of Tsar Nicholas I. When he formally requested of his uncle the permission to marry Harriet, he was sent to the battlefront and Harriet was arrested and ordered out of the country. They would never see one another again and she would die alone at thirty-eight while the grand duke was declared insane and banished by his family to Tashkent.

Although not every match was an exchange of cash for titles, there can be no doubt that the chief attraction was the mighty dollar. The beautiful Minnie Stevens was first engaged to the Duc de Guiche, eldest son of the Duc de Gramont, who sent an agent to New York to inquire into the Stevens's finances. When it was learned that her dowry was not as large as she had led others to believe, the engagement was broken. As Lady Waldegrave wrote to Lady Strachey, "I must say I think this business very cruel, but at the same time I can't help thinking she deserved a snubbing as she told me she had £20,000 a year and would have more and she told me that sum in dollars as well, so there is no mistaking the amount." The Duc de Guiche wisely chose the financial advantages offered by a de Rothschild marriage

while Minnie contented herself with Colonel Arthur Paget who was later knighted, at least giving Minnie the comfort of having "Lady" in front of her name. In time Minnie would introduce Consuelo Vanderbilt to her husband, the 9th Duke of Marlborough, for which she was probably compensated.

What would prompt a self-made millionaire to part with so much of his hard-earned money for the sake of daughter's marriage to a royal or noble husband? Very often it was a wife who had dreams of grandeur or, far more often, one who had been socially snubbed at home and decided to try her luck abroad. There was something cleansing about the miles of ocean between the two continents. As Ruth Brandon has written of the era, "All Americans were more or less equally unacceptable. One might therefore pick the richest without compunction."

A peer's paid advertisement in New York's *Daily World* in 1901 sought an heiress wife, stipulating that, "her age and looks are immaterial, but her character must be irreproachable," and even included the amount to be paid up front as well as an admonition that she should also have "sufficient wealth besides to keep up the rank." The practice became so commonplace that Virginia Cowles wrote, "To the aristocracy it became an opportunity for profitable matrimonial alliances which resulted in a general refurbishing of family coffers."

While some were considered "love matches," there was no harm in falling in love with a girl who also had money. Department store heiress Mary Leiter was the best thing that ever happened to her husband, George Curzon, the future Marquess Curzon of Kedleston, with

Left: George Curzon, "a most superior person," became Marquess Curzon of Kedleston and made great use of his wife's fortune. Right: His American wife, Mary Leiter, with their two daughters. After her death Curzon married another American.

Katherine, to the Duke of the Abruzzi was followed in the newspapers as assiduously as that of today's media stars. The duke, a famous mountain-climbing explorer, was a son of the Duke of Aosta who was King of Spain during the 1870's civil wars, while his grandfather was Italy's King Victor Emanuele II. During protracted negotiations with both families, there was even a call by the Albanian people that the duke become their king and make Katherine their queen. But the senator was highly insulted when he learned that the duke's family might not approve of a marriage to his daughter, publicly stating, "Seeing that the Duke does not want to come to this country and work like any other American gentleman, I would prefer that my daughter marry a Randolph County schoolmaster." He intercepted Katherine's

whom she was completely besotted. Her money allowed his brilliance to be displayed to a wider audience. When he was appointed viceroy of India, as Vicereine Mary became the highest-ranking woman in that country other than the queen. Still, several duchesses refused to curtsey to her at the coronation durbar in 1903. When Mary died in 1906 after becoming ill in India, her husband married another American.

Some fathers were unwilling to pay the price asked for their daughter's elevation to a title, among them the very wealthy U. S. Senator Stephen B. Elkins. The engagement of his beautiful daughter,

mail and returned a ruby ring to the duke without showing it to his daughter. So strongly was he publicly condemned that his budding campaign for the Republican presidential nomination was ended. For his part, the duke of the Abruzzi never married while the twice-married Katherine stipulated in her will that she be buried in a bracelet given to her by the duke.

Finally, why were there only a handful of marriages of wealthy American men to titled European brides? Chiefly because marriage almost never offered the husband a title (for one exception see the entry for Cecilia Ulman). One of the few marriages of a wealthy

Left: Sumner Moore Kirby was an heir to the Woolworth's fortune and died in a Nazi concentration camp.
Right: His wife, Princess Leonida Bagration, by her second marriage became mother of the claimant to the Russian throne.

daughter, Grand Duchess Maria, is widely regarded as the current claimant to the Russian throne. The other possible claimant, Prince Dimitri Ilyinsky, is the grandson of American Audrey Emery.

We are not likely to see such a flurry of international marriages again. Admittedly they still happen on occasion, such as the daughters of duty-free magnate Robert Miller, one of whom is the mother of the heir to the non-existent Greek throne. But, as Consuelo Vanderbilt's husband, the 9th Duke of Marlborough, wrote, such unions "no longer appeal with the same force and vigour to the American feminine mind as they did in the closing years of the Victorian era."

husband was that of Sumner Moore Kirby (1895 – 1945), an heir to the Woolworth department store fortune, who married in 1934 Princess Leonida, daughter of Prince George Bagration of Moukhrani. They met in Nice where both were learning French. The couple divorced in 1937 and he remained in Nice where he was captured by the invading Nazis and placed in a concentration camp for the crime of "plutocracy." Although an imprisoned doctor did his best to prevent Kirby's being sent to hard labor in the mines, Kirby died in camp at Leau bei Bernburg on 7 April 1945. His former wife, Princess Leonida, married in 1948 Grand Duke Vladimir of Russia and their

On the whole, the exchange of dollars for titles was crassly commercial. Of course there were exceptions, but they prove the rule. As U. S. Senator Chauncey Depew observed of the appeal of an American heiress at the height of the phenomenon, "She gives him more pleasure in one hour, at a dinner or ball, than he thought the universe could produce in a whole life-time. Speedily he comes to the conclusion that he must marry her or die. He knows nothing of business, and to support his estate requires an increased income. The American girl whom he gets acquainted with has that income, so in marrying her he goes to heaven and gets – the earth."

American Women

First to marry a future King – Betsey Patterson (King Jerome Bonaparte of Westphalia)

First to marry a King Consort/King Regent – Elise Hensler (King Ferdinand II of Portugal)

First to marry a Crown Prince – Hope Cooke (Chogyal Palden of Sikkim)

First to become a Queen – Hope Cooke (Gyalmo of Sikkim)

First to marry a Reigning Prince – Alice Heine (Prince Albert of Monaco)

First to marry a Reigning King – Lisa Halaby (King Hussein of Jordan)

First to be mother of a Prince Imperial – Alice Green (Prince Augustin of Mexico)

First to marry a former Prince Imperial - Mary Louise Kearney (Prince Augustin of Mexico)

First to marry a Maharaja – Nancy Ann Miller (Sir Yeshwant Rao II Holkar XIV Bahadur, Maharaja of Indore)

First to marry a formerly reigning King – Wallis Simpson (Duke of Windsor, formerly King Edward VIII of Great Britain)

First to be created a Royal Princess in her own right – Nancy Stewart Leeds (Princess Anastasia of Greece by King George II of Greece)

First to be recognized as a Princess in her own right by another sovereign – Anita Stewart (Princess de Braganza by Emperor Franz Josef I of Austria)

First to be mother of a Queen – Gladys Steuart (Queen Geraldine of the Albanians)

First Princess to be born in the White House – Princess Cantacuzene (Julia Dent Grant)

First to be buried with a royal family – Peggy Green, Princess Viggo of Denmark

First for whom a Prince renounced his title to marry – Mary Esther Lee (Prince Friedrich of Schleswig-Holstein)

First whose son succeeded as head of a mediatized royal house – Nancy Leishman, Duchess of Croy

First whose grandchildren would be in the line of succession to the British throne (if they were not Catholic) – Elsie Moore, Duchess of Torlonia

First whose children were allowed princely titles – Elizabeth Reid Rogers, Princess Christian of Hesse-Phillipsthal-Barchfeld

First to marry princely brothers – Louise Astor Van Alen (Mdivanis)

First to marry a French royal duke – Peggy Watson (the Duc de Nemours, later Duc de Vendome et d'Alencon)

Last Crown Princess of Korea – Julia Mullock

Crowning Glory

AMERICAN WIVES OF PRINCES AND DUKES

Dorothy Adriance, born 5 March 1893, was the eldest child of William Allen Adriance and Mary Horton Adriance of Poughkeepsie, New York. Her father was a partner in the harvester manufacturing firm of Adriance, Platt and Company in Poughkeepsie that was sold in 1913 to the Moline Plow Company of Illinois. At the time of the sale, his firm boasted 1,250 employees and was the most successful company in the city. Moline Plow over-extended itself and was bankrupted by the refusal of the new Soviet revolutionary government to pay for hundreds of plows it purchased and the company's Poughkeepsie plant closed in 1923. The Adriances kept an apartment in New York City on Riverside Drive and gave a dance at Sherry's in December of 1911 to present their daughter to society.

Dorothy was touring Europe with her mother during the winter of 1923 when she met **Stefano, 6th Prince of Cellamare, 10th Prince of Villa, 17th Prince of Santobuono, 10th Duke of Gesso, 11th Duke of San Elia, 17th Duke of Castel di Sangro, 7th Marquess of Alfedena**, born in Capri, 6 March 1885, died 26 October 1965. They were married on Palm Sunday on the isle of Capri in 1923. In August of 1924 the young couple arrived in New York to spend six months visiting her parents. At the time she disembarked Dorothy was wearing a string of three hundred pearls said to have been a wedding present from her husband. In 1937 she led a group of women in New York City sponsoring a benefit theatre party for the Charities Aid Association. She took a home in Lenox, Massachusetts, for the 1940 season and entertained there. Stefano, who was the seventh of fifteen children but the eldest son, was a grandson of Giuseppe, 5th Prince of Cellamare of

Dorothy Adriance's father was Poughkeepsie's largest employer. After he and his partner sold out, his company was bankrupted by the new Soviet regime.

the 9th line of the Caracciolo family. He succeeded his uncle in 1905 as Prince of Cellamare but there were no children and the title passed to a cousin, the current (9th) Prince of Cellamare, who has only a daughter and a sister. Another cousin of the 10th line of the Caracciolo family, Filippo, 8th Prince of Castagneto and 3rd Duke of Melito, married American **Margaret Clarke.**

In later years Dorothy, Princess di Cellamare, kept a home in Lumberville, Pennsylvania, where her mother died in 1941, having gained notice as a painter of landscapes working from her home in Ogunquit, Maine. The princess also had a home in New York City and, late in life, another in Nantucket. She had a brother, William, who was vice president and art director of Brook, Smith, French & Dorrance art agency in New York City. The Adriance Memorial Library in Poughkeepsie is named in honor of her family.

Estella Dolores Alexander, daughter of Lyman and Sophie Alexander, was born in Sonoma, California, 18 August 1872, and reared in San Francisco. She first married Sidney B. Veit of Chicago, who managed the Paris office of his father's millinery importing firm based in New York City where his father lived on Fifth Avenue. At the time of their marriage she was reportedly a chorus girl. After they divorced in Paris in January of 1904 Veit brought suit against her seeking to recover more than $30,000 of insurance proceeds she collected on his policies. She married in Chicago, 14 August 1906 **Robert, Prince de Broglie,** born in Paris, 23 Nov 1880, died Coyoacan, Mexico, 24 Feb 1956, grandson of Albert, 3rd Duc de Broglie, 4th Prince de Broglie. He had previously been married in 1901 to the literary Baroness Deslandes, who was fourteen years older than he and the divorced wife of Count Fleury. The baroness and the prince were divorced the next year and his father accepted his repentant son back into the family, although a religious divorce was out of the question in the strictly-Catholic de Broglie family.

Estella met the prince in Paris and, after their marriage in Chicago, his wealthy and influential father had it declared void by a French court because of his disapproval. The court found that no notice of the marriage had been posted and that the groom had not secured his parents' consent. In the year of their marriage Estella sang in New York City while her husband conducted the orchestra. In 1907 she appeared in *George and the Dragon* at Edinburgh's King's Theatre. The couple was then remarried in Paris, 10 December 1907. Estella, a lyric soprano who sang on the stage under the name of Manitza, was sometimes accompanied by her husband. They had a daughter, Jassemonde, and Estella returned to the stage at Ostend.

Prince Robert de Broglie's grandmother was the beautiful Pauline, Princess de Broglie, painted here by Ingres in 1853. She had already died by the time her husband became the influential French ambassador in London.

The prince eventually yielded to his family's wishes and left his wife and child, and she alleged that she had been supporting him financially while he was "idling away his time at Chamonix and other resorts." She brought a divorce action against him in 1908 seeking financial support for herself and their daughter and the divorce was granted in 1909. She then refused the sixty dollars per month she had been awarded as alimony. In 1913 his family brought a legal action against her to prevent her using the de Broglie name on posters and programs for her performance at the Imperial Theatre in the Champs Elysee. In 1929 she returned to New York City and was living at the Hotel Lombardy when she petitioned to regain her American citizenship.

The prince married two more wives but had no children. Estella, formerly Princess Robert de Broglie, returned to France and died in an internment camp at Drancy, 27 March 1944. Their daughter, Jassemonde Estelle, served as a French army officer in Viet Nam and died unmarried in 1981. Prince Robert's first cousin, Prince Louis (1892 – 1987, later Duc de Broglie), won the 1929 Nobel Prize in Physics for having postulated the wave nature of electrons, one of the bases of quantum physics. In 1930, Prince Robert de Broglie's mother, who possessed one of the largest fortunes in France, married Prince Louis Fernando de Bourbon-Orleans, paternally a great-grandson of King Fernando VII of Spain and maternally a grandson of Queen Isabella II of Spain. The bride, who was thirty-two years older than her groom (who was eight years younger than her own son), lived another thirteen years, outlived by her husband by only two. The groom's mother, the very social Infanta Eulalia, counted many Americans among her friends and was often a visitor to the U.S. and officially opened Chicago's Columbian Exposition of 1893. She cut short a visit to Mrs. Potter Palmer because she was only "the wife of an innkeeper." Eulalia's brother, the Duke of Galleria, married Princess Beatrice of Edinburgh, a granddaughter of Queen Victoria. Eulalia's nephew, Spain's King Alfonso XIII, married Princess Ena, another granddaughter of Queen Victoria, and they barely escaped a bloody assassination attempt on their wedding day.

Josephine Angela, born San Francisco, 24 August 1888, daughter of Joseph Angela and Elizabeth Mary Hinton Angela, married in Paris, 18 November 1940, as his second wife, **Louis Emmanuel, 14th Duc d'Uzes, 15th Count of Crussol,** first duke and peer of France, born Paris, 15 September 1871, died Neuilly, 28 September 1943. He succeeded his brother, Jacques, in 1893. His first wife had been Therese d'Albert de Luynes, by whom he had two children, including his son who predeceased him. His grandson, Emmanuel, succeeded as **15th Duc d'Uzes** and married two Americans, **Carolyn Baily Brown** and **Margaret Bedford,** but had only daughters and his cousin succeeded him as 16th Duke. The boy's mother, although born in London, was an American citizen when she fled with him just three days before the Nazis reached Paris. They traveled on the Exochorda, accommodating forty more passengers than the ship was equipped for, arriving at New York City after stopping in Bermuda where the ship was boarded and three German passengers were taken into custody. Her father-in-law, the duke, refused to leave Paris and his American wife remained with him. The duke's mother, the famous dowager duchess, was active in politics, having contributed three million francs to Boulanger in an effort to revive the French monarchy.

She was also a sculptor of note as well as a poet, novelist, and dramatist, and served as president of the Lyceum of France. Josephine, as Duchess d'Uzes, remained in Paris with her husband during the German occupation. He died in 1943 and she spent part of the occupation in a German prison camp. After the liberation of Paris

Alice Astor was one of her day's greatest heiresses. Her dashing husband had first been a son-in-law of Russia's Tsar Alexander II.

Above: Alice was reared by her beautiful but distant mother in a palatial mansion on Fifth Avenue. Right: John Jacob "Jack" Astor, IV perished on the *Titanic* but his much-younger pregnant wife was saved.

she received a citation from the U. S. government for her Red Cross activities. Josephine returned to the U. S. in 1947 and died of a heart ailment at eighty at the Dresden-Madison Nursing Home in New York City in September of 1966.

(Ava) **Alice Muriel Astor,** born New York City, 27 July 1902, died New York City, 19 July 1956, was the daughter of John Jacob Astor IV, "Colonel Jack," who died on the *Titanic* (his pregnant second wife, who was younger than Jack's son, was rescued). A society stalwart named Hatch was widely rumored at the time to be Alice's real father. Alice's mother was the famously beautiful Ava Willing of Philadelphia who

later married England's Lord Ribblesdale, whom King Edward VII nicknamed "The Ancestor" because he looked so much like an old master. Alice married in London, 24 July 1924 (divorced 1932), as his second wife, **Serge, Prince Obolensky-Neledinsky-Meletsky,** born Tsarskoie-Selo, 20 September 1890, died Grosse Pointe, Michigan, 29 September 1978. Prince Serge's first wife had been Catharina, Princess Yurievsky, daughter of Tsar Alexander II of Russia. Serge was a decorated soldier for England in World War I, then fought for the U. S. in World War II as a paratrooper, making his first five jumps at the age of fifty-three. He became a hotel official in New York City where he was a familiar sight at the St. Regis, the Plaza, and the Sherry-Netherland. In 1958 he wrote his memoirs, *One Man In His Time,* in which he described Alice on their first meeting as "twenty, brilliantly educated, and had the darkest hair I'd ever seen - she looked like an Egyptian high priestess as it swirled about her shoulders in great blue-black folds … she had a fantastic knowledge of art and literature, music - anything you could think of - and she combined this with a fierce and wild determination to win at golf."

Alice was one of the first four people to enter the tomb of King Tutankhamen and believed herself to be a reincarnation of an Egyptian royal. Her mother strongly opposed Alice's marriage to a penniless prince, preferring her candidates, Lord Ivor Churchill (second son of the American Duchess of Marlborough, Consuelo Vanderbilt), Lord Cochrane, and wealthy American Bob Huntington, brother of Helen Astor. But Alice's will matched her mother's and, once Alice reached

Ava Astor was a celebrated beauty. When she married Lord Ribblesdale in the same year in which his horse won the Derby, a friend telegraphed him, "Only heaven left."

the age of twenty-one and came into her own inheritance, the marriage took place in London with Prince Paul of Serbia as best man. She wore diamond earrings that Marie Antoinette had sewn into her corsage when she fled to her eventual death - a gift from Alice's brother, Vincent, who also deeded her a ninety-nine-acre part of his estate at Ferncliff in New York where she built a house for herself and Serge. When Vincent sailed home from Germany on his new 2,000-ton yacht, the *Nourmahal,* in 1928, his brother-in-law, Serge, was part of the all-male party.

Alice and Serge divorced after eight years (Serge retained custody of their son while Alice kept the daughter, who was born after their divorce proceedings began) but remained friends and he married third, at Arlington, Virginia, 3 June 1971, **Marylin Fraser Wall**, born Detroit, Michigan, 13 August 1929. Alice married three more times and professed to love each of her husbands. The second was Raimund von Hofmannsthal, son of the Austrian poet and dramatist who wrote the libretto for several Strauss operas including *Der Rosenkavalier,* while the next was a soldier, Philip Harding, whom she married in 1940. During the war years Alice entertained lavishly in London and frequently hosted a Bohemian set of friends including Edith and Osbert Sitwell, Aldous Huxley, and Frederick Ashton, and was a generous patron of Sadler's Wells Ballet Company. Her final husband, married in 1946, was David Pleydell-Bouverie, grandson of the 5th Earl of Radnor. Alice and Serge's son, Prince Ivan, married Americans **Claire McGinnis** (who was excommunicated from the Catholic Church for her marriage in a Russian ceremony) and **Mary Elizabeth Morris,** while the second husband of their daughter, Princess Sylvia, was **Prince Azamat K. Guirey** (descended from the Khans of Crimea).

The day after Alice died in 1956 at her Ferncliff home, two extortionists appeared at the door of her brother, Vincent, demanding money to keep silent their charge that Alice had died by suicide. Vincent ordered an immediate autopsy that confirmed she died naturally of a heart attack. Alice rewrote her will the day before she died in 1956 but her attorney misplaced it for several months. Her estate totaled $5,305,000. The trust fund she had inherited upon reaching her age of majority was $5 million. Alice's mother, Lady Ribblesdale, lived until 1958 and left $25,000 to her son and the remainder of her $3 million estate went to Alice's children, Ivan Obolensky of New York City, Sylvia Von Hofmannsthal Guirey of New York City, Romana von Hofmannsthal McEwen of New York City, and Emily Harding. Prince Serge Obolensky outlived his former wife by twenty-two years, dying in 1978. He walked to work well into his eighties and his morning calisthenics always included standing on his head. Even at that advanced age, he was said to possess "a charming, lip-licking way of looking at a woman."

Margaret "Peggy" Wright Bedford, daughter of Margaret Wright Stewart Bedford and Frederick Henry Bedford (he was a director of Standard Oil of New Jersey), was born in New York City, 18 October 1932 and made her debut there in 1951. She married first in New York City, 14 April 1951, Thomas M. Bancroft Jr. of New York City, and they had one daughter, Margaret "Muffie" Bancroft, before divorcing in Alabama, 10 May 1960. She married second, at Paris, 29 December 1960, **Prince and Duke Charles d'Arenberg,** born Paris, 27 May 1905, died Paris, 11 June 1967, son of Prince and Duke Pierre d'Arenberg, and grandson of the 6th Duke of Arenberg. They had one son, Prince Pierre d'Arenberg, born at Bern, 7 October 1961, who was married in a spectacular society wedding in 1997 to Silvia de Castellane. Several months after her husband's death, Peggy met Emmanuel de Crussol, the **15th Duke d'Uzes, 16th Count of Crussol,** the premier duke and peer of France, whose first wife had been American **Carolyn Baily Brown** (later Mrs. Geoffrey C. Doyle, by whom he had two daughters; at his death in 1999 he was succeeded by a first cousin). They were married at Marrakesh, 5 July1968, (she was the second of his three wives). The bride's witness was the Maharaja of Jaipur, the Indian Ambassador in Madrid, and the only other guest was the French consul at Marrakesh. The bride and groom were the guests of his close friend the Countess de Breteuil, who lived at Villa Taylor in Marrakesh, a palatial home built in 1923 by the Taylors of Rhode Island, who came to Morocco on a steam yacht, and hosted such guests as Rita Hayworth, Charlie Chaplin, Winston Churchill, and Franklin D. Roosevelt.

Some news reports referred to Peggy as "the Double Duchess" but, in her first husband's family, only the head of the house was usually referred to as "Duke" while the other sons were called "Prince." The Duke and Duchess d'Uzes were estranged during the last year of her

Peggy Bedford married both a prince and a duke and was sometimes referred to as a "Double Duchess."

Jennie Berry purchased historic Nemi Castle and offered to donate it to the Vatican but died before her plans were accomplished.

life and she was killed in an auto accident in France returning from a party just before her forty-fifth birthday on 16 October 1977. Her funeral was held in New York City's St. James' Episcopal Church. The Duke of Uze's grandmother was the famous Dowager Duchess who was active in politics, having contributed three million francs to Boulanger in an effort to revive the French monarchy. She was also a sculptor of note as well as a poet, novelist, and dramatist, and served as president of the Lyceum of France. Peggy Bedford's husband's grandfather, from whom he inherited the titles, married as his second wife American **Josephine Angela.** Peggy's daughter by her first marriage, Muffie Bancroft, married C. M. Amory Jr., then W. Stephen Murray.

Eugenia "Jennie" Enfield Berry, born 1863/1870, daughter of cotton broker Col. Thomas A. Berry of the Confederate Army and of Frances Margaret Rhea Berry, was born and reared on Oak Hill Plantation near Rome, Georgia. She married first Henry Bruton of Nashville, Tennessee, former head of the American Snuff Company. He died in 1893, leaving her a wealthy widow and she married in Washington, 2 March 1901, **Prince Enrico Ruspoli,** born in Rome, 25 July 1878. He was a son of Prince Luigi Ruspoli, whose brother, Paolo, married Americans **Florence York** and **Rosalie van Zandt.** The year of Jennie's birth varied widely but the bride was as much as fourteen years older than her second husband. Prince Enrico died 4 December 1909 and his widow was involved in protracted litigation against the Italian government over the historic castle of Nemi, about twenty miles south of Rome, which she purchased from the Orsini family. She sought compensation for damages done to the medieval castle both by squatters and by occupation troops during the Second World War. She contributed heavily to Catholic causes and had promised to donate Nemi castle to the Vatican for an American-Italian educational institution if her claims were settled. At the time of her death, they were not. She was twice decorated by the Holy See for her work in philanthropy, receiving the Cross of Benemerenti and an order Pro Ecclesia et Pontifice. She also supported the Berry schools in Georgia that were founded by her sister, Martha. Automaker Henry Ford, who was a close friend of Martha Berry and a patron of her school, accompanied Eugenia, Princess Ruspoli, to her sister's funeral.

The Princess died at her home at 1020 Fifth Avenue in New York City at the age of eighty-one in 1951, leaving an adopted daughter, Maria Theresa, Princess Alexis Droutzkoy. Many exceptional examples of Princess Ruspoli's furnishings are now in the Martha Berry Museum in Rome, Georgia. In 1928 her niece, **Marian Berry,** was married at Princess Ruspoli's villa in Rome to **Sigismondo, Prince di Capagnano.** The aunt had promised her niece an annual financial settlement of 120,000 lire, a promise the niece registered at the U. S. Consulate in Rome. When the aunt ended the payments the following year, she was sued by her niece who, in 1933, won a court case ordering full payment with interest. Her aunt was ordered to pay 590,000 lire immediately and to continue the annual payments.

Marian Berry, niece of American Jennie Berry, Princess Ruspoli, born Oak Hill, Georgia, 9 September 1901, married at Nemi 16 July 1928, **Sigismondo, Prince di Campagnano,** born Rome, 12 December 1894, died Rome, 24 December 1982, who succeeded his father in the additional titles. He was the only son of Ludovico, 8th Prince Chigi-Albani della Rovere, 8th Prince di Farnese and di Campagnano, 4th Prince di Soriano, 8th Duke of Ariccia and di Formello, Marchese di Magliano Pecoraeccio, and his wife, Antoinette, Princess of Sayn-Wittgenstein-Sayn. Prince Sigismondo's father was the Grand Master of the Order of Malta. Marian and Sigismondo were married at her aunt's chateau in Rome and immediately afterwards were received in private by

Pope Pius who imparted the apostolic benediction. They lived in Rome and had a son, Prince Agostino, born at Ariccia in 1929, and a daughter, Princess Francesca, born at Arricia in 1933. His grandfather, Mario, 6th Prince Chigi-Albani, Marshal of the Conclave, was convicted in 1900 of unlawfully selling out of Italy the valuable Botticelli Madonna, which had been in the family art gallery for more than a century. He was sentenced to pay a fine of $68,000 and it was some time before the picture reappeared in the Chigi gallery. Marian and Sigismondo's son, Prince Agostino, succeeded as 10th Prince of Farnese, Prince of Campagnano, Prince of Soriano, Duke of Ariccia, Duke of Formello, Marquess of Magliano Pecorareccio, etc., and remained unmarried until his death in July of 2002. He was succeeded by his only male second cousin who has a son.

Florence Binney, born in Boston, 4 February 1865, was a daughter of William Greene Binney. Her grandfather was the naturalist Dr. Amos Binney who founded the Boston Society of Natural History. He was the nation's leading authority on the subject of land mollusks and used his own funds to hire artists to draw and create plates so that the data could be published and shared. His son, William Greene Binney (Florence's father), continued his work and distinguished himself as a conchologist. William and his father were responsible for assembling and donating the collection of American shells at the Harvard Museum. Florence Binney first married before 1887 Albert Alexander Kingsland, a son of Ambrose C. Kingland, the mayor of New York City who first conceived and set aside land for Central Park. Florence and her first husband had a son, Albert Alexander Kingsland, in 1887. He lived near Genoa, where he was called Alessandro, and had problems in the 1960s relating to his growing marijuana on his estate.

After Florence and her first husband divorced, he married Jennie

Florence Binney's first father-in-law conceived and set aside land for New York City's Central Park. She was later the Princess di Camporeale.

Travis and died at Washington's Willard Hotel in 1917. His nephew, Walter Kingsland, married in 1928 as her second husband, Princess Marie-Louise d'Orleans, daughter of the Duke de Vendome and granddaughter of the King of Belgium. After Florence's divorce from Albert Kingsland she then married in Burlington, New Jersey, 6 September 1888, **Pietro, 7th Prince di Camporeale, Duke of Adragna, Marquis di Alvatilla, Marquis di Sambuca, Baron di San Giacomo, Signor di Macellaro, Pietralunga, Sparacia, Dammusi, and Mortilli.** born Naples, 26 April 1852, died Rome, 30 April 1918. Florence and her second husband lived at the Villa Camporeale in Palermo and had a daughter, Maria-Anna, born at Rome, 5 July 1895, who received authorization on 15 April 1920 to succeed to her father's titles. Maria-Anna Beccadelli di Bologna, Princess di Camporeale, married 20 March 1920 Filiberto Sallier de La Tour, Prince di Castelcicala (who inherited the title from his mother), and had a daughter who died young as well as a son, Pietro Paolo, born 29 January 1928, who married Costanza Mastrogiovanni Tasca. The son and his wife had Filiberto, Ariane, and Gherardo. In 1920 the by-then widowed Florence and her son, Alberto Alexander Kingsland, traveled on the *Patria* from Palermo to New York City. The Camporeale family is extinct in the male line but Florence's grandson, Paolo, is the Prince of Castelcicala and Duke of Calvello. Florence, Princess di Camporeale, died on 3 January 1944 and is buried in Rome.

Lida Lacey Bloodgood, born New York City, 2 February 1923, daughter of John von Schaick Bloodgood and Lida Louisa Fleitmann Bloodgood, married Rome, 8 January 1947, **Prince Dominik Radziwill,** born Balic, 23 January 1911, died Geneva, 19 Nov 1976. Lida's mother was an award-winning cross-country rider who was crushed under her horse in 1915 while competing at Piping Rock. She suffered double fractures of her legs but the next year she was chosen as the best cross-country rider at the Meadow Brook Hounds. The bride's maternal grandmother was Lida Heinze Fleitmann, who wrote several books about horses and was the sister of F. Augustus Heinze, who became the dominant figure in Montana copper mining. He arrived in New York City in 1906 with a verdict settlement of $15 million from Amalgamated Copper and purchased controlling interest in the Mercantile National Bank of which he became president. He was eventually sued for malfeasance by Edwin Gould, who won a verdict for $1.2 million shortly before Heinze's death. Prince Dominick's mother, Renata, was an Archduchess of Austria, and his father, Prince Hieronymus, died in a prison camp in Alezewskoye in 1945.

Prince Dominick's first wife, whom he married in 1938 and divorced in 1946, was Princess Eugenie of Greece and Denmark, daughter of Princess Marie Bonaparte, granddaughter of King George I of the Hellenes, and a first cousin of Prince Philip, Duke of Edinburgh. By her he had a son and a daughter. Lida and Prince Dominick had three daughters, one of whom married Don Antonio of the Princes di Paterno while another married Prince Innocenzo Odescalchi.

(Caroline) Lee Bouvier, born New York City, 3 March 1933, was a daughter of John Vernou Bouvier III and Janet Lee Bouvier (later Mrs. Hugh D. Auchincloss) and sister of Jacqueline Bouvier Kennedy Onassis. She attended Miss Porter's School in Connecticut, then Sarah Lawrence College. She married first, in 1953, Michael Temple Canfield. He was rumored in a small royal circle to be an illegitmate son of Prince George, Duke of Kent, and strongly resembled his purported uncle, the then-Prince of Wales (later King Edward VIII/ Duke of Windsor). Another rumor had him as a son of the diplomat Lord Acton. Canfield was adopted by Cass Canfield, senior London editor of Harper & Row, who moved among the British social circle centered upon the Royal sons. The younger Canfield served in the U. S. Marines and was seriously wounded in the Iwo Jima landing. He graduated from Harvard in 1951 then served as private secretary to John Hay Whitney and Winthrop Aldrich when they were the U. S. Ambassadors to Great Britian. The new Mrs. Canfield joined her husband at his London post after their marriage. She obtained a civil divorce in 1958 and there were no children. Canfield then married Laura Charteris, grand-daughter of the 9th Earl of Wemyss, whose first and second husbands were the 2nd Viscount Long and the 3rd Earl of Dudley (Dudley's next wife was Grace Kolin of the shipping family who then married Prince

President John F. Kennedy and his family on Christmas Day, 1962, in Palm Beach. Mrs. Kennedy's sister, Lee, and husband, Prince Stanislaus Radziwill, are on the right with their children.

Stanislaus Radziwill, future husband of Lee Bouvier Canfield; after Laura Charteris's marriage to Michael Canfield, she married the 10th Duke of Marlborough, son of Consuelo Vanderiblt, seven weeks before his death). Canfield died at the age of forty-three after suffering a heart attack on a BOAC flight from New York to London.

On 19 March 1959, Lee Bouvier Canfield married at the county courthouse in Farifax County, Virginia, Prince Stanislaus Radziwill,

Princess Lee Radziwill and her sister, First Lady Jackie Kennedy, in Pakistan in March, 1962.

born Spanow, Poland, 21 July 1914. It was his third marriage and he had a son by his second wife, the former Grace Kolin, later the Countess of Dudley. The prince campaigned in Polish-American neighborhoods for his new brother-in-law, John F. Kennedy, during the 1960 presidential campaign. In June of 1961 the Radziwills entertained the Kennedys at their home in London. During the visit the president stood as godfather for the christening of the Radziwills' daughter, Anna.

In November of 1962 Lee Radziwill secured a Vatican annulment so that her second marriage would be recognized by the church. She and Prince Stanislaus had two children, Anthony and Anna Christina. Anthony was particularly close to his cousin, John F. Kennedy Jr., and served as best man at his 1996 Georgia wedding to Carolyn Bissette. Within weeks of the young Kennedy's death with his wife and her sister in an airplane he was piloting, Anthony Radziwill, who had been an Emmy-award winning television producer, died of cancer. Prince Stanislaus Radziwill, who did not remarry after his divorce from Lee Bouvier on 23 July 1974, died 27 June 1976.

Lee Bouvier Radziwill reportedly had an affair with Greek shipping tycoon Aristotle Onassis, who then married her sister, Jacqueline. Lee Bouvier Radziwill became a close friend of ballet star Rudolf Nuryev, as well as writer Truman Capote before their public feud. She then married movie producer Herbert Ross (1927-2001) whose films included *Footloose, Pennies from Heaven,* and *Steel Magnolias.* He attempted to lure the American-born Grace Kelly, Princess of Monaco, out of retirement for his 1977 film *The Turning Point,* but her husband would not allow her to accept.

Suzanne "Susie" Bransford, born 19 January 1868 in Crescent Mills, California, was a daughter of Sarah Cooper Bransford and Confederate veteran Milford Bransford, who moved west from Missouri after the War. Her father struggled through a string of poor business decisions and her mother was forced to take in boarders. Susie proudly proclaimed to be a member of an old Virginia family and, at sixteen, was sent to a finishing school in San Francisco. With her father's continued failures, Susie was forced to accept work as a seamstress and hairdresser and sang in a local lyceum. At the age of twenty-five, Susie knew her days as a belle were numbered. She moved to the mining community of Park City, only thirty miles from Salt Lake City.

She later insisted that family and friends burn any of her letters from her early days in Park City as she was determined to have no proof that she worked as a common laborer there. Her luck changed, however, when she met a bookkeeper named Albion B. Emery, who was thirteen years older than she and unmarried. He and Susie were married on 11 November 1884 and rented a modest house. Susie adopted her younger sister's son when the sister died after childbirth at the age of eighteen. While traveling to Boston to visit her husband's family, Susie visited an orphanage and convinced her husband to adopt a two year-old girl they named Grace. Using borrowed money, Emery, in partnership with two other men, purchased the Mayflower Silver Mine. They soon struck it

Left: Sisters Jackie and Lee Bouvier photographed in London by Cecil Beaton.

Right: Lee and her first husband, Michael Canfield, who was rumored to be an illegitimate member of the British royal family.

rich and any question of Susie's working for a living was permanently banished. Emery was elected to the Utah House of Representatives and quickly became its Speaker. Susie and her newly-wealthy husband paid off their creditors and moved to Salt Lake City where Susie began to climb the social ladder.

At her husband's death on 14 June 1894 he left no will. Susie relied upon the insurance benefits left to her as the complicated issues of ownership of the Silver King mine were litigated in court. Susie and their daughter won her claim to all Emery's money but the hard-fought battle did little for her public esteem and made bitter enemies

The often-married Susie Bransford was known as the "Silver Queen."

largest home in Utah (it had previously belonged to Brigham Young's favorite wife) and she hired an expert from Marshall Field in Chicago to redecorate its forty-three rooms. In 1904 Susie added a wing to house her growing art collection while an increasing number of cars was garaged below. Her adopted daughter, Grace, did not fare so well during her mother's frequent absences that she came to resent with intensity. Susie placed her in a Washington-area boarding school and, having already witnessed the closed doors of New York society, decided to tackle those in the nation's capital. As the *New York Herald,* reported, however, "… this Western woman has everything money can buy except family lineage to back her, and even her escutcheon is soiled by the sinister Bar of labor. She was a milliner."

Susie and Col. Holmes jointly financed a new shipping business that quickly increased their wealth (they were aided by influence from Susie's brother, John, who eventually was mayor of Salt Lake City). Susie's daughter, Grace, reached her majority at eighteen and demanded her share of her father's vast wealth but was rebuffed by her mother. She also insisted upon marrying Susie's nephew, Wallace Bransford (Grace still had not been told that she was adopted and Susie tried to convince her that she could not marry her genetic first cousin). They were married anyway in modest circumstances as Susie refused to pay for any of the wedding, even though she did abide by the law which dictated that she had to give her daughter half the Emery estate. Grace was told on her honeymoon by her husband that she was not Susie's biological child and her relationship with her mother, never good at its best, rapidly deteriorated. Susie built a home, El Roble, in Pasadena, California, and increasingly made it her permanent residence, although she also purchased a summer home, Oakwood, in East Millcreek, Utah.

Grace died childless as a young woman, never having reconciled

of her late husband's partners. It wasn't long before her wealth earned for Susie the public moniker of "Silver Queen" which she would retain until her death. Her second husband was the widowed Colonel Edwin F. Holmes. Born in 1843, he was sixteen years older than she and had retired from the lumber and shipping business with $7 million. They were married in New York City on 12 October 1899 and held a reception at the Waldorf-Astoria. After giving his bride several pieces of expensive jewelry, the couple left for a six-month European honeymoon that included a presentation to the tsar and tsarina in St. Petersburg.

Susie returned to Salt Lake City where she became known for her lavish entertainments at his wedding gift to her—Gardo House, the

with Susie who did not attend the funeral nor even send flowers. Graces's will left most of her inheritance to her husband (who was also Susie's nephew). Susie was so angered the money did not revert to her that she moved permanently to Pasadena and announced that she was suing her son-in-law to recover the funds and was naming as her heir her brother's niece-by-marriage who was an aspiring actress. Not only did Susie lose the legal challenge to her daughter's will, but she was publicly castigated by the judge for her callous indifference as a mother and mother-in-law. She and the Colonel sold all their holdings in Utah (except the rapidly-depleting silver mine) and moved permanently to Pasadena. Col. Holmes died in October of 1925 having left his daughters by his first marriage what few resources had not been exhausted by several years of international travel with Susie.

Unable to bear living at the palatial home in Pasadena she had only recently renovated and extended at great expense, Susie moved to the Plaza Hotel in New York City where her previously-announced heir, her brother's niece-by-marriage, also lived with her young daughter. Susie fell prey to a string of "walkers" who were after a good time and possible inheritance. She began to be courted by **Prince Nicholas Engalitcheff** (1864 - 26 March 1935), a former Russian consul in Chicago who was called "the melancholy Slav" in New York society. He had previously been married to Chicago heiress **Eva Pardridge** (see her separate entry) by whom he had a son before she divorced him and retook her maiden name (the son probably committed suicide). In December of 1916 Prince Nicholas Engalitcheff married a French woman, Melanie de Bertrand Lyteuil, who claimed to be immensely wealthy but was arrested for fraud stemming from purchases she made in Paris for which she never paid. Engalitcheff then courted the widow of Oscar Hammerstein who later sued him to recover money she

advanced him. He then turned his full attention to Susie and competed for her affections with another fortune-seeker, Prince Georges Dadiani (who eventually married American heiress Lucy Tew).

Engalitcheff and Susie announced their engagement in the *New York Times* and booked the Russian Orthodox Church. Only when they arrived at the Marriage Bureau to obtain their license were they told that the prince was still married to his second wife. Susie was horrified and called everything off before sailing for Europe.

Caught on the rebound, she married on 20 July 1930 Dr. Radovan Delitch, a Serbian physician who was a decorated War veteran – and also thirty-one years younger than she. The first service was held in the Russian Orthodox Church followed by a later civil ceremony in Paris. Although he gave up his medical practice and was reportedly attentive to Susie, he was unhappy as a kept man and eventually committed suicide by hanging on board a cruise ship returning to America on Christmas Eve of 1932. Susie responded by holding a massive sale of all her California holdings in the depth of the Depression, realizing only $100,000 total when her palatial home, El Roble, was worth more than a million. Meanwhile, Prince Nicholas Engalitcheff had obtained an Enoch Arden divorce from his missing wife and immediately came courting at Susie's feet. On 18 October 1933, Susie married **Prince Nicholas V. Engalitcheff** in the New York Municipal Court building followed by a ceremony at the Russian Orthodox Church. He was fifty-nine and she was seventy-four, although she gave her age as fifty-eight (one newspaper reported, "…when she was married to Dr. Delitch in Paris in 1930 dispatches said she was 71."). Among those guests attending the reception afterwards were the American-born Princess Obolensky and Princess Troubetskoy, as well as Prince Matchabelli.

In January of 1934 the couple left on an around-the-world

honeymoon cruise. The Prince immediately returned to womanizing and even began an affair with their nurse while onboard and charged a necklace for the nurse to Susie's ship account. When the nurse was fired and returned to Denver, Engalitcheff followed her there but she was no longer interested as he no longer had access to Susie's rapidly-dwindling fortune. Susie, however, continued to pay all his bills even though they lived apart and he reportedly hired a limousine to take him to his weekly manicures. When he died of a stroke in March of 1935 at the Hotel Barclay in New York City, his wife was reported to be too ill to be at his side. Susie remained close to her named heir, Adele Blood, and was devastated when she took her own life with a gun. Adele's seventeen year-old daughter, Dawn, discovered the body, and two years later took her own life by the same means. Through an intermediary, Susie began selling her jewels to pay her bills, replacing each one with paste imitation, but her travels to all the world's society destinations continued unabated. She began borrowing from a bank that believed her estate was still considerable and, within six months, had borrowed more than $20,000 for living expenses. She died of a drug overdose at eighty-three in 1942 in distressed financial circumstances while staying at an inn in Norwalk, Connecticut, and probably took her own life as she left a note with instructions for her business manager. She was buried with her parents and her first husband in Salt Lake City's Mt. Olivet Cemetery. Although $65,000 was left in her estate, her outstanding bills totaled more than that amount.

Catherine Britton, born Washington, D.C., 27 March 1892, died Vienna, 21 June 1929, daughter of Alexander Britton and Louise Reed Britton, married as his first wife, at Washington, D.C., 14 December 1916, **Prince Alfred Hohenlohe-Schillingsfurst,** son of Prince Konrad Hohenlohe-Schillingsfurst and Countess Franziska von Schonborn-Buchheim. At the time he was serving as an attache' at the Austro-Hungarian Embassy in Washington. The service was held at the bride's parents' home officiated by a Catholic priest although the bride was not Catholic. The prince's parents opposed the marriage as did his government and they were only reconciled after the end of the War when Austria re-established diplomatic relations with the U. S. Among the guests at their wedding was the German ambassador and his wife, Count and Countess von Bernstorff (she was the American-born **Jeanne Luckemeyer**).

Catherine Britton's family opposed her marriage as did her husband's government. Their son also married an American heiress.

The bride's father was a partner at the Washington law firm, Britton & Gray, founded by his father, and was also president of the exclusive Chevy Chase Club. He served as the attorney for the Santa Fe Railway in Washington, D.C. The groom was immediately assigned to his country's San Francisco consulate, having earlier served as chamberlain to the emperor. The bride was an army nurse in Europe at the outbreak of World War I but before the United States entered the conflict. They had three children and he was at her bedside when she died in Vienna in 1929. Almost five years later the prince married again but had no more children and he was killed in an airplane crash at Prestwick, Scotland. Their eldest son, Prince Alexander, married wealthy American **Peggy**

Schulze. Their second son, Prince Konrad, died of wounds received in action at Lake Lagoda. In 1921 Alexander Britton attempted to deduct from his income taxes as "bad debt" a substantial loan advanced to his son-in-law but the Board of Tax Appeals denied his request and the ruling was later upheld by the District of Columbia Court of Appeals.

Ethel Julia Bronson, born New York City, 6 June 1870, was a daughter of Isaac Bronson Jr. Her grandfather, Isaac Bronson, founded both the New York and Ohio Life Insurance and Trust Companies and, by 1828, was already worth $250,000. Among his ten children was Ethel's father, Isaac, who increased his inheritance in banking and land speculation. Ethel's cousin, Mrs. Lloyd Griscom, was the wife of the U. S. Ambassador to Italy. Ethel's mother lived in Rome in an apartment at the Borghese Palace and died one evening on the way home from the theatre. Ethel married 16 May 1903, **Giambattista, Prince Rospigliosi,** born Rome, 5 May 1877, died Santa Marinella, 5 April 1956, later mayor of Civitavecchia. He was a son of Prince Camilo, who was a younger brother of **Marie Parkhurst's** husband, Prince Giuseppe, and grandson of the 2nd Prince Rospigliosi. Ethel's husband's family was well-known as a member of the "Black," or papal aristocracy. Giulio di Girolamo Rospigliosi was made a cardinal in 1637 and elected pope as Clement IX in 1667. Giacomo, the pope's nephew, was made a cardinal by his uncle in 1667.

Although Ethel was well-received in society, her fellow American, Marie Reid Parkhurst, was shunned when she married the head of the Rospigliosi family as she was divorced from her former husband, Governor Frederick Parkhurst of Maine. Marie's legal entreaties to the Vatican to recognize her princely marriage wound through the processes for years before finally being decided by the pope, who overturned a decision of cardinals. Although Marie's son finally succeeded to the titles, he married two Americans and died childless and Ethel's son eventually became the 10th Prince Rospigliosi. Ethel and Giambattista lived at the Villa Rospigliosi in Rome and had a son and three daughters. She died at Rome, 5 November 1924 and her son succeeded to both Italian princely titles as well as to Scottish noble ones. The son, Giulio, succeeded an uncle as 10th Prince Rospigliosi, 13th Prince of Castiglione, 10th Duke of Zagarolo, Marquis of Giuliana, Count of Chiusa, Baron di Valcorrente e della Miraglia, etc., and succeeded his cousin as the Scottish 11th Earl of Newburgh, Viscount of Kynnaird, and Lord Levingston of Flacraig. His son, Ethel's grandson, is the current 12th Earl of Newburgh and also holds the Italian titles. Giambattista's brothers Prince Francesco, Prince Ludovico, and Prince Clemente married Americans **Laura Macdonald Stallo, Mildred Haseltine,** and **Claire Weil.**

At Ethel's death, she left a substantial estate in U. S. stocks. After her death Giambattista married secondly, in 1926, Donna Faminia, Princess Odeschalchi. Ethel's grandson, the 11th Prince, has only one daughter who is heir to the Scottish titles, and a younger brother who is heir to the Italian titles. Ethel's daughter, Elena, married Antonio, Duke of Lante Montefeltro della Rovere, whose grandmother was American **Mathilde Davis.**

Mary Gwendoline "Mamie" Caldwell (1863 – 1910), was a daughter of William Shakespeare Caldwell and Elizabeth Breckenridge Caldwell of Louisville, Kentucky. She and her sister, Mary Elizabeth "Lina" Caldwell, lost their mother when they were quite young, and she left them her half-million dollars. Their father, who had converted to Catholicism, died not long after, leaving each of them $5 million. They were brought up by their maternal aunt, Mrs. Donnelly, and educated at European convents. After her debut in Louisville (at which her dress was unfavorably commented upon because it was too low in the bosom - even though she had worn it to be presented to Queen Victoria) she went to Italy and, in 1887, met **Prince Joachim Murat,** grandson of the King of Naples and his wife, sister of Napoleon I. They became engaged and, during the financial negotiations, he attempted to gain control of her fortune. She was indignant and announced that she had intended settling upon him $50,000 per year but would now reduce that amount to $25,000. The engagement was broken and she gave her entire trousseau - bearing the insignia of the King of Naples - to the poor and returned to America were she presented $300,000 to the Catholic University in Washington, D.C.

Mamie then married 19 October 1896, the 7th **Marquis des Monstiers-Merinville,** in the same year in which her sister, Lina, born 1865, married **Baron Kurt von Zedtwitz,** a member of the German Diplomatic Corps at Washington. Immediately after his marriage Baron von Zedtwitz was appointed the German Minister to Mexico, but within a year he was killed by the fall of the mast of his private yacht, the *Isolde,* which came into collision with the yacht *Meteor,* owned by the emperor of Germany, during the Royal Albert Regatta at Southsea, England, in August 1896. After Mamie's 1896 marriage to the Marquis, he used her fortune to renovate his estates in France and Brittany. The marriage was not happy and she returned to the United States in 1904 where she lived with little remaining money at the Buckingham Hotel in New York City. Also in 1904, her sister, Baroness von Zedtwitz, shocked everyone by renouncing Catholicism and writing a book entitled, *The Double Doctrine of the Church of Rome.* Mamie shared her sister's new opinion. She suffered several illnesses and lost her hearing and most of her sight. She died in December 1910 only one year after the death of her sister, who was succeeded by a son, philanthropist Baron Waldemar von Zedtwitz (the greatest bridge champion of the 1930s and preferred partner of Harold S. Vanderbilt).

The sisters are both buried in Louisville's Cave Hill Cemetery beneath larger-than-life Greek marble statues. Several buildings at Washington's Catholic University are named for Mamie who also gave the original funds to establish the University's School of Theology. Although an old Louisville family, much of the Caldwell estate was confiscated during World War I by the Alien Property Office (because von Zedtwitz's widow was adjudged to be German) and became Louisville's first airport and an adjacent city park. There are teaching chairs in medicine at Yale University endowed by Lina's son, Baron Waldemar von Zedtwitz.

Eleanor Calhoun, born approximately 1861 in Visalia, California, was an actress and author. A great-grandniece of John C. Calhoun, she was a daughter of Laura Davis Calhoun and Judge Ezekial Ewing Calhoun. Eleanor made her debut as Juliet in *Romeo and Juliet* at the old Grand Opera House in San Francisco. She then played in Shakespeare and other classic roles throughout the South. She was reportedly the mistress of William Randolph Hearst until his father forced him to give her up as a condition of his being handed control

Eleanor Calhoun was a serious actress who transferred her considerable talents and energy to her husband's Serbian people.

of the *San Francisco Examiner* (his mother did the same in 1895 when she agreed to give him the money to buy the *New York Journal* in exchange for giving up another female companion). Eleanor made her London debut in 1882, appearing with Sir Johnston Forbes-Robertson and other stars in the Haymarket Theatre (Theatre Royal).

She married in London, in 1903, **Prince Eugene Lazarovich-Hrebeljanovich** (his first wife was the Countess Marie Serurrier, a descendant of the Napoleonic Marshal; she died in 1900), who was a descendant of the Serbian tsar. From 1371 to 1389 Lazar I Hrebeljanovich was the ruling princely monarch of Serbia. He united several allies to resist the Ottoman invasion of the Balkans in the fourteenth century and stood as the last bulwark against Islamic invasion of Europe. He and his armies were defeated at the battle of Kosovo, 15 June 1389, and he was executed by the Turks. His body, including his decapitated head, were preserved at the Serbian Orthodox monasteries at Ravainica and Gracanica for many years but were recently removed to Belgrade, Yugoslavia. His descendant, Prince Eugene, was a Serbian statesman, author, and lecturer and was a member of the Austrian General Staff before the First World War. By his first wife he had three children: Prince Doushan, who later lived with his step-mother in New York City; Princess Mara, who lived in Heidelberg; and Prince Stephen, who ran away from home to fight for the Allies and was never heard from again.

After her marriage in 1903 Eleanor left the stage and assisted her husband in seeking the liberation of Serbian lands in Macedonia then under Turkish rule. She convinced Alexander Smith Cochrane in 1908 to finance the Danube-Aegean Waterway Project and also was responsible for Sir Ernest Cassel's underwriting of a loan of five million pounds to the Sultan of Turkey to pay for her husband's plan of agrarian tax collecting and settlement for European Turkey in the interest of "Christian population." While on a visit to the U.S. in 1912, Prince Eugene delivered a course of lectures at Stanford University. Eleanor took advantage of their U. S. visit to appear in *The Mission Play*, a historical pageant underwritten by Henry Huntington, at a newly-built playhouse near Mission San Gabriel outside Los Angeles. The Governor of Georgia created Eleanor an Officer of the Old Guard of Georgia and, in memory of her great uncle, John C. Calhoun, decorated her with a jeweled Gold Cross of Honor in the presence of a review of troops for the Calhoun family. During a visit to New York City in 1912, Professor Pupin of Columbia attacked the couple for using a princely title that he insisted no longer existed. Renowned scientist Nicola Tesla immediately came to their defense, writing to the *New York Times* of the prince's esteemed heritage and of the couple's contributions to his homeland.

Eleanor assisted the prince in writing the two-volume work, *The Serbian People: Their Past Glory and Their Destiny*. She wrote her memoirs, *Pleasures and Palaces*, in 1915, and lived in New York City. Another work, *The Way: Christ and Evolution*, appeared in 1926. At her death her step-son, Prince Doushan, was still alive. Prince Eugene died in Heidelberg, Germany, 15 July 1941 at the age of seventy-one. Princess Eleanor died at the age of ninety-two in New York City on 9 January 1957. Her only child, a daughter, Zora, predeceased her.

Jane Allen Campbell, daughter of George W. Campbell of New York City, was born in Montclair, New Jersey, in 1863. In 1895 she accompanied her widowed mother and aunt, the Baroness Westenberg, on a grand tour of Europe. Mrs. Campbell and the baroness were known as the beautiful Watson sisters from Florida. The baroness first married a Mr. Brikhead and stood helplessly on the beach at

"Princess Jane" painted by Constantin Alajalov in 1938, the year of her death.

Westhampton watching her only child, a son, drown, as did a Mr. Post who tried to save him. After she was widowed she married the Baron de Westenberg, who was the ambassador of the Netherlands to the United States before assuming that post in Rome. There his wife and, later, his widow, assumed an important social position and was particularly favored by Queen Margherita. She settled her large inheritance on her niece and introduced Jane to the Italian court. The beautiful young woman married at Geneva 7 June 1897, **Carlo, 3rd Prince di San Faustino, Marquis del Monte Santa Maria,** born Rome, 6 June 1867,

Princess Jane wore full mourning for more than twenty years, including this visit to Loelia, Duchess of Westminster, at the Lido in Venice in 1926.

died 25 May 1917, a descendant of an old Roman noble family, who succeeded his father in the titles in 1892.

Jane was well-known for shocking society for more than forty years in Rome by ignoring established social traditions. At one of her first functions as hostess in Rome, she discovered just before the guests were to arrive that the punch to be served was lemonade instead of the champagne which she desired. Her husband refused to give her the keys to the wine cellar and she had insufficient cash to purchase champagne. She immediately pawned an heirloom gold necklace and the guests were served champagne. At one of her dinners, she had a Foreign Office expert arrange seating according to rank. When the guests arrived she had mistakenly reversed left from right and all the guests were seated incorrectly. Sir Oswald Mosley wrote of her salon as "a university of charm, where a young man could encounter a refinement of sophistication whose acquisition could be some permanent passport in a varied and variable world. If he could stand up to the salon of Princess Jane, he could face much."

She was particularly helpful to the young Barbara Hutton in establishing social connections in Venice. One of Hutton's biographers, C. David Heymann, however, adjudged Princess Jane's influence in Venice "as the first and last word on who rated and who did not, and her judgments in such matters were not only final but frequently cruel." Hutton wrote in her own diary that Princess Jane "was a wonderful juggler. She could keep numerous activities going at once, planning a dinner party while listening to a conversation while playing backgammon while reading a book while knitting a sweater while berating the cabana boy while recounting the latest gossip…" In 1902 she was accused by a maid of having beaten her so badly that she needed ten days to heal. Jane put herself in danger in 1908 when, during student riots outside the Austrian embassy in Rome, she and a friend stepped onto the balcony of the embassy and laughed at the rioting students below.

A great beauty in her younger days, Princess Jane wore deep mourning after her husband's death –always in white –for more than twenty years. Persistent rumors of their oft-impending divorce were met with strong denials although she admitted late in life that, had her husband been American, she probably would have divorced him soon after their marriage. Her granddaughter, Susanna Agnelli, in her 1975 memoir, *We Always Wore Sailor Suits,* as a child recalled that her grandmother, whom she called "Princess Jane," "adores people and parties and gossip and strange mix-ups of life. She says atrocious things at which people tremble, but she can make anyone's life fun if she decides to look after them." Biographer Hugo Vickers wrote that Jane was "noted for her boundless hospitality, wit and humor," while the Duchess of Sermoneta said that she "collects human beings as others collect postage stamps or moths." In 1929 she received the Red Cross Gold Medal for her charitable work for a sun-cure colony for tubercular children. At the time it was the highest award ever given to a woman for such work in Italy.

Just before her death she wrote her memoirs that were published serially in a weekly newspaper. She and her husband had a son, Don Ranieri, and a daughter, Donna Virginia. The son succeeded as the 4th Prince of San Faustino and married two Americans, **Catherine Sage** and **Lydia Bodrero Macy,** and had a son by the second marriage who is the current prince, although he and his American wife have no children (by Lydia's last marriage to Roland L. Redmond, President of the Metropolitan Museum of Art, she became an aunt of John Bryan whose highly-publicized affair with Sarah, Duchess of York, and the resulting tabloid photographs effectively ended her marriage). Virginia, daughter of Jane and the prince, married Edoardo Agnelli, an heir to the Fiat fortune, and was the mother of famed playboy Gianni Agnelli, the eventual Chairman of Fiat (whose wife was a daughter of the American-born **Margaret Clarke,** Princess di Castagneto). The senior Agnellis' daughter, Clara, married Prince Tassilo von Furstenberg (whose second wife was American oil heiress **Cecil "Titi" Blaffer Hudson),** grandfather of **Prince Alexandre von Furstenberg,** who married the American-born **Alexandra Miller,** sister of the current Crown Princess of Greece. Jane, Princess di San Faustino, died of pneumonia in Rome on 23 June 1938.

Marguerite Gibert Chapin, born in Waterford, Connecticut, 24 June 1880, was a daughter of Lindley Hoffman Chapin and Leila M. Gibert, and step-daughter of Cornelia Garrison Van Auken Chapin of New York City. The bride inherited a fortune in her own right from her late grandfather, Frederick Gibert, and her mother died when Marguerite was only five, followed by the loss of their family home to fire when she was fourteen, and the death of her father when she was sixteen. Her father's second wife was Cornelia Van Auken by whom Marguerite had two half-sisters and one half-brother. Marguerite's new step-family was Protestant and she later said that her attendance at Catholic mass with the family servants instilled in her a feeling of isolation. The family estate, Aeolia, at Goshen Point near Waterford, Connecticut, included a Catholic Chapel containing a Cellini chalice in honor of Marguerite's mother, Lelia Gibert. Marguerite's childhood neighbors and friends, the Miller twins, recalled her as "oh, so very handsome with her long dark curls and her perfectly beautiful dresses.... We'd rather be Marguerite Chapin than anybody on the earth."

Marguerite made her debut in New York City then, having reached her majority and inherited her own private fortune, went abroad with a companion and chaperone and made Paris her home while studying music and art. In 1910 she met and befriended the artist Edouard Vuillard whom she commissioned to design for her a five-panel screen now known as La Place Vintimille in the collection of Washington's National Gallery of Art. Marguerite married at London, 30 October 1911, **Roffredo, 1st Prince di Bassiano** (Italian title of 17 April 1903 granted by King Victor Emanuel), and later **17th Duke of Sermoneta** and **8th Prince di Teano** of the Caetani family, Chevalier of the Order of Malta, born Rome, 13 October 1871, died 4 April 1961. He was the son of the 15th Duke of Sermoneta and younger brother of Leone, later 16th Duke of Sermoneta, Prince di Teano, etc., whose wife was lady in waiting to Queen Helena. Another brother was at that time in charge of Italian affairs in St. Petersburg. The wife of the Italian ambassador, Marchese Imperiali di Francavilla, and the Earl of Lathom (Roffredo's mother was British, of the Earls of Lathom and Barons Skelmersdale) were among those present at the wedding that had been shrouded in secrecy for days. The bride had been staying for one week at the Ritz Hotel with the Baroness Grenier, sister of the groom, whose husband was at that time Belgian Minister to Peking.

The Caetani family was identified with the history of Italy for ten centuries and gave Boniface VIII to the papacy. The Caetanis owned the famous Pontine Marshes near Rome for over 600 years before they were sold to the Italian government under Mussolini for drainage and settlement. The groom's father, the Duke of Sermoneta, was a prominent Italian statesman and well-known archaeologist. It was he who brought to King Victor Emanuel II in Florence the result of the plebecite of the Roman people declaring their acceptance of the Kingdom of Italy, thus completing the unification of the country. Roffredo, who walked in Liszt's funeral procession (and some thought he was a son of Liszt), was a gifted composer and was considered both handsome and a true marital prize. He pursued American **Gladys Deacon** for more than two years before she finally rebuffed him to seek a marriage proposal from Prince Torlonia (who eventually married American **Elsie Moore** while Gladys became the second wife of the **9th Duke of Marlborough,** former husband of **Consuelo Vanderbilt**).

When Gladys learned that Roffredo had married, she wrote to her mother, "Isn't all this marriage, taking in marriage a gorgeous sight? There is something so healthy and cattle-like about it." Marguerite and Roffredo had a daughter, Lelia, born in Paris, 4 October 1913, and a son, Camillo, born in Florence, 20 October 1915. They lived at the Caetani Palace in Rome as well as in Paris and Versailles. As Marguerite Caetani, she was known to the literary world as the editor of *Botteghe Oscure* (Dark Shops, a street name in Rome), a biannual review that published original poetry and fiction from the United States, England, Germany, Italy, France, and Spain in their original languages. Andre' Malroux, Albert Camus, Paul Valery, Ignazio Silone, Robert Graves, Archibald MacLeish, e. e. cummings, Dylan Thomas, Tennessee Williams, and Marianne Moore were among many writers whose works appeared in *Botteghe Oscure,* which ceased publishing only in 1961 when Marguerite Caetani was in ill health. From 1920 to 1935 she published the French review *Commerce* with Paul Valery and others. She became, in the words of her nephew, Schuyler Chapin, formerly the General Manager of the Metropolitan Opera and Commissioner of Cultural Affairs for the City of New York, "the Diaghilev of literature."

She took a keen interest in the gardens of Ninfa, the estate owned by the Caetani family since 1297 and rescued from neglect by her English-born mother-in-law. It was said that, while at Ninfa, she could look up to several hills overlooking the estate, each of which the family owned as well as the villages atop them, each bearing the name of one of her husband's ducal or princely titles. Marguerite Caetani, Duchess of Sermoneta (her husband had succeeded his elder brother as the 17th Duke) and Princess of Bassiano, died at the age of eighty-three in Rome, 18 December 1963. She had retained her American citizenship and left a daughter, Donna Lelia, who succeeded to her father's titles and was Mrs. Hubert J. Howard (of the Lords Howard of Penrith), and two half-sisters, Mrs. Francis Biddle of Washington, D. C., (the poet Katherine Chapin), wife of President Franklin D. Roosevelt's U. S. Attorney General, and Cornelia Chapin, a sculptor.

Marguerite Chapin, Duchess of Sermoneta, published original works by Malroux, Camus, MacLeish, and other emerging talents. She has been called "the Diaghilev of literature."

Her son, Prince Camillo, was a student at Harvard just before World War II began. While there he fathered an illegitimate daughter by "a proper New England girl." He was killed in service in Albania on the orders of Mussolini because of his mother's strong anti-Facist sentiments. Although his family was told that he was killed in battle, his body had only one gunshot wound behind the ear fired from close range. His mother never spoke of him again after his death. Her brother-in-law, Prince Michaelangelo, died several months later, leaving only a daughter and there were no male heirs in the principal Caetani line. Ninfa was lovingly cared for by her daughter, Lelia, who died without heirs and established a foundation to ensure its well-being. The gardens are now open to the public. Her papers are at the Palazzo Caetani in Rome. One of Marguerite's poets, the Austrian Hugo von Hofmannsthal, wrote to her, "It is an exquisite pleasure to think of you. You surround yourself with poets and artists, and the air around you remains very pure and very clear, with no shadow of snobbishness. You talk to dogs as one should talk to dogs, you talk to plants as it is fitting to talk to plants, you talk to poets as one should talk to poets—and you remain yourself, of an unfailing grace. You are admirable."

(Esther) **Millicent Clarke,** daughter of Richard and Annie Watt Clarke, was born in Yokohama, Japan, to American parents on 2 September 1921. In 1923 her family was caught in the immense earthquake, tidal wave, and fire that flattened Yokohama and Tokyo in which 130,000 people were killed. They escaped to Kobe and then were refugees to Shanghai in 1924. After a series of calamities they reached Peking, where her father died in 1927, leaving her mother with three small children in a country whose language she did not speak. On Millicent's thirteenth birthday she was told that she had an incurable disease with no hope of recovery and, on the day Japan declared war on China in 1937, her mother died. During a full bombing raid, Millicent's brother was barely able to retrieve their mother's body from the hills where her death took place. Because the railroads were being bombed, they could not escape but buried their mother themselves, using tombstones for cover while bullets flew overhead. The family then made the dangerous trip to Tiensin and took a boat to Kobe and

The Duke and Duchess of Doudeauville with her daughter. The duke had only an illegitimate son.

eventually to Hong Kong where they remained for almost two years. Millicent and her sister then sailed to Manila where her fatal diagnosis was confirmed on her eighteenth birthday when she was told she had six months to live. While listening to the radio announcement that Pearl Harbor had been bombed, her building was struck when bombs rained on Manila. Escaping with her life, Millicent was imprisoned at two internment camps, Santo Tomas and Los Banos, for three years and two months. Only when General McArthur returned to Manila was she freed just before an order to execute all prisoners was

The Duchess of Doudeauville's early life of adversity reads more like a modern spy novel than that of the heiresses of her day.

to be implemented. After a further five-week stay in an abandoned Filipino prison, she and other former internees were taken on a troop ship traveling five weeks under a blackout and finally reached Port San Pedro, California. On that voyage she met her first husband by whom she had a daughter.

Exercising her right as the daughter of American parents, Millicent became a U. S. citizen in 1949. Believing, however, that Europe offered a more stable environment for her daughter after her separation from her husband, Millicent moved there and eventually met **Armand de la Rochefoucauld** who was then fifty-five and had never been married. She married at Saanen, Switzerland, 5 February 1957, Armand, 7th Duke of Doudeauville, 4th Duke of Bisaccia, born 22 September 1902, died Ajijic, Mexico, 29 April 1995, son of the 5th Duke of Doudeauville, Duke of Estrees, Grande of Spain, and of Princess Louise Radziwill. Ludwig Bemelmans, creator of the "Madeleine" character, dedicated his 1952 book about Lord Cucuface, *How To Travel Incognito,* to Armand, Duke of Doudeauville. The duke's sisters married H.R.H. Prince Sixtus of Bourbon-Parma (brother of Empress Zita of Austria) and the 6th Prince-Duke de Poix/Duke de Mouchy (their son married as his second wife American **Joan Douglas Dillon**) while his aunts married the 9th

Prince of Ligne and the 10th Duke of Harcourt. Armand succeeded his elder brother to the dukedom in 1973 and they lived in Florida for eight years before moving to Mexico where the duke died at the age of ninety-three. Prior to his marriage, Armand had an acknowleged illegitimate son, Armand, in 1944 by Renee Brandt. The son was a continuing source of despair for his father and cost him a great deal both financially and emotionally. The son eventually served prison time for his financial improprieties. The duke and Millicent had one daughter, Lise (named after his mother), who married Jean-Pierre Ribes, and there is no male heir in the family.

The Dukes of Doudeuville are a younger line of the Dukes of la Rochefoucauld, Dukes of Liancourt, Dukes of Anville, and Princes of Marcillac. As of this writing, Millicent, the last Duchess de Doudeauville, is still living well into her eighties, decades after she was told her life would be short. She is, in her opinion, "a very lucky woman God has chosen to bless."

Margaret Clarke, born Peoria, Illinois, 6 July 1897, died Sirmione, 30 July 1955, daughter of Charles C. Clarke and Alice Chandler Clarke, married at Florence, 8 January 1925, **Don Filippo Caracciolo, 8th Prince of Castagneto and 3rd Duke of Melito,** born Naples, 4 March 1903, died Rome, 16 July 1965, who was president of the Italian Automobile Club and a member of one of the most prominent Neapolitan noble families. Don Filippo's younger brother, Don Mario, married American **Myriam Crosby.** During World War II, Margaret's villa at Lugano, Switzerland, was a reception center for anti-Fascist refugees and a listening post of the Italian Resistance movement. The prince was successful in crossing the German lines to serve as undersecretary of the Interior in Marshal Pietro Badoglio's pro-Allied government in southern Italy. The princess once secretly crossed the border to visit him at Cannabio. When a Fascist group occupied their town the locals hid her by disguising her in men's clothing, then secreted her back to Switzerland under the cover of night. They lived at the Villa Cancelli in Florence, and she died of a heart attack at Sirmione on Lake Garda at fifty-eight in July of 1955. Their son, Don Carlo, the 9th Prince of Castagneto and 4th Duke of Melito married in 1996 but had no children except an illegitimate daughter who married Fabio Borghese, Prince di Leonforte. His younger brother Don Nicola, succeeded and has a young son. Margaret's daughter, Marella, married Fiat magnate Gianni Agnelli, a grandson of the American-born **Jane Campbell**, Princess di San Faustino.

Grace King Connelly, of Augusta, Georgia, daughter of Grace Sterling King Connelly (whose sister, Mary "Minna" Livingston King, married Henry Paget, **4th Marquess of Anglesey**) and John McPherson Berrien Connelly, and granddaughter of John Pendleton King (1799-1888), U. S. Senator from Georgia, married Ugo Gregorini-Bingham, **Duc del Garigliano et di San Cesareo.** One of their daughters, **Adela Luisa Gregorini**, born Bologna, 3 April 1896, died 9 February 1974, succeeded to her father's titles as Duchess del Garigliano et di San Cesareo. She married in London in 1918, **Don Piero, Prince Colonna,** governor of Rome and gentleman to Her Majesty the Queen of Italy (Don Piero's uncle, Don Fabrizio, married American **Jeanne Marie Beard Perkins**). Their elder son, Don Francesco, succeeded as Duke of Garigliano while his younger brother, Don Ugo, succeeded as Duke of San Cesareo and married as his second wife American **Avery Johnine Leigh** (his son by his first wife, Oddone, is the current duke). Adela Luisa's sister, **Mary Grace Gregorini** (born Casalecchio, 20 September 1896, died Haroue' Castle 19 August 1970), married **Charles Louis, 6th Prince of Beauvau-Craon,** born Saint Assise Castle, 6 May 1878,

The Sikkim royal family. Hope Cooke's husband is the center child in the front row while his father is in glasses and a bowler hat behind his wife.

died Paris, 15 September 1942. Their son, Marc, succeeded his father as 7th and last Prince of Beauvau-Craon. He married first, Dona Cristina de Borbon, daughter of the 3rd Duke of Durcal and a Grande of Spain, and had only two daughters, Minnie and Diane. The 7th Prince of Beauvau-Craon married once more and had no children. At his death in 1982, the line became extinct in the male line. Dona Cristina's sister, Dona Isabel, married Sir James Goldsmith and was the mother of his daughter, Isabelle, whose husband disappeared off the coast of Taiwan in 1984.

Hope Cooke, a daughter of John J. Cooke and Hope Noyes Cooke (formerly Mrs. James Mulford Townsend, Jr.), was born in San Francisco, California, 24 June 1940. Her father left the family soon after her birth. After her parents were divorced in 1941, she and her half-sister, Harriet, were reared by their maternal grandparents, Helen and Winchester Noyes (he was president of the international shipping brokerage firm of J. H. Winchester & Co.). In January of 1942 their mother died when the small plane she was piloting crashed. Suicide was strongly suspected and Hope never knew whether there were mortal remains of her mother or where they might have been buried. Brought up by a series of cruel nannies, she and her sister lived in an apartment across the hall from their formal and distant grandparents. After their deaths (he, when was Hope was twelve, followed by the grandmother three years later), Hope and Harriet became the wards of their maternal aunt and uncle, Mary Noyes Chapin (1902 – 1984) and diplomat Selden Chapin (1899 – 1963), who was U. S. ambassador to the Netherlands, Panama, Iran, and Peru. He had earlier served as minister to Hungary from 1947 to 1949 until he was declared persona non grata by the Communist government because of his alleged participation in the Mindszenty affair and was recalled to Washington.

Hope finished high school while living with her aunt and uncle in Iran and, while in her late teens, had her first visit to India, an experience she found revelatory. She enrolled at Sarah Lawrence College in Asian Studies and, while attending a course in Darjeeling in 1959, she met at the Windermere Hotel Palden Thondup Namgyal, the widowed Crown Prince of Sikkim, Asia's smallest kingdom (at the death of his elder brother in 1941 he was named Crown Prince and Heir Apparent). He was almost twice her age with three children, their mother having died on 17 June 1957. After a courtship of two years, Hope Cooke married on 20 March 1963, the then-Crown Prince **Palden Thondup Namgyal,** (later) **12th Chogyal (King) of Sikkim,** who was born at the Royal Palace in Gangtok, 22 May 1923. The ceremony was held in the Royal Chapel of the Buddhist Tsuk-La-Khang monastery (Hope, a

Hope Cooke and her husband are behind his three children with a younger son by Hope in the front. Their daughter would later complete the family.

former Episcopalian, had been a practicing Buddhist since her teen-age years in Iran). When the king died the same year on 3 December 1963, Hope's husband ascended the throne as Chogyal (ruler/king) and she became Gyalmo (queen). Their "palace" was a five-bedroom home in the 6,000-foot altitude of Sikkim's capital, Gangtok. She was an active step-mother to her husband's three children, Tenzing, Wangchuk, and Yangchen, and had her own son, Palden, on 19 February 1964 and daughter, Hope Leezum, on 28 February 1968.

The king worked to improve his country, resulting in a literacy rate twice that of his neighboring nations of Nepal, Bhutan, and India, and maintained an uneasy measure of independence for so small and unprotected a country. At the same time, he drank heavily and his extramarital affairs included a mistress in Europe. Prior to his marriage with Hope he already had a natural son and daughter with a Sikkimese woman (the daughter, Omo, married an American). Hope attempted to champion Sikkim's cottage industries producing rugs and jewelry for export but suffered from her marital unhappiness. When India made plain its intention to dissolve Sikkim's independence and make it another of its member states, no nation would come to its defense. After the death of Prime Minister Nehru, who was a supporter of Sikkim, his daughter, Indira Gandhi, came to power and intensified her country's efforts to undermine Sikkim. As Hope Cooke later wrote in her painfully-honest autobiography, *Time Change,* "Little countries were powerless to help. Big ones, including America, too preoccupied to care."

Realizing that the end was near, Hope left Sikkim with her two children and her step-daughter, while the eldest son, Crown Prince Tenzing, remained with his father. The two were soon placed under house arrest and the Sikkimese were forced at gunpoint to raise the Indian flag. Sikkim was absorbed by India as its twenty-second state in 1973. Its three hundred-year-old monarchy was abolished and the royal family was deposed. Cooke relocated to New York City and finally divorced in 1980. Her former husband died of cancer in New York City on 29 January 1982 at the age of fifty-eight. His eldest son, Crown Prince Tenzing, was educated at Harrow and Cambridge and was killed in an auto accident near Gangtok on 11 March 1978. The next eldest son, Wangchuk, was educated at Harrow and the University of London. After his elder brother's death he became crown prince and, at his father's death in 1982, he was formally consecrated at the Royal Chapel in Gangtok as Chogyal (king) although he is not recognized by the Indian government. He spends much of his time in meditation practicing Buddhism with his teachers in Sikkim and Bhutan.

Although the Indian government would prefer that he fade into obscurity, the Sikkimese people (who now comprise a minority in their own country) hold an annual festival offering Cham, a sacred traditional dance. Although the dance is not held to attract tourists, it nevertheless has become a popular attraction that produces much-needed revenue. The Indians have attempted to hold it without the presence of the Chogyal, but the Sikkimise, who consider it a sacrament, will not even begin the dance unless the members of the royal family are in attendance. Several years ago the Indians ordered him to stay away and told the dancers to begin because the Chogyal was "running late and would arrive shortly." They were too wise to be fooled, however, and refused to dance until he was firmly seated in his presiding chair. His sister, Princess Yangchen, attended Finch College and graduated from Connecticut College before marrying a British advertising executive, Simon N. Abrahams, and for a while they operated an upscale children's shop in New York City. She was to

Lucy Cotton made good copy and her name was rarely out of the newspapers.

receive a kidney transplant from her eldest brother but he was killed before the operation took place and the kidney eventually came from her first cousin, Princess Sonam Yuthok, whose mother was the late king's sister.

The son and daughter of Hope and the king were educated in the U.S. Prince Palden, a 1986 graduate of Georgetown University, was a managing director at J. P. Morgan Chase. He and his wife, Kesang, live in Bronxville, New York, with their three daughters. His sister, Princess Hope Leezum, graduated from Georgetown University with a degree in International Relations before modeling in New York City. She first married diplomat Thomas Reich Jr., step-son of concert pianist Daniel Ericourt who premiered Aaron Copland's "Passacaglia." Reich was at the time the head officer for Burmese affairs at the U. S. State Department. He and Princess Hope Leezum later divorced and he became U. S. Consul in Okinawa. She remarried a Sikkimese deputy police commissioner, Wangyal Tobden, and returned to Sikkim in 1993 where she is known as "Semla" ("Daughter of our Country," a designation used for princesses). They have a son, Kalzang. Hope Leezum heads TrekSikkim with offices in New York City and in Gangtok. Princess Hope Leezum organizes and leads enervating treks into the Himalayan Mountains, usually accompanied by her husband. Her mother, the first American queen, became a public local historian in New York City. She ran the walking tour program for the Museum of the City of New York, was a weekly columnist for the *New York Daily News,* taught history at Yale and Sarah Lawrence College, and made a documentary about the history of Manhattan's lower east side. She also reviewed books for the *New York Times* as well as the *Chicago Times* and was an international lecturer on East-West relationships. In addition to *Time Change* (1981), she also wrote *Seeing New York:*

Lucy Cotton moved from stage to screen and was an early movie star. Her first marriage made her wealthy and her fifth gave her a title but none made her happy.

History Walks for Armchair and Footloose Travelers (1995) as well as, with dancer/choreographer Jacques D'Amboise, *Teaching the Magic of Dance* (1983). She married historian Michael Wallace, a professor at the John Jay College of Criminal Justice, who won the Pulitzer Prize for History for his book, *Gotham: A History of New York City to 1898.* They divorced in 2002. She no longer lives in New York and is researching a book at the British Library.

Lucy Cotton, born Houston, Texas, approximately 1891, daughter of Adelaide Wisby Cotton and Warren Jefferson Cotton, was an actress who performed on Broadway and then in a series of early movies. In 1916-1917, her first stage appearance was in *Turn to the Right!* She was then given a starring role in *Up in Mabel's Room* in 1919 and afterwards left the stage for good. The titles of her successive movies give a fair indication of the type of roles in which she was cast: *Blind Love, The Devil, The Misleading Lady, Divorced, Life Without Soul, Roses and Thorns,* and *The Sin That Was His.* She married on 10 October 1924 in Paris Edward Russell Thomas, owner of the *New York Morning Telegraph,* a Yale graduate whose father, General Samuel Thomas, left a fortune of $20 million enabling an annual trust fund of $180,000 for Edward. The son reportedly made $2 million on his own by by creating a corner in the cotton market. In the 1907 financial panic he was forced to sell his renowned racing stables but eventually recovered his fortune.

In 1902 Thomas was the first driver in America to kill someone with an automobile when his Daimler, formerly owned by William K. Vanderbilt Jr., struck a seven-year-old child and dragged the body three blocks. Years later Thomas would be seriously injured in another auto accident from which he took months to recover and his daughter also died in the same manner. Edward R. Thomas first married in

Prince Vladimir Eristavi-Tchitcherine's princely title was somewhat dubious but he wore it proudly.

Newport, Rhode Island, a seventeen-year-old Virginian, Linda Lee. After their divorce she took her sizable financial settlement and married the composer Cole Porter. The story of their highly social relationship, largely financed by her funds, was told in the movie *DeLovely*. Edward R. Thomas's second wife, by whom he had a son, Samuel Finley Thomas, was Elizabeth Finley. Thomas and Lucy had a daughter,

Lucetta Cotton Thomas, in May of 1925, the year before he died on 6 July 1926 at the age of fifty-two. For a short while his widow assumed management of his profitable newspaper.

His extensive estate included a $50,000 bequest to his sister's husband, Rhode Island Governor Livingston Beeckman, and his second wife sued the estate to increase the amount left to his young son (who was eventually to become chief of neurology at New York's St. Luke's Hospital). Thomas's infant daughter by Lucy received a trust fund of approximately $2 million with the remaining amount, slightly over $1 million, to his wife. She frequently entered into litigation with his estate over the succeeding years in an effort to receive some of her daughter's income. In 1934 Lucy gave a ninth birthday party for the girl at her fifteenth-floor apartment at the Hotel Pierre. The party lasted twelve hours and more than five hundred guests paid $2.50 each to join the festivities, with the proceeds going to a pianist who was a protégé of Lucy. Two singers from the Metropolitan Opera performed during the party and Lucetta was seen clutching a big doll before being led away to bed by a governess while the party continued for seven more hours.

Lucy Cotton Thomas married Lyton Grey Ament in 1927 and Charles Hann, Jr. in 1931. Both marriages were performed by the same minister in Towson, Maryland, and both ended in divorce. In 1933 she married William Magraw, president of Manhattan's Underground Installations Company. Immediately after that marriage kidnappers demanded $150,000 in ransom not to abduct Lucy's daughter, Lucetta. Lucy moved to south Florida where her late husband owned substantial property and, in 1934, she purchased the Deauville resort at Miami Beach consisting of a hotel, casino, swimming pool, and bathing beach. The sales price was said to be $3 million. She ran it for two seasons before leasing the resort to the owner of *True Confessions* magazine.

THRONES WHOSE HEIRS ARE DESCENDED FROM AMERICAN WOMEN:

Albania – Gladys Steuart (daughter of John Steuart, U. S. Consul at Antwerp)

Austria – Mathilde Price (daughter of Delaware railroad president James Price)

France (Capet) – Josephine Mary Curtiss (daughter of Joseph D. B. Curtiss)

Greece – Marie-Chantal Miller (daughter of duty-free magnate Robert Miller)

Great Britain – Frances Work (daughter of Cincinnati stockbroker Frank Work)

Monaco – Grace Kelly (daughter of Philadelphia contractor John Kelly)

Netherlands – Johanna Magdalena Oswald (daughter of NYC baker Philipp Oswald)

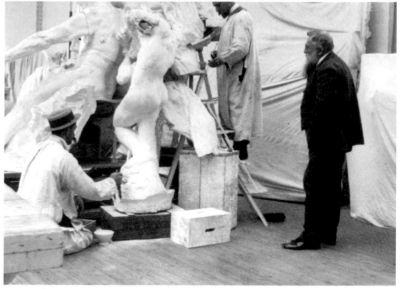

Claire Coudert enhanced Rodin's stature and his commission prices while she was his mistress.

During World War II it was used by the Coast Guard for anti-invasion beach patrol; it never recovered its glory days and was demolished in 1956.

On 3 May 1941 Lucy divorced William Magraw and, three hours later, in Key West, Florida, married **Prince Vladimir Eristavi-Tchitcherine,** born 19 October 1881 in Orel, Russia, who had been working in a jewelry store at the time of their meeting. The Tchitcherines were a Russian noble family with medieval roots, although not a royal one, while the Eristavis were a Georgian royal family, and Vladimir added the second name to his own after his first marriage before World War I to Clementine de Vere. She was divorced from her first husband and father of her son, Herman Wirtheim, a tiger tamer and circus artist known as Herman Weedon. Prince Vladimir married second in March 1929, **Diane Rockwood** who was from Indianapolis, Indiana, and they were also divorced. Lucy and Prince Vladimir were re-married in a religious ceremony on 15 June 1941 in New York City's Russian Orthodox Cathedral officiated by the church's dean. Afterwards a reception was held in the penthouse of the St. Regis Hotel. The couple lived in Miami and were divorced there on 12 October 1944. On 12 December 1948 her butler found her unconscious in her bed with an empty bottle that had held 100 sleeping pills. Lucy Cotton Thomas Ament Hann Magraw Eristavi-Tchitcherine was declared dead upon reaching the hospital. Prince Vladimir died in February of 1967 in New York City.

Lucy's daughter, Lucetta Cotton Thomas, left home upon reaching her majority and had no further contact with her mother. Having been taunted for years by the nickname, "Miss Cotton Panties," she changed her name to Mary Frances Thomas and married Kenneth Oscar Bailey. They lived in Luray, Virginia, where she died in an auto accident on 20 January 1980. She had no children and most of her estate went to charity.

Claire Coudert, daughter of Charles Coudert of New York City, a noted international attorney, married at St. Patrick's Cathedral, New York City, 12 March 1891, the **Marquis (later Duke) de Choiseul.** The archbishop of New York performed the ceremony and announced the personal blessing of the pope. The 1500 invited guests were required to present cards to be admitted. The couple lived in the Chateau de Menilles near Paris. At the time of their marriage, the Atlanta, Georgia, newspaper wrote, "The New York papers are of the opinion that the visit of the Marquis de Choiseul was ostensibly for the purpose of marrying a rich wife, which he succeeded in doing. An announcement has been made in the leading society paper of New York City stating that the home occupied by Mr. Charles Coudert, the father of the newly made marquise, has been offered for sale which goes to strengthen the report that a sum of money had to be settled on the marquis in exchange for his title." In 1904 Claire met in London the sculptor Rodin and began to champion his works, eventually increasing his annual income from 60,000 francs to 400,000 francs. The two became lovers in 1906 and in 1908 he sculpted an unfinished bust of her. While many credited her with reviving Rodin's career, others accused her of isolating him from his friends and family. After a trip to Italy in 1912 Rodin ended their relationship.

Claire's family was founded in America by a Bonapartist refugee from France and eventually formed one of the nation's most influential law firms. Its members represented several European nations, including France and Italy, in their American transactions and litigation. Among its clients was American-born Anna Gould in her divorce action against her first husband, Count Boniface de Castellane. One of Claire's sisters, Marie Aimee, married the Baron Brenig of Germany while another, Constance, married publisher Condé' Nast. Another sister, Grace, never married and died while visiting Claire and her husband in France. At the time, she left her estate in the care of the duke. Her sisters eventually challenged the will charging that their brother-in-law had exerted undue influence over their sister in her dying days.

During World War I Claire devoted herself to the care of tubercular French prisoners returning from German war camps. In 1917 she was given a silver medal by the French government for her work and, in August of 1918, she received a gold medal for her continuing hospital work. Her last visit to America was in 1916 when she went to New York to raise funds for repatriated French soldiers. Claire Coudert, Duchess de Choiseul, died suddenly of pneumonia at her home at 3 Avenue Sylvester Sacy in Paris on 7 March 1919. Her husband's assumption of the title of Duke of Choiseul was greatly disputed by the Choiseul-Praslin family but, as there were no children, the controversy ended at his death. At the time of Claire's wedding, the head of the Choiseul-Praslin family was married to American-born **Marie Elisabeth Forbes,** whose son, the 7th Duke, also married an American.

Florence Crane, born Chicago, 25 February 1909, died New York City, 21 October 1969, was a daughter of Florence Higinbotham Crane and Richard T. Crane, Jr. (1873-1931). Her father was president of the family's extensive bathroom fixture manufacturing company that was founded by his father. Under his leadership the firm expanded to 20,000 employees and had facilities in two hundred showrooms around the world. During his lifetime he distributed $12 million of his company's stock to his staff and his will left additional stock to long-time employees who had never sold his original gift. He was reputedly the second-wealthiest man in Chicago. His wife, Florence,

The Grand staircase of St. Petersburg's Belosselsky-Belozersky Palace.

Top left: Florence Crane.

Top right: Crane Cottage at the exclusive Jekyll Island Club retreat.

Bottom: "Castle Hill" in Massachusetts. Both it and their Jekyll home were designed by David Adler.

was a daughter of Harlow Higinbotham, a partner of merchant prince Marshall Field, who served as president of the Chicago Worlds's Fair and Columbian Exposition of 1893. Florence's mother's sister was married to Joseph Medill Patterson, editor and publisher of the *Chicago Tribune* and of the *New York Daily News*. The Cranes built an elaborate "cottage" at the exclusive Jekyll Island Club off Georgia's coast as well as the palatial "Castle Hill" in Ipswich, Massachusetts (with fifty-nine rooms requiring nineteen servants inside the house). Both were designed by society architect David Adler. At Florence's mother's death in 1949, she bequeathed Castle Hill and two thousand acres to a non-profit organization charged with its preservation, while the remaining two thousand acres went to her two children. Part of the estate is now operated as an inn.

Florence's uncle, Charles R. Crane, was an accomplished diplomat who was largely responsible for beginning the import of oil from the Middle East. He was ambassador to China and became intimately involved in the creation of Czechoslovakia (his daughter married the son of that country's founder). Florence married in New York City, 27 November 1943 (as his second wife) **Prince Serge S. Belosselsky-Belozersky,** born St. Petersburg, Russia, 23 June 1895, died New York City, 23 October 1978, son of Prince Serge C. Belosselsky-Belozersky and of American-born **Susan Whittier,** daughter of General Charles H. Whittier (who died on the **S.S. Mauretania** in 1908). Prince Serge's first wife, by whom he had no children and from whom he was divorced in 1928, was Countess Elisabeth N. Grabbe (1893-1982). Prince Serge's father was ADC to Grand Duke Vladimir and then a major-general assigned to the personal suite of Tsar Nicholas II. Florence and Prince Serge had two daughters, Princess Marina who married in 1962 Vladislav Kasarda (their three children use the hyphenated

last name Beloselsky-Belozersky-Kasarda) and Princess Tatiana who married in 1974 Juan Adolfo Bezamat. They also have three children. The Belosselsky-Belozersky family is extinct in the principal male line. Florence's cousin, John Crane, married Countess Teresa Martini Marescotti.

Martha "Sunny" Sharp Crawford, daughter of George W. Crawford and Annie Laurie Warmack Crawford, was born at Manassas, Virginia, 1 September 1931. Sunny's father, who was the founder and chairman of the Columbia Gas and Electric Company, died when his only child was three, leaving a fortune of $75 million. Her mother purchased Tamberlane, an estate in Greenwich, Connecticut, and a Fifth Avenue apartment. Sunny graduated from Chapin School in New York City, then was removed to Europe when she fell in love with a Russian translator from a noble but penniless family. Sunny's mother remarried Russell Aitken in 1957 and they took Sunny with them to the Schloss Mittersell in the Austrian Alps where she met her future husband. She married as his first wife on 20 July 1957, **Prince Alfred von Auersperg,** born Salzburg, 20 July 1936, died Salzburg,19 June 1992. The wedding was performed at Tamberlane, her family estate in Greenwich, Connecticut, by a Catholic priest. Sunny's daughter, Annie-Laurie "Ala," married as her second husband 9 June 1989, American banker Ralph Isham, born 17 Apr 1956. Sunny's son, Prince Alexander "Alex," married New York City, 10 June 1995, American **Nancy Louise Weinberg,** born Norfolk, Virginia, 10 May 1959. Prince Alfred and Sunny Crawford divorced and he married two more times and had an additional daughter by his third marriage.

Martha married second, in New York City, 6 June 1966, Claus Borberg, born in Copenhagen, 11 August 1926, who was adopted and used his mother's name of Bulow altering it to "von Bulow." He was

Top left: Aimee and her fourth husband, Prince Alexandre Miskinoff.

Top right: The Crocker mansion in Sacramento.

Bottom: Aimee, Princess Mstislav Galitzine.

an attorney in London and served as vice president of Getty Oil. The story of their marriage and her subsequent coma was told in the book and movie *Reversal of Fortune.* Claus was charged with her attempted murder but subsequently acquitted after a lengthy, expensive, and well-publicized legal battle. Sunny and von Bulow had a daughter, Cosima, who sided with her father in his trials for the attempted murder of his wife. Sunny's mother, whose estate was worth $90 million, had drawn her will so that her three grandchildren would share equally at her death. Mrs. Crawford rewrote her will excluding Cosima and dividing her $90 million equally between Sunny's two children by Prince Alfred. Cosima and her father continue to live in Sunny's homes and to draw income from her estate while Sunny is in a persistent vegetative state.

Aimee Crocker (1863-1941), born Sacramento, California, was an heiress to gold and railroad fortunes and a daughter of Judge Edwin B. Crocker (1818-1875), legal counsel for the Central Pacific Railroad, Justice of the California Supreme Court in 1865, and founder of the Crocker Art Museum, the longest continuously operating art museum in the West. Her father was a brother of Charles Crocker, one of the "big four" California railroad barons. The family embarked on a grand European tour from 1869 to 1871 then returned to Sacramento to move into the mansion that had been built for them during their journey. Aimee (originally Amy) married five times, beginning in 1887. She wrote of her family in her 1937 memoirs, *Without Regret,* "The Crocker family needs neither introduction nor comment. For those who never read the papers I might say that we were exceedingly wealthy." In her teens she was infatuated with several suitors in her first trip abroad. She became engaged to one, a German prince in uniform, after a relationship of one month. She broke the engagement and later wrote of the prince, "I recall that he did not commit suicide."

She was retrieved from Europe by her mother after presentation at court in Dresden. Back at home, two friends, R. Porter Ashe and Harry Gillig, played a game of poker for her hand and Ashe won with four aces. She married him in 1887 and divorced him one year later. Aimee then chartered a yacht and sailed to Hawaii having met its king, David Kalakaua, in Europe. She remained there almost a year and the king gave her an island of her own, where she was named princess of its three hundred inhabitants. Returning to San Francisco, she then married Harry Gillig who had earlier lost her hand in the poker game. That marriage, too, ended in divorce.

Traveling abroad years later with her daughter, Gladys Ashe, she met two brothers, Jackson and Powers Gouraud. She married Jackson Gouraud and he died several years later. Her daughter, Gladys (born 21 November 1885), married his brother, Powers Gouraud (thus becoming her mother's sister-in-law), and they also divorced. On 11 June 1914 Aimee married **Prince Alexandre Miskinoff,** a Russian nobleman. They separated in 1915 and he divorced her the next year when she contested the suit. He alleged cruel and inhuman treatment as well as desertion and that her actions had made him ill. One of his written charges was that, although he "always behaved in a calm and respectful manner," toward his wife she made great scenes "and arrogantly claimed that her great fortune gave her the privilege to abuse her husband." Her reply was that her husband had become infatuated with a fifteen-year-old girl in her family and that he had misled her prior to their marriage concerning his social standing. The strangest allegation in the suit was that a baby girl was born to the couple on 11 April 1915, a charge his wife denied. Miskinoff replied that he had a letter in his wife's own hand announcing the baby's birth but that his wife immediately left their home at the Hotel McAlpin with the baby because she did not

Nina Crosby was first married to the son of a U. S. senator from Louisiana who served as American ambassador to France.

want her daughter from an earlier marriage to know of the child. He alleged that his wife then kept the baby at the Hotel Endicott in the charge of nurses. He stated that he purchased a baby carriage for $80 and for several weeks proudly pushed his daughter around the sidewalks near the Hotel but his wife then became jealous of his attentions to their daughter. He asked for visitation rights to the child but his wife continued to deny her existence and the divorce was granted. On 22 September 1925 in Paris Aimee married **Prince Mstislav Galitzine, Count Ostermann** of Russia, born Kiev, 21 January 1899, died Paris, 28 February 1966. They were divorced in 1927 in Paris when she charged infidelity. Opposing the suit Prince Galitzine said that their marriage "was purely a commercial one, animated by the American woman's desire to be a Princess," adding that he "married for a financial settlement on condition that the union be one in name only." After their 1927 divorce he remarried a Frenchwoman and had a daughter and Aimee retained the name Princess Galitzine. She later became very active socially in New York City and had her gowns designed in Paris. While in Java she "wore the native costume and lived in a native hut." During her stay in Japan she lived in a paper house. While there a young British officer reportedly stole for her a sacred Buddha from a temple and "the affair was hushed up." She died at seventy-eight at the Hotel Savoy Plaza in New York City in 1941. Her daughter, Gladys C. Ashe, died in Santa Barbara in 1947, having lived in Beaumont, France, at her Chateau de Baudiment and left a son, Gerald Morgan Russell.

Nina Crosby, born New York City, 1 March 1881, died Monte Carlo, 19 February 1966, was a daughter of Walter Floyd Crosby and Louise Gauthier Sutton Crosby (whose grandfather, railroad developer Dudley S. Gregory, was the first mayor of Jersey City and later congressman) of New York, and the widow of James Biddle Eustis

Jr. Nina's first husband, whom she married in 1904 and by whom she had a son, was the son of the Chief Justice of Louisiana, U. S. senator from Louisiana 1877-79 and 1885-91, and U. S. Ambassador to France 1893-97. His father's brother, George, was secretary to the Confederate legation in Paris during the American Civil War.

After she was widowed Nina married 24 October 1917 in the Lady Chapel of St. Patrick's Cathedral in New York City, **Prince Melchior, Marquis de Polignac,** born Joigny, 27 September 1880, died Neuilly 18 December 1950, a cousin of Prince Edmond who married **Winnaretta Singer.** The bride converted to the Catholic faith before her marriage to de Polignac. At their wedding, the best man was Andre' Tardieu, head of the French High Commission, of which the groom was a member (Tadieu would later serve three terms as France's premier). Melchior's great-grandfather, Auguste, Duke de Polignac, was created a prince of Rome by the Pope in 1822 and was granted the rank of prince by the King of Bavaria in 1838. Marquis Melchior de Polignac was a noted sportsman and member of the International Olympic Committee as well as a member of an important champagne producing firm and president of the Champagne Producers Association in France. He was the grandson of the famous Madame Pommery who invented dry champagne when she unsweetened dessert wine so that she could drink it with her meals. He became head of the family firm in

Left: Nina Crosby when she was Mrs. James B. Eustis.

Right: Nina with her second husband, the Marquis de Polignac, head of the family's Pommery champagne firm.

Left: The Curtiss sisters - on the left is Bessie, Duchess de Dino, and on the right is Josephine, Princess di Poggio-Suasa.

Right: Josephine Curtiss whose granddaughter, Emmanuela, married the second son of Spain's King Alfonso XIII.

who was active in the resistance to the Nazis in WWII and had three sons. Nina died in Monte Carlo, 19 Feb 1966. Their son, Dalmas, was CEO of Pommery Champagne and a member of the International Olympic Committee. Melchior's first cousin, Pierre, was created Duc de Valentinois and Prince of Monaco in 1920 when he married the illegitmate Charlotte, Hereditary Princess of Monaco, and they were the parents of Prince Ranier of Monaco, husband of American Grace Kelly. Nina's grandson by her first marriage was American diplomat Charles "Chip" Eustis Bohlen.

Elisabeth Curtiss, born 12 November 1847, was a daughter of Joseph Davis Beers Curtiss (whose father, Lewis, was an early stockholder and trustee of Atlantic Mutual Insurance Company) and Elisabeth Shipton Giles Curtiss of New York City (thus a sister of **Josephine Mary Curtiss** who married Emmanuele, **Prince of Poggio-Suasa**). Elisabeth "Bessie" Curtiss married at Nice, 18 March 1867, Maurice, later the **4th Duke of Dino,** born 25 January 1843, third son of the Marquis de Talleyrand-Perigord, who received the ducal title from his father in 1887 in anticipation of his own eventual title as Prince de Sagan. She made the mistake of taking him to Newport in the summer of 1881 where he was drawn to the much larger fortune of **Adele Stevens** (see her separate entry) who shocked society by leaving her husband

1907 at the death of an uncle and his wife worked in New York City to promote her husband's Pommery champagne. The marquis organized in Reims in 1910-1911 the first "aviation weeks" which evolved into the international air show. He was also responsible for rebuilding much of the city, including its famous cathedral, after it was destroyed in World War I. The marquis was an excellent polo player who in 1913 organized at Reims the first open-air school of athletics in France to teach French youth exercise and competition. He enlisted in the infantry in WWI and fought at Verdun but transferred to the aviation division. He accompanied Andre' Tardieu on a special mission to Washington and returned to Europe six months before the war was over where he acted as liaison officer between the French and American forces. The couple lived in Paris and in Reims. He died in Paris at seventy in December of 1950 and was survived by their son, Dalmas, born 1920,

Don Jaime, briefly Prince of the Asturias before renouncing his rights, married Josephine Curtiss' granddaughter.

and children behind to join him in Paris. The couple divorced 11 August 1886 and he married in Paris 25 January 1887 American **Adele Livingston Sampson** (daughter of Joseph Sampson and formerly the wife of Frederic William Stevens) and he died at the Villa Perigord in Monte Carlo, 5 Jan 1917. His uncle was the famous Prince de Sagan, one of the most noted fashionables at the court of Napoleon III. One of his cousins married **Helen Morton**, daughter of U. S. Vice President Levi P. Morton. Another cousin, the Baron Raymond de Selliere, married the widowed Mrs. Charles A. Livermore, who was a stepdaughter of American banker John O'Brien. Elisabeth Curtiss and the Duc de Dino had a daughter, Pauline Palma, born in Venice 1871, who married at Paris, 25 September 1890, Mario Ruspoli, son of the Prince de Poggio-Suasa by his first marriage. Elisabeth died in Rome at the home of her sister, the Princess of Poggio-Suasa, on 30 March 1933. Their family estate, Chatsworth, in Burlington County, New Jersey, covered more than five thousand acres. It eventually became a country club where the Astors, Cuttings, and other social New York families gathered before being sold for back taxes in 1908.

Josephine Mary Curtiss, born New York City, January 1861, was a daughter of Joseph D. B. Curtiss and Elizabeth Shipton Giles Curtiss (thus a sister of **Elisabeth Curtiss** who married the 4th **Duke of Dino**). Josephine married as his second wife in Paris, 18 June 1885 Emmanuele, **Prince of Ruspoli and 1st Prince of Poggio-Suasa, Duke of Morignano.** Their children were Francesco, born 1891; Vittoria, born 1892; and Eugenio born 1894. A son by the prince's first marriage, Mario, married in 1890 the step-daughter of Josephine's sister, Elisabeth, and the 4th Duc de Dino. Josephine and Emmanuele's eldest son, Don Francesco, succeeded to his father's titles and his grandson, who will eventually succeed him, married the Duchess of Plasencia in her own right, enabling him to add the title of Duke of Plasencia to his own. Josephine and Emmanuele's daughter, Donna Vittoria, married the Duke of San Lorenzo and their daughter, Emmanuela, married (non-dynastically in Spain as he renounced his Spanish rights due to his having been born unable to speak or hear) Infante Jaime, second son of King Alfonso XIII of Spain and Queen Ena (who was a granddaughter of England's Queen Victoria). Jaime was briefly Prince of the Asturias, heir to the Spanish throne, after his elder hemophiliac brother renounced his rights to marry a Cuban dancer. Don Jaime was created Duke of Segovia by his father in 1935.

Following the death of his father, he assumed the title Duke of Anjou and became the senior Capetian pretender to the French throne. He also assumed the title Duke of Madrid and sought to reclaim his Carlist right of succession to the Spanish throne that he had earlier renounced (to no avail as his younger brother's son, Juan Carlos, is now King of Spain). The two sons of the Duke of Segovia/Anjou in 1962 brought a legal action against their father charging that he was squandering his share of King Alfonso's estate. The court ruled against

The Spanish royal family. Don Jamie is seated on the far left.

briefly engaged to American heiress **Dolly Fritz** who later took her own life (she reportedly would not return the heirloom diamond and sapphire engagement ring—a claim her family denies—when Don Gonzalo's mother refused to let them marry). He was granted the title Duke of Aquitaine by his father and, though married three times, had only an illegitimate child by an American woman. Although Josephine Curtiss' granddaughter, Emmanuela, divorced the Duke of Segovia/Anjou (he later married an opera singer) and married again, she retained the title Duchess of Anjou and Segovia as her Romanian and Italian divorces from Don Jaime were not recognized in Spain. As of this writing she is still living. In 1975 the Duke of Segovia/Anjou was visiting the tomb of his mother, Queen Victoria Eugenie, at Lausanne when he fell and was seriously injured. He had two operations for a blood clot in his brain but remained in a coma and died 20 March 1975 at St. Gall, Switzerland. His

the sons and the family was later reconciled. Of the two sons of the Duke of Segovia/Anjou, the eldest, Don Alfonso, Duke of Cadiz, married General Franco's granddaughter and was granted the style "His Royal Highness" in 1972, a right that was deprived him in 1987 when the Spanish government also announced that the title of Duke of Cadiz would die with him. He was ambassador of Spain to Sweden 1969-1973 and was decapitated in a skiing accident in Colorado in 1989. His eldest son, who was granted the title "Dauphin" by his father, was killed in an auto accident (caused by his father) in 1984 and that title passed to his younger brother, the Duke of Tourraine.

The second son of the Duke of Segovia/Anjou, Don Gonzalo, was

grandson, Don Luis Alfonso, born 1974, is the current Capetian pretender to the throne of France and Carlist pretender to the Spanish throne and is styled Duke of Anjou and Bourbon. He is considered by one contingent to be head of the Royal House of Bourbon. Alfonso, Duke of Cadiz, and his brother and son were also all French citizens by virtue of their mother, and the French government accorded them each French passports all bearing the style "Royal Highness" with the titles of Duke of Anjou, Duke of Aquitaine, and Duke of Anjou respectively. Luis-Alfonso continues to enjoy the title in his French passport. Prince Emmanuele's elder brother, **Prince Paolo**, married in 1888 the American widow **Rosalie Van Zandt Riggs**.

Mathilde Barclay Davis, born New York City, 11 July 1841, died Rome, 8 February 1917, was a daughter of Hon. Thomas E. Davis and Anna Power Davis. Her English-born father was an early developer and land speculator in New York City. He built the entire block of St. Mark's Place (East 8th Street) between 2nd and 3rd Avenues and, in 1833, sold a home there to Col. Alexander Hamilton, son of the first U. S. Secretary of the Treasury. The senior Hamilton's widow lived her last nine years there with her son. Davis then purchased the entire northeastern end of Staten Island, which he developed and called New Brighton. There he built five Greek Revival mansions referred to as "Temple Row" (one is still in existence). Davis was also an early investor in the development of Texas. In 1834 he was one of a group of men who purchased a strategic high peninsula overlooking the San Jacinto River at the head of Galveston Bay. They called their project the "New Washington Association" and began shipping trade to New Orleans until the outbreak of the Texas Revolution when the Mexican army burned the project to the ground.

At Davis's death in 1878, his estate exceeded $2 million. Other than his widow, who then lived in Paris with their unmarried daughter, Nora, and their daughter Mathilde in Italy, his other surviving daughters were Isabel Sanford, Marie D'Heursel, and Annie La Montagne, also of Paris, and **Lizzie, the Marquise Gavotti,** of Florence, Italy. Davis's other daughter, Catharine, pre-deceased him and married William H. Gebhard, who made his own fortune as a New York City importer of fine wines and liquors. The Gebhards' son, Frederick, was one of the founders of steeplechasing in America. He was the lover of famed English actress Lillie Langtry, formerly the mistress of King Edward VII while Prince of Wales. Lillie had an illegitimate son by Prince Louis of Battenberg but hoped to marry Gebhard after her divorce from Edward Langtry. Freddie Gebhard bought for her a brownstone in New York City as well as a private railway that reportedly cost almost $1 million. In 1888 he and Lillie purchased adjoining estates in the wine-growing country north of San Francisco. Although they eventually married it was not to one another. Mathilde Davis married in the private chapel of the Marquis Gavotti Verospi at Rome, 28 April 1866 **Prince Don Antonio, 9th Duke Lante Montefeltro della Rovere, Prince of Cantalupo, & a Grandee of Spain,** born Bagnaia, Viterbo, 25 April 1831, died Rome, 7 July 1897. Her dowry was reported to be $3 million. Their eldest son and heir, **Prince Don Pietro,** married at Homburg vor der Höhe, 11 September 1899, **Anita Russell Allen,** born St. Louis, Missouri, 7 March 1878, died Rome, 16 February 1953, daughter of Bradford Russell Allen and Helen Armstrong Allen.

At his father's death in 1897, Don Pietro succeeded to the titles. In 1911 King Victor Emmanuel and Queen Helena visited the younger duke and his American-born duchess, Anita, at their historic Villa Lante at Bagnaia, near Viterbo. The newspapers took note that such an unprecedented royal visit was a great honor. The Villa Lante was considered one of the best examples of patrician Renaissance villas in Italy and began to take its present form in 1564 when it was the property of Cardinal Gambara. When Mathilde's husband, Duke Lante Montefeltro della Rovere, died, the *New York Times* reported rather crassly his entire obituary as, "Duke Lante Della Rovere is dead. He was a descendant of Pope Julius II and married a rich American named Davis." The son of Don Antonio and Anita Allen, Don Antonio, succeeded his father in 1953 and his wife was the daughter of American **Ethel Bronson,** Princess Rospigliosi. The third son of Mathilde Davis and Don Antonio, **Prince Don Ludovico,** born

Top left: The Lante Montefeltro della Rovere family at Villa Bagnaia, 1905. Anita Allen is on the far left and her husband on the far right.

Bottom left: Don Lodovico.

Bottom center: Natividad Terry, wife of Baron Alberto Blanc.

Top right: Don Lodovico's wife, Susanna Tilghmann.

Dorothy Deacon, whose father killed his wife's lover when he caught them in the bedroom. Her mother was already having the affair at the time of Dorothy's birth.

gardens are beautifully evoked in Edith Wharton's *Italian Villas and Their Gardens* as well as in Vernon Lee's travel classic *The Enchanted Woods*. The gardens were heavily damaged by bombing in World War II but were later restored after the family sold the estate.

Dorothy Evelyn Parker Deacon was born in Paris of American parents, Florence Baldwin Deacon and Edward Parker Deacon, on 12 April 1891. Her maternal grandfather, the wealthy Admiral Charles H. Baldwin (1822 – 1888), was the official U. S. representative to the coronation of Alexander III as Emperor of Russia. Dorothy was born during the time that her mother was having an affair with a Frenchman, Emile Abeille, whom the Deacons met in 1888. Her mother unwisely admitted to a well-known American gossip Kate

Rome, 17 September 1871, died Rome, 23 June 1923, married at Bryn Mawr, Pennsylvania, 10 January 1900, **Susanna Tilghmann**, born Philadelphia, Pennsylvania, 14 July 1874, died Rome, 9 September 1945. Their daughter married Baron Giulio Blanc, son of King Victor Emmanuel II's Secretary of State.

A great-grandson of Mathilde Davis is Marchese Giulio Sacchetti who served for many years as Delegato dello Stato della Citta del Vaticano (the highest-ranking layman in the Vatican). Villa Lante's

Moore (mother of **Elsie Moore, Duchess of Torlonia**) that she swung naked on a swing in Abeille's apartment for his enjoyment. Abeille's former mistress, the Countess du Bari, wrote to Edward Deacon to ensure that he was aware of his wife's relationship with Abeille. After two years of her denials, Deacon caught her in a nightgown with Abeille in her room at the Hotel Splendide in Cannes. He shot the lover three times then, when his wife begged for her own life, Deacon responded, "I will not shoot you for the sake of our children. I have caught you at last, and now leave you to give myself up." A gravely wounded Abeille verbally changed his will on his deathbed to benefit his former lover, Florence Deacon, before dying. In custody, Edward Deacon was told that he could prosecute his wife for adultery but refused when he learned that she would be arrested. He also insisted that he had merely meant to injure Abeille and not kill him. During the subsequent legal actions, Deacon changed his will to exclude his wife and to establish a trust fund for his four daughters (it was to remain in effect, producing income, until the death of his eldest daughter in 1977). He was sentenced to one year in prison as the court found that he had meant only to injure Abeille.

Gladys and Dorothy were first sent to their grandmother, then entered into a convent school in Paris. Within months Edward Deacon's release was secured by American diplomats and, upon his departure from prison, he sued his wife for adultery to ensure that he would receive custody of their four daughters. After extensive legal machinations, Edward Deacon was given the three eldest daughters while the youngest, Dorothy (who was perhaps not even his child), was awarded to her mother. The next years were spent in a tug-of-war between Florence, who sought to regain her daughters, and Edward, who was adamantly opposed. After Edward's death in 1901, the girls all joined their mother, who in 1904 took an apartment in the Palazzo Borghese in Rome and remained there for nine years. Her intimate companion until his death in 1914 was the married Prince Alfonso Doria Pamphili, a relationship that caused much talk of disapproval among society. Dorothy Deacon married at the Roman Catholic Church of St. Mary's in Cadogan Square, London, 5 July 1910, **Prince Antoine "Aba" Albert Radziwill, Duke of Nieswiez, Comte de Mir,** born Berlin, 30 October 1885, died Warsaw, 18 December 1935,

who succeeded his father in 1910. Aba was a grandson of Princess Marie, whose husband was adjutant to Emperor William I and a great leader in German society. Princess Marie was visited every year on her birthday and at New Year by Emperor William. Aba Radziwill was the son of Princess "Bichette" Radziwill who had befriended Dorothy Deacon's mother when she came to Rome.

Hugo Vickers related a conversation in his biography of Dorothy's sister, Gladys, concerning Dorothy's mother-in-law, "Once, throughout an entire dinner the Princess remained in black silence, and when asked what the matter was she replied: 'Do you expect me to enjoy myself with an impotent man on one side and a homosexual on the other?'" Prince Radziwill was first smitten with Dorothy's eldest sister, Gladys, but gave her up for Dorothy. The slighty-miffed **Gladys Deacon** (see her separate entry) did not attend the wedding but eventually married the **9th Duke of Marlborough,** former husband of American **Consuelo Vanderbilt,** who had been Gladys's friend. After Dorothy Deacon married Prince Aba Radziwill, the groom's mother immediately sent a notice to the Almanach de Gotha stating that the family did not recognize the marriage. In August of 1911 she became reconciled to the union and recognized it officially. The couple eventually divorced and the marriage was annulled in Rome, 13 May 1921. They had a daughter, Elizabeth, who married Prince Witold Czartoryski and then Jan Tomaszewski. Dorothy attended her sister Gladys's 1921 marriage to the 9th Duke of Marlborough although their other surviving sister, Edith, refused to do so as did any member of the groom's family.

Dorothy Deacon married second, at Rome, 15 January 1922, **Count Francois de Paula Palffy d'Erdod.** In 1926 she sued her former husband in New York City seeking funds for their daughter. She and the notorious womanizer Count Palffy d'Erdod divorced 15 June 1928. He married eight times and his third wife, **Eleanor Green Roelker** (1890-1952) was also an American. Dorothy was known to collaborate with the Germans during World War II in exchange for such mundane favors as fine soap. She lived at a hotel in Lausanne and died there 17 August 1960 succeeded by her daughter by the first marriage, Elizabeth "Betka" Tomaszewska, and a son and daughter by the second marriage, John Palffy and Caja Palffy Valtorta.

Gladys Marie Deacon, daughter of Edward Parker Deacon and Florence Baldwin Deacon, was born of American parents on 7 February 1881 at the Hotel Brighton in Paris (see entry for her sister, **Dorothy Deacon,** for their parents and childhood). Gladys was the most beautiful and alluring of the four Deacon daughters. When she was fourteen, Gladys read about the engagement of Consuelo Vanderbilt to the 9th Duke of Marlborough and wrote in her diary, "O dear me if I was only a little older I might 'catch' him yet! But Helas! I am too young … And I will have to give up all chance to ever get Marlborough." The diarist Chips Channon wrote that Gladys was, in her heyday, "the world's most beautiful woman … the toast of Paris, the love of Proust, the belle amie of Anatole France." In fact, Proust said of Gladys, "I never saw a girl of such beauty, such magnificent intelligence, such goodness and charm." In 1897 the 9th Duke of Marlborough met Gladys Deacon for the first time and invited her to stay at Blenheim where Gladys met his American-born wife, **Consuelo Vanderbilt,** resulting in a friendship that lasted for many years. Consuelo was to write of her eventual successor as Duchess of Marlborough, "Gladys Deacon was a wonderful girl endowed with a brilliant intellect. Possessed of exceptional powers of conversation, she could enlarge on any subject in an interesting and amusing manner."

In 1901 the Prussian Crown Prince William came to England (his father, the Kaiser, had visited Blenheim and later asked the Marlboroughs to host his eldest son) and fell in love with Gladys. He gave Gladys his ring and she returned the favor by giving him her bracelet. Upon his return to Germany his angry father insisted that the gifts be returned as he could never countenance such an unequal mésalliance. In September 1902 Consuelo and Gladys toured through Germany where they were escorted by an Imperial A.D.C. (Consuelo wrote that he was "a man impervious to a woman's charm") whose assignment was to assure that no meetings took place between the crown prince and Gladys. The crown prince said shortly before his death in 1951 that he had been in love with an American woman—presumably Gladys—but was not allowed to marry her. In the same year as Gladys's visit to Germany she was so well-known that "Miss Deacon" cardboard dolls were sold to the public. Her next suitor was Lord Francis Hope, owner of the Hope Diamond and the eventual 8th Duke of Newcastle (whose former wife was American **May Yohé**). In August 1906 Gladys declared that she was engaged to Lord Brooke, heir to the Earl of Warwick (Daisy, the Countess of Warwick, was the long-standing acknowledged mistress of the Prince of Wales, later King Edward VII), but the marriage did not take place.

Her next rumored suitor was Prince Roffredo Caetani, 1st Prince Bassiano (and later 17th Duke of Sermoneta) who eventually gave up pursuing her and married American **Marguerite Chapin.** Gladys's many suitors and admirers included Auguste Rodin and Bernard Berenson and the Dukes of Norfolk and Camastra as well as Prince Arthur, Duke of Connaught, a son of Queen Victoria. The strained marriage of the Duke of Marlborough to Consuelo Vanderbilt finally failed in January 1907 when they were legally separated, eventually

Gladys Deacon was a legendary beauty who was a great friend of Consuelo Vanderbilt and her husband, the 9th Duke of Marlborough, before replacing Consuelo as duchess. She wed the duke at the Paris home of an American cousin.

to be divorced in 1921. A Catholic rota declared that the marriage was annulled because the bride had been forced against her will to marry the duke. Not only was Consuelo then free to marry Jacques Balsan but the duke, who had converted to Catholicism, was also allowed to marry again. Gladys Deacon married as his second wife on 25 June 1921 in Paris Charles Richard Spencer-Churchill, **9th Duke of Marlborough**, born at Simla, India, on 13 November 1871, and known all his life by the nickname "Sunny," not for his disposition but for his courtesy title of Earl of Sunderland. His parents had divorced in 1883 in a very public scandal after the 8th Duke fathered a child by the Countess of Aylesford in 1881. Sunny's father, the 8th Duke, was re-married in 1888 in a blatant exchange of money for titles to American heiress **Lillian Warren Price,** the widowed Mrs. Louis Hammersley (see her separate entry). The 8th Duke died unexpectedly at the age of forty-eight, leaving Sunny as 9th Duke just four days before his 21st birthday.

The marriage of Gladys and her longed-for duke was not happy. Finally, in 1933, he cut off electricity and gas to their London apartment and attempted to have Gladys declared insane. He was negotiating with the Duke of Alba to retire permanently as a layman to a Benedictine monastery in Spain but died of cancer on 30 June 1934 before taking that drastic step. One obituary of him likened the late duke to "a lonely peacock struggling through deserted gardens." Gladys, who had severely disfigured her famously-beautiful face with paraffin injections, lived in seclusion until 1962 when she was taken from her home to a psychiatric hospital where she remained until her death. She retreated into obscurity where she would have remained had not young author Hugo Vickers discovered and befriended her there. After months of patience, he was able to coax

from her the basis for an excellent biography, *Gladys, Duchess of Marlborough,* published in 1979. Gladys died 13 October 1977 in her ninety-seventh year. Although rumors had insisted that she was destitute, an auction of her possessions produced well over $1 million.

Joan Douglas Dillon, born New York City, 31 January 1935, was the daughter of C. Douglas Dillon and Phyllis Ellsworth Dillon. In 1931, her father became a member of the New York Stock Exchange and, in 1938, director of Dillon, Read. From 1953 to 1957, he was U.S. ambassador to France then served as undersecretary of state from 1957 to 1959. He was treasury secretary for the Kennedy and Johnson administrations from 1960 to 1965. After twelve years of government service, Douglas Dillon returned to New York in 1965 and became president of the Metropolitan Museum. He died in 2003 at the age of ninety-three. His daughter, Joan, married first, in 1953, James B. Moseley. They had one daughter, Joan Moseley, and divorced at Washoe, Nevada, 12 December 1955, and the marriage was annulled ecclesiastically at Rome, 22 June 1963. She married second in London at the Roman Catholic Church of St. Edward the Confessor in Guildford, 1 March 1967 **Prince Charles of Luxembourg,** born 1927, brother of Grand Duke Jean of Luxembourg. By Prince Charles she had two children, Princess Charlotte, born in New York City in 1967, and Prince Robert, born 1968, who married at Boston in 1994 an American, Julie Ungaro, who was created Princess de Nassau in 2004.

Prince Charles died 26 July 1977 and she married third, at Isleboro, Maine, 3 August 1978, Philippe de Noailles, **7th Duke de Mouchy, Prince-Duke de Poix, 9th Marquess of Arpajon, 8th Count of Nogent le Roi, 5th Count of Noailles** (who had three children, including his heir, the Prince of Poix, by his first wife, a granddaughter of American **Anna Gould, Marquise de Castellane**). She now lives in New York

City and in Paris and is president of Château Haut-Brion, one of the few remaining family owned domains of the Bordeaux region with a history dating to the sixteenth century. In the early 1970s, she began extensive renovation and decoration at the chateau and, in 1975, succeeded her cousin as president of Domaine Clarence Dillon, which was founded by her grandfather.

Margaret Preston Draper, born Boston, 18 March 1891, was a daughter of General William F. Draper (1842-1910) of Hopedale, Massachusetts, whose family was the largest manufacturer of cotton machinery in the United States, and his second wife, Susan Christy Preston Draper. General Draper's father, George, invented the Draper power loom that was found in most textile mills throughout the nation. General Draper's brother, Eben, was governor

Left: Prince Andrea gambled and won – he kept his first wife's money then married his original fianceé. Right: Margaret paid for the right to keep her title after the divorce.

of Massachusetts 1909-1911. Margaret's parents had the unusual distinction of being a Union general and the daughter of a Confederate general, as Susan Preston Draper was a daughter of Kentuckian William Preston who was a member of Congress and U. S. Ambassador to Spain before fighting as a general in the War and then serving as the Confederate ambassador to Emperor Maximilian's court in Mexico. Margaret Draper's maternal grandmother's family, the Wickliffes, were the largest slaveholders in Kentucky. At Margaret's debut costume party in Washington, she wore her mother's $500,000 necklace of which the largest jewel was a gift from Margaret's godmother, Queen Margharita of Italy.

Margaret was rumored to be engaged to several continental suitors, including Count de la Tour d'Auvergne, before she married in Washington, D.C., on 25 October 1916, as his first wife, **Andrea, Prince Boncompagni-Ludovisi-Rondinelli-Vitelli, Marchese di Bucine,** born Rome, 3 February 1884, died Montreaux, 10 December 1948. The young couple met in their childhood when her father was the U. S. ambassador to Italy, 1897-1900, under President McKinley. Prince Andrea's grandfather was Rodolfo, 7th Prince Piombino and Duke di Sora, and Andrea inherited the di Bucine title from his mother. They were married by Cardinal Gibbons at the home of the bride's widowed mother overlooking Farragut Square in Washington, D.C.

Her cousins, Edith and Minna Blair, were bridesmaids. Margaret was received into the Catholic Church days before her wedding. At her mother's home were displayed ancient tapestries purchased by General Draper when he was ambassador after serving in the U. S. Congress. They had originally hung in the Ludovisi Palace in Rome, which was at that time the American Embassy. The chief justice of the United States and his wife attended the wedding, as did the Russian, French, and Italian ambassadors. The bride wore point lace—originally the property of a queen of Spain—which was purchased by her father when he was minister to Madrid. As the *New York Times* reported, "The bridegroom, although an army officer as well as a Prince, wore neither uniform nor orders."

The groom was the senior member of a family reported to suffer under a curse since the seventeenth century. The senior male member of the family at that time, who was totally without funds, abducted a wealthy cousin and forced her to marry him, telling her that her fiance' was dead. Hearing of the girl's marriage, the fiance' hanged himself and the young bride cursed the family to remain poor. Young Prince Andrea certainly fulfilled the prophecy. His wealthy grandmother died in mysterious circumstances, along with four of her five children, in 1840 (it was rumored that her mother-in-law, the imperious Princess Borghese, had her poisoned). It was from the only remaining child that the Boncompagnis descend. Margaret's groom, Prince Andrea, was first engaged to a beautiful Swede, Blanceflor Bildt, whose grandfather had been Prime Minister of Sweden. Her father was the Swedish Minister to Italy where the young couple met. Andrea's family had, however, arrived at a financial arrangement with the Draper family for Margaret's hand. The heart-broken groom was reportedly offered the following consolation: if the marriage remained childless after ten years, they would divorce, Margaret would retain the title of princess, and he would be given permanent control of two American trust funds established for him.

Perhaps bowing early to the inevitable, the marriage was annulled at St. Siege in 1924 after only eight years and he married his Swede that same year. At Prince Andrea's death in 1948, the two trust funds reverted to Blanceflor as well as their palazzo in Rome and an estate in Umbria. At her death in 1972, her estate funded the Blanceflor Foundation in Stockholm that still grants funds for Swedish and Italian philanthropic purposes. There were no children by either marriage and Margaret, still called Princess Boncompagni, died in Washington, D.C., in 1973. Her double first cousin (their fathers married sisters), Wickliffe, funded the right-wing Pioneer Fund to advance research in genetic engineering and eugenics. He was said to have supported Hitler's views on race. Margaret's nephew, William F. Draper, was known as the "dean of American portrait artists," having painted presidents Kennedy and Nixon as well as the Shah of Iran.

Grand Duke Dmitri was a first cousin of Tsar Nicholas II and the two were reared almost as brothers. He was considered the ideal candidate to marry the tsar's daughter, Olga.

Audrey Emery, born New York City, 4 January 1904, died Palm Beach, Florida, 25 November 1971, was a daughter of John J. Emery and Leila Alexander Emery of Cincinnati, Ohio. Her father was a multi-millionaire developer who, with his brother, Thomas J. Emery, made a fortune in candles, soap, chemicals, and real estate, eventually changing the face of Cincinnati. By the early 1900s, the Emery fortune was said to be the largest west of New York City. In 1908 John J. Emery gave his extensive painting collection and an endowment of $200,000 to the Cincinnati Art Museum and in 1925 his widow gave the museum a new wing to house the art collection she left at her death. Their daughter, Audrey, was voted one of the ten most beautiful women in America. She married at Biarritz, 21 November 1926, **Grand Duke Dmitri Pavlovitch Romanov,** captain in the Russian cavalry and aide-de-camp, born 18 September 1891. His father, Grand Duke Paul, was murdered at St. Petersburg in 1919 but spent most of his life away from his son. His mother, Princess Alexandra, was a daughter of George I, King of the Hellenes, and died in childbirth.

Dmitri grew up as a younger friend of his first cousin, Tsar Nicholas II, and was a nephew of Tsar Alexander III, a grandson of Tsar Alexander II, a brother of the Grand Duchess Marie of Russia and a half-brother of the Princess Paley. He was a ward of the sadistic Grand Duke Sergei and his beautiful English wife, Ella, but Sergei was assassinated and Ella entered a convent, so much of his upbringing was spent with the Tsar's daughters. He was supposedly considered the ideal candidate to marry the Grand Duchess Olga, the eldest daughter. It was said that, if the Tsar's hemophiliac son did not survive to adulthood, Olga and Dmitri might rule Russia together. As a youth Dmitri was devoted to the ballet and later became a champion sharpshooter. As a young man he became infatuated with an American, **Miss Alice Durham,** whom he met at a skating rink in St. Petersburg in 1914, and there were American rumors that the couple would marry. Later that year he became enamored of Princess Belosselsky, the former **Susan Whittier** of Boston, and he was banished from Russia for four months. With Prince Felix Youssoupoff, Dmitri was said to have participated in killing Rasputin. His resulting banishment by the tsar from the country was the only reason he was not killed along with the rest of the royal family. In 1917 he was arrested in a counter-revolutionary plot in Petrograd but escaped to Paris where he lived almost penniless until discovered by society.

Audrey Emery's son would eventually serve as Mayor of Palm Beach.

Although Dmitri's marriage to Audrey was morganatic, on 28 July 1935, she was created H. S. H. Princess Romanovsky-Ilyinsky and their son was also accorded the style of Serene Highness. They had a son, Prince Paul, in 1928, and divorced at Bayonne, France, 6 December 1937. In 1939 she was married to a Georgian, **Prince Dmitri Djordjaze,** whose previous wife had been another American, **Elizabeth Warner.** Grand Duke Dmitri died of tuberculosis 5 March 1942 at a Swiss sanitarium in Davos at fifty after a kidney ailment. Their son, Paul, born 27 January 1928, was naturalized as a citizen of the U. S. and became a permanent resident of Palm Beach, Florida, with his wife and children in the 1950s and from 1981 served more than a decade on the Town Council and three terms as mayor using the name Paul R. Ilyinsky. His son, Michael, a Cincinnati photographer, in 1997 organized eight of his grandfather's descendants to take part in the opening of a St. Petersburg exhibition of the Romanov family. In the next year he and other members of his family were present for the re-burial of the assassinated Imperial family at St. Catherine's Chapel inside the walls of the Peter and Paul Fortress. An American television crew accompanied his father during that trip.

In the weeks before Prince Ranier of Monaco married Grace Kelly, there were persistent rumors that he would wed the widowed Audrey Emery but she insisted that they were just friends. Audrey's sister, **Leila Emery,** born Bar Harbour, Maine, 1 July 1902, died Rome, 29 December 1962, first married Alastair Mackintosh, whose first wife had been the actress Constance Talmadge. Leila married second at Paris, 30 August 1938, **Helie, 7th and last Duke of Talleyrand, 7th Duke of Dino, 6th and last Prince of Sagan,** born Florence, 20 January 1882, died in Rome, 20 March 1968. Although Leila Emery's daughter by her first marriage married the Count de Rochembeau, she had no children by Talleyrand and the titles are extinct except for the Dukedom of Dino, which was confirmed in 1912 by King Umberto II of Italy and granted to Helie's sister's son. Helie's brothers, the **5th Duke of Talleyrand** married American **Anna Gould,** while the **6th Duke of Talleyrand** married as his first wife, American **Helen Morton,** whose father was United States Vice President Levi P. Morton. Audrey and Leila's brother, John J. Emery Jr., married Irene Gibson Post, daughter of Charles Dana Gibson and niece of **Nancy, Lady Astor.**

Elizabeth "Bessie" Hickson Field, born New York City, 14 April 1846, died Rome, 11 April 1909, daughter of J. Hickson Field and Mary Elizabeth Bradhurst Field of New York City, married in Rome, 3 March 1870, **Don Salvator Brancaccio, 1ˢᵗ Prince Brancaccio, 5ᵗʰ Duke of Lustra and 2ⁿᵈ Prince of Triggiano, Marquis of Brancaccio and Bajada,** and a Spanish grandee of the first class, born 18 July 1842, died Rome, 14 July 1907, who succeeded his father 25 August 1868.

She was considered a great beauty and served as lady-in-waiting to Queen Margherita of Italy. Her brother, Hickson, was a student at Georgetown University and was at Ford's Theatre the night Abraham Lincoln was assassinated. He helped carry Lincoln to a room across the street and took away the bloodied vest the president was wearing when he was shot. In 1880 Elizabeth built the last Roman Patrician Palace, the Palazzo Brancaccio, on Calle Oppio near the famous Seven Hills. The palatial mansion was designed by Gaetano Koch and decorated by the painter Frecesco Gay. As many as nine hundred guests could be seated in the interior and up to fifteen hundred in its gardens. Restored in 1969, the Palazzo is now rented for lavish entertainments. Elizabeth's first son, Carlo Hickson, was born nine months after their wedding and died before succeeding his father. Their second child, Maria, born 1875, married at Rome, 1895, Prince Francesco di Arsoli of the Princes Massimo. Their third child, Marcantonio, was born 1879, and was named Prince di Roviano by royal decree of 14 April 1904 with primogenture of 8 July 1897. He succeeded his father as 2ⁿᵈ Prince and Duke Brancaccio, 2ⁿᵈ Prince of Triggiano, 2ⁿᵈ Duke of Lustra, and a patrician of Rome. He lived at the Brancaccio Palace in Rome

Bessie Field was so embraced by Italian society that she served as lady-in-waiting to Queen Margherita.

Bessie's parents, Mr. and Mrs. J. Hickson Field. Their son, Hickson, was at Ford's Theatre and helped carry a wounded President Lincoln across the street to his deathbed.

and at the chateau de San Gregorio outside Rome and never married.

Though her family is extinct in the male line, through her daughter, the Princess d'Arsoli and Massimo, her descendants include a union with the royal family of Italy through the marriage of the 5th Prince di Arsoli to Princess Maria Adelaide, daughter of the 2nd Duke of Genoa and great-granddaughter of King Carlo Alberto, King of Sardinia after the abdication of King Victor Emanuele. By a 1978 Decree, a descendant in the female line, Don Fabrizio Massimo, born 1963, added the surname Brancaccio and bears the titles Prince of Triggiano, Prince of Roviano, and Duke of Lustra. He has three children, including a son. Elizabeth's aunt, Eleanor Kingsland Field, married John Jay, grandson of the Chief Justice of the U. S. Supreme Court.

Marie Elisabeth Forbes, born New York City, 29 May 1850, died in Paris 3 November 1932, was a daughter of Paul Forbes and Valerie Wright Forbes. She married at Geneva, 17 December 1874, Gaston, **6th Duke of Praslin, 2nd Duke of Choiseul-Praslin, Count of Chevigny, Count of Choiseul-Praslin,** born 7 August 1834, died Menton, 12 February 1906. Gaston's father, the 5th Duke, in 1847 murdered his wife, the duchess. She had announced that she planned to divorce him over his multiple affairs. He attacked her in her bedroom at their Château de Vaux-le-Vicomte where he slashed her throat with a knife and beat her to death with a pistol as she fought back. He claimed innocence, but the presence of bloodstains in his room as well as examination of the pistol confirmed what took place. He had planned to marry the governess, who in turn fled to the United States and married the Reverend Henry M. Field, editor of the *New York Evangelist.* The Duke de Choiseul-

The Chateau where the 5th Duke of Praslin brutally murdered his wife. He planned to marry the governess but she ran away to America and he took his own life.

Menton-Garavan. Of their seven children, their eldest son, Gaston, born in 1876, succeeded as 7th Duke and married in London 29 November 1910 as his second wife, American **Lucie-Marie Tate,** widow of Charles Paine, whose daughter, **Elisabeth Paine,** married **Aleksander, Prince Sapieha-Kodenski.**

The 7th Duke had no children by either marriage and was succeeded at his death in 1937 by his younger brother, Gabriel, born 1879, as 8th Duke. Marie and Gaston's third son, Count Claude, was charged in a Paris police court in 1911 with mortgaging worthless copies of priceless paintings as authentic items in the famous Choiseul collection. The count had pledged as collateral a pearl necklace worth $19,000 but he gave the necklace to his mistress who later sold it for less than half the purchase price. The current 9th Duke, born 1945, is Marie and Gaston's great-grandson and has three daughters and a son. His father, Rene, Marquis

Praslin then killed himself with a dose of arsenic before he could be arrested for murdering his wife (Bette Davis played the role of the governess in the 1940 movie *All This and Heaven Too*). There were even reports that the duke actually lived in hiding until his eventual death in 1870. Marie and her husband lived at the Villa Bosano in Menton.

Marie Elisabeth Forbes was a childhood friend of **Jenny Jerome** who became Lady Randolph Churchill, American-born mother of Winston. Marie lived as a widow in Paris and at the Villa Terza in

de Choiseul Praslin, served as French ambassador to the Seychelles Islands. Gaston's younger brother, **Count Horace de Choiseul-Praslin,** married as his second wife in Paris, 25 May 1906, **Mary Hooper,** born Cincinnati, 8 February 1866, died Viry-Chatillon, 16 December 1948, who was the widow of **Paulo, Marquis d'Adda Salvaterra.** The inventor of the praline was Caesar Gabriel Choiseul, Duke de Praslin (1598-1675).

Caroline Forster, wife of Joseph Stickney of New York City, was born in Waltham, Massachusetts, 17 July 1869, and died at New York City,

October 1936. According to the *New York Times*, Caroline was "a poor but charming girl" prior to her marriage to coal baron Joseph Stickney, who was many years her senior. They had two children, Forster Reynolds and Caroline Reynolds, and lived at 874 Fifth Avenue in New York City. In 1881 he bought Mount Pleasant House and ten thousand acres of land in New Hampshire in view of Mt. Washington (later called Bretton Woods), then used two million board feet of timber and employed 250 Italian artisans to build the Mount Washington Hotel. At its opening in 1902 he said to reporters, "Look at me, gentlemen, for I am the poor fool who built all this." One year later he was dead, leaving Caroline a fortune in excess of $10 million. She sailed for Europe soon after and took a town house in London. While there in 1912 she gave a dinner and musicale for Ambassador and Mrs. Whitelaw Reid at her town house at 5 Chesterfield Gardens, which she leased for the season from the Earl of Donoughmore. Each year she would spend a part of the late summer and autumn in the U. S. in the White Mountains at the Mount Washington Hotel.

She met Prince Aymon Faucigny-Lucinge in Paris in 1913 and he immediately began pursuing her hand in marriage. She accepted him in June and, two weeks later, they were married in the Catholic Cathedral in London (although the bride was Protestant). She married on 2 July 1913, **Prince Aymon Faucigny-Lucigne,** born Paris, 30 May 1862, died Chateau de Chardonneux, 1 August 1922. He was a first cousin of Prince Guy, who married American **Natividad Terry.** Among those present were

Caroline Forster was "a poor but charming girl" before her marriage to a wealthy husband. When widowed, she married a prince but returned every year to her hotel in New Hampshire.

the U. S. Ambassador and Mrs. Page and French Ambassador Cambon, as well as several family members of the groom. Following the ceremony there was a wedding breakfast at her Chesterfield Gardens home and then the couple departed for a brief honeymoon at Knole Park, the Kent home of Lord and Lady Sackville. The groom's parents had only recently died and his affairs were still unsettled. The couple lived at the Chateau de Chardonneux at Ecommoy, Sarthe, France, and had no children. He was killed in World War I at the Battle of Verdun and Caroline retired to her Mount Washington Hotel in New Hampshire where she had her own royal suite and a private dining room. She died in New York in 1936 and her portrait still graces the lobby of the Hotel.

Caroline Fraser, daughter of Thomas Fraser and Anna Lauton Fraser, born Charleston, South Carolina, 13 April 1810, died Paris, 10 February 1879, married at Bordentown, New Jersey, 18 August 1831, **Prince Lucien Murat, Prince of Naples, Prince of Cleves and of Berg, Prince de Ponte-Corvo,** born Milan, 16 May 1803, died Paris, 10 April 1878. He was the second son of Prince Joachim Murat, Grand Duke of Berg and Cleves and King of Naples, and of Princess Caroline Bonaparte, sister of Napoleon I. In 1848 Prince Lucien was a successful candidate for the National Assembly from the Department of Lot and was elected by a large majority. On 3 October 1849 he was made minister to Turin and was elevated to senator in 1852. By a decree of 25 January 1852 (under the presidency of his cousin, Napoleon III), he assumed the title of prince and his wife was accorded the title of princess. He at one time sought to rule Italy but was not successful. He lived virtually all his life off his wife's meager earnings and she eventually was reduced to teaching children in her home. Two of their sons married Princess Dadiani of Mingrelia and a daughter of the Duke of Wagram and one of their daughters married the Duke de Mouchy.

Prince Lucien's brother, Prince Achille, married American **Catherine Daingerfeild Willis.** Lucien and Caroline's grandson, Prince Michel, born 1887, married at Paris, 6 February 1913, American **Helen Stallo,** while a great-grandson, Prince Charles, born Paris, 16 June 1892, died Morocco, 24 November 1973, married (twice) **Margaret Rutherfurd,** daughter of Lewis Morris Rutherfurd and Anne Harriman Rutherfurd and formerly the wife of Sir Paul Dukes and of D. Ogden Mills. Two of Caroline and Lucien's great-granddaughters, Princess Laetitia and Princess Caroline, married Americans Charles Codman of Boston and Raymond Guest, grandson of steel industrialist Henry Phipps. Guest was the U. S. ambassador to Ireland from 1965-1968.

Margaret A. "Gogo" Geary, born Harrisburg, Pennsylvania, 1863, died New York City, August 1945, was a daughter of Mary Church Geary, the second wife of General John W. Geary. He was the first mayor of San Francisco, governor of the Kansas Territory (where a county is named in his honor), and was twice elected governor of Pennsylvania following his service as a Union general. He ended his army career as military governor of Savannah where he oversaw the city's surrender. His daughter, Margaret, first married Charles Henry Scott of Philadelphia by whom she had a son, Charles H. Scott Jr. She then married **Prince Constantin Toumanoff,** born 1867, died at Cannes, 4 February 1933, a former general in the Imperial Russian Army. The couple lived at the Villa des Anglais in Cannes, France, and had a home on Fifth Avenue in New York City as well as a summer home near Hancock, New Hampshire. Margaret wore her title proudly, and one relative recalls being made to wait in an antechamber until she could be formally presented to her great-aunt.

Alice Gibson, born in New York State, 20 January 1894, died New York City, 25 August 1960, was formerly the wife of a Mr. Coburn. She married morganatically in 1932 as his second wife, **Leopold, Archduke of Austria, Prince of Hungary, Prince of Tuscany,** who was naturalized in the United States as Leopold Habsburg Lorraine in 1953. Born in Agram, Austria, he was a son of the Archduke Leopold Salvator and of Blanca of Castille, Princess de Bourbon, an Infanta of Spain. His great-uncle was the Emperor Franz Joseph of Austria. He first married Baroness Dagmar Podrinska in 1919 and they divorced after having a daughter, Gabrielle. He served in World War I at the Battle of Medeazza and was said to be the youngest person to receive the Order of the Golden Fleece.

He came to the U.S. in 1927 and became a "bit" player in Hollywood. Three years later he was cleared in New York City of a charge of grand larceny for selling a $450,000 necklace that had been a gift of Napoleon I to his wife, Marie Louise, on the birth of their son. The necklace later came into the possession of Leopold's aunt, the Archduchess Maria Theresa. After she sent it to him in America to sell for her, he enlisted the assistance of a couple, the Townsends, who skipped town after selling it to a jeweler for much less than the archduchess thought it was worth. Leopold's commission was $20,000 and he was acquitted by a jury for his part in the transaction. During the trial, the *New York Times* reported that "Mrs. Alice Coburn of Sutton Place" had stood by him throughout the ordeal and he was seen to kiss her hand at the jury's announcement. After their marriage, Leopold then worked in a factory in Willimantic, Connecticut, where he lived in a small house. He was in line as a pretender to the Spanish throne in the Carlist branch but renounced those rights in favor of his younger brother who was married to Princess Ileana of Roumania, a great-granddaughter of Queen Victoria. Several years before his death he inherited a small amount of money, which helped alleviate his distressed circumstances. He and Alice were known in Willimantic as "Mr. and Mrs. Lorraine." They divorced but remained on good terms and she was at his bedside at his death in Willimantic, Connecticut, 14 March 1958.

Maud Staples Ely-Goddard, a daughter of Leonard W. Goddard and Adelaide Ely-Goddard of New York City, was born at New Brighton, 17 August 1859, died Brussels, 14 April 1922. Her maternal grandfather, Smith Ely, was a retired furniture manufacturer from New Jersey who invested in the copper business and became president of the Vermont Copper Mining Company. By 1880 his mines employed more than one thousand workers with an annual production of more than three million pounds of copper. In 1878 Ely purchased the Union mine in Corinth, Vermont, and named it the Goddard mine in honor of his grandson, Ely Ely-Goddard, Maud's brother.

Maud married at Paris, 4 April 1884, **Charles, Prince Poniatowski**, born Paris, 2 March 1862, died New York City, 5 May 1906, eldest son of the 5th Prince Poniatowski and Prince di Monte Rotondo and of his wife, Louise le Hon, who was the illegitimate daughter of the Duke de Morny, who was himself the illegitimate son of Auguste, Count de Flauhaut, by Queen Hortense of Holland. They lived in Mexico and did not have children.

Charles would have inherited the Poniatowski family titles but he died two years before his father. They were instead inherited by his younger brother and his American wife, **Elizabeth Helen Sperry**. A first cousin of Maud and Ely, **Romaine Goddard**, married the **Baron de Overbeck** of Germany. In 1878 Baron de Overbeck was put in charge of the steamship *America* when it was chartered by a British company. Later that same year the Baron was conferred the title of **Maharaja of Sabah** by the Sultan of Borneo, after concluding successful negotiations for the cession of territory to his London-based company. The Baroness de Overbeck's father was Daniel

Convers Goddard, first assistant secretary of the newly-created U. S. Department of the Interior, who died only a few years into his marriage. His widow, Madeleine Vinton, was a daughter of Congressman Samuel Finley Vinton (1792-1862) and Romaine Madeleine Bureau Vinton. A well-known author, she opposed women's suffrage and, by her first husband, had Vinton Augustine and Romaine Goddard.

After her husband's death she married secondly, 1865, Admiral John Adolph Dahlgren, famous U. S. naval officer and inventor of the Dahlgren cannon. Their sons, John Vinton and Eric, married respectively **Elizabeth Drexel** and Lucy Drexel, daughters of Joseph W. Drexel of Philadelphia, and their daughter, Ulrica, married Josiah Pierce and was the mother of **Romaine Dahlgren Pierce** who married the **3rd Marquess of Milford Haven.** John Dahlgren died shortly after his marriage to Elizabeth Drexel and his widow eventually married society leader Harry Lehr, who informed her on their wedding night that he was homosexual. After his death, she then married the **5th Baron Decies,** widower of American **Helen Gould,** a granddaughter of railroad baron Jay Gould by his eldest son, George. A cousin of John and Eric, **Margaretta Drexel,** married the **14th Earl of Winchilsea and Nottingham.**

Mary "May" Goelet, born New York City, 6 October 1878, died London, 26 April 1937, was a daughter of real estate heir Ogden Goelet (1846 – 1897) and Mary Rita Wilson. Her mother was one of the "Marrying Wilsons" of Georgia, who were celebrated for contracting such advantageous marriages (the mother's sisters married Cornelius Vanderbilt and Sir Mungo Herbert, British ambassador to the U. S., while their brother married a daughter of "the" Mrs. Astor). May

May Goelet was such a prized marital catch that one duke announced his engagement to her even though they had never met. Hers was considered one of the few "love matches" of the era.

was such a prized marital catch that the impecunious 9th Duke of Manchester announced his engagement to her to ward off his creditors even though he had never met her. In what was said to be one of the few "love matches" of the day (despite her $20 million dollar dowry), May married in New York City on 10 November 1903, Henry John Innes-Ker, **8th Duke of Roxburghe**, born Broxmouth Park, 25 July 1876, died Wilton 29 September 1932. May's fortune restored Floors Castle where the current Prince Andrew, Duke of York, became engaged to Sarah Ferguson. The duke's younger brother in 1907 married American heiress **Anna Breese** and they were said to be highly disappointed when May finally had a male heir in 1913. May had been a bridesmaid at the marriage of Consuelo Vanderbilt to the 9th Duke of Marlborough (their husbands were cousins) but May's marriage, unlike Consuelo's, was happy. Perhaps that is why Consuelo wrote that May's "chief interests were needlework, salmon fishing and bridge. To those diversions she devoted a good brain which might perhaps have been used to better purpose." The current duke is May's grandson.

Anna Gould, born New York City, 5 June 1875, died at Neuilly, 29 November 1961, was the youngest daughter of railroad financier Jay Gould and Helen Day Miller Gould. After the death of her parents she was reared largely by her elder sister, the pious Helen, as well as her far-from-pious eldest brother, George, and his very social wife, Edith. So vast was the empire built by their late father, one of the most notorious of the "Robber Barons," that Anna and her five siblings at one time were each collecting $115,000 every week in dividends

The dandy Count Boniface de Castellane with his "light that failed," the vastly wealthy Anna Gould.

and interest alone. Her inheritance was reported to be as high as $80 million but perhaps was closer to $15 million. She was an obvious target for the infamous dandy, Count Boniface de Castellane, who was the model for Proust's character of Saint Loup.

Reared in opulence at his grandmother's chateau of Rochecotte, "Boni" needed a great deal of money to achieve the lifestyle to which he aspired and professed not to care that, along with her millions, Anna Gould inherited the dark, swarthy looks of the Goulds (even though he later called their marital bedchamber 'le chambre expiatoire'). Robert de Montesquiou said of her, "Elle a les yeux d'un singe, un singe qu'on a pris en captivité" – She has the eyes of a monkey, a monkey taken in captivity.

Boni deliberately put himself in Anna's path and they were introduced in Paris in 1894 by Fanny Read, a well-connected but impecunious American woman, who was known to make such introductions in exchange for compensation. Boni's memoirs (in which he calls Anna, "my Light that Failed") admits that, before he met his future wife, "Gossip credited Miss Gould with the possession of boundless wealth; she was worth milliards instead of millions." (i.e., hundreds of millions). Had her father been alive, there is little doubt that she would not have been captured. Anna Gould married in New York City on 14 March 1895 **Count (later Marquis) Boniface de Castellane,** born Paris, 14 February 1867, died Paris, 12 December 1932. She wisely refused to convert to Catholicism (even though Archbishop Corrigan officiated at the ceremony) and was said to have settled $2 million immediately on the groom.

Above: de Castellane was Proust's model for the dandy Saint Loup.

Top left: Anna's second husband and their only son.

Top right: Anna's second husband as a young man.

While Anna was busy over the next decade with the birth of a daughter and two sons (Marie Louise, Boniface Jay, and Georges), her husband spent as much as $8 million of her inheritance. His memoirs admit, "True, I spent her millions but, I have actually represented a more than profitable investment for her." Their primary residence was Paris's opulent pink marble Palais Rose complemented by the chateau du Marais at Essonne (with 1,200 hectares of land) and the chateau de Grignon at Vauclose. There was also a yacht, the *Valhalla,* for transporting them to Russia and Norway, and later the *Anna* for competing at the Cowes regatta. During their years of marriage Anna was reportedly the only person who did not know about Boni's many affairs and the expensive gifts purchased with his wife's money that were lavished on his mistresses. He arrived at the Palais Rose one evening to find it emptied of furnishings and his family; even the electricity had been disconnected. Anna divorced him at Paris on

11 April 1906 and the marriage was finally annulled after years of legal challenges of which *Time* magazine opined "Probably not since Henry VIII tried in vain to get an annulment of his marriage with Catherine of Aragon has a matrimonial case been so long in the courts of the Roman Catholic Church." A special court of nine cardinals was eventually required to render a final decision and the marriage was held to have been valid (even though she wasn't Catholic) and the annulment granted on 17 July 1915 was finally upheld in 1924.

Boni set his sights on Anne Morgan, the immensely wealthy daughter of J. P. Morgan, but she shared his sexual interest in women and had no need or desire for a husband, living rather openly with literary agent Elisabeth Marbury and society decorator Elsie de Wolfe. During the intervening years of annulment appeals, Anna married at London, 7 July 1908, her former husband's first cousin, **Helie de Talleyrand-Perigord, 5th Duke of Talleyrand, Duke of Dino, Prince of Sagan,** born at Mello 23 August 1859, died at Paris 25 October 1937. They had a son, Howard, and a daughter, Helene Violette. The son and heir took his own life in 1929 when his parents, citing his young age, refused to let him marry the woman of his choice. Their daughter eventually inherited her father's title as Duchess of Sagan and, at her death on 6 March 2003, the title ended with her. She married as her second husband Gaston Palewski (1901 -1984), vice president of the National Assembly, minister, ambassador, and constitutional council president of France, and right-hand man to De Gaulle in the Free French movement (Palewski was also a lover of Nancy Mitford who made him the hero of her novels; when he was

France's ambassador to Italy from 1957 to 1962, the Romans called Palewski ''L'Embrassadeur'' because he chased women through the halls of the French Embassy).

Anna's second marriage was far happier than her first. The prince/ duke died 26 October 1937, and Anna lived as a widow for another quarter century. In 1916, Anna and her younger brother, Frank, sued their four siblings for mismanagement of their father's vast estate. After eleven years of litigation, the courts finally decided that George had mismanaged the estate and a judgment for $50 million was entered against the four elder siblings as trustees (the settlement was reduced by compromise to $20 million). In the closing days of litigation, eldest son George died, leaving an estate of only $15 million which was whittled down by taxes and judgments to $5 million and promptly became the source of another legal battle between his seven legitimate and three illegitimate children. Anna and Frank were then left with the task of collecting their court-ordered money from the three surviving siblings. At one point, almost every major law firm in New York City was involved in the litigation.

Anna spent her last years alternating between France and her father's residence in Lyndhurst, New York, where she was aloof and isolated. One great-granddaughter recalls that she was kinder to her servants than to her family. She died at Neuilly on 29 November 1961. Boni de Castellane, a notorious womanizer in his youth, reportedly converted to homosexuality in his fifties and lived openly with another man in his chateau. His last years were plagued by ill health and his mother, who outlived her son by two years, was said to visit him every day. He died in Paris on 12 December 1932. A son of Anna and Boni, Boniface Jay, was a diplomat who married a daughter of Jules Patenôtre, the first representative of France to the United States to be accorded the title of ambassador, and of his American heiress wife, Eleanor Elverson whose family owned the *Philadelphia Inquirer*. Boniface Jay was posted to Berlin and London before becoming French minister to Morroco.

One of Anna's descendants from her first marriage, Diane de Castellane, married the 7th Duke of Mouchy, **7th Duke of Poix, 9th Marquess of Arpajon**, whose second wife was American **Joan Douglas Dillon.** Diane's son by the duke, currently the Prince of Poix, is the heir to his father's titles. Anna's grandson by her daughter of the second marriage, Helie de Pourtales, married as his second wife **Countess Marie Eugenie de Witt**, daughter of Count Serge Witt and Clotilde Bonaparte, Princess Napoleon, and granddaughter of Victor, Prince Napoleon and Princess Clementine of Belgium. Thus Countess Marie is a great-granddaughter of Leopold II, King of the Belgian, as well as of King Jerome of Westphalia, brother of Emperor Napoleon Bonaparte. And, because of her descent from Electress Sophia of Hanover, she is listed in the order of succession to the British throne.

Julia Dent Grant was born in the White House on 7 June 1876 while her grandfather, Ulysses S. Grant, was president. Her parents were General Frederick Dent Grant and Ida Honore' Palmer Grant, sister of the wealthy and socially prominent Mrs. Potter Palmer of Chicago. In 1888 Julia's father was appointed U. S. minister to

Julia Dent Grant had a family name but no wealth. She wrote perceptive first-hand accounts of a changing world order.

Left: Julia Dent Grant as Princess Cantacuzene. Right: Born in the White House while her grandfather was president, Julia is pictured in her mother's arms.

Austria and for the next five years she lived in Vienna, learning to speak German with a Viennese accent.   Julia was received at court and was introduced to her father's hunting partner, Emperor Franz Joseph, and his empress, and was presented to Queen Victoria on the family's journey. Her return to the U. S. at the end of her father's term was a decided let-down after such an exciting era and Julia eagerly accepted an invitation from her wealthy aunt, Mrs. Potter Palmer (who attended the coronation of Tsar Nicholas II in Moscow in 1896 where she met both the tsarina and the Queen of Greece), to accompany the Palmers on a trip to Europe and Egypt in 1898.

At the very end of their journey Julia met in Rome Prince Michael Cantacuzene who was temporarily assigned to the Russian embassy while recuperating from a horse-show accident. The Palmers left Rome for Cannes and within a week Prince Michael followed them; two days later he was engaged to Julia. The Grants had no money and Julia's father was then posted to the Philippines. Prince Michael's mother (his father was deceased) was said to be unconcerned that Julia brought no dowry and gave her consent to the marriage. **Prince Michael Cantacuzene** was born 29 April 1875 in Odessa, Russia, and died 25 March 1955 in Sarasota, Florida. He was reportedly descended from John VI Cantacuzenos, Emperor of Byzantium (1341-1355), whose descendants emigrated to Moldavia and Wallachia and were qualified with a princely title in 1856 and 1865, confirmed in 1893. On 19 May 1872, his father was authorized to revive the name and title of his maternal grandfather, statesman Count Michael Speransky (1772 – 1839), who died without sons. The Cantacuzenes were not wealthy but had inherited from the Speranskys a substantial estate of Bouromka in the Ukraine.

Mrs. Palmer took charge of her niece's wedding and the ceremony was held in Newport on 25 September 1899. The groom wore his parade white uniform with red and silver trim and high boots, topped with a golden helmet crowned by an Imperial eagle. The couple left the next day for Russia where Prince Michael re-entered military life and was gravely wounded in the First World War. They barely escaped the Revolution with their lives and their son and two daughters and the jewels Julia was able to sew into her clothes. All of their real estate in Russia was forfeited. Prince Michael had little aptitude for work in his injured condition and only through the generosity of Mrs. Palmer, who died shortly before her niece's return and left Julia a modest inheritance (including a home in Sarasota), were they able to survive. Julia's grandfather, President Grant, had not been a wealthy man and lost what little funds he had in 1884 when duped by a business partner. Dying with cancer, he forced himself to write his memoirs so that his wife would not be destitute in her last years. He died three weeks after the memoirs' completion and his widow lived comfortably until 1902.

Julia set about to emulate her grandfather and began writing a succession of memoirs to support her family. Hers were among the very few American eye-witness accounts of the Russian Revolution and their accuracy was later confirmed by other sources. Prince Michael traveled briefly to Russia to join a counter-revolution but, when it was unsuccessful, he returned permanently to the U. S. where he obtained citizenship. He and Julia retreated to Florida where he helped manage orange groves for the Palmer family. When the Palmers organized their own bank in Sarasota, he became an officer there. Julia and Prince Michael divorced in 1934 and she took the name Julia Cantacuzene Grant; he married Jeanette Drapter, who was a clerk at the bank. In that same year Julia petitioned to regain her American citizenship, which she had relinquished upon her marriage. She moved to Washington where she continued writing for magazines and newspapers and became a frequent lecturer against Communisim.

Julia's eldest child, Michael, graduated from Harvard, became a stock-broker, and was a successful equestrian and shooting expert. He and his wife had two children before their divorce and her suicide.

Their son, Rodion, married a granddaughter of cereal heiress Marjorie Meriwether Post. Julia's younger daughter, Zenaida "Ida," married Sir John Hanbury-Williams in a Washington wedding attended by President and Mrs. Coolidge, as well as the chief justice, the secretary of state, and the British ambassador. Their daughter, Barbara, married Prince Michael M. Cantacuzene from another branch of the family. Prince Michael Cantacuzene, Julia's former husband, died in Sarasota, Florida, on 25 March 1955, at the age of seventy-nine, still married to his second wife. For a 1970 White House luncheon honoring descendants of American presidents, Alice Roosevelt Longworth, daughter of President Teddy Roosevelt, declined saying, "I'm cutting down on going out." Princess Cantacuzene replied, "Cutting down? Well think of that. Why, she's only eighty-six!" The princess was almost ninety-four at the time. Her sight began to fail at the age of seventy and she suffered five operations before becoming blind at eighty. Days before her ninetieth birthday she awoke with partial vision after a retina in one eye dropped without medical explanation. In 1970 a census-taker called Julia's grandson for help, explaining that she seemed confused by his questions. When asked for specifics, the grandson was told, "She seems to think she was born at 1600 Pennsylvania Avenue in the year of America's centennial." The reply was, "But then, there's no reason for me to come over as that is perfectly correct." Julia lived just short of a full century, dying at the age of ninety-nine at her home in the Dresden Apartment Building in Washington, D.C., on 4 October 1975.

Stevens "Stevee" Anna Greeff was a daughter of Catherine Stevens

Greeff and Theodore Greeff of Greenwich, Connecticut, and of Tucker's Town, Bermuda. Her father founded Greeff Fabrics in 1933 and his company became known for creating and manufacturing fabrics and wallpapers based upon historically accurate patterns such as Audubon's birds. Mr. Greeff died in 1980 and the company was purchased in 1996 by F. Schumacher & Company. Stevee attended Briarcliff College and the University of Lausanne in Switzerland. She married on 17 August 1968 in Banksville, New York, **Diego, 9th Duke de Vargas Machuca, 6th Marchese di Vatolla, 11th Marchese di San Vicente and a Grande of Spain first class, 11th Conte del Porto, 20th Conte di Urgell, 27th Signore di Vargas and 14th Signore di Varguillos,** born 22 June 1941. A reception was held afterwards at Document Hill, the bride's family home in Greenwich.

The couple met when the bride was working at her father's London offices. At the time of their marriage the groom was a vice president in the Milan offices of the advertising firm McCann-Erickson. At the engagement announcement, Diego's father was still living and the wedding was scheduled for June of 1968. The 7th Duke died in April, the young duke succeeded to his father's titles, and the wedding was delayed until August. At the time of the marriage, the bride's mother remarked to the *New York Times* that the marriage "is so completely un-American." The couple had a daughter in 1970 and a son in 1974 who is styled Count of Porto and Hidalgo until he succeeds his father. The duke and duchess were divorced in 1995 and she lives in the United States.

Alice Green, daughter of John Green of "Rosedale," (now 3501

The Empress Carolota and Emperor Maximilian of Mexico had no children and adopted as prince imperial the son of an American mother.

Newark St., N.W.) Washington, D.C., and Nancy Forrest Green, and granddaughter of Rebecca Plater Forrest and Major-General Uriah Forrest and great-granddaughter of George Plater III, sixth governor of Maryland (who voted as a presidential elector for George Washington in 1789), married at "Rosedale," 9 June 1855, **Prince Don Angel de Iturbide y Huarte,** born Queretaro, 2 October 1816, Mexican Prince, who was granted the style, "His Highness" on 22 June 1822. Prince Don Angel was the second son of H. M. Augustin I, Emperor of Mexico, who took the constitutional oath 21 May 1822 and was crowned with his wife at the Cathedral of Mexico City, 21 July 1822. He had been the author of Mexico's separation from Spain and was enthusiastically pressured to accept its new throne (even though he still recognized

The Kearney house in Georgetown, home of the first American-born wife of a prince imperial.

Spain's Ferdinand VII as his king and wanted him or another Bourbon to accept the throne of Mexico). Congress voted 77 to 15 to offer Augustin the crown and later voted unanimously to make its succession hereditary for the Iturbide family. After plots against the crown by disaffected military leaders, the emperor abdicated 19 March 1823, and went into exile in Italy and England, but returned a year later and attempted to regain the throne. He was arrested and shot without trial on 19 July 1824, and was buried at Padilla, then re-interred at Mexico City Cathedral in a ceremony on 28 October 1838.

When the emperor's eldest son, the prince imperial, died unmarried (leaving an illegitimate daughter who eventually became the first lady of Peru) in New York City in 1866, the next son, Don Angel (husband of Alice Green), would have become head of the family and heir to the throne had he not abdicated his rights in favor of his only son, Prince Don Augustin de Iturbide y Green, Prince Imperial of Mexico, only a year before on 13 September 1865, in exchange for the adoption of his son by Mexico's new emperor. Don Angel died at Mexico City 21 July 1872 and his wife, Alice, died 28 January 1892. The only son of Alice Green and Prince Don Angel was **Prince Don**

Augustin de Iturbide y Green, born 2 April 1863. He was educated at Ascot School in England and at Georgetown University where he received a degree of Bachelor of Philosphy. Emperor Maximilian (brother of Emperor Franz Joseph of Austria) and his wife, Empress Carlotta, took the throne of Mexico in 1863 with the support of the French troops of Napoleon III. They invited the Iturbide family back to Mexico and, when it became obvious that the couple would have no children, they adopted young Don Augustin and his first cousin, Don Salvador. The two boys were granted by Emperor Maximilian the title of Prince of Iturbide with the qualification of "Highness" on 13 September 1865. They were reared apart from their parents and from one another in an effort to ensure the throne's succession by keeping them safe from dangers and jealous intrigues. The elder, Don Augustin, became prince imperial, head of the royal house and heir to the throne, making Alice Green the first American mother of a prince imperial. She vehemently protested the loss of her son but her highly-compensated family overruled her objections. Emperor Maximilian thought that, by offering the Mexican people an heir who was a member of their formerly-ruling family, they would more easily accept his own reign. His plans were for naught.

At the fall of the new empire and Maximilian's execution in 1867, Don Augustin's birth family took him first to England and then to the United States to live. He married on 5 July 1915 at St. Matthew's Cathedral in Washington, D.C., as his second wife (his first, by whom he had no children, was English-born Lucy Eleanor Hatchett, 1862-1940) **Mary Louise Kearney** (making her the first American-born wife of a former prince imperial), born Washington, D.C., 25 September 1872, daughter of Brig. Gen. James Kearney of "Quality Hill" in Georgetown, Washington, D.C. Don Augustin, the former prince imperial, renounced his claim to the throne and returned to Mexico. He served as an officer in the Mexican Army in 1894 and was subsequently exiled for publishing a protest against the government of President Porfirio Diaz for which he was imprisoned. He was later a professor of French and Spanish at Georgetown University. He had a nervous breakdown, which eventually led to his complete physical decline. He died without children at Washington, D.C., on 3 March 1925 and was buried in Philadelphia next to his grandmother, the empress, at the Catholic Church of St. John the Evangelist. The former Iturbide empress had moved to Philadelphia in 1824 after the execution of her husband, where she lived quietly with a modest pension from the Mexican government. She visited President Polk at the White House in 1848 seeking to restore the pension she had previously been remitted by the Mexican government but he was unable to help her, although he wrote in his diary, "She is an interesting person." Don Augustin's widow, Mary Louise, lived until September of 1967. His first cousin, Don Salvador, who was also adopted by Emperor Maximilian, was largely reared in Hungary and Italy, where he was a close friend of the Duke of Madrid, Carlist pretender to the Spanish throne. He married in 1871 the Baroness Gizella de Tarradhaza and their descendants mainly live in Australia. An Austrian descendant of another Iturbide brother is considered head of the Imperial house of Iturbide and heir to the non-existent Mexican throne.

Eleanor Margaret "Peggy" Green, born New York, 5 November 1895, died Copenhagen, 3 July 1966, was a daughter of James Oliver Green, president of Western Union Telegraph, and Amy Beaumont Hewitt Green, a granddaughter of New York City Mayor Abram S. Hewitt, and great-granddaughter of philanthropist Peter Cooper, founder of the Cooper Union. In 1923 Eleanor visited her cousin, Baroness von Schilling, in Copenhagen, and there met her future husband, the youngest son of Prince Valdemar and Princess Marie of Orleans. She married in New York City's Calvary Church 10 June 1924, **Prince Viggo of Denmark,** born Copenhagen, 25 December 1893, died Copenhagen, 4 January 1970. He renounced his rights of succession along with the title prince of Denmark and the qualification of royal highness and assumed the style His Highness Prince Viggo, Count of Rosenborg, 21 December 1923. He was a major general in the Danish Army and his grandfather was King Christian IX of

Prince Viggo of Denmark renounced his rights to marry his American wife.

Princess Peggy, as she was affectionately known, became greatly loved in her adopted home.

Denmark, brother of George I, king of the Hellenes. His aunt was Queen Alexandra of England, consort of Edward VII. At the time of their wedding the *New York Times* stated, "There has probably never been recorded a marriage in the history of New York society of such importance, and it is the first time that a person of royal birth has taken an American bride in this city." About fifteen hundred guests attended the reception in the Hewitt mansion at 9 Lexington Avenue. A room in her parents' country estate, Ringwood Manor, was decorated especially for their honeymoon. She learned to speak Danish fluently with little accent and, after their marriage, she became heavily involved in charity work and was very popular in Denmark, where she was referred to as "Princess Peggy." She was an active horsewoman and was usually accompanied by at least three dogs. The couple enjoyed bicycling and always took an annual cycling vacation through Jutland. She attended charity bazaars where she drew portraits of guests, and for many years packed Christmas baskets for the needy. Peggy had wonderful jewelry including "a massive diamond choker" which was a wedding gift from her father. One jeweler in Denmark who often dealt with her recalls her as "very sweet. She looked like a charwoman but was great fun. All the royals here relaxed with her as she had no snobbery or protocol." The same source said that Prince Viggo was "dry ... with little charm." Peggy was extremely active in relief work during World War II and, with the prince, often represented the king and queen of Denmark at official functions. In 1961 the king bestowed upon her the Order of the Elephant, the highest order of the nation, which was instituted in the fifteenth century. In 1962 she and Queen Ingrid of Denmark were patrons of the "Creative Craft in Denmark Today" exhibition at the Cooper Hewitt Museum in New York City, which included her mother among its founders. In 1931 she gave a collection of forty-two gowns with accessories to the Brooklyn Museum. Peggy died in Denmark at the age of seventy on 3 July 1966, having had no children. Her funeral service in Denmark was attended by King Frederik IX, Prince Viggo's nephew, and Queen Ingrid. She was buried as Her Highness Princess Viggo, Countess of Rosenborg, in the old cathedral at Roskilde where Danish royals are traditionally interred.

Lisa Halaby, daughter of Najeeb Elias Halaby and Doris Carlquist Halaby (an American of Swedish ancestry), was born in Washington, D.C, on 23 August 1951. Her paternal grandfather, Najeeb Halaby, was a Syrian immigrant who came to the United States with his family as a teenager. He and his Texas-born wife, Laura Wilkins, founded a successful antiques boutique, Halaby Galleries, in Dallas that Neiman-Marcus offered to house in their expanded department store in the mid 1920s. The Halabys' son, Najeeb, went on to become a private and Navy test pilot, lawyer, public servant, businessman and NGO leader. He was appointed by President Kennedy as presidential advisor and the highest ranking minority head of a U. S. agency when he became director of the Federal Aviation Administration, and later, president and chair of Pan American World Airways.

Left: Lisa Halaby was a cheerleader in Princeton's first coed class. Right: Lisa Halaby became "Noor al Hussein" upon her marriage and was given the title of queen.

His eldest daughter, Lisa, attended schools in New York, California, and Washington, D.C., before graduating from Concord Academy in Massachusetts. She entered the first co-educational class at Princeton University where in 1974 she received a B.A. in Architecture and Urban Planning. After university she worked on international urban planning projects in Australia and Iran before undertaking research throughout the Arab world for a Pan Arab aviation project based in Jordan. Lisa first met her future husband, **King Hussein,** on a brief visit to Jordan with her father at a ceremony marking the acquisition of the country's first Boeing 747. As Lisa went about her business in Amman she would have several fleeting encounters with the king; a lunch invitation one day turned into an entire day's conversation. The striking young woman was assiduously courted by the king who had been widowed the year before and a whirlwind courtship ensued. Lisa Halaby embraced Islam and upon her engagement King Hussein gave her the name "Noor," which became Noor al Hussein – Light of Hussein - on her wedding day, 15 June 1978. She became the first American woman to have the title of "Her Majesty."

King Hussein, a direct descendant of the prophet Muhammed, was a member of the Hashimite family who ruled, in various forms,

Top: King Hussein and Queen Noor surrounded by all his children, the youngest four of whom are hers.

Right: King Hussein and Queen Noor in unaccustomed formal dress. They both preferred to be casual and usually drove themselves when in their own country.

over the Hejaz (the Western part of Arabia which includes the holy cities of Mecca and Medina) from the time of the Caliph Ali in the seventh century until 1925. On 20 July 1951, King Hussein was with his grandfather, King Abdullah I, when he was assassinated at the al-Aqsa mosque in Jerusalem. A medal King Abdullah had recently given to young Prince Hussein, which he wore at his grandfather's insistence, saved Hussein from the assassin's bullet that deflected off the medal. King Hussein's father suffered from mental illness and ruled only for a brief time before Hussein was proclaimed king on 11 August 1952 and ruled under a regency until assuming full powers at the age of eighteen on 2 May 1953. At his death, he was the longest-reigning monarch in the world. He accomplished extraordinary progress in his country by advancing universal education, exemplary health care, the role of women, and a participatory and pluralistic system of governance, all within the framework of Arab and Islamic principles. He struggled throughout his forty-seven-year reign to secure a comprehensive, just, and lasting peace in the Middle East. Under his guidance, Jordan was transformed from a pre-industrial state to a modern model of political, economic, and social progress in two generations and in the process became a sanctuary of peace, stability, and moderation in the Middle East. During the Gulf War, however, when he called for Iraq's withdrawal from Kuwait and for an Arab resolution of the crisis he was portrayed as anti-American. During that time, Queen Noor was a valuable advocate for her country, often appearing on television and in the halls of Congress to present the Jordanian perspective.

King Hussein's first marriage, in 1955, was an arranged one with an Egyptian-born cousin of his father and they were divorced in 1957. In 1961 he married his second wife, the British-born Toni Gardner, who was given the title Princess Muna. They divorced in 1972 but she was allowed to retain her title. His third wife, Queen Alia, whom he married in 1972, was killed in a helicopter crash in 1977. By his first three wives King Hussein had four sons and three daughters as well as one foster daughter. By Queen Noor, King Hussein had four children, Prince Hamzah (who was crown prince of Jordan from 1999 to 2004), Prince Hashim, Princess Iman, and Princess Raiyah.

Over the past thirty years, Queen Noor has initiated and sponsored programs and projects in Jordan to address specific national development needs in the areas of education, culture, women and children's welfare, sustainable community development, environmental conservation, human rights, and conflict resolution. The Noor Al Hussein Foundation (NHF), founded in 1985 to consolidate and integrate the Queen's diverse development initiatives, has received international recognition for its institutions and programs, particularly in the areas of empowering women, community development, and micro-finance. Additionally, Queen Noor is actively involved in a number of international organizations advancing global peace-building and conflict recovery, and advises the United Nations on these issues. She is president of the United World Colleges, chair of the United Nations International Leadership Academy, advisor to Women Waging Peace, Seeds of Peace, and the International Campaign to Ban Landmines, patron of the World Conservation Union, trustee

of the Aspen Institute, Conservation International, World Wildlife Fund International, Refugees International, Mentor Foundation, and a member of the International Commission on Missing Persons.

When King Hussein's cancer became life-threatening, she held the family together during his hospitalization in the U.S. and remained with him throughout months of treatment. Shortly before his death the king changed the long-standing succession to the throne, replacing his brother, Prince Hassan, with King Hussein's eldest son, Prince Abdullah (now King Abdullah II). After the king's death, she founded the King Hussein Foundation, a non-profit, non-governmental organization that promotes cross-cultural dialogue and understanding and, building on efforts in Jordan, advances social, economic, and political opportunity in the Arab and Muslim world. She has published two books, *Hussein of Jordan* in 2000 and *Leap of Faith* in 2003, her best-selling memoir, which was published in fifteen languages.

Elizabeth Frances Hanan was a daughter of shoe manufacturer James and Annie Dalton Hanan and sister of John Henry Hanan of New York City, who was a well-known yachtsman. Her brother had an impressive home on New York City's Fifth Avenue as well as "Castlewood," his estate in Newport, Rhode Island. His family's highly successful shoe company was established prior to 1886 when it became the first manufacturer to stamp the company's name on its shoes. In addition to New York City, the company had offices in London and Paris. He also founded the Brooklyn Manufacturers Trust Bank. Elizabeth was cruising the Mediterranean with her brother and sister-in-law when she met the Italian **Duke Arturo de Majo Durazzo**

(and purportedly **Prince of Achaia**, although that principality was absorbed by the Byzantine Empire in 1432). She was fifty-three and he was thirty-nine at the time. They were married amid great pomp on 17 February 1914 at St. Thomas's Church on Fifth Avenue in New York City. Less than nine months later, on 7 October 1914, she filed suit for divorce, alleging fraudulent representation of his background and that he was a fugitive from justice in France, where he had been convicted of larceny and sentenced to imprisonment. The suit contended that, prior to their marriage, he had been a cashier for the owner of the Hotel Richmond in Paris when, in 1912, he embezzled substantial funds and stole marketable securities. The money was supposedly lost by gambling. He was charged with larceny but left Paris before being taken into custody.

After his marriage, when he and his wife accompanied the Hanans on their yacht, they docked in Monoco where he was recognized by the local police when he was arrested on a disorderly conduct charge. He was then retried on the original charges and sentenced to prison for six months although he served only six weeks and repaid the funds. His brother-in-law advanced all costs and obtained the best legal representation for the duke, who was then instructed that he was not to see his bride again. After his release, the duke made his way to New York where he repeatedly made attempts to reconcile with his wife. When she refused, he threatened to make the matter public unless she paid him fifty thousand dollars. At that point John H. Hanan disclosed the fact that his sister had been duped and threatened with blackmail. Hanan made it clear that he had paid all costs in Monoco

only on the condition that the duke never see his bride again. Among Hanan's statements to the press was that, prior to the marriage, the duke waived all rights to his wife's substantial fortune and that, "He was not a purchased duke." The groom asked the court to dismiss her suit on the grounds that the court had no jurisdiction over him as he was not a U. S. citizen. On 4 June 1915 she withdrew the suit but at the time her attorney said there had been no reconciliation and that the Hanan family had not made a financial settlement upon the duke.

On 12 July 1915 the couple arrived together at Narragansett Pier, Rhode Island, where they had taken a cottage. There appears to have been no divorce but she was known as "Mrs. de Majo Durazzo" for the remainder of her life and did not use the title of duchess. In 1916 the duke sued the estate of a friend for ten thousand dollars, claiming that he had been seriously injured when he stepped through a door where an elevator was supposed to be but fell to the bottom of the shaft. The court awarded him $750. John H. Hanan was not without his own legal and marital discord. He was divorced by his wife and mother of his two sons in 1903 (she died in 1907) then, two months later, he married a wealthy widow, Edythe Evelyn Briggs (Mrs. Charles Talbot Smith), before his final divorce decree was signed. He and his new wife became prominent in social circles and were known for dispatching their yacht, the *Edythia,* to Providence to pick up the governor and his wife for dinner. They also had mansions in Miami and in Brooklyn and would dispatch private railway cars to transport guests to their lavish parties. In 1905 the U. S. Navy's North Atlantic

Squadron detoured from maneuvers to anchor in Narragansett Bay while their admiral and his officers dined with the Hanans.

In 1915 the Hanans gave a dinner at their Shore Acres estate in honor of Rhode Island governor R. Livingston Beeckman, with the dining room decorated as a huge bird cage with canaries, parrots, and doves loosed in the room and the coat of arms of Rhode Island displayed in flowers and lights. But the frivolity came to an end in January 1920 when influenza settled into the Hanan family mansion on Fifth Avenue. John H. Hanan was the first to become ill and soon his entire family was infected, including his wife's three sisters. Edythe, his wife, died first, followed two weeks later by her twenty-eight-year-old son, who had been adopted by Hanan. The son's widow was also near death and unable to attend her husband's funeral. Within weeks John H. Hanan was also dead and, in January of 1921 the remaining members of the family were all involved in a complicated legal suit seeking their share of the accumulated fortune. Elizabeth, Mrs. de Majo Durazzo, was a defendant in the suit and then faded out of public view. The duke's family achieved notoriety again in 1925 when the Marquesa Amanda Durazzo, wife of the Italian minister to Peking, was accused of attempting to murder Maria Cioci, mistress of Captain Petri, the Italian military attache at Peking. The marquesa was repatriated to Italy and confined first to prison then to a lunatic asylum. Captain Petri committed suicide. The marquesa's husband died in 1930 in Brussels where he was the Italian ambassador. The Majo Durazzo family is now extinct in the male line.

Mildred Haseltine, born in Rome (of American parents) on 9 February 1879, died Rome, 9 November 1946, was a daughter of Phildelphia-born artist William Stanley Haseltine (1835-1900) who studied at the University of Pennsylvania and Harvard. His New York studio, where he worked from 1858 to 1866, was near that of his contemporary, Alfred Bierstadt. He studied landscape painting in Duseldorf and became noted for his use of light with particular focus upon natural landscapes. In 1866 he moved to Paris then permanentaly in 1869 to Rome where his daughter was born. He was best known for his Italian landscapes. His works are in the collections of the National Gallery of Art, the Cleveland Museum of Art, the Smithsonian Museum, and the National Academy of Design, to whose board he was elected.

Mildred married in Rome, 17 April 1904, **Prince Ludovico Rospigliosi,** born Rome, 16 October 1881, who was killed in action at Pozzuoli on 30 October 1917, during World War I. He was a son of Prince Camilo, who was a brother of **Marie Parkhurst's** husband, Prince Giuseppe. His brothers, Prince Francesco, Prince Giambattista, and Prince Clemente married Americans **Laura Macdonald Stallo, Ethel Julia Bronson,** and **Claire Weil.** Mildred and Prince Ludovico separated by mutual consent (but did not divorce) in May 1912, with a court decree granting custody of their children to her for ten months a year and to their father for the remaining two months. At the time the legal decree was considered highly unusual and the court went so far as to issue a statement that no aspersions were cast on the actions of either husband or wife. Their eldest son never married but there are numerous descendants from their daughter and other two sons.

Dorothy Haydel, born St. Louis, Missouri, 29 May 1893, died Kitzbühel, Austria, 11 April 1961, was a daughter of Mr. and Mrs. Harry Haydel of St. Louis. She first married in Biarritz, France, in 1925 Hermann Oelrichs II of New York City and Newport. His father, who died at sea in 1906, was president of the shipping line that bore his name. The son graduated from law school in 1914 and moved to a ranch in California, having inherited a large fortune from his father. His mother, Tessie Fair, was one of two daughters of U. S. Senator James G. Fair of California. The other daughter was Mrs. William K. Vanderbilt, II, sister-in-law of Consuelo Vanderbilt, **Duchess of Marlborough.** Dorothy's parents were both deceased and she spent much of her time with her sister in California. Hermann Oelrichs II died in New York City in 1948 and his widow, Dorothy, married at Long Island, New York, 21 August 1950, as his third of four wives, **Ferdinand, Prince of Liechtenstein,** born Salzburg, 18 January 1901, died Neuilly-sur-Seine, 7 July 1981, who made his home in Sweden (his brother, Prince Jean, married first, American Aleene McFarland and second, American Jean Ann French).

Prince Ferdinand's first wife, who was British, was created Countess von Rietberg when they married morganatically. She was a first cousin once removed of HRH The Duchess of Kent. His second wife received no title, nor did Dorothy in his third marriage. His fourth wife, however, who was French, was created Princess of Liechtenstein in 1975, seven years after their marriage. Of his four wives, he had children by his first and second, and his eldest child,

Count Christopher von Reitberg, married American **Kathleen Mahan.** Dorothy's first husband was a first cousin of Natalie Oelrichs, who married **Duke Heinrich of Mecklenburg Schwerin.** At Dorothy's death in 1961, her obituary incorrectly referred to her as "Princess Dorothy Liechtenstein" and made no mention of her divorce nor her husband's remarriage.

Zefita Suzanne Hayward, born New York City, 5 April 1849, died Paris, 29 February 1896, was a daughter of Zefa and Henry Hayward, a very wealthy New Yorker (including Southern land holdings) who lived with his family much of the year in Paris. Henry's brother was known for having permanently lamed August Belmont in a duel defending a woman's honor against a remark made by Belmont. Zefita's younger brother, Frank, "was born to indolence" with an independent income and ended his own life by shooting himself in the temple in the presence of a friend in the family's mansion on then-fashionable 21st Street while his mother and sister were in Paris and St. Moritz. He was twenty-seven, and had earlier been forced to marry a girl who was pregnant with his child. Zefita was a cousin of the old-New York Cuttings and Livingstons. She married first, on 2 May 1876, **Albert-Louis de Gallatin,** who was born 19 September 1850. He was a grandson of the Swiss-born U. S. secretary of the treasury Albert Gallatin (a noble entitled to use "de" as part of his name although he did not) and a cousin of **Adele Stevens,** who married the 4th Duke of Dino. Gallatin died 12 February 1880, leaving his widow $100,000. His brother, James F. Gallatin, sought to challenge the bequest as he was deeply in debt. Zefita withdrew her legal objections when the court ordered that she be guaranteed for life the income from a corpus of $100,000.

She married at Paris, 6 June 1888, as his second wife, **Guy de Rohan-Chabot, 1ˢᵗ Duc de Ravese, Count de Chabot,** born Paris, 8 July 1836, died Paris, 4 October 1912, son of Gerard, Count de Chabot. According to a family member, Guy de Rohan-Chabot was not close to the head of the Rohan family because he "bought from the Pope a roman title of Duke which was found not valuable for our family." Although French, he was authorized on 13 May 1907 to bear the Spanish ducal title with primogeniture. The family received the title Duc de Rohan, Prince de Leon, when Henri Chabot (1616-1655) was created Duc de Rohan after his marriage to Marguerite, Duchess de Rohan. The 1ˢᵗ Duke of Ravese's son by his first wife succeeded him but had only one son, Gilbert, who was killed in action in 1918. The Dukedom of Ravese is now extinct in the male line but the Dukedom of Rohan continues. At Zefita's death, she left her husband, the duke, only twenty francs, while ten thousand dollars went to her attorney. The remainder of the large estate was left to her mother, then to descendants of her aunt. Her nephew and others in the family contested her will but to no avail.

Rita Hayworth (born Margarita Carmen Cansino), daughter of Eduardo Cansino and Volga Haworth Cansino, was born Brooklyn, New York, 17 October 1918. The daughter of a Spanish-born dancer and his partner, Hayworth became a professional dancer with her father's nightclub act at the age of twelve and appeared as Rita Cansino in several films, beginning in 1935. She was billed as her father's

Rita Hayworth was one of the most glamorous stars of Hollywood.

wife rather than his daughter and, during those years, she endured her father's repeated sexual abuse. She escaped her plight by marriage to a man twenty-two years older than she. On the advice of her first husband, Edward Judson (who became her manager; they were married 1937 - 1943), she changed her name and dyed her hair auburn, cultivating a sophisticated glamour that first registered in *Only Angels Have Wings* (1939), *Strawberry Blonde* (1941), and *Blood and Sand* (1941). The musicals *You'll Never Get Rich* (1941) and *You Were Never Lovelier* (1942), both with Fred Astaire (who said in his memoirs that she was his favorite partner and "danced with trained perfection and individuality"), and *Cover Girl* (1944), with Gene Kelly, made her a star and a favorite pinup girl of American servicemen. The sexual allure of Hayworth's performance rose to its peak in *Gilda* (1946), which caused censorship issues because of the so-called striptease in which she was filmed singing "Put the Blame on Mame" (the dubbed voice was not hers). Rita was called "The Great American Love Goddess" and was featured on the cover of *Time* magazine in 1941. In that same year a photo of her in *Life* magazine became the most-requested G. I. pinup, selling more than five million copies. In

Left: Rita Hayworth once said of her most famous role, "Men go to bed with Gilda but they wake up with me." Top: In 1977 before Alzheimer's Disease took its toll. Bottom: Rita was expecting their child, Princess Yasmin, when she wed Prince Aly Khan.

a reference to her status as a bombshell, Rita's likeness was placed on the first atomic bomb to be tested after World War II at Bikini Atoll. Her later films included *The Lady from Shanghai* (1948), directed by her second husband, Orson Welles (to whom she was married 1943 – 1948 and had a daughter, Rebecca), as well as *Affair in Trinidad* (1952), *Salome* (1953), *Miss Sadie Thompson* (1953), *Pal Joey* (1957), *Separate Tables* (1958), *The Money Trap* (1966), and *The Wrath of God* (1972). Rita was in the south of France in 1948 when she was invited to a party she did not want to attend given by Elsa Maxwell in Cannes. She dressed all in white and arrived late and, from the moment Prince Aly Khan saw her, he was smitten although both were still married. His sexual appetite was voracious but selfish (Alastair Forbes said of him, "Aly's idea of premature ejaculation was about the same as Father Christmas's - i.e. one should only come once a year.").

Rita announced she was leaving films and married (she was visibly pregnant at the time) on 27 May 1949 (as his second wife) **Prince Aly Aga Khan**, born Turin, Italy, 13 June 1911, died France, 12 May 1960, son of Prince Sultan Mohammed, Aga Khan III, leader of the world's Shia Ismaili Muslims, and his second wife, Theresa Magliano, an Italian ballet dancer. Through his father, Aly Khan was a direct descendant of the prophet Mohammed by his daughter, Fatima. They had one child, Princess Yasmin Aga Khan, who was born 28 December 1949 in Lausanne, Switzerland. Aly Khan was expected to succeed his father despite his well-known tastes for fast cars and beautiful women. But when his father, the Aga Khan, died in 1957, his will designated Aly Khan's eldest son, Karim, then a student at Harvard, to succeed him. Aly Khan was then named as head of Pakistan's delegation to the United Nations despite criticism of his not being Pakistani. Aly Khan was killed in an automobile accident 12 May 1960 in suburban Suresnes, France, when the Lancia he was driving was hit by an oncoming car as he was driving to the home of his half-brother, Prince Sadruddin, near the Saint-Cloud golfcourse. A former French model, known as Bettina, was seated next to him and was slightly injured. Aly Khan's chauffeur, who was seated in the rear seat while his employer drove, escaped with minor injuries. Rita's marriage to Aly Khan failed in 1951 and they divorced in 1953. She returned from Europe to the States and resumed her film career, leaving the screen again during her marriage to singer Dick Haymes from 1953 – 1955. Her final marriage, to director James Hill, was from 1958 to 1961. She once said, "Men go to bed with Gilda but they wake up with me." For some fifteen years before her death, Hayworth suffered from Alzheimer's disease. Her daughter, Princess Yasmin Aga Khan, assumed all responsibility for her mother and made public the fact that she was suffering from the disease—the first time many people were made aware of its ravages. Rita Hayworth died at her daughter's apartment in Manhattan on 14 May 1987 and was buried in Holy Cross Cemetery in Culver City, California. Since 1985, the Rita Hayworth Galas, chaired by her daughter, Princess Yasmin Aga Khan, have raised more than $44 million. One hundred percent of those funds go toward research and support programs for Alzheimer's disease. Actor Joseph Cotton said of Hayworth, ""No matter how bad the film, when Rita danced it was like watching one

Florence Hazard brought a large dowry derived from ketchup to her marriage with a bankrupt prince.

of nature's wonders in motion."

Florence Ellsworth Hazard, born New York City, 25 December 1882, was a daughter of the "ketchup king," Edward Clarke Hazard (1831-1905) and of Florence Adeline Frothingham (1863–1923). The father was a successful wholesale grocer who, from 1868, owned the exclusive distribution rights in the northeast for McIlhenny Tabasco sauce although, contrary to folklore, there was no truth to the rumor that Hazard's cousin, General John. G. Hazard, discovered the sauce while in New Orleans and brought it to the attention of E. C. Hazard. Florence married at her parents' home at Shrewsbury Manor, New Jersey, 14 June 1899, **Franz, Prince Auersperg,** born Paris, 11 December

1869, died Rzeszow, 16 February 1918, grandson of the 7th Prince. Her dowry was reported to be $1 million. The groom's father was prime minister of Austria and his brother head chamberlain and grand marshal to the emperor of Austria. Prince Franz's sister was brought up at the Austrian court as the companion of the Archduchess Valerie and was later married to Count Ferdinand Kinsky, grand master of the horse to Emperor Franz Joseph.

After resigning from the Austrian army, Prince Franz relocated to America where he graduated from the Long Island Medical College and lived in a boarding house in Brooklyn immediately prior to his marriage. He had been declared bankrupt in 1898 having "squandered an immense fortune before he was twenty-six years of age and disappeared from society." The *New York Times* reported in 1902 that Prince Franz left the army "to pursue the delights of wild dissipation. He was frequently to be seen in cafés of doubtful reputation, recklessly gambling with low associates, and his escapades made it necessary for him suddenly to leave Vienna three years ago under circumstances not altogether creditable. The prince worked his way across the Atlantic as a cabin boy and then became a liftboy in a Philadelphia hotel." After the announcement of his engagement to an heiress, however, "the Prince's august relatives are now prepared to welcome him as a redeemed prodigal."

In 1901 Prince Franz was declared bankrupt in a New York court when it was disclosed that he owed almost $300,000 in debts and had no available assets. Only his clothes and his medical instruments were protected from the court's seizure. The following year a process server seeking to deliver a writ for non-payment had to pretend to be ill and schedule a doctor's appointment in order to serve Prince Franz. In 1902 Florence converted to the Roman Catholic faith, having been reared in the Episcopal Church. Their marriage was declared unequal and they lived together in Manhattan while he practiced medicine at Bayonne City Hospital. A year after their marriage a man acting as an electrician entered their home and stole ten thousand dollars in jewels which had been given to her by her husband's family as a wedding present. Eight years after their marriage, she alleged that, after her father's death, she refused her husband's insistence that she place her large inheritance in his name. She left their home to join her mother in Seabright, New Jersey, while Prince Franz first went to Texas and then returned to Austria where he joined the Red Cross as a medical officer. They had no children and she sued him for divorce, winning a final decree in 1915. Although they had no children, Florence's niece, Florence Hazard Little, lived with her aunt at her home on Park Avenue before being married to Roger Mellick in 1950. Prince Franz's elder brother succeeded their uncle as 9th Prince d'Auersperg,

Alice Heine was a duchess at seventeen then the first American princess of Monaco. She helped turn the principality into a haven for the arts.

Duke of Gottschee, and Princely Count of Wels. On 1 May 1915 Florence married at her sister's home in Seabright, New Jersey, John J. Murphy, whose sister, Julia, was the wife of Hugh J. Grant, mayor of New York City from 1889 to 1892. Their father was former state senator Edward Murphy Jr., of Troy, New York. Florence and her last husband lived in New York City and at Kings Point on Long Island before he died on 23 April 1935. She lived until 10 December 1960 and is buried in Troy, New York.

(Marie) Alice Heine, daughter of Michael Heine and Marie Amelie Miltenberger Heine, was born in the French Quarter of New Orleans, Louisiana, on 10 February 1858, at her mother's family home consisting of three joined houses at 910 Rue Royale. Michael Heine's grandfather, Heymann Heine, was a banker in Hannover who nurtured his three sons (one of whom was

Princess Alice converted from Judaism before her first marriage but publicly advocated for Alfred Dreyfus, a Jewish French military officer. Right: Alice painted by her brother.

the father of the poet Heinrich Heine) into various branches of the family firm. Son Isaac went to Bordeaux to deal in wine and cotton and eventually dispatched his two sons, Michael and Armand, to New Orleans to open an American office. After Michael's marriage to his beautiful half-Creole wife from a wealthy and influential German family, the couple had a son and a daughter, Alice, and spent part of each year in Paris. By 1863 A&M Heine was one of the most important banking houses in France. The firm lent France the necessary funds to fight the Franco-Prussian War and the Heines became frequent visitors at the court of Napoleon III where Mrs. Heine was befriended by the Empress Eugenie. The beautiful blonde Alice was presented at court at

the age of sixteen and was immediately deluged with invitations. Her cousin Paule Heine-Furtado, eleven years her senior, had married in 1866 the 3rd Duke of Elchingen (after his death in 1881 she married the 5th Prince d'Essling/4th Duke of Rivoli, becoming the mother of the 4th Duke of Elchingen/5th Prince de la Moskowa as well as the 6th Prince d'Essling/5th Duke of Rivoli). Paule took her cousin under her wing and, with Alice's fortune and beauty, she became a great marital prize. Alice married first on 25 February 1875, after converting from Judaism to Catholicism, Armand de Chapelle de Jumilhac, 7th Duke de Richelieu (1847-1880). They had a son (the 8th and last Duke) in 1875 and and daughter in 1879 before the duke's death the next year. Alice was left a very wealthy widow at the age of twenty-two. She became Proust's model for the Princess de Luxembourg, whom he described as "tall, redhaired, handsome, with a rather prominent nose" and a voice "so musical that it was as if, among the dim branches of the trees, a nightingale had begun to sing." Perhaps most important, he considered her "a woman of the soundest judgment and the warmest heart." She led a fabled salon in Paris where only the bright and the beautiful were welcomed.

Alice met Monaco's introspective Prince Albert, heir to his blind father, Charles III, the sovereign Prince of Monaco (a tiny principality Somerset Maugham described as "a sunny place for shady people"). Prince Albert cared far more for his oceanographic studies than the prospect of ruling his country and he was often away onboard his yacht (his charts of the Mediterranean were used by the Allies for their landings in the Second World War). His first marriage had been arranged to Lady Mary Hamilton (1850 – 1922) by whom his son and heir was born. She was a daughter of the 11th Duke of Hamilton & Brandon and of Princess Marie of Baden, a second cousin of the Emperor Napoleon III as Lady Mary's maternal grandmother was Stephanie de Beauharnais, the adopted daughter of Napoleon I. Although she brought a large financial settlement to the marriage, she and her husband were both unhappy and Mary was kept virtually a prisoner while legal negotiations continued over her dowry. In a letter she later referred to "the bitterness of the weeks I spent in Monaco." In 1870 she left for a cure in Baden-Baden and never returned nor did she see her husband for more than five years. The marriage was

nullified by the Vatican after eight years with a special provision rendering their son, the eventual Prince Louis II, legitimate. Mary was already pregnant when she then married her long-time lover, the Hungarian Count Tassilo Festetics de Tolna (by whom she was the great-grandmother of fashion designer Egon von Fürstenberg).

Prince Albert became a constant visitor to the young widowed Alice, Duchess

Prince Albert of Monaco cared more for his ocean explorations than for ruling over his small principality. He struck his wife at the opera because of her long-standing affair.

de Richelieu, and would have married her except for his father's vehement objection to the duchess's liberal salon (her friend Oscar Wilde dedicated to her one of four fairy tales in his "A House of Pomegranates") as well as her Jewish background. Prince Charles III died on 10 September 1889 with his daughter by his bedside. His son Albert was, as usual, at sea but altered his course for home when informed that he was now Monaco's reigning prince. On October 23 he accepted the oath of loyalty in the courtyard of the palace he had tried so hard to escape. There were no celebratory court balls as Albert quickly made his way to Alice. There, in Paris on 30

October 1889, Alice married **Albert, Prince of Monaco,** born Paris, 13 November 1848. Only a few friends were present and the couple left for a quiet honeymoon before returning to Paris. In February of 1890, the newlyweds arrived by train in Monaco where they were met by crowds who looked forward to a renewal of court life not seen during the years of Albert's father. Princess Alice became a generous patron of the arts when Monaco, for the first time, began to emerge as more than a gambling oasis. The Prince of Wales was an annual vistor and he befriended Alice. Eventually, his wife, the future Queen Alexandra, did the same and they remained life-long friends.

Prince Albert continued his sea voyages leaving Alice to her artistic pursuits. Her father re-negotiated even more lucrative casino contracts to Monaco's benefit including the full price to build and operate Alice's new opera house. She employed Raoul Gunsbourg to direct the Monte Carlo Opera and he produced nine operas in his first season (one with Nellie Melba in the lead) as well as six comedies (two with Sarah Bernhardt) and four operettas. Unfortunately for Prince Albert, Gunsbourg hired composer Isidoro de Lara, formerly Isidore Cohen, who became Alice's lover. In 1902, at the opening of de Lara's *Hunchback of Notre Dame,* Alice entered the Opera House on her husband's arm. De Lara whispered to her on the stairs and Prince Albert, in full view of the attendees, slapped his wife across the face. With great aplomb, Alice lifted her head and ascended the stairs as her husband left the building. Within days she moved out of the palace into a London hotel. They separated judicially on 30 May 1902 in Monaco and 3 June 1902 in France but never divorced.

Princess Alice continued her literary and musical salon in London where de Lara had a suite on the same floor.

Prince Albert died in Paris on 26 June 1922 and Alice became the dowager princess of Monaco. She died at the Hotel Crillon in Paris on 22 December 1925. Her son by her first husband, the 8th (and last) Duke de Richelieu, married American **Elinor Douglas Wise** (see her separate entry). Prince Albert's son would become Monaco's Prince Louis II at his father's death. A new treaty with France in 1918 required that, should the Grimaldi family not have a French or Monegasque heir, Monaco would become a French possession. Prince Louis II had only an illegitimate daughter, Charlotte, born in 1898 to a nightclub hostess, Marie Louvet. In 1919, Alice's husband, Prince Albert, had his son legally adopt the girl so that the family line might continue. A handsome younger son of the de Polignac family was found and he was created a prince the day before he was married to Charlotte in 1920. Their marriage, too, was unhappy but produced a daughter and a son, the future Prince Ranier, husband of **Grace Kelly,** who became the second American-born princess of Monaco.

Elise Friedericke Hensler, born on Boston's Carver Street in 1836, was a daughter of tailor Conrad Hensler, a German immigrant who recognized Elise's musical talent at an early age. From 1848 until 1852, the family lived in Springfield, Massachusetts, where Elise began her music studies. Through the intervention and financial assistance of friends, she studied in Paris and Milan from 1853 until 1855 when she made her debut at La Scala's early carnival season. She returned

to the U.S. and in January of 1856 made her Boston debut in *Linda di Chamounix*. On 24 March 1856 she made her New York City debut at the prestigious Academy of Music, creating the female lead in Luigi Arditi's *La Spia*, based upon James Fennimore Cooper's *The Spy*. A Boston reviewer, noting that she returned to the U.S. because of her father's ill health, noted, "Although her voice is not large ... it is a very pleasant and sympathetic voice, resonant and equal in its registers." A New York reviewer called her debut there, "triumphantly successful," noting, "The quality of Miss Hensler's voice is sympathetic and sweet. It does not command admiration but beseeches it, and is

Left: Elise Hensler in her days as an aspiring singer.

Center: Elise in a "trouser role" at the opera.

Right: Elise in her domestic days as the wife of a former king.

precisely the voice to strengthen with practice and study."

Elise returned to Europe where, on the evening of 29 October 1857, she was engaged for opening night at the Royal Opera House in Lisbon. Occupying the royal box to celebrate his birthday was King Fernando II of Portugal, the king regent and former king consort of Portugal. Born Ferdinand, **Prince of Saxe-Coburg-Gotha,** (and later) **Prince of Kohary,** on 29 October 1816, he was a first cousin of both Queen Victoria and her consort, Prince Albert, a nephew of King Leopold I of Belgium, and great-uncle of the eventual King Ferdinand of Romania. In 1836, the year of Elise Hensler's birth, he married Maria II (Maria da Gloria), queen of Portugal, who was born in 1819 and proclaimed queen at her father's abdication in 1826. After a bloody civil war ensued, she regained the throne in 1834, two years before her marriage to Ferdinand. After the birth of their first child, Prince Ferdinand was created **King Consort Fernando II of Portugal** on 16 September 1837. When Queen Maria II died in 1853 (having produced 11 children), Ferdinand was proclaimed king regent because their eldest son was only thirteen years old. The son became King Pedro V in 1861 and his father was a valuable guide and teacher to the young man who was considered progressive in his reign. Ferdinand was an accomplished artist and singer who was rumored to collect pornographic literature.

At the time of Elise's appearance at the Lisbon Opera, Ferdinand was still a very powerful king regent. He asked for an introduction to the young woman and she was summoned to a party at the home of Ferdinand's aunt, the Infante Isabella. In the genteel language of the day, Elise "accepted his patronage" – she became his mistress. She was moved into a cottage at Ferdinand's Pena Castle at Sintra, a fantasy of styles built by Ferdinand in 1838, but was not received by society because of her unmarried status. They had a daughter, Alice, even though her birth year is usually listed as 1855 – two years before Elise met Ferdinand. In 1862 Ferdinand was offered the throne of Greece when Otto I abdicated but he declined. Finally, on 10 June 1869, in the royal chapel of Pena Castle, Elise married Ferdinand. Just prior to the wedding his brother, the Duke of Saxe-Coburg, created Elise the **Countess of Edla.** In the same year, the throne of Spain was offered to Ferdinand but he refused when he learned that his wife could not be queen. The couple lived happily at Pena Castle where he imported trees from Elise's native Massachusetts to make her feel at home. There they entertained the Brazilian emperor and empress, General and Mrs. U. S. Grant, and the king and queen of Spain.

In 1877 an American friend received a note from Elise written on stationery "engraved with a capital E, drawn as though it were a flowering branch and having a crown perched on it, rather like a hat on a rack." King Ferdinand died on 15 December 1885 and Elise made only one more public appearance at the marriage of her step-grandson, the Duke of Braganza (later King Carlos who was assassinated along with his eldest son in 1908). She lived in quiet solitude and became so well-loved that, at the passing of the Portugese monarchy, the new Republican government made a special request that she remain in her adopted country. Her daughter, Alice, married in 1883 Manuel de Azevedo Gomes and had three children who still have descendants in

Portugal. Elise Hensler, countess of Edla, lived until 21 May 1929, dying at Pena Castle at the age of ninety-three.

Margaret Hirsch was a daughter of Harry B. Hirsch of Melrose Park in Philadelphia, president and general manager of the Belmont Iron Works. She graduated from Smith College and held a fellowship at Bryn Mawr College. She then studied as an advanced student in international law at the University of Pennsylvania. In 1922 while traveling in Palermo, she met her future husband. In August of 1923 she and her father journeyed to Paris to meet her suitor and in October of that year they met his parents at their estate near Palermo. In the fall of 1924 Margaret Hirsch married **Don Corrado Valguarnera, 9th Prince of Niscemi, 4th Prince of Castelnuovo and 9th Duke delle'Arenella,** born Palermo, 10 December 1901, died 30 April 1966. His father was a member of the Italian Senate for twenty years and his mother was a lady-in-waiting to the queen of Italy. His parents were the models for the characters of Tancredi and Angelica in Tomasi di Lampedusa's novel *The Leopard.* From their home at the Villa Niscemi they became well-known personalities in the social life of Palermo. For two months prior to the wedding the groom worked in a radio manufacturing shop in Philadelphia then joined the General Electric Company in Schenectady, New York. He later escaped fascism and became a U. S. citizen living in Philadelphia.

Their daughter, Maria "Mimi," born 29 November 1931, graduated from the Convent of the Sacred Heart in Oakbrook, Pennsylvania, then studied at the Philadelphia Museum School of Industrial Arts while working part-time as a jewelry designer and manufacturer for Schiaparelli. She won a scholarship to the School of Applied Arts in Paris and in the 1950s formed a partnership with designer Arnold Scaasi. She opened her own jewelry business in New York City in 1960 under the name "Mimi di N." Mimi married at New York City, 23 February 1971, **Prince Alexander Romanov,** born 1929, died London, 22 September 2002, whose grandmother was a sister of Tsar Nicholas II of Russia. The best man was the groom's brother, Prince Nikita, who had married in 1961 American-born **Janet Schoenwald.** Their father, Prince Nikita, was chosen in 1929 as the Russian pretender to the throne by the Supreme Russian Monarchist Council meeting in Paris. At the time he was a bank clerk who rode the Metro to work. Prince and Princess Niscemi were survived by two daughters and the titles were inherited at his death by a nephew.

Virginia "Ella" Hobart, born 22 December 1875, in San Francisco, California, and died there, 17 August 1958; she was a daughter of Walter Scott Hobart and Mary Baker Rounds Hobart. She first married 7 July 1896 in San Francisco, art collector Charles A. Baldwin (brother of the mother of Gladys and Dorothy Deacon), son of Rear Admiral Charles H. Baldwin, a Mexican and Civil War veteran who commanded the Mediterranean Squadron. He built his estate, Broadmoor, at Colorado Springs and modeled it on the Petit Trianon, the royal villa at Versailles. They had two sons, Charles and John. Her father was a California gold mine operator and partner in the Comstock Lode at Virginia City, Nevada, who owned the rich Utica mine at Angels Camp. After her first husband died in 1936, she divided her time between San Francisco and her home in Colorado Springs.

She married second, in 1949, race car enthusiast **Prince Zourab Tchkotoua**, a Georgian prince who was a cavalry officer under the tsars. His family, rulers of the province of Samourzakani, were hereditary princes of the Russian Empire and one of the oldest West Georgian feudal families. He was eighteen years younger than she. They were separated but not divorced in 1953. She died at the age of eighty-four at San Francisco, and he continued his career as a race car driver. Her nieces were **Gladys Deacon,** who married the 9th Duke of Marlborough (after he was divorced by Consuelo Vanderbilt), and **Dorothy Deacon,** who married Prince Antoine Radziwill, then Count Francois de Paula Palffy. Prince Zourab's stepdaughter, Jana Doletti, married Prince Nicholas, brother of King Carol of Roumania. Prince Zourab's cousin, Prince Nicholas Tchkotoua, married automobile heiress **Carol Marmon** of Indianapolis, Indiana.

Claire Huntington, born Sacramento, California, 1860, was born Clara Elizabeth Prentice, daughter of Edwin Prentice and Clarissa Stoddard Prentice. Her father was drowned in a flood in the Sacramento Valley when she was less than a year old. She was adopted by her mother's sister, Elizabeth T. Stoddard, the first Mrs. C. P. Huntington, and was fifteen before she learned, through an accidental remark, that she was adopted. Collis Potter Huntington, son of William and Elizabeth Vincent Huntington, was born April 16, 1821, in Harwinton, Connecticut. He married first, September 16, 1844, Claire's aunt, Elizabeth T. Stoddard, of Cornwall, Connecticut, and she died in 1883. He married second, July 12, 1884, Mrs. Arabella D. Worsham. Huntington died at his camp, Pine Knot, in the Adirondacks,

Above: Claire's enormous dowry came from her step-father's railroad fortune. She was very social and was often invited without her husband.

Opposite page: Collis P. Huntington was the only man who could ride over his own railroad tracks from the Atlantic Ocean to the Pacific.

Their next endeavors were the Southern Pacific from San Francisco through Los Angeles to New Mexico and Texas and the completion of the Chesapeake and Ohio Railroad. Eventually, Huntington became the only man in America able to ride in his railroad car over his own tracks all the way from the Atlantic Ocean in Virginia (where he founded the City of Newport News by investing more than $7 million in a ship-yard) to the Golden Gate on the Pacific coast. At Clara's adoption her name was changed to Claire Huntington. She was traveling in Europe with her chaperone in the summer of 1889 when she met the heavily-in-debt young **Prince Francois Hatzfeldt,** born 15 June 1853, son of Alfred, 1st Prince Hatzfeldt-Wildenburg, a member of the Hereditary Chamber of Deputies in Prussia. In announcing the engagement, the *New York Times* headline read "Another Prince in Luck" with the opening sentence, "Another American heiress has been captured by one of Europe's impecunious nobility." They were married at London's St. Wilfred's Chapel, Brompton Oratory, on 28 October 1889. The couple left for a wedding trip to Italy then moved into his family's home, Hatzfeldt Castle, at Shoenstein-on-the-Rhine. He became so enmeshed in debt that he was forced to repatriate to England where creditors pursued him.

The princess became a favorite of King Edward VII, who often issued her invitations that did not include her husband. Prince Francois would have succeeded his father as 2nd Prince Hatzfeldt but he died 3 June 1911 before his father and the title passed to a nephew, son of American **Helen Moulton.** Claire's dowry to her husband was reported to be $5 million. At her adoptive father's death, his estate in New

on August 13, 1900. C. P. Huntington first entered the hardware business with Mark Hopkins, then later joined Leland Stanford and the Crocker brothers in the railroad business (Edwin B. Crocker's daughter, Aimee, married as her last husband Prince Mstislav Galitzine). The result was the Central Pacific Railroad Company, which perfected the entire California system of 8,900 miles of railroad track. They also completed the trans-continental line from Portland, Oregon, to New Orleans, Louisiana.

York alone was valued at more than $28 million. Claire received $2 million outright, an amount later raised to $8 million by her adoptive mother. Her eventual inheritance after Mrs. Huntington's death was estimated at as much as $75 million. As a widow she entertained at her mansion at 33 Grosvenor Street in London and later lived at Draycot House in Chippenham, Wiltshire. At her death on 17 December 1928, she left her entire estate to friends and employees in Europe (including $10,000 for the care of her pets) with only $25,000 for her American relatives. Several contested her will, led by a grand-nephew who sought $5 million. The suit was eventually settled out of court.

Helen Husted, born New York City, 1 February 1933, was a daughter of New York-based architect Ellery Spaulding Husted, who helped plan Washington's Dulles International Airport. Helen married in Washington, D.C., 13 September 1952 as his first wife, **Prince David Chavchavadze,** born London, 20 May 1924, son of Paul, Prince Chavchavadze (born 1899, St. Petersburg, died 1971, Hyannis, Massachusetts) and his wife, Princess Nina, daughter of Grand Duke Georgi Romanov who was murdered at St. Petersburg 1919, and his wife, Princess Maria, daughter of George I, king of the Hellenes. Thus Prince David Chavchavadze was a great-grandson of Emperor Nicholas I of Russia and also a grandson of George I, king of the Hellenes, as well as a great-grandson of King Christian IX of Denmark. Prince David's father, Prince Paul, was a well-known writer who translated the memoirs of Stalin's daughter, Svetlana. At his 1922 marriage to Princess Nina, there were seven members of the Russian royal family in attendance and the English royal family sent

Barbara Hutton married against her father's wishes one of the "Marrying Mdivanis."

representatives and wedding gifts. Prince David graduated from Yale where he was a member of Phi Beta Kappa. He and Helen Husted had two daughters, Maria and Alexandra, and divorced in 1958. She lives in Wellfleet, Massachusetts, as "Nell Husted." He then married second, in Cincinnati, Ohio, on 28 December 1959 (divorced 1970) **Judith Clippinger,** born Cincinnati, Ohio, 25 March 1929, died Great Falls, Virginia, 21 October 1997. By his second marriage there was one daughter, Princess Catherine, who married American John Alan Redpath, and one son, Prince Michael. Prince David married third, in Washington, D.C., in 1979, **Eugenie de Smitt,** born

Top: The car in which Prince Alexis Mdivani was killed.

Bottom left: Barbara Hutton at her first marriage.

Bottom right: Barbara appears unconcerned at the lucrative marriage contract being signed by her husband.

New York City, 12 July 1939. In 1989 he wrote *Crowns and Trenchcoats: A Russian Prince in the CIA*. In 1990 he authored *The Grand Dukes*. He and his third wife are socially prominent and active in the nation's capital. His mother's sister, Princess Xenia, married William B. Leeds, son of American **Nancy Stewart Leeds** who married **Prince Christopher of Greece** and was created Princess Anastasia in her own right.

Barbara Woolworth Hutton, born New York City, 14 November 1912, was a daughter of Franklyn L. Hutton and Edna Woolworth Hutton. At her mother's suicide when Barbara was less than five, she inherited $5 million from her mother's Woolworth's fortune; when she turned twenty-one, she inherited more than $42 million. On 20 June 1933 in Paris, she married first, against her father's wishes, Russian **Prince Alexis Mdivani,** and they were divorced less than two years later (see Louise Van Alen). For the ceremony she wore a single-strand pearl necklace that consisted of forty-one perfect pearls; it set a world record when it was sold at Christie's in Geneva in 1999 for $1.48 million. Alexis died in an auto accident in 1935 which injured his lover, Maud, Baroness Thyssen, step-mother of the late art collector.

Barbara married second, 14 May 1935, the Danish **Count Kurt Haugwitz-Reventlow,** whom she later described as the cruelest of her seven husbands. They had a son, Lance, who was Barbara's only child, born 25 February 1936, in London. She renounced her American citizenship and became a Dane in December of 1937.

The Reventlows were divorced in 1941 and, on 8 July 1942, she married screen star Cary Grant. The media immediately dubbed them "Cash and Cary." They were reintroduced by the wealthy and highly-social American-born Dorothy, Countess di Frasso, after the two women returned from a trip to Hawaii (Grant eventually accompanied di Frasso's body from Los Angeles to New York City after she died in her sleep on a train from Las Vegas where she had been visiting Marlene Dietrich). A week before Grant married Hutton, he legally changed his name from Archibald Leach to Cary Grant and officially became an American citizen (he was born in England). He also, at his own insistence, signed a waiver to all future claims on Hutton's fortune in the event of a divorce.

Although Hutton later said that she loved Grant more than any of her husbands, the Grants were divorced in 1945 and she married fourth, 1 March 1947, **Prince Igor Troubetskoy,** born Paris, 18 August 1912, of Lithuanian descent (Prince Igor's brother, Prince George, an American Army officer and actor, also married an American, **Maria Stranahan**).

They were divorced in 1952 (he then married Christianne Murat) and she married fifth, 30 December 1953, Panamanian playboy Porfirio Rubirosa (who also married heiress Doris Duke). They divorced 53 days later and ended a marriage that cost her a reported $2 million.

She married sixth, 8 November 1955, tennis star **Baron Gottfried von Cramm,** an old friend who was homosexual. They divorced in 1960 and she married seventh, in Cuernavaca, 7 April 1964, Raymond Doan, who was born of a French mother and a Vietnamese father. Shortly before their marriage, she appeared at the Laotian Embassy in Rabat, Morocco, to attempt to purchase a title for her next husband. A clerk recalled an impoverished Laotian prince and Hutton paid him $250,000 to adopt Doan, thus creating him **Prince Vinh Na Champassak.** Champassak was a city approximately 200 miles west of Angkor, near Bangkok, in what is now Thailand. He assumed regal pretensions and, in a French magazine article in 1972, attempted to document that he was actually descended from the royal family whose name had been purchased for him. They legally separated in 1969 but she continued to use his last name.

She died in San Francisco, 11 May 1979 after several illnesses and many operations. Barbara's father was a brother and partner of E. F. Hutton of the stock brokerage firm who married cereal heiress Marjorie Meriwether Post. Of several biographies of Barbara Hutton's life, one was entitled *In Search of a Prince.*

Evangeline Johnson, born 1897 in New Brunswick, New Jersey, was a daughter of Evangeline Brewster Johnson and Robert Wood Johnson, who was the founder of Johnson & Johnson. In 1876 he learned that, due to postoperative infections, at some hospitals as many as 90 percent of patients died after surgery. He searched for a solution and, in 1886, founded Johnson & Johnson with his two brothers and began manufacturing surgical dressings. Four years later they added a talcum product called baby powder. When Robert Wood Johnson died in 1910, his brother became president until 1932 when Evangeline's brother, Robert Wood Johnson II, took control of the company.

Today Johnson & Johnson is the world's largest health and medical care products conglomerate and its product lines, including Band-Aids, Tylenol, Tampons, and Neutrogena, account for more than $30 billion in annual sales. Evangeline Johnson graduated from Miss Spence's School in Manhattan in 1916 and became an instructor in first aid and then a lieutenant in the City's Red Cross Ambulance Corps. She was decorated by President Wilson for her services in World War I.

Evangeline waged a personal battle against the city of Palm Beach in the early 1920s for its refusal to allow women to wear shortened bathing suits in public. She flew her own plane over the area throwing out handbills in protest. She first married in 1926 conductor Leopold Stokowski (1882-1977) whom she divorced in 1937 during the time he was having an affair with the actress Greta Garbo (Stokowski's next wife was heiress Gloria Vanderbilt from 1945 to 1955).

She then married in Phoenix, Arizona, in January of 1938, **Prince Alexis Zalstem-Zalessky,** of Russian descent, who died in 1965, and

Conductor Leopold Stokowski was the first husband of Evangeline Johnson. His next wife was heiress Gloria Vanderbilt.

they lived in Palm Beach and in New York City's Carlyle Hotel. At the time of their marriage the prince was described as "a student of tropical agriculture." Their Palm Beach home, next door to the Kennedy compound, became well-known in 1984 when a Venezuelan tanker ran aground there and stayed for three months. In 1972 Evangeline attended a gala ninetieth birthday party for her former husband, Leopold Stokowski, in New York City, along with their two daughters.

As a widow, she married in 1975 Charles Merrill, a much-younger artist and eccentric, and they lived in Dublin, Ireland, where they produced a quarterly arts magazine before moving to North Carolina. She died 17 June 1990, at the World's Edge Apple Organic Farm in Hendersonville, North Carolina, at the age of ninety-three, leaving two daughters by Stokowski, Lyuba Rhodes of Geneva and Dr. Sadja Greenwood of San Francisco, as well as five grandchildren. After her death her widower became the partner of another man. The foundation established by Evangeline's brother, Robert Wood Johnson II, annually distributes approximately $250 million in healthcare grants.

Prince Karl-Victor's father, Wilhelm (here with his wife), was briefly the reigning Prince of Albania.

Islip, Long Island. Her father was hired as head gardener and caretaker of two large adjoining estates on Long Island. Eileen grew into a very beautiful woman and, at nineteen, began taking the train into New York City where she worked as part of the war effort. The owner of "The Willows," one of the two adjoining estates, was the fifty-one-year-old Andre' de Coppet, who had watched her mature and finally met her on the train. Andre' de Coppet was head of the Wall Street brokerage house of de Coppet and Doremus which was founded by his father. A collector of rare books and letters, he lent to Princeton University in 1935 a collection of ten letters written by Napoleon and five letters written by Empress Marie Louise. De Coppet purchased them from the private papers of Prince Eugene Beauharnais, Napoleon's stepson. In addition to his brokerage firm, he also grew

Evangeline's great-nephew, Robert Wood "Woody" Johnson IV, owns the New York Jets.

Eileen Johnston was born at Chester, England, 3 September 1922, but moved to the U. S. when she was three years old; she was the daughter of George Johnston and Alice Percival Johnston of sisal in Haiti on his Plantation Dauphin, which was, at 450,000 acres, the largest singly-owned plantation in the world, initially employing four thousand people and increasing to twelve thousand workers during the height of World War II. De Coppet was traveling to Panama when his ship stopped at Port-au-Prince and he first saw Dauphin Plantation.

When Manilla was captured by the Japanese, Plantation Dauphin became the largest source for making rope for the U. S. Navy. Eileen and Andre were married in 1941 and had two daughters, Diane and Laura. Andre' de Coppet died at Lausanne, 1 August 1953, and the plantation was sold to the Haitian American Sugar Company.

His widow married in New York City's St. James Episcopal Church on 8 September 1966, **Karl-Victor, Hereditary Prince of Albania, Prince of Wied,** born Potsdam, 19 May 1913, died Munich, 8 December 1973, son of Wilhelm, reigning prince of Albania (1914), and Sophie, Princess von Schonburg-Waldenburg. He was born as H.S.H. Karl Viktor Wilhelm Friedrich Ernst Günther, Prince zu Wied, and was raised to the title of hereditary prince of Albania and the style of His Highness on 7 March 1914. His best man was his uncle, Prince Ludwig of Wied. Karl-Victor and his wife were both given the qualification of "Highness." He was known to play the piano as well as a professional pianist and also spoke six languages fluently. They lived mainly at Munich until his death. After Prince Karl-Victor died, his widow lived at Claridge's Hotel in London for two years until she returned

ALMOST AN AMERICAN-BORN PERSIAN EMPRESS

Florence Breed (1875 – 1950), a daughter of Francis W. and Alice Ives Breed, was described as "a Boston debutante." Her father was a successful shoe manufacturer with factories in Lynn, Massachusetts, and in Rochester, New Hampshire, who produced approximately seven thousand pairs of shoes a day. Florence married in 1904 Mirza Ali-Kuli Khan (1879 – 1966), an early advocate of the Baha'i faith, and they lived in Iran immediately after their marriage. He was sent to the United States as a Baha'i translator and teacher and then headed the Persian legation at Washington, successfully convincing President Wilson to allow Persia to send a mission to the Peace Conference at Versailles. Ali-Kuli Khan was a member of that delegation and later became head of the court of the then-crown prince regent of Persia. In 1910 Florence was with her husband when he presented his credentials at the U. S. State Department in Washington. Among their children was a daughter, Marzieh, who accompanied her parents to a posting in Tehran where she was presented at the court of the then-crown prince regent, Soltan Ahmad Shah, who in 1909 was declared shah at the age of nine at the abdication of his father during a turbulent revolution. He was to be the last shah of the Qajar/Kadjar Dynasty and was overthrown in 1925 by Reza Khan (later Reza Shah Pahlavi). Soltan Ahmad Shah asked for the hand of young Marzieh Khan but she had other plans. She attended Vassar, then graduated with highest honors from Stanford University where she was a member of Phi Beta Kappa (her classmates called her "our Persian princess") before earning an MA from the University of California at Berkeley. Fluent in several languages, Marzieh was the first woman to work on the staff of a Tehran newspaper. Also a proponent of the Baha'i faith, she spent ten years in Europe researching the Middle Ages and the Renaissance. She died in 1993, never having children by either husband. Her would-be suitor, the last shah of his dynasty, never had children and died in exile in 1930. He is buried in Iraq and his brother became the claimant to the throne.

to the U.S. The prince's only sibling, a sister, died in an internment camp in Romania. Neither Karl-Victor nor his sister had children, and their father was deposed as king of Albania after a reign of only seven months. Karl-Victor was considered to be head of the princely house of Albania (Wied) and sovereign grand master of the Order of the Black Eagle, but those titles became extinct at his death. Eileen died at New York City's Stanhope Hotel on 1 September 1985.

Martina Potter Jones, daughter of Dr. John Davies Jones and May Potter Jones, was born in Cincinnati on 3 September 1884, and died in Florence, 22 June 1955. She married in Florence, 8 December 1904, **Don Giuseppe Lanza, Prince di Trabia,** born Palermo, 8 March 1880, died Florence, 9 February 1945, grandson of the 10th Prince de Trabia and Prince di Butera. They lived in Florence and had a daughter and a son who was authorized by royal decree of 1927 to bear the title Marchese Lanza di Ajeta. The current (14th) Prince of Trabia is also 4th Prince Lanza Branciforte as well as Prince of Santo Stefano, of Mistretta, of Pietraperzia, of Scordia, of Campofiorto, of Scalea, della Catena, Duke of Camastra, Duke of Santa Lucia, of Branciforte, of Militello, Marquess of Barrafranca, della Ginestra, of Misuraca, of Mussomeli, of Sommatino, of Mazzarino, and also holds many titles of count and baron. At the death of Martina's mother in 1913, her will disclosed that she had settled $100,000 on her daughter, provided she married the groom. Martina was left an annual income of only three thousand dollars, while the remainder of the substantial estate went to Martina's husband and children.

Nancy Southgate Jones, daughter of Southgate Jones and Nancy Amorette Green Jones, was born at Durham, North Carolina, on 11 June 1927. Her father, Southgate Jones, was a banker and real estate developer in Durham, and was president of the North Carolina Joint Stock Land Bank at his retirement and head of the real estate firm bearing his name. Nancy married at Durham, North Carolina, 2 September 1949, **Charles "Charlie," Prince de Rohan,** born Budweis, 5 December 1924. He died in Cincinnati, 27 February 2005. Prince and Princess Rohan had a son and two daughters, all of whom married Americans. They divorced in Somerville, New Jersey, 10 February 1975, and he married second, in Cincinnati, Ohio, 5 April 1975, **Virginia Putnam Durrell,** born Mount Pleasant, Michigan, 29 January 1938, daughter of James Durrell and Pauline Osborn Durrell and formerly the wife of J. Osborn. Nancy Jones de Rohan married in the Episcopal Church of St. John on the Mountain in Bernardsville, New Jersey, on 1 March 1975, John Van Rensselaer Strong, an attorney in the New Brunswick firm of Strong, Strong & Gavarny founded by his grandfather in 1852. She now lives in Far Hills, New Jersey.

Agnes Elisabeth Winona Leclercq Joy, born Swanton, Vermont, 25 December 1840 (though she later claimed 1844), was a daughter of William Leclercq Joy and his second wife, Julia Willard Joy. Tales of her adolescence—that she was a circus rider (she was, in fact, a skilled equestrienne), that her mother was a captured Indian squaw, that she was a New York actress, that she spent several years in Cuba—were deliberately encouraged by her in an apparent attempt to obscure her background. What is known is that she traveled to Washington, D.C., in 1861 to visit her sister, Della, and her husband, Edmund

Johnson. Agnes toured the Virginia encampment of Brigadier-General Louis Blenker's "German Division" and was introduced to her future husband. She spoke no German or French and he spoke no English but Agnes later wrote that they spoke in "the more universal language of the eyes."

Agnes married in Washington's St. Patrick's Catholic Church on 30 August, 1862, **Prince Felix Constantin Salm-Salm,** born in Anholt, Westphalia, on 25 December (a birthday he shared with his wife) 1828. He was the third son of the reigning Prince zu Salm-Salm and was a soldier of fortune who fought in Prussia, Austria, and Denmark before his mounting debts forced him to leave his country. Upon his arrival in the U. S. he was appointed chief-of-staff to Brigadier-General Louis Blenker with the rank of colonel. Within weeks of their marriage, Agnes first exhibited her own powers of persuasion when she visited New York's governor and emerged from his office with a commission for her husband to command his own regiment. Agnes joined her husband in the field where their usually squalid living conditions were akin to what one observer called "a combination of barroom and brothel." When President Lincoln and his family paid a formal visit to the troops, Agnes pulled his head toward her and kissed him on the cheek.

After the prince's regiment was dismissed, Agnes once again went to work securing another coveted command for him but only if he would raise his own troops—a task Agnes immediately fulfilled. As a rival

Agnes Joy enjoyed her notoriety and deliberately tried to embellish the facts of her life.

Top left: Prince Felix Salm-Salm's military career was greatly enhanced by his wife.

Top right: Agnes at the height of her fame.

Right: Agnes in later life lived on a pension from the Austrian emperor.

noted jealously, the prince's "beautiful wife had done the talking—and a good deal of smiling and coaxing." Many contemporaries whispered that Agnes's powers of persuasion extended to the bedroom although there was never any eyewitness report to confirm that assumption. The prince finally saw battle late in the War and acquitted himself well. Agnes went to Washington and procured for him a promotion to the rank of brigadier general, later writing, "He had given me his name and made me a princess, but notwithstanding his name and rank ... I procured for him the command of the 8th, and raised for him the 68th Regiment, and now he had become a general through my exertions." As the War wound to its close, the prince was stationed at Dalton, Georgia, and Agnes joined him there, riding the final distance from Chattanooga to Dalton on a locomotive's cowcatcher. While there Agnes' sister, Della, had a second son and gave him to Agnes, who named him Felix. But the baby would not thrive with a nurse and had to be returned to his mother (years later he was joined by a sister named Agnes Winona Johnson who spent much of her time with her Aunt Agnes in Europe).

At War's end the prince was named acting military governor of Atlanta and Agnes assisted in trying to find provisions for the area's conquered residents. They moved on to Savannah where he was finally discharged from his duties. With no desire to remain in the U.S. in peacetime, he offered his services to Mexico's Emperor Maximilian, an Austrian archduke who was placed on the throne by Napoleon III. His wife, the Empress Carlota, was a first cousin of England's Queen Victoria. Maximilian had already begun his descent into defeat but the Salm-Salms pledged allegiance and both joined him in Mexico. Salm became the emperor's chief aide with the rank of colonel and was with him when they were surrounded by forty thousand troops and had to take refuge in the Convent of the Cross at La Cruz near Quaretaro.

The prince was also with the emperor when they were captured and sentenced to die. Agnes rode alone on horseback with only her small dog to ask Mexico's president to spare their lives. She was assured that the matter would be taken under advisement then rode again through enemy lines to reach her husband. She was presented for the first time to the captured emperor who was being kept in wretched conditions with no legal representation. Again she traveled to seek a delay so that attorneys could plead his case and once more was successful. Maximilian decorated both Agnes and her husband but his fate was pre-ordained. Days before his scheduled execution Agnes tried to bribe his captor with $100,000 in gold. When that offer was unsuccessful she unbuttoned her blouse and exclaimed, "Isn't the sum enough? Well. Colonel, here am I!" The horrified officer would not relent. The next day Agnes' arrest was ordered by General Escobedo who ordered her out of the city and was reported to have said, "I would rather face a whole Imperialist battalion than an angry Princess Salm."

At dawn on 19 June 1867 Emperor Maximilian was led to his execution, exclaiming, "What a glorious day! I have always wanted to die on just such a day." He absolved his executioners and even offered smelling salts to his fainting priest. Prince Salm, whose life had been spared, was kept away lest he should attempt useless heroics. Agnes and her husband returned to Europe where he resumed his career as a soldier of fortune. He was killed in action at Gravelotte on 18 August

1870 and the Austrian emperor awarded Agnes a lifetime pension in memory of his brother Maximilian. On 16 September 1876 she married Charles Heneage, secretary of the British legation at Berlin, and a brother of the first Baron Heneage. They separated not long afterwards and he died in 1901. Agnes visited the U. S. in 1899 under the name of Princess Salm-Salm to restore the flags of her late husband to his regiments. She returned again in 1900 to raise funds for the relief of the Boer War wounded.

Agnes wrote her voluminous memoirs with more of a view of history than of truth. One contemporary military officer wrote of Agnes, "Besides her great beauty, the Princess was known for her remarkably free and easy manners, her determined ways and daring horsemanship, and of course other ladies considered her a mere adventuress; but in reality she was only a very shrewd woman, whose motto was the same as that of the Jesuits: 'The end justifies the means.' ... Proud and politely cold with ordinary men, she was seductive only with influential people and a few personal friends." Agnes died at Karlsruhe on 20 December 1912.

(Margaret) **Brooks Juett,** born Lexington, Kentucky, 27 August 1930, daughter of Mr. and Mrs. Brooks Juett, married Lexington, Kentucky, 12 September 1952, **Martin, Prince Lobkowicz,** born London, 21 December 1928, grandson of Ferdinand, 9th Prince von Lobkowicz and Duke of Roudnice. Martin's father, Prince Maximilian, was the Czechoslovakian envoy to London and died in Dover, Massachusetts. Brooks and Prince Martin had three sons and a daughter, all born in the United States. Brooks and her husband live in Dover, Massachusetts, and do not use their title. Prince Martin's first cousin, who was in line to succeed to the titles, in 1920 renounced his line's right of succession. Prince Martin's grandfather was succeeded at his death by his cousin, Jaroslav, as 10th Prince von Lobkowicz. Martin's younger brothers, Prince Dominik and Prince Oliver (who was killed in an auto accident in Greenwich, Connecticut), married Americans **Louise Brooks, Sarah Stefanoni,** and **Marjorie Hunter.** Emperor Joseph II bestowed upon the 7th Prince Lobkowicz the title Duke of Roudnice in 1786. He remains best known as a great lover of music and patron of Beethoven, who dedicated numerous works, including the 3rd (Eroica), 5th and 6th (Pastoral) Symphonies, the Opus 18 String Quartets, and the Triple Concerto, to Lobkowicz.

Maximilian Lobkowicz (1888-1967), Prince Martin's father and the last heir to occupy Roudnice, was a lawyer, politician, and diplomat. He supported the new Czechoslovak state of 1918, even when it abolished official titles and redistributed family properties. During the Second World War, all of his holdings were confiscated by the Nazis because he represented the Czechoslovak government in exile as ambassador to the Court of St. James in England. He again had to flee in 1948 after the Communists took over, when he permanently settled in America.

After the 1991 law providing for the return of confiscated property, Prince Martin and his son, William, began the daunting task of tracing down and reclaiming most of the treasures that had been taken from the family. Much of the Lobkowicz collection has been reassembled at Nelahozeves Castle. The collection, "Six Centuries of European Art Patronage," opened to the public in 1997 in the presence of President Havel. The Lobkowiczes owned a priceless collection of Amati, Stradivari, and Guarneri violins. Not until 1992 was the family given an inventory of their items and at that time discovered that their 1617 Amati violin had been sold and was in America. It was being carried by virtuoso Rachel Barton in 1995 when she was pinned underneath a train that crushed her legs (although the violin was undamaged). Despite legal challenges by the Lobkowicz family, it was claimed by the Stradivari Society and is currently on loan to a German violinist. The Lobkowiczes have established a non-profit "American Friends for the Preservation of Czech Culture" operating from Dover, Massachusetts.

Elise Cragin Kay, born New York City, 27 April 1910, died Cannes, 2 February 1968, was a daughter of Lt. Col. D'Arcy Kay and Jeanne Cragin Kay. She married as his first wife in Brussels (civil) 19 July 1932 and (religious) 20 July 1932, **Robert, 8th Prince de Béthune-Hesdigneul,** born Louvaine, 12 December 1900, died Woluwe-St.-Lambert, 26 September 1943. At the time of their marriage her husband was a count but he succeeded to his father's princely title in 1933. They divorced in 1937 and he married again but there were no children by either marriage. She married as her second husband a Mr. Lassetter. Prince Robert's younger brother eventually succeeded as 9th Prince but had no sons and the current holder is a cousin. The princely title was first recognized in the Netherlands in 1781, by France in 1781 and 1818, and by Belgium in 1888.

Elise was a niece of the Reverend Howard K. Bartow, rector of St. Stephen's Episcopal Church in Cohasset, Massachusetts. Her father's sister, **Violet Kay,** was a well-known horsewoman who married the **Marchese Alberto Godi di Godio** of Rome. In 1938, she was convicted of attempting to smuggle one million lire out of Italy by hiding it in the mattress of her bed on the midnight express train from Rome to France. She was arrested at the French border and, along with her husband and an exchange broker, paid a fine of almost three million lire.

Grace Patricia Kelly, born in Philadephia, Pennsylvania, 12 November 1929, was the third child of John "Jack" Brendan Kelly (1889-1960) and Margaret Majer Kelly (1898-1990). Her father was a self-made millionaire building contractor and Democratic Party leader who had been a triple gold-medal winning Olympic rowing champion

Grace Kelly's cool beauty and natural talent brought her to the attention of Monaco's Prince Rainier.

Left: Grace Kelly won the Best Actress award in 1955.

Grace and her husband became extremely close and he was devastated at her accidental death.

who lent his brother the money to begin his construction business. Grace's brother, Jack Jr., represented the U. S. in the 1948, 1952, 1956, and 1960 Olympic Games. He would win the bronze medal in the single scull at the 1956 Olympics (he gave the medal to his sister, Grace, as a wedding present) and eventually was appointed as president of the United States Olympic Committee. Grace Kelly studied at Raven Hill Academy in Philadelphia, a convent run by the Sisters of the Assumption, and later at Stevens School in Philadelphia. She entered the American Academy of Dramatic Art in New York, and graduated after two years. Her parents opposed her choice of an acting career and she began as a model. Her stage debut took place in

(he was the first American to win the single sculls race). While overseas in World War I he defeated twelve heavyweight boxing champions and only a broken ankle kept him from fighting Gene Tunney, a Marine who would later defeat Jack Dempsey. Kelly served as Democratic Party chairman in Philadelphia but later lost the nomination for the U. S. Senate. In 1940, he introduced Franklin D. Roosevelt at the National Democratic Convention for his third term nomination. His brother was American playwright George Kelly, a Pulitzer Prize winner

New York where she played the role of Raymond Massey's daughter in Strindberg's play, *The Father.* After several parts in the theatre and in television, she went to Hollywood. She appeared in her first film role, *Fourteen Hours,* when she was twenty-two. Among her succeeding films were *High Noon, Mogambo* (during which she supposedly had an affair with co-star Clark Gable), *Dial M for Murder, Rear Window, High Society, To Catch a Thief, The Swan,* and *The Country Girl,* for which she received an Oscar in 1955. Grace was on the Riviera at the annual Cannes Festival when she was asked to meet Monaco's Prince Rainier. The meeting was suggested by Father Francis Tucker, an American who had been assigned by the Vatican as the prince's private chaplain. Amid cameras poised to record the event the two made polite conversation and she was given a tour of the palace and grounds. Later, while discreet inquiries were being made by the Catholic Church, Grace and the prince were secretly corresponding. He made his first trip to America to visit Grace on the set of *The Swan*, a film about a mother who wants her daughter to marry a prince. Rainier then visited the Kellys in Philadelphia and his proposal of marriage was accepted. Grace's father paid a $2 million dowry for a state wedding and established a trust fund for his daugher's benefit. The marriage contract also stipulated that any children of the marriage would remain with their father should the union end. Because Grace had four years remaining on her acting contract, MGM agreed that, in order to release her, she would complete *High Society,* then the studio would be given exclusive rights to film the wedding. Jack Kelly paid all costs for the trans-Atlantic crossing of sixty-six members of his family and their friends to travel to Monaco. On the night before the wedding, Prince Rainier's father, Pierre de Polignac, Duke de Valentinois (who became very fond of his daughter-in-law and was a great source of support early in her marriage), gave her a magnificent drop pearl encircled with rubies topped by a diamond crown. It had belonged to her predecessor, the American-born **Alice Heine,** Princess of Monaco (see her separate entry). As he gave it to Grace, he declared, "You will be her worthy successor." Grace Kelly married at Monaco's royal palace (civil) on 18 April 1956 and (religious) in Monaco's Cathedral of St. Nicholas on 19 April 1956, **Ranier III, Prince of Monaco,** born Monaco, 31 May 1923. She assumed the style "Her Serene Highness Princess Grace of Monaco." That evening an impressve hour-long fireworks display was paid for by Aristotle Onassis who is said to have quipped as the bride arrived in Monaco, "A prince and a movie star. It's pure fantasy." (Onassis also paid for many costs of the wedding, allowing Rainier to keep most of the Kelly dowry). They left for a six-week honeymoon on board the royal yacht and Grace returned pregnant. She and her husband became extremely close in succeeding years even though he would not allow her to return to her film career as she wished. She was not accepted by some segments of European aristocracy who continued to view her as a parvenue. Britain's Princess Margaret was reported to have looked her up and down and commented, "Well, you don't *look* like a movie star," to which Grace hotly replied, "Well, I wasn't *born* a movie star." Her children came quickly: Princess Caroline was born in 1957, Prince Albert in 1958, and Princess Stephanie in 1965. Grace encouraged the arts in her adopted country and assisted her husband in luring many new companies to Monaco, resulting in a principality with one of the highest per-capita incomes in the world. On September 13, 1982, Princess Grace was driving her youngest daughter from their "farmhouse" high above Monte Carlo when she complained of a sharp pain in her head. As the car veered her daughter tried unsuccessfully to apply the handbrake and the car crashed over an embankment, landing 120 feet below. Princess Stephanie was injured but able to exit the smoking car. Princess Grace was found to have irreversible brain damage and her family agreed to remove her from life support; she died on 14 September 1982. Although the world's royal families had snubbed her wedding, they were heavily in attendance for her funeral, including the Princess of Wales who had been compared to her. Princess Caroline, who had been considered a difficult and rebellious young woman, stepped forward in her mother's place and her grief-stricken father was rarely seen without her. In her third marriage, to Ernst, Prince of Hannover and Duke of Brunswick, she had a daughter who became the first Grimaldi to be born a Royal Highness. Prince Rainier died in Monaco 6 April 2005. His only son and heir is now Monaco's reigning Prince Albert II, named for his great-grandfather whose second wife was American beauty Alice Heine. He is as-yet unmarried but has acknowledged a child born out of wedlock, just as was his grandmother through whom he inherited his titles.

Helen Kelly (1885 – 1952), daughter of Edward Kelly, commodore of the New York Yacht Club, and granddaughter of financier Eugene Kelly, in 1902 married Frank Jay Gould, youngest son of railroad financier Jay Gould. They had two daughters, Helen and Dorothy (who were reared mainly by Frank Gould's sister, Mrs. Finley Shepard). The girls wed Swiss Barons, Jean-Daniel de Montenach and de Graffenried de Villars. Helen Kelly Gould married second, in July 1910, Ralph Thomas, wealthy treasurer of the Sugar Trust, forfeiting half her annual alimony from Gould. He died five years later at the age of thirty-two (supposedly leaving her $2 million, although she denied it) and, in June of 1917, she married in Paris, the Albanian **Prince Noureodin Vlora,** whose father had been the Ottoman prime minister. He was born in

Constantinople but the family estate was in Valona, Albania. His father, Ferid Vlora Pasha, was Vizier of Turkey under Abdul Hamid. Prince Noureodin's sister, Djellalleddin Pasha, was the wife of the ex-Khedive of Egypt.

Helen and Noureodin met in Biarritz in December of 1916. Within months, she was pictured in American newspapers arriving on the *S. S. Aquitania* as "Princess Vlora of Albania" with accompanying press assertions that she "may sometime be Queen of Albania." Vlora did not appear at their Paris divorce proceedings in 1922 but Helen evidently maintained a certain fondness for the prince. Some years later, when he was imprisoned along with twenty-three rebels who resisted a coup led by King Zog, Helen appealed to the American legation to intercede in his behalf. Consul Robert Murphy tried to comply but all communications had been cut off with the capital of Tirana, and Prince Vlora was eventually executed.

Helen married again in 1926 soap manufacturer Oscar F. Burke. Among the guests at their reception were Mr. and Mrs. Kingdon Gould (he was the nephew of Helen's first husband, Frank). The Burkes also divorced and Helen retook her maiden name and died a few years before Frank Gould, her first husband, on 8 August 1952, in Barbizon, France. At one time, the much-married Ziegfeld girl, Peggy Hopkins Joyce, announced her engagement to Prince Vlora but he was not among her six husbands. Peggy's then-husband, millionaire lumberman James S. Joyce, charged in their 1921 divorce that his wife's plan had been to secure one million dollars from him and then to wed Prince Noureodin Vlora.

Top left: Helen Kelly while married to Jay Gould's youngest son, Frank.

Top right: Prince Noureodin Vlora was executed in a coup led by Albania's King Zog.

Left: Helen with her two Gould daughters.

Agnes Raffaella Kennedy, born in New York in 1901, was a daughter of Robert Davidson Kennedy and May Nutting Kennedy, and granddaughter of wealthy Brooklyn merchant Col. Andrew Jackson Nutting. She married first in 1928, Clare Van Neck who, unknown to her, was suffering from tuberculosis. They divorced and she married one week after her divorce, on 1 December 1932 in London's Savoy Chapel, **Edward, 7th Duke of Leinster, Marquess of Kildare and Earl of Offaly, and Viscount Leinster of Taplow,** the premier (indeed the only) Duke of Ireland, born 6 May 1892. His mother was a famously lovely daughter of the 1st Earl of Feversham and she was usually referred to as "the beautiful tubercular Hermione." His father died when Edward was nine months old, followed by Hermione's death when Edward was less than two. As the third son, he was considered to have little chance of succeeding to the titles and, early in life, developed a great propensity for debt. He married first, against his family's wishes, in London on 12 June 1913, an actress and chorus girl, May Etheridge. They had a son the following year before separating for seventeen years, during which time she was not allowed to see her son, and divorced in 1930 (she died alone five years later by placing her head in a gas oven; her son did not attend the service after being told by a fellow officer, "You cannot possibly go to a pauper's funeral.").

During that time the Leinster trustees, aware of his inability to manage money, were unwilling to grant him a lavish allowance. Even though he was a third son, Lord Edward entered into a contract with a wealthy businessman, Sir Harry Mallaby-Deeley, who gave him a one-time payment of £60,000 in exchange for all the income Edward would receive in his lifetime should he ever become duke. Edward quickly spent the entire amount and, after his second eldest brother was killed in action in World War I (where Edward was also wounded) and his eldest brother (who had succeeded their father as duke) died of a brain tumor, Edward succeeded in 1922 as the 7th Duke of Leinster. He was given an annual payment by Mallaby-Deeley of £1,200 (which was not required under their contract) but all the remainder of the estate's annual income – more than £80,000 – completely bypassed him. He was not even allowed to live in the family's stately home, Carton House, as it was rented and the amount given to Mallaby-Deeley. In 1923 he appeared in bankruptcy court owing £23,500 with an income of £20 per week. A few months later he was convicted of obtaining credit under false pretenses. He immediately went to the United States for six months in an open search for a wealthy heiress to marry. He later testified in court that he wooed two possibilities but neither agreed to marry him and secure his financial security.

He met Raffaella while in New York City. Although her autobiography, *Duchess from Brooklyn,* insists that her mother had gone through all the family funds, a fact that was supposedly known by the duke ("I only looked expensive," she stated), he insisted on marrying her. Immediately upon their return to England, she offered her engagement ring to pay for his outstanding hotel bill when he was detained by a hotel manager. The duke eventually owed more than £300,000 and incorporated himself as "The Dukedom of Leinster Estates, Ltd." to escape prosecution. Rafaella brought a divorce action against him for infidelity in 1939 but a Scottish court found that it had no jurisdiction over him as he was not domiciled there. At the time, the duke told the court he left Scotland "to suit my wife. She said she could not live with black-faced sheep and lochs and I saw a certain amount of truth in that."

Raffaella was a close friend and companion of the asthmatic Princess Maud, granddaughter of King Edward VII. If the duchess's autobiography is to be believed, she even wrote Princess Maud's obituary at the request of her family. Rafaella and the duke divorced in 1946 and he married third, 11 March 1946, Jessie Smither, who died in 1960. He married fourth in 1965 Vivien Irene Felton, born 19 February 1920, died Brighton 1992, daughter of a motor mechanic. She had been the duke's housekeeper in the block of small apartments where he lived (she was still married at the time). Her attempts to help him achieve financial success only resulted in additional debt. He also had an acknowledged illegitimate son, Adrian, by Yvonne Probyn in 1952. Yvonne's letters to him were intercepted by Vivien, his last wife, and

Richard Morris Hunt designed this Fifth Avenue mansion for Josephine Kleiner Schmid.

he later accused Vivien of having tricked him into marrying her when he should have married the mother of his son.

Because the duke had been an undischarged bankrupt for forty-five years, he lost his right to sit in the House of Lords and was precluded from participating in the coronation ceremonies of 1937 and 1953. In 1964 he was finally discharged from his bankruptcies and on 15 July 1975 first took his seat in the House of Lords (Vivien wore a borrowed coronet for the State Opening of Parliament). He came under the sway of a publicity agent who engineered his Parliamentary appearance and arranged a press tour. The duke became so depressed after a fight with his son and heir that he committed suicide with a cocktail of whiskey and nembutol in a basement flat in Pimlico on 8 March 1976. Rafaella, formerly Duchess of Leinster, died in London, 28 December 1993, at the age of ninety-two. By the Duke of Leinster's first wife to the actress May Etheridge, he had a son who succeeded his father in 1976 as the 8th Duke. That son had a son, the Marquess of Kildare, who succeeded as the 9th Duke in 2004. But the 9th Duke's only son, the Earl of Offaly, born in 1974, was killed in an auto accident in Ireland in 1997 and had only two sisters. The heir presumptive to the titles is the 9th Duke's brother who does have a son.

Josephine Kleiner of Covington, Kentucky, (her father was a German immigrant to Cincinatti, where the Jackson Brewery on McMicken Avenue at Elm Street was organized in 1853 by brothers Meinrad and Fridolin Kleiner), was born 21 April 1862, and died at San Remo, 8 October 1937. She graduated from a convent in Montreal when she was eighteen and married Swiss immigrant Auguste Schmid, a member of the firm of Bernheimer & Schmid who owned the Lion Brewery in New York City. A one-dollar per barrel tax on American-made beer largely financed the Union government during the Civil War but bankrupted many small breweries. Schmid and his partner were able to expand and their beer continued to be made until 1941. Their brewery was located at 107th to 108th Street and from Columbus Avenue west almost to Amsterdam Avenue. When he died of pneumonia in June of 1889, his wife and their two young daughters were in Europe. His obituary noted at the time that he was worth approximately $5 million. In February of 1893, one of the two daughters, Josephine, died at the age of twenty-one, having just come into her inheritance of one-third of her father's estate, and an elaborate funeral service was held in St. Patrick's Cathedral with many prominent German-Americans in attendance.

Mrs. Schmid took her late husband's place in his firm and, in 1903, bought out his partner for $1.4 million and converted it to a corporation called Lion Brewery of New York City. She owned all the stock and completely reorganized the workforce. She purchased a great deal of property on lower Broadway and on Cortlandt and Warren Streets. She built for herself on Fifth Avenue at 62nd Street an impressive mansion designed by Richard Morris Hunt, who also designed for her a country estate at Tarrytown, New York. Josephine Kleiner Schmid married as his second wife (his first marriage was annulled in 1901) at the Church of the Sacred Heart of Jesus and Mary in Brooklyn, 22 May 1909, **Giovanni-Battista, Prince del Drago, Marquess of Riofreddo**, born Rome, 12 August 1860, died Rome, 1 March 1956, fourth son of the

3rd Prince del Drago, Prince of Mazzano, of Antuni, and of Trevignano, Count of Ascrea. At the time newspapers reported in their headline that the bride was fifty and the groom twenty-seven and that the bride was worth $10 million. Josephine's only living child, Pauline (Mrs. Hugh A. Murray), did not attend. She had sued her mother in 1908 for an accounting of the estate, claiming that Josephine had deprived her of her portion of her late father's fortune which should have been at least $3 million more, and that, while she was still a minor, her mother had forced her to sign documents relinquishing her right to the funds. One of the allegations in the suit was that Josephine paid herself an annual salary of $500,000. The suit came to trial but was halted after several days when the parties reached an undisclosed settlement.

Josephine's new husband, Prince Giovanni, had come to New York City after his first Swiss marriage to a singer (by whom he had a son) was annulled. It was said that he brought with him only a diamond diadem that had belonged to his grandmother. Its supposed sale to George Gould enabled the young man to live in some degree of comfort. For a time he was rumored to be engaged to Sylvia Green, daughter of the immensely wealthy Hetty Green, "the witch of Wall Street," but she married an Astor grandson instead (he signed a prenuptial agreement insisted upon by his mother-in-law that prevented him from inheriting his wife's fortune; his own smaller fortune of $2 million made him acceptable to Hetty). The prince then became a clerk in a Wall Street firm. Even though a younger son of a small but admittedly ancient house, his royal connections were impressive. His grandmother, the Princess Maria Christina of Bourbon-Two Sicilies, had first contracted a

morganatic marriage to an Englishman before marrying King Fernando VII of Spain. They were the parents of Queen Isabel II of Spain. King Fernando's widow later married the Duke of Rianzaro and of that marriage Giovanni's mother had been born. He was thus a cousin of the King of Spain and had peripheral connections to several other royal houses. Within days of Josephine's marriage to Giovanni, the *New York Times* insisted that, although he was a grandson of the Spanish Queen, Giovanni was not accorded a princely title. They continued to refer to her as "Mrs. del Drago." It was customary, however, for younger sons to be given a courtesy title of prince even though Giovanni had little chance of succeeding as head of his house.

Josephine and her new husband lived in New York City and at the Palazzo Colonna in Rome. At first it seemed that they would be shunned by Italian society but the widow of Giovanni's eldest brother (whose youngest son married American **Anne Marie Wallace**) took them up and soon they were a part of Rome's social world. It was rumored that Josephine offered the Italian government $2 million in the hope of increasing her access to the Italian royal family. The American ambassador, Thomas N. Page, leased the entire first floor of the Palazzo del Drago as his official residence. In 1917, Josephine was again sued by her only surviving daughter, Pauline Schmid Murray, seeking $3 million for the alleged diminution in value of the brewery since her mother had assumed total control. Mrs. Murray was slated to be the sole owner of the brewery after her mother's death. The *New York Times* headline read, "Brewery Princess Sued for $3,000,000" even though its first line began, "Mrs. Josephine del Drago, sometimes referred to as Princess del Drago...". In December of 1931 Josephine's daughter, Pauline, and her husband, Hugh A. Murray, as well as their chauffeur, were killed near their country estate in South Carolina, where they had journeyed immediately after the marriage at their New York City home of their daughter, Paula, to attorney Frederic R. Coudert, Jr. (later a U. S. Congressman).

After Josephine's death in San Remo in 1937, her granddaughter, Paula Murray Coudert, filed a legal challenge to the will under which she received only a diamond tiara. The principal heir was the widower, Giovanni, who received $300,000 outright plus a life interest in her residuary estate. The principal of the trust, after Giovanni's death, was to go equally to the children of his brother, Mario del Drago. A separate trust of $200,000 was established for Giovanni's son, Marcello, with the principal at his death to be distributed to his children. Giovanni's son, Marcello, served several posts as Italian ambassador and married American **Geraldine Parrinello.** At the time of his father's 1956 death in Rome at the age of ninety-six, Don Marcello was the Italian ambassador to Japan. When Giovanni's nephew, Rodolfo, married American **Anne Marie Wallace** in Rome in 1932, the service was conducted by Cardinal Pacelli, papal secretary of state, and the couple was privately received immediately afterwards by Pope Pius, who gave the bride a gold rosary.

Jacqueline ("Jackie") Lane, born 16 May 1943, in England (although she worked and lived mainly in the U.S.), married as his second wife at Las Vegas, Nevada, 3 May 1973, **Prince Alfonso Hohenlohe-Langenburg**, born Madrid, 28 May 1924, son of Prince Egon Hohenlohe-Langenburg and Dona Maria de la Piedad Iturbe y Scholtz, Marquesa de Belvis de las Navas. Born Jocelyn Lane, she changed her name after a successful modeling career in London when she took up acting. She appeared with Elvis Presley in *Tickle Me* in 1965. Her television appearances included *The Wild Wild West*, *Hawaii Five-O*, and *The Man From U.N.C.L.E.* They were divorced at Stanfield, Connecticut, 18 March 1985 (he married again in 1991 to American **Marilys Healing**), having had one daughter, Princess Arriana, born at London, 1975. He also had an illegitimate daughter, Desiree, in 1980 by Heidi Balzer. Prince Alfonso's first wife, by whom he had two sons, was only eighteen at the time they were married. She was Princess Virginia "Ira" zu Furstenburg, whose grandmother was American **Jane Campbell**, Princess di San Faustino. Princess Arriana, daughter of Jackie Lane and Prince Alfonso, married in a high-profile ceremony at Marbella, Spain, on 30 June 2002, D. Dixon Boardman, who was thirty years her senior. The guest list included many society names as well as dozens of royals. Boardman is a great-grandson of Isidor Straus, who founded Macy's department store, and his wife, Rosalie Blum Straus, both of whom died on the *Titanic*. Boardman's daughters by American banking heiress Pauline Munn Baker, Serena and Samantha, are often pictured in society columns and are older than their step-mother.

Marguerite Lawler and her husband, the 14th Maharaja of Indore.

Marguerite Lawler, born Fargo, North Dakota, 13 July 1904, was a daughter of J. B. Lawler of Minnesota, a switchman for the Northern Pacific Railroad. Marguerite was educated at the Sacred Heart Convent in Lake Forest, Illinois, at the Romona Convent in Alhambra, California, and at Hunter College in New York. She trained

H. H. Maharaja Yeshwant Rao II Holkar Bahadur, 14th Maharaja of Indore (he was called "Junior" within his family). His father also married an American wife.

chronic insomnia, and drug addiction (opium poppies grew in abundance in his princely state of Indore).

He was born 6 September 1908, and was educated at England's prestigious Cheam School and at Christ Church, Oxford. There he used his great wealth in an unsuccessful attempt to buy friendships and subsequently nursed a grudge against the English for the remainder of his life. Junior succeeded on the abdication of his father on 26 February 1926 (see separate entry for **Nancy Ann Miller**) and was installed at the Juna Rajbada, Indore, on 11 March 1926. He reigned under a council of regency until he came of age before being invested

as a nurse at St. Mary's Hospital in Minneapolis and was later employed with the Union Pacific Railway and at the Good Samaritan Hospital in Los Angeles before becoming, from 1927 till 1937, personal nurse to Mrs. Alexander Pantages, widow of the theatre entrepreneur who eventually controlled more than seventy vaudeville theatres on the west coast (and was also the lover and business partner of brothel-keeper "Klondike Kate" Rockwell). Marguerite, who by that time had married John Branyon, was hired to care for **H. H. Maharaja Yeshwant Rao II Holkar Bahadur, 14th Maharaja of Indore** (he was called "Junior" within his family), who suffered from depression,

with full ruling powers at the King Edward Durbar Hall in Indore on 9 May 1930. As her patient, he convinced Marguerite to leave her permanent job and to obtain a divorce from her husband, John Branyon, citing his supposed adultery. Marguerite married Junior in Mexico City on 19 September 1938. He had married his first wife, daughter of the Chief of Kagal-Junior, when he was fifteen and she was eleven. They openly detested one another but had a daughter, Usha Devi, to whom he was devoted, and the girl's mother died in a Swiss clinic in 1937 at the age of twenty-four. He built for them a lavish home in Santa Ana, California, for the then-considerable sum of $500,000. His daughter, Princess Usha, attended the local public school, although a servant slept outside her door in the hall each night.

In April of the following year he took his new wife, Marguerite, to Indore where they received a darshan, a form of blessing, from the family priest. Marguerite impressed his subjects and the British Resident described her as "a sensible, serious lady over thirty, with a genuine desire to use her new position for the benefit of the State and its people." Because she was divorced, officials declared her marriage to be morganatic and she was denied the style of "Her Highness" and was called "Maharani Holkar." The British decided that, because she was not named as the guilty party in her divorce, she could be received and mix socially even though she could not receive the highest-styled title. Princess Usha, who was only five when her father re-married, became very close to her step-mother and accompanied her back to California when Marguerite left him the first time as a result of his continuing misbehavior and drug abuse.

In the 1930s the Romanian sculptor Constantin Brancusi worked on an ambitious public sculpture project, an unrealized temple in India, for the Maharaja of Indore who owned the original of Le Corbusier's Chaise Lounge Experimental Prototype and used it in his palace with a mattress covered in leopard skin. He also owned the famous Porter Rhodes Diamond, which was sold by Sotheby's in 1987. In 1930 he commissioned the German architect Eckart Muthesius to design a new art-deco palace in northern India as well as its furnishings. It was called Manik Bagh ("Jewel Gardens") and boasted the first air

conditioning in India. Muthesius worked with the most avant-garde European designers—Jacques Ruhlmann, Eileen Gray, Louis Sognot, Marcel Breur, and Hans Luckardt—to design the furnishings that were sold by Sotheby's in Monaco in 1980. Methesius also designed a private railway car and the interiors of two airplanes for the Maharaja. Marguerite and Princess Usha spent most of their time at their home in California. The

The 14th Maharaja of Indore with his second American wife, "Fay" Watt Crane.

subjects of Indore, however, did not want their young princess to live in the United States. Bowing to the fact that Marguerite could not give him another heir, the couple divorced in 1942 (Marguerite later married as her third husband at Las Vegas, Nevada, 15 January 1945, Charles W. Masters, a postman who was in the Coast Guard. They divorced only six months later and she joined the WAVES. She died at Corona del Mar, California, 2 May 1963).

While she was still married to the maharaja, during his wife's increasingly-frequent absence, Yeshwant had been seeing the American-born "Fay" Watt Crane, wife (since 5 July 1936) of Frank Arthur Crane, an executive at an aircraft factory in Bangalore where they lived with their daughter, Gwyneth. Posing as his secretary, Fay had accompanied him on one of his trips to the U.S. to see his wife and daughter. Fay and her daughter stayed with the maharaja in a Washington hotel under the name of "Mr. and Mrs. Holkar." Hoping to protect their daughter from negative publicity, Fay's husband stated publicly that his wife and daughter had gone to visit her mother. The maharaja offered his wife, Marguerite, a generous financial settlement as well as custody of his daughter if she would agree to be named the guilty party in a divorce. He checked into a dude ranch near Reno, Nevada, in order to establish residency and, on 3 July 1943, he obtained a divorce from Marguerite, citing her "extreme cruelty." The British Resident in Indore, Sir Kenneth Fitze, termed the agreement "a monstrous lie" and lamented that "Hollywood standards" had "governed recent events."

Only hours after his divorce from Marguerite, the maharaja then married at Reno, Nevada, 6 July 1943, **Euphemia "Fay" Watt Crane**, born 1 July 1914, formerly the wife of Frank Arthur Crane. He broke his agreement with his former wife and took his daughter, Usha Devi, back to Indore with him. The maharaja was described by the press as "a lounge lizard and a liar" and one British source wrote that he had "seduced another man's wife in circumstances that would preclude for life any Englishman who had so behaved from the presence of the Sovereign!" The British government decreed that not only was she not to be "Her Highness," but she would also be denied the title of Maharani as she "was not to be treated as a respectable member of society ... in view of the fact that she had traveled to America with the Maharaja and stayed with him in a hotel." On 18 May 1944 Fay had a son, Richard, by the maharaja, although the boy was precluded from the succession. In November of 1946 Britian's India Office reprimanded King George VI's staff for referring to Fay in the king's official telegram as the maharani. In August of 1947, after her husband's opium addiction had only gotten worse, Fay left for California, taking their infant son, Richard, with her. The maharaja became such a frequent visitor to the U. S. and was seen so rarely in his principality that the British Resident opined that his state anthem should be "One Day My Prince Will Come." Bowing to the inevitable, the maharaja and Fay were divorced in 1960. He died of cancer at Breach Candy Hospital in Bombay on 5 December 1961. Fay died in California on 2 May 1963.

Their son, Richard, was educated at Stanford University where he met his first wife, **Sally Sue Budd.** They were married in Dallas, Texas, 11 August 1966 (she was renamed "Shalini Devi"), and had a son, Randall, and a daughter, Sabrina, before being divorced. Richard then became engaged to Pamela, former wife of movie producer Conrad Rooks. She is the daughter of a Hindu father and a Sikh mother. Richard became a jewelry designer and has been involved in the restoration of a traditional style of weaving (the Maheswari sari), running a co-op operated by women weavers. His elder sister, Princess Usha, born in Paris, 20 October 1933, succeeded their father as Maharani of Indore after having lived for most of her early years in a mansion in Santa Ana, California. She had been declared heir-apparent in preference to her brother (who was designated as heir by his father) by special gazette in 1950. The decree was signed by

India's president and home minister, contrary to Hindu traditions, precedents, and religious sanctions (even after India's constitution had become effective).

After ruling for ten years, she was deprived of her rank, titles, and honors by the Government of India on 28 December 1971, thus ending her family's reign that had begun in 1733. She married a wealthy industrialist, Satish Chandra Melhotra, and formerly lived at Lal Baug Palace, the Holkar family's home, which was begun in 1886 and completed in 1921. Comprising twenty-eight acres, it boasts Italian marble columns, Persian carpets, Belgian stained glass windows, and a wooden ballroom floor mounted on springs. As a precaution against fire, the pantry and kitchen are located across a rivulet and a mechanical trolley services the residence. A replica of the gates of Buckingham Palace, but twice their size, emblazoned with the Holkar emblem, stands at the entrance. The palace now serves as a museum and cultural center while the family lives in a fashionable area of Mumbai. The maharani's husband, S. C. Malhotra, is chairman of Empire Industries, a multi-faceted manufacturing company based in Mumbai with more than $50 million in assets. They have two sons, both of whom are officers in the family corporation. Neither is in line for succession to the titles as their mother married into a different gotra (i.e., caste lineage system). Although some refer to their uncle Richard as the current maharaja, his birth as the son of an American wife and product of a morganatic marriage precludes his succession as well.

Frances Alice Willing Lawrance, born Bayshore, New York, 22 July 1901, died 1989, was a daughter of Francis Cooper Lawrance Jr., and his second wife, Susan Willing Lawrance. His first wife, Sarah Eggleston Lanier, who died in 1893, was a daughter of Charles Lanier, the very wealthy founder of the banking firm of Winslow, Lanier and Company and a director of many corporations. Francis Lawrance Jr., died of Bright's disease at his villa in Pau, France, in 1904 at the age of forty-five. His sister, Kitty Lawrance, married W. Averill Harriman, eldest son of the president of the Union Pacific Railroad. Frances Lawrance married in Paris, 27 December 1919, **Prince (John Willard) Marie-Andre' Poniatowski,** born San Francisco, California, 13 December 1899, died 30 November 1977, third son of Prince Andre' Poniatowski and his American wife, **Elizabeth Sperry.** Frances's father was deceased when her 1919 engagement was announced and her attorneys applied to the Surrogates Court in New York City for an increase in her allowance in order to marry the prince. At the time, the groom was an officer in the French army and his income was stated to be only 20,000 francs per year.

Frances's trust fund left to her by her father was valued at $200,000 with a yearly income of $10,000. Additionally, she had a trust fund from her grandfather with an annual yield of $10,000. She stated in depositions that her living costs would be 160,000 francs per year, including 28,600 for clothes, 22,000 for an automobile and chauffeur, and 42,000 for food and household supplies. Her mother stated that she had "spared no expense" in rearing her daughter but that her own costs for maintaining her home in Paris made it impossible for her to give more to her daughter. She also stated that her daughter's "friends and acquaintances are people of the highest standing" and that the mother approved of the marriage. The groom was born in San Francisco, his mother's home, where his father made many trips during World War I "in the interest of Franco-American banking." He and his two brothers served in the French Army during World War I and the groom later joined the Polish army. The couple's eldest son was killed in action in Holland in 1945.

Frances's mother, Susan Willing of Philadelphia, was a sister of the famously beautiful Baroness Ribblesdale, born Ava Willing, whose first husband was Jack Astor who was lost on the *Titanic*. Thus Frances's first cousin was **Alice Astor** who married **Serge, Prince Obolensky-Neledinsky-Meletsky.** Frances's aunt, **Frances "Fanny" Lawrance,** married in 1885, the **7th Baron Vernon** of England. Frances had three cousins who were reared by their Lawrance aunt when their parents were killed in a freak yachting accident. **Florence, Marcelite,** and **Edith Garner** married respectively, **Sir William Gordon-Cumming, 4th Baronet** (of the Tranby Croft scandal), the **Marquis de Breteuil,** and the Danish **Count Moltke Huitfeld.**

Mary Esther Lee, born in New York City, 3 October 1837, was a daughter of Anne Duryce Phillips Lee and wealthy merchant David Lee of the merchant firm of Lee, Dater and Miller. After her father's death in January of 1853, her mother took Mary and her three sisters to Europe, where one of the sisters married **Baron Waechter-Lauterbach.** Mary was befriended by the American-born Marquise de Chasseloup-Laubat, originally from New Orleans, who was a favorite of the Empress Eugenie. The Marquis, a godson of Napoleon I, was at that time in

Top: Mary Esther Lee's first husband, Prince von Noer, left her even wealthier.

Bottom: Her second husband, Count von Waldersee, who led the Allied forces in the Boxer Rebellion.

charge of Napoleon III's navy, having previously been minister for Algeria and the Colonies. His wife was known to have an affinity for fellow Southern women and was a valuable ally in introducing them to the French court. It was there in 1864 that Mary Esther Lee met Prince Friedrich of Schleswig-Holstein, who was on a mission to explain the difficult border disputes involving his country. He was immediately taken with the twenty-seven-year-old woman and asked for her hand in marriage. She accepted when Emperor Francis Joseph agreed to create him and his new wife a prince and princess.

Mary married in Paris, 3 November 1864, as his second wife the much older **Prince Friedrich Emil August of Schleswig-Holstein,** born Kiel, 23 August 1800, died Beirut, 2 July 1865. Her family opposed a morganatic marriage so, less than a month before his wedding he relinquished his title as a prince of Schleswig-Holstein to marry her and was given by the emperor of Austria the title of **Prince von Noer** (a village in Schleswig, Prussia), created 6 October 1864, a title he could share with her as she was Princess von Noer.

Mary Esther Lee became so close to her first husband's niece, the Empress of Germany, and so influential with her husband, the emperor, that jealous courtiers intrigued against her. She never asked anything for herself nor for her husband.

He had a son and two daughters by his first wife (Mary Esther was younger than his eldest son). His son also renounced his inheritance in order to marry and was also created Prince von Noer. Prince Friedrich died in Beirut, leaving his wife of less than a year $4 million. On 14 April 1874 at Lautenbach, Wurtemberg, she married **Alfred, Count von Waldersee**, born 8 April 1832, died 3 May 1904, General Field Marshal who commanded the allied international forces in the Boxer Rebellion in China in 1900. She was particularly close to her first husband's niece, the Empress of Germany, and became an intimate friend of the emperor, who often visited her to seek her opinion—a practice that aroused intense jealousy from the remainder of the royal court. According to many reports, she was one of the emperor's closest advisors and he enjoyed dropping in on her unannounced to seek her counsel. Her salon in Berlin was famous for the influence she was able to exert and she was her second husband's active partner in the political and military quarrels that raged around him during the days of Bismarck's power. The memoir of one palace insider recalled her as "a remarkable woman. She was singularly gifted and noted for her wonderful tact...The Empress Augusta Victoria treated her as one of her best friends, both ladies having sympathies in common."

It was largely through the empress that Emperor Wilhelm came to rely so heavily upon the American woman. According to the memoir, the emperor "liked her frankness, the simple, earnest way in which she spoke to him, making use of the privileges that her age and her relationship with the Empress gave her, but never at the same time forgetting the distance that separated her from her Sovereign, nor

the respect which she owed to him." Perhaps unsurprisingly, jealous courtiers eventually drove a wedge between the countess and the emperor but she never betrayed the great trust he had placed in her, nor did she make any request of him either for herself or her husband. The emperor's personal physicians were attending von Waldersee when he died. In 1903 she and her sister, Baroness Waechter-Lauterbach, traveled to New York City to see their dying brother, David Bradley Lee. It was her first return to her homeland in almost fifty years. In her widowhood she devoted herself to church and philanthropic work and died at her home in Hanover at the age of seventy-seven on 4 July 1914. She left her entire estate of $750,000 to German relatives, including her sister's daughter, Blanche, Baroness von Palm. Her family mansion in Hanover was left to establish a home for women's aid called the Waldersee Institute.

Amanda Leigh was a daughter of Wolfram Lewis, a financial consultant in Santa Fe, New Mexico, and of Elsie (Mrs. Douglas) Leigh of New York City. Her step-father was among America's most celebrated sign and lighting designers. Moving to New York City from his native Alabama at the age of twenty-eight, Douglas Leigh eventually designed the twenty-five-foot high steaming coffee cup sign for A & P, an effervescent billboard for Bromo-Seltzer, and a 120-foot Pepsi-Cola waterfall. His most famous creation, however, was the Camel cigarette smoking-ring sign that remained on Times Square for twenty-six years and was copied in twenty-two other cities. Leigh also lighted the Empire State Building, the Citicorp Building, and the Waldorf-Astoria Hotel. At one time he owned One Times

Square from which the ball is dropped on New Year's Eve, and in 1976 he made New York City's fountains flow red, white, and blue during the National Democratic Convention. He died at the age of ninety-two in 1999 and the Borghese family gave more than eight hundred objects from his advertising collection to the American Sign Museum.

Amanda met at a wedding in Madrid and later married **Prince Francesco Borghese, 6th Duca di Bomarzo, 17th Prince di Sant Angelo & Prince di San Paolo, 12th Marquess di Monticelli, 12th Count di Chia, Lord of Attigliano & Mugnano,** born Castelvecchio, 18 December 1938. Their daughter, Ilaria (born 1969), married in Summit, New Jersey, 11 July 1998, Steven Charles Winn, and is an occupational therapist in New Jersey. Francesco's mother, born Marcella Fazi, in 1956 founded the Princess Marcella Borghese cosmetics company with Charles Revson that became a division of Revlon. She died in 2002 and was buried in the Borghese family chapel in the Basilica of Santa Maria Maggiore in Rome. Prince Francesco's father, whom he succeeded in 1985, was president of General Motors Company in Italy. The Borghese family produced Pope Paul V and Rome's most famous public park as well as the acclaimed art gallery, the Galleria Borghese. Prince Francesco's twin, Prince Livio, married American **Susanna Keyser** and they live in New York City. Francesco and Amanda's youngest son, Prince Lorenzo (born 1972), has his own line of cosmetics for dogs. He was featured as the eligible prince on American television's Bachelor program in the fall of 2006.

Nancy Leishman, born Pittsburgh, Pennsylvania, 2 October

Nancy Leishman's father was president of Carnegie Steel and ambassador to several countries. It was the perfect training for her future role.

Nancy spent her adolescence in Germany where her father was ambassador.

Istanbul on the assumption that he would be reimbursed by Congress. When he returned to Washington he was dismayed to learn that there was neither the will nor the resources to repay him. Leishman then invited the Speaker of the House, several congressional leaders, and key members of the foreign relations and the appropriations committees to an elegant stag dinner. After they had been sufficiently wined and dined, they began playing poker and the ambassador lost large sums of money to them. At that point he challenged them that he would drop his request to be repaid for the ambassadorial residence if he lost the remainder of the game, while they would appropriate the necessary funds if he defeated them. Only then did Leishman begin playing in earnest and, before the evening was finished, he had secured the necessary votes. The Palazzo Corpi became the first U. S. government-owned diplomatic premises in Europe.

Nancy's elder sister, **Marthe Leishman**, married in 1904 **Count Louis de Gontaut-Biron**, a marriage reportedly arranged by a Paris attorney for a fee. They were negotiating a divorce when the count died and the attorney brought a civil action for his payment. In 1910, when Leishman was ambassador to Italy, his wife gave a luncheon in Rome for first lady Mrs. Theodore Roosevelt at which nine of the eighteen guests were American women married to titled husbands, including Countess Gianotti (Frances Kinney, wife of the prefect of the palace of the king), the Duchess de Arcos (Virginia Lowery), Princess Poggio-Suasa (Josephine Curtiss), the Marchesa de Viti de Marco (Etta Dunham), the Duchess Lante della Rovere (Mathilde Davis), Princess Ludovico Lante della Rovere (Anita Allen), Countess

1894, died Copenhagen, 11 January 1983, was a daughter of Julia Crawford Leishman and John G. A. Leishman (1857 – 1924) who was president of the Carnegie Steel Company and U.S. minister to Switzerland 1897-1901, Turkey 1900-06, U.S. ambassador to Turkey 1906-09, Italy 1909-11, and Germany 1911-13. When Leishman was ambassador to Turkey, he purchased with his own funds ($2.5 million in today's currency) as the ambassador's residence the Palazzo Corpi in

Left: Nancy (right) and her sister, Marthe. Nancy is next to her second husband. Right: The 13th Duke of Croy. His second wife was also American.

di Brazza (Cora Slocomb), the Duchess di Torlonia (Elsie Moore), and Princess di San Faustino (Jane Campbell).

Nancy Leishman lived in Germany while her father was ambassador, and married on 27 October 1913 at the Little Catholic Church of St. Joseph in Geneva, Switzerland, **Karl Rudolf, the 13th Duke of Croy, Duke of Arenberg, Duke of Meppen, Prince of Recklinghausen**, born Brussels, 11 April 1889, died Feldafing, 2 August 1974. More than two thousand people strained for a view of the couple and the priest performing the ceremony was forced to ask the crowd to be silent so he could officiate over the rites. The duke's mother arrived at the last moment and his sister did not attend the ceremony. There were news reports that his family had made one last attempt to prevent his marriage and they were very public in their pronouncements that

Nancy could never be called "duchess." At the time the Almanach de Gotha declared their marriage "unequal"—it was the first time the official handbook went to such an extreme as to call a marriage a "misalliance." Years later the duke's uncle brought suit to prevent the Croys' son from inheriting the estates, though the son was eventually allowed to inherit the title. Rumor had it that Kaiser Wilhelm II's eldest son, the crown prince, was very interested in Nancy Leishman and the kaiser urged the Duke of Croy to marry her instead. Within months of the wedding the crown prince paid an official call on the couple in spite of the Gotha's pronouncement of their unequal marriage. The crown prince could have made an informal visit but purposely announced his schedule so as to bestow his public blessing on the marriage.

The Croys' first son was born in November of 1914 while his father was with the German army at the front. They had another son and two daughters, the youngest of whom married three American husbands. The Duke of Croy later gave his sister-in-law, Marthe, in marriage to society stalwart and heir James Hazen Hyde on 25 November 1913, in the American Church of the Holy Trinity in Paris. After the birth of her children, the duke supposedly treated Nancy badly and, as the rumor circulated, the final insult was his gift

Nancy's father, Ambassador John Leishman, with the Queen of Italy. He was ambassador to that country from 1909-1911.

of her furs to their governess. She knew that, having had a Catholic marriage, a divorce would be difficult, but was finally able to secure the approval of two archbishops and the divorce was granted with even the duke's payment for costs. The Croys divorced at Wiesbaden, 19 June 1922, confirmed 20 December 1922. Nancy's father, former Ambassador John G. A. Leishman, died in Monte Carlo on 27 March 1924. In 1936 Nancy married Andreas d'Oldenberg, minister of Denmark to France and recipient of the Legion of Honor. He died 9 September 1939.

Nancy lived in Paris, then in Copenhagen at the time of her death in 1983. The Duke of Croy married second, American **Helene Lewis,** of Albany, New York, who later married **Count Anthony de Bosdari** of Italy, a second cousin of King Victor Emmanuel of Italy. Bosdari's next wife was **Josephine Fish** of Chicago.

Bertha Emma Lewis was born at New Orleans, Louisiana, 16 March 1872, and died at Santa Margherita, near Rapallo, 22 April 1939. She was educated in Paris at the Convent of Sacre' Coeur and spoke French fluently. Bertha married at London, 24 August 1895, **Prince Karl Isenburg-Birstein,** born at Offenbach, 18 February 1871, died Rapallo, 6 January 1951, son of the reigning 5th Prince of Isenburg and Marie Louise, Archduchess of Austria. After the marriage they lived at the fifteenth century Chateau de Seeburg, on the Rhine near Leoni in Bavaria, and at Birstein, and had no children. It was said that their wing of the family palace held no fewer than 170 rooms. She was reported to be a great horsewoman and an excellent shot. Her Paris home was a salon of prominent musicians and she was a sponsor and patron of many musical festivals that she always attended. She arranged for the Paris reception of the Abbe' Perosi, who succeeded Palestrina as musical director of the Sistene Chapel, after he appeared in the Paris Trocadero to present his own compositions.

Prince Karl was a chevalier of the Maltese Legion of Honor. His brother, Franz Joseph, succeeded their father as 6th Prince of Isenburg, a princely family founded in the middle of the seventeenth century. Princess Karl died at her villa at Santa Margherita, near Genoa, at the age of sixty-seven. In 1892 Prince Karl's eldest brother, Prince Leopold,

Bertha Emma Lewis became an active patron of music.

heir to the titles, traveled to the United States in an avowed search to find an heiress for a bride. The prince borrowed heavily against his future inheritance and the fortune he planned to marry. One of the heiresses he named as a target of affection was Consuelo Vanderbilt (although there is no indication that he ever met her), who in 1895 instead married the 9th Duke of Marlborough. Another was Mary Pullman, daughter of the sleeping car magnate, but her thrifty father was said to oppose the marriage. When he returned without a wife, Prince Leopold convinced a cousin, Archduke Francis Salvator, to guarantee for him yet another loan from the same moneylender to whom he was already heavily in debt. Despite protracted litigation and a great deal of unflattering publicity, the debts were never repaid.

In 1898 the unsuccessful Prince Leopold renounced his rights in favor of his next brother, Prince Franz Joseph, who eventually succeeded their father. Meanwhile, their cousin, Princess Alexandra Isenburg (born 1855), who had married yet another cousin, Prince Adalbert Isenburg (born 1839), enjoyed a high social profile enabled by their joint fortunes. But Princess Alexandra fell in love with a Lieutenant Pagenhardt who was described as "a man of plebeian birth, penniless and not even good looking." She was divorced by her husband who named Pagenhardt at the co-respondent. The couple married and Princess Alexandra was able to retain most of her $5 million dowry and to have her new husband created a baron. They kept numerous palaces and were even said to have entertained one hundred guests for dinner on fifty consecutive evenings. They enjoyed a yacht and a private railroad car and she was famous for her expensive jewels. She inherited several other bequests and in only a few short years the couple had spent $8 million. They amassed massive debts that were finally called in and unable to be paid. Within ten years of marriage, they were divorced.

The princess was forced to sell off properties one by one until she was absolutely destitute. She was arrested by a bailiff when walking down a Berlin street and was searched for any cash or valuables that could be retained for her creditors. The resulting scandal caused her relatives, who had given up any tie to her, to offer her an annual allowance of $2,500 if she would leave the country (although they would not settle her debts). She lived quietly for several years before becoming a regular at the gaming tables at Monte Carlo where she lost heavily. Her relatives were forced to cut off her allowance when they learned she had again borrowed great sums of money. When the German courts announced that the princess had debts of $15 million and no assets, one of her creditors took his life. She was reduced to keeping a boarding house where she greeted each guest with the smallest bow of her head.

Helene Lewis, born Albany, New York, 14 February 1898, daughter of Thompson H. Lewis and Mrs. Lindsay Lewis, married in Munich, 23 Oct 1924, Karl Rudolf, the **13th Duke of Croy, Duke of Arenberg, Duke of Meppen, Prince of Recklinghausen**, born in Brussels, 11 April 1889, died Feldafing, 2 August 1974, formerly the husband of American **Nancy Leishman** (whose son inherited the titles). They had no children and were divorced in 1931 and he married twice more after Helene. She then married **Count Anthony de Bosdari** of Italy, a son of Count Anthony who was a second cousin of King Victor Emmanuel of Italy and a nephew of the Count de Bosdari who was Italian ambassador to Germany. Count Anthony de Bosdari had been married in 1928 to **Josephine Fish**, daughter of Mrs. Charles King Corsant of Chicago and that marriage was dissolved several months later when he announced his engagement to the actress Tallulah Bankhead (a marriage which never took place after she learned that the engagement ring he gave her was not his and that he was still married). In 1903 their kinsman, Count Maurice de Bosdari, forged the signature of J. P. Morgan on a number of bills purported to have been given as payment for pictures. The bills were then sold to moneylenders at a discounted rate. He had sold a painting to Morgan and thus obtained his signature on a check. When a warrant was issued for de Bosdari's arrest, he fled to Alexandria, Egypt, but was captured and returned for trial where he was sentenced to three years in prison.

Helene Lewis married as her last husband Nicholas Horthy Jr. (1907 – 1993), former Hungarian envoy to Brazil and to Chile and younger son of the regent of Hungary from 1920 to 1944, the elder of whom was styled "His Serene Highness the Regent of the Kingdom of Hungary." Horthy Sr. (1868 - 1957) was commander in chief of the Austro-Hungarian fleet during World War I and helped organize the anti-Bolshevik counter-revolution in 1919. As a result, he was made commander in chief of the Nationalist Army and, on 1 March 1920, he was chosen regent (or governor) of Hungary. He twice prevented former Emperor Charles I (Charles IV in Hungary) from regaining his Hungarian throne, once by negotiation and once by force. When Charles was banned from the throne and forced into exile, Horthy found himself regent of a kingless kingdom. When Nazi troops invaded Hungary on 19 March 1944, Horthy was forced to remain in his position as a figurehead. Horthy's eldest son, Stephen, who had been vice-regent, was killed when his plane crashed on the Russian front in 1942.

The German secret service knew of the anti-Nazi activities of the regent's younger son, Nicholas Horthy Jr., and a Croat spy was planted among his close collaborators (the son was reported to have told the regent, "Father, if we don't do something soon, we will have to leave the palace with a shopping bag in hand.") The Nazis learned of a meeting by young Horthy on October 15 with emissaries of Tito, who themselves were agents of the German secret service. A trap was prepared and Nicholas Horthy Jr., was kidnapped after a shooting and struggle in which Horthy Jr., was seriously wounded and some of his guards killed. The regent and his son were captured by Nazi officers who had rescued Benito Mussolini from imprisonment the year before. After being seriously wounded by gunfire, Horthy Jr. was taken from the palace rolled up in a carpet and sent to Mauthausen and then Dachau, where he was eventually liberated by U.S. troops in the same liberation that included Prince Frederick Leopold of Prussia and Prince Philip of Hesse (whose wife, Princess Mafalda of Savoy, was killed in the Buchenwald Camp). German SS and paratroopers arrested Horthy and, in order to secure his son's safety, the regent signed a document which made his archrival, the Arrow Cross leader Ferenc Szálasi, his successor. Horthy and his family were then put on a train to Bavaria where they were held under house arrest. They eventually lived as permanent exiles in Portugal where the regent remained in death until he was finally re-interred in Hungary in 1993. Helene Lewis, Mrs. Nicholas Horthy Jr., died in Palma de Mallorca in the Balearic Islands of Spain.

Anita Lihme, the daughter of Christian Bai Lihme and Olga Hegler Lihme, born Peru, Illinois, 4 November 1903, died New York City, 14 May 1976, married at Watch Hill, Rhode Island, 29 August 1925, **Prince Edward Joseph Lobkowicz**, born Scholl Hradiste, 20 June 1899, died Freiburg, Germany, 2 January 1959, whose father was imperial chamberlain of the Austro-Hungarian Empire. Prince Edward was a member of an ancient Bohemian family and served in action in World War I against the Italians as a lieutenant in the Austro-Hungarian Army. He was a partner in a Paris brokerage house until World War II broke out when he fought in North Africa as a captain with the Czechoslovak forces attached to the British army. He was made a chevalier of the French Legion of Honor and

Anita Lihme and her husband, Prince Edward Lobkowicz, whose father was imperial chamberlain of the Austro-Hungarian Empire.

received the French Croix de Guerre and the British, French, Czechoslovak, and Polish Military crosses for his service in the Second World War. He became a broker at Fahnestock & Company in New York City and also had a home in Watch Hill, Rhode Island. He died at the age of fifty-nine and left a son, Prince Edward, who married Francoise, Princess of Bourbon-Parma, daughter of Xavier, Duke of Parma, prince and head of the Royal House of Bourbon-Parma, as well as a daughter, Anita, who graduated from Radcliffe then married Count Charles Louis de Cosse' Brissac.

Mathilde Elizabeth Lowenguth, born Strasbourg, 29 November 1870, died New York City, 10 July 1948, at Tranquility Farms, Allamuchy, New Jersey, married first, **Count de Wassenaer,** a Dutch nobleman who left her a young widow. She married second, on 16 June 1902, in St. George's Chapel in London, Rutherfurd Stuyvesant. His original name was Stuyvesant Rutherfurd but he changed it by an act of the legislature (in the year in which he graduated from Columbia) to suit the will of a wealthy uncle who left him a fortune on that condition. His brother was Winthrop Rutherfurd, who married a

Mathilde Lowenguth was first the Countess de Wassanaer, then Mrs. Rutherfurd Stuyvesant, before marrying Prince Alexandre de Chimay.

daughter of Vice President Levi Morton, and his sister was the wife of Henry White, U. S. ambassador to France. The Stuyvesants made their home opposite Stuyvesant Square and at Tranquility Farms that included a two thousand-acre game park with four hundred deer, fifty elk, and five thousand English pheasants. They also had a house in Paris on the rue Dumont d'Urville, where he died on 4 July 1909. Their sons were Alan Stuyvesant and Lewis R. Stuyvesant, the latter of whom was the American consul at Calcutta and pre-deceased his mother.

Mathilde married third at Paris, 19 August 1933 (as his second wife), **Prince Alexandre de Chimay,** born Paris, 9 March 1873, died Paris, 21 March 1951, third son of the 18th Prince de Chimay and Prince de Caraman. His sister was the first lady in waiting to the queen of the Belgians. During World War II Mathilde was treasurer of the American Fund for the Charite' Meternelle de Paris. Prince Alexandre had a son by his first wife, Helene, Princess Bassaraba Brancovan, but no children by Mathilde. His eldest brother, the 19th Prince de Caraman-Chimay, married American **Clara Ward,** whose son died before succeeding his father. Tranquility Farms, a forty-seven-room mansion built on five thousand acres, is still in Allamuchy. The Rutherford Mansion, currently called the Villa Madonna, was built with twenty-three rooms in 1903 on one thousand acres. In 2001 the majority of the property was permanently preserved by the New Jersey Nature Conservancy.

Virginia Woodbury Lowery (1855 – 1934) was a daughter of Frances A. Woodbury Lowery and Judge Archibald H. Lowery of Washington, D.C. Her grandfather was Levi Woodbury (1789-1851) of Portsmouth, New Hampshire, governor, secretary of the Navy, secretary of the Treasury, and associate justice of the U.S. Supreme Court. Virginia's uncle, Montgomery Blair, was postmaster-general under President Lincoln as well as the great-grandfather of actor Montgomery Clift. Virginia married in June 1895, in Washington, **Jose Ambrosio Brunetti y Gayoso,** 15th Duke de Arcos, born 6 February 1839, son of Count Lazare Fernando Brunetti-Salvioni, the Austrian ambassador to Spain, and of Marquise Maria de Gayoso y Cobos.

The title of Duke of Arcos and Grandee of Spain is an ancient one, having been created in 1498. The groom's maternal great-grandfather, Don Pedro VI de Alcantara Tellez-Giron y Pacheco, was the 9th Duke of Osuna and married the 12th Duchess of Benavente, 14th Duchess of Gandie, 13th Duchess of Bejar, and 12th Duchess of Arcos. The titles were passed down in the maternal line and Jose became the 15th Duke of Arcos after his first cousins, the 13th and 14th Dukes of Arcos (as well as the 11th and 12th Dukes of Osuna), died childless. The Lowerys were an old Washington family and their home at 1000 Vermont Avenue, at the corner of K Street, was a frequent site for entertaining. The couple met when he was first secretary at the Spanish legation. He was then transferred as minister first to Montevideo then to Santiago. At the time of their marriage, he was the Spanish minister to Mexico. In 1899 the duke was appointed ambassador to the United States and returned to Washington where his wife was particularly useful to him and to her adopted country (although she never relinquished her citizenship). His arrival marked the resumption of diplomatic relations since his predecessor left in 1898 at the outbreak of war.

President McKinley received the duke and duchess at the White House on 3 June 1899 at the same time that the United States' ambassador to Spain was presenting his credentials in Madrid. In 1901 the duke exchanged treaties with the U. S. secretary of state, ceding claims to the Philippine Islands and laying out details of a peace treaty between the two nations. In the next year the duke was called home to Spain to serve in his nation's government before ending his service as ambassador to the Quirinal. At his retirement in 1907, he and the duchess settled in Rome where they took a large apartment in the Palazzo Brancaccio, built by the American Mrs. J. Hickson Field for her daughter, the Princess Brancaccio. The previous American ambassador had lived in the apartment for the prior five years. The widowed duchess died there on 8 March 1934, having stipulated that she be buried in Rock Creek Cemetery in her native Washington. She left $1 million to American philanthropies, including hospitals and libraries, as well as a further half-million to Italian charities. The impressive art collection she had assembled over the years was left to Washington's National Gallery of Art, along with her fan collection and a fund for a room to display them. The Prado Museum in Madrid received paintings, including those by Romney, Raeburn, and Lebrun, as well as the duke's book collection and papers. The duchess also added $50,000 to Harvard's trust fund founded by her late brother, Woodbury Lowery, for the study of history. The Lowery mansion in Washington was given to establish a free medical clinic and emergency treatment center. A substantial remainder was also left to her Blair cousins.

Her brother, Woodbury Lowery (1853-1906), a Washington patent attorney and historian, assembled a collection of three hundred original maps relating to former Spanish possessions in the United States and it was given to the Library of Congress. The residence of the duchess's cousin, Woodbury Blair, opposite the White House, is the official residence for visiting heads of state. The duke and duchess had no children and the title is now held by Doña Angela Maria de Solis-Beaumont y Tellez-Giron, Duchess of Arcos.

Evelyn "Eva" Bryant Mackay, born Downieville, Nevada, 12 November 1861, was a daughter of Mrs. John W. Mackay by a prior marriage to Dr. Bryant, a cousin of William Cullen Bryant. John W. Mackay was an Irish immigrant to New York City who sailed to California in 1851. He had missed the California gold rush but moved to Virginia City, Nevada, where he eventually formed the Bonanza Firm along with James G. Fair, James C. Flood, and William S. O'Brien. There they developed the famous Comstock Lode and became enormously wealthy (one mine alone, the Big Bonanza, produced more than $400 million in ore in just four years). On 28 October 1879 former President Ulysses S. Grant descended with Mackay into his Big Bonanza Mine where temperatures reached as high as 120 degrees. After coming out of the mine Grant was quoted as saying, "That's as close to hell as I hope I'll ever get." Mackay's monthly income from the mine was estimated at $500,000. Jay Gould once said of him after a particularly nasty rate war, "You can't beat Mackay, all he has to do when he needs money is go to Nevada and dig up some more."

By 1877, when the mine was depleted, he and his family moved to San Francisco, then to Paris and London, and finally returned to the U. S. in 1920. Mackay formed the Commercial Cable Company with James G. Bennett and, while on a business trip to London, died in 1902. His widow and children commissioned the sculptor

Left: Clarence Mackay, Jr., with James Gerard, U. S ambassador to Germany. Right: Eva Mackay's niece, Ellin Mackay, and her husband, composer Irving Berlin.

Gutzon Borglum (known for sculpting Mt. Rushmore) to create a statue of Mackay. It was originally intended for the State Capitol grounds in Carson City but, after some opposition from politicians, the site was withdrawn. The president of the University of Nevada offered a site and his generosity was rewarded by Mackay's donation of the Stanford White-designed quad buildings to house the Mackay School of Mines. In 1930 the family donated the Mackay Science Hall and its endowment still supports the School of Mines. In 1882 Mrs. Mackay had her portrait painted by society artist Leon Bonnat dressed in a robe manufactured for the Empress Eugenie as a gift from the municipality of Paris. It was said to have taken fourteen years to complete by the first five hands at the Chantilly atelier.

"Eva" Mackay was educated at the Convent of the Sacred Heart in Paris. She married 11 February 1885, at Paris, **Don Fernando di Colonna, 8th Prince of Stigliano, Prince of Galatro and Aliano, Prince of Paliggiano, Prince Colonna, Marquis di Castelnuevo, Baron di Alianello,** etc., and a Spanish grandee of the first class, and became the Princess **di Stigliano,** although the U. S. press often referred to her as the Princess Colonna, a title which was not hers. The *New York Times* enthused of the garments, "for beauty of material, elegance of design, and perfect fitness and appropriateness to its future wearer has seldom been approached in the annals of Parisian toilet." Of the guest list, they insisted that, "The reception was especially distinguished by the quality of the guests, among whom were included about every person of distinction and worth in French society."

She lived at the Castello Costa, at Santa Margherita Ligure, Italy, and was engaged in hospital work with the Red Cross throughout the War. Her daughter, Biana, married Count Jules de Bonvouloir and lived in Paris, and there were two sons, Andrea (Prince di Aliano) and Marc Antonio, who served in the Italian army in WWI. The marriage was not happy and they spent much of their time living apart while the children divided their time between their parents. The prince borrowed large sums of money and had all his bills sent to his wife. In 1893 there was a separation after she received bills for women's lavish gifts that had not been given to her. When she reproached her husband for his actions, he reminded her of the social

station to which he had been born as opposed to her own lowly state. In reporting the breach, the *New York Times* reported that the prince's "morals improved only as he was paid out of the Bonanza King's strongbox." Eva obtained a divorce decree in 1895, retained custody of their children, and settled an income of 60,000 francs per year on the prince. Her mother and all of her children were with her when she died of influenza in 1919. Her eldest son, Andrea, succeeded his father in 1926 as 9th Prince di Stigliano, 9th Prince di Aliano, 9th Marchese di Castelnuovo, etc., but had no children and the titles passed to descendants of Don Fernando's younger brother. Eva's niece, Ellin Mackay, married songwriter Irving Berlin and wrote a book about her grandmother, *Silver Platter: A Portrait of Mrs. John Mackay.*

(Helen) Isabelle McMillin, born New York City, 7 September 1889, died Paris, 7 February 1958, was a daughter of Helen Frisbie McMillin and Emerson McMillin Jr. Her grandfather, capitalist Emerson McMillin (1844 - 1922) was the twelfth of fourteen children and had little schooling. He worked as a manual laborer in an iron foundry while teaching himself at night. He moved up the company ladder but in 1861 volunteered for the Union Army at the outbreak of war. He was one of six brothers known as "The Fighting McMillins" who all volunteered for the War—three were killed outright in battle or later died of wounds. He later said that looking at the stars at night while on guard duty gave birth to his great interest in astronomy. After the War McMillin returned to work in the gas works, married Isabel Morgan, and had five children. In 1888 he became president of the

Columbus Gas Works where he became "the gas magnate of Ohio." McMillin then founded the American Light and Traction Company. Having made his first fortune in Ohio, he moved to New York City in 1891 and started the banking and investment firm that bore his name. McMillin also incorporated the East River Gas Company at Long Island City. He manufactured gas at his Ravenswood gas plant, excavated underneath the East River, and transported his product in a drill-and-blast tunnel passing beneath Blackwell's Island. McMillin sold his company in 1894 and by 1897 it was part of J. P. Morgan's New Amsterdam Gas Company.

He had been an early financial supporter of Ohio State University and in 1891 he offered to pay for building and equipping an astronomical observatory for the institution. It was opened in 1896 when McMillin made an additional bequest to endow a fellowship in the school of astronomy. Further gifts would follow over the years until his death in 1922. The 12.5 inch refracting telescope was the largest in Ohio when it was built in 1895 and is still used today by Heidelberg University. McMillin had a summer home on the Rangeley Lakes in Maine as well as an estate called Darlington near Mahwah, New Jersey, a 45,000 square-foot mansion containing seventy-five rooms. Darlington eventually was sold to the Catholic Diocese of New Jersey who used it as the Immaculate Conception Seminary. Isabelle was reared by her grandfather after her parents' death. She married in Paris 25 September 1939 as his second wife, **Prince Michel Murat,** born 7 February 1887, son of Prince Louis Napoleon, and grandson of American **Caroline Fraser** and Lucien, 3rd Prince Murat.

The bride's aunt, **Baroness Ubaldo Traverso** (Estelle McMillin, formerly Mrs. Stanley Stewart), was the only family member present as both the bride's parents were already deceased. Prince Michel died at Paris 8 June 1941 and he had no children by Isabelle. His first wife had been American **Helen Macdonald Stallo,** born Cincinnati, Ohio, 5 September 1893, who died at Paris, 1 April 1932, daughter of Edmund K. Stallo and Laura Macdonald Stallo, by whom he had one daughter. Helen Stallo's sister, **Laura Stallo,** married **Francesco, Prince Rospigliosi.** Isabelle's aunt, Baroness Ubaldo Traverso, worked at the American Hospital in Florence where she also sang to entertain the troops. She was later decorated for her war work. Her husband was head of the Red Cross Hospital Number 6 in Italy during the War. At the baroness's death in 1948, her estate of more than $4 million was left to various U. S. charities with three-quarters of that amount for the United Hospital Fund and Presbyterian Hospital. She and her husband are buried with the McMillin family in New York's Woodlawn Cemetery.

Vernon Marguerite Rogers Magoffin (1886 – 1956) was a daughter of Samuel McAfee Magoffin and Elizabeth Moran Rogers Magoffin, and a descendant of Kentucky's first governor, Isaac Shelby, as well as a cousin of Governor Beriah Magoffin who attempted to prevent Kentucky's siding with the Union in the American Civil War. Vernon Magoffin first married in 1911 Chester Peter Siems (1884-1918) who built the Trans-Siberian line prior to World War I. The Siems-Carey Railway and Canal Company owned the largest single spruce production effort of World War I, producing 250 billion board feet

Vernon Magoffin's first husband built the Trans-Siberian railroad but died at thirty-three, leaving her with three children under the age of five. Prince Irbain Khan-Kaplanoff was a former tsarist cavalry officer.

of spruce in the Pacific Northwest. The railroad extension built to service it cost $10 million. Siems died at the age of thirty-three in the flu epidemic of 1918, leaving his widow with three children under the age of five. She married on New Year's Day, 1920, Rushton Peabody.

After their divorce three years later she married George Drexel Steel. After their May 1932 Reno divorce in which she clamed cruelty, she married in January of 1933, in Greenwich, Connecticut, **Prince Irbain Khan-Kaplanoff** (1887 – 1947) a former Tsarist cavalry officer who was wounded twice in the first world war. He came to the United States in 1923 and was in business with Prince Matchibelli. A family member described him as "a blue-eyed Caucasian." The couple lived on Park Avenue and at Vernon Hall, her estate in Southampton, Long Island. The prince's step-children, whom he taught to ride horses in the English style, were fond of him. Her last husband, whom she married in 1948 after the prince's death, was E. Dudley Haskell, an official with the American Red Cross and former publisher of the *Boston Herald*. The bride's daughter was her only attendant. Haskell died in June of 1955, followed by his widow in April of 1956. Her daughter, Dorothy Siems, married James Abercrombie de Peyster whose mother, at the time of the marriage, was the Countess Bohdan de Castellane. Prince Irbain escorted his step-daughter down the aisle.

Estelle Romaine Manville, born Pleasantville, New York, 26 September 1904, died Stockholm, 28 May 1984, was a daughter of Henrietta Estelle Romaine Manville and of the asbestos king H. Edward Manville, president and chairman of Johns-Manville Company,

of New York City. She married on 1 December 1928, **Count Folke Bernadotte of Wisborg,** born Stockholm, 2 January 1895, assassinated at Jerusalem, 17 September 1948, son of Prince Oscar of Sweden, Duke of Gotland, and grandson of King Oscar II of Sweden and Norway. He was a descendant of the Napoleonic marshal Jean Bernadotte, who in 1810 was elected crown prince of Sweden and in 1818 succeeded to the throne as King Charles XIV.

Estelle Manville's father made his fortune in asbestos.

Count Folke's father had renounced his rights of succession to marry a commoner and assumed with royal authorization the title of Prince Bernadotte with the qualification of highness. The father was created Count Wisborg by Grand Duke Adolphe of Luxembourg and his children were styled Counts and Countesses Bernadotte of Wisborg. Count Folke represented Sweden in 1933 at the Chicago Century of Progress Exposition, and in 1939-1940 was Swedish commissioner general at New York World's Fair. He was also vice chairman of the Swedish Red Cross and in that capacity he supervised the exchange of disabled British and German war prisoners.

The couple's engagement was announced at Hi-Esmaro, the

Pleasantville estate of the bride's parents. In a wedding ceremony with military honors, the bride wore the wedding veil of the groom's grandmother, Queen Sophie of Sweden, topped with a specially-made nine-pointed coronet of diamonds made by the Swedish court jeweler. They were married in St. John's Episcopal Church in Pleasantville, which could only seat 250 guests, while the reception afterwards at her parents' estate included one thousand guests. The best man was Prince Gustav Adolf, eldest son of the Swedish crown prince. The day after their wedding the couple attended a White House luncheon given by President and Mrs. Coolidge for the members of the Swedish royal family who had attended the ceremony. The Manvilles then entertained the Swedish royals on their yacht.

Count Folke and his American wife had four sons, two of whom died young. The eldest surviving son was born in New York and is a physician in Sweden while his younger brother lives in London. Estelle's father, along with Howard Hughes, was instrumental in establishing and endowing the University of Nevada School of Medicine. Estelle's parents had an extra-long bed installed in their 266 foot-long yacht, *Hi-Esmare,* in case their son-in-law's uncle, the King of Sweden, might visit. In 1932, when the King of Sweden's nephew, Prince Lennart, renounced his rights to marry a commoner, it was Estelle, Princess Bernadotte, who was credited with having convinced the king to accept the marriage and give his blessing. She was seen walking arm-in-arm with the king into a jewelry shop in Nice to help him purchase the couple's wedding gift, a dinner set of gold engraved with the royal coat of arms. In the spring of 1945, while working in the Swedish legation's

Count Folke Bernadotte was assassinated by an organization of extreme Zionists while trying to negotiate peace in the Arab-Jewish conflict.

temporary headquarters at Friedrichsruh, Germany, Count Folke was summoned by Heinrich Himmler, head of the Gestapo. They met at Lübeck, Germany, when Himmler insisted that Hitler was dying and that Himmler had authority to offer the complete surrender of

Germany to Britain and the United State, provided Germany was allowed to continue resistance against Russia. The Swedish foreign office transmitted Himmler's offer to Prime Minister Churchill and President Truman, who notified Premier Stalin, advising him of the British-American decision to accept only an unconditional surrender to the three Allied governments. Count Folke recounted the experience in his 1945 book, *The Curtain Falls.*

On May 20, 1948, the five super powers of the United Nations Security Council agreed to choose Count Bernadotte as mediator to seek peace in the Arab-Jewish conflict in Palestine. Ten days later he initiated conferences with Arab and Jewish leaders in Palestine and Arab leaders in Cairo, Egypt, and Amman, Jordan. He succeeded in obtaining agreement to a four-week truce commencing June 11 and, two weeks later, submitted to the Arab League and the Israeli government a peace plan that both sides rejected. On July 12 he made a report to the United Nations Security Council in New York City and shortly thereafter returned to Palestine. On September 17, Count Bernadotte and Colonel Andre P. Serot of the French Air Force were assassinated in Jerusalem by members of the Stern group, an organization of extreme Zionists, who had committed numerous atrocities over a period of years against the British and Arabs. Three days after his death, Count Bernadotte's final report on his peace efforts was published in Paris. It gave the United Nations General Assembly his suggested terms for a peace that was to be imposed by the United Nations and won the immediate support of the United States and Britain. Count Folke was also president of the Swedish Red Cross and the Swedish Boy Scouts and was heavily decorated for those efforts. He is most widely remembered for his successful negotiation of the release of 15,000 prisoners, mostly Scandinavian, from German concentration camps in World War II. He wrote *The Fall of the Curtain, Instead of Arms,* and *To Jerusalem.*

The Manvilles' yacht, which was originally launched in 1929, was transferred to the U. S. Navy in 1940, converted to a gunboat, and renamed the *Niagara PG-52.* After serving as a convoy escort in Pearl Harbor, she was converted to a torpedo boat tender and was badly damaged by a Japanese air attack in 1943 off Cristobal Island, then sunk by torpedoes. Estelle and her brother, H. Edward Manville Jr., donated in their father's memory a dormitory at the University of California Berkeley known as Manville Hall. The Folke Bernadotte Academy, located on the high coast of Sweden, is a Swedish government agency dedicated to improving the quality and effectiveness of international conflict and crisis management with a particular focus on peace operations. Estelle's father's will established a multi-million dollar fund for philanthropic purposes and left his son and daughter each one-third of his substantial estate. He died in 1944 followed by his widow in 1947. Estelle married second, at Stockholm 3 March 1973, Carl-Eric Ekstrand, and was active in the Girl Scouts and the International Red Cross. She lived in Sweden and France and died at St. Paul de Vence on 28 May 1984, leaving two sons and six grandchildren.

Mary McCormic, born Bellville, Arkansas, 1885, died 10 February 1981 in Amarillo, Texas, was a blonde opera singer reared in Texas and

a protégé of Mary Garden at the Chicago Civic Opera. She made her debut in 1920 as Micaela opposite Mary Garden as Carmen. She became principal singer at the Chicago Opera House, which was built specifically for Mary Garden by her lover, utilities tycoon Samuel Insull. *Musical America* described Mary McCormic's voice then as having "limpid, colorful tones, warm, tender and powerful, with exquisite pianissimo shadings and an effortless swelling to her full voice." After a few successful seasons she moved to Paris where she was very well-received. She returned to Chicago triumphantly in 1930 as Madama Butterfly. One current critic (Peter G. Davis, *The American Opera Singer,* 1997) has written that McCormic's early recording of *Thais's* "Mirror Aria" "does give an idea of her urgent style, personal magnetism, and the appealing tug in her voice." She married 27 April 1931 at Phoenix, Arizona, **Prince Serge Mdivani,** formerly the husband of silent film star Pola Negri, whom he divorced when her career began to wane. At the time of their marriage, Mary's voice had begun to fade but she was extremely wealthy.

Mary McCormic was a principal singer at the Chicago Opera House but was unfortunate enough to marry one of the Mdivanis.

The press still referred to her as "the baby diva" because her bee-stung lips gave her a youthful appearance.

In 1932 a scandal arose concerning the mis-spending of corporate funds by Prince Serge and his brother, Prince David Mdivani (see separate entry for **Mae Murray**). Both Mary McCormic and Mae Murray began divorce proceedings against their husbands and the brothers were eventually indicted by a grand jury on fourteen counts of grand larceny. Barbara Hutton, who was then married to the third Mdivani brother, paid their bonds of $10,000 each. Mary's husband counter-attacked by charging that she was having an affair with Samuel Insull, the utilities tycoon who had been the lover of Mary's mentor, Mary Garden. Insull, who had been Thomas Edison's private secretary, made several fortunes as electricity became commercially viable. In the ensuing publicity, Mary slapped a female reporter who claimed that she had been struck in the jaw.

At the divorce proceeding, Mary McCormic, who had once publicly called her husband "the world's greatest lover," on the witness stand referred to him as "the world's worst gigolo." She admitted having hit and scratched him, contending, "Why deny it? They ought to give me the Congressional Medal of Honor for it!" She listed for the court her husband's many indiscretions and added that he had never made any effort to support her financially. "It was left to me to take care of the household bills," she testified. "And he refused to let me have any friends. He said that I must remember that I was a princess and I could no longer associate with common people. At the same time, he made it obvious that he felt he was associating with a common

person by being married to me. He told my friends that I was beneath his station in life." She told the court that she had lent him $40,000 for a business investment that he then refused to repay. His response to the court was, "Ridiculous! How can a man borrow money from his wife? If one has money, the other uses it." He also insisted that, far from his having committed adultery, the guilty party was his wife, "But I'm too polite to name names."

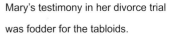

Mary's testimony in her divorce trial was fodder for the tabloids.

Their divorce was granted 13 November 1933 and Prince Serge immediately began pursuing Louise Van Alen, the wealthy former wife of his brother, Alexis. When Mary read the news, she told the *Daily Mirror,* "The Mdivanis are suave and cosmopolitan but they are Georgians, and Georgians are Asiatics. The Asiatic male regards himself above all as a male and his wife as a slave. When I married Serge the continental veneer soon came off and I knew I was hooked. Once he stormed at me, 'I hate work and I hate you because you want me to work.' He told a simple truth and it was so obvious I actually sympathized with him. But not in the same way I can sympathize with a girl who is married to one of them."

Prince Serge did marry Louise Van Alen, his former sister-in-law, before dying on the polo field, having been kicked in the head by his pony. In the same year in which her divorce was granted Mary appeared in Janet Gaynor's film, *Paddy the Next Best Thing,* playing herself (although her scenes were deleted). Mary married on 25 November 1936, Homer V. Johannsen and they were divorced the following 14 July. She lived quietly in Texas and died in 1981.

Alexandra Miller, born New York City, 8 October 1972, is a daughter of Robert Warren Miller who was born in Quincy, Massachusetts, and became a billionaire through his lucrative duty-free shopping network of stores. His New England heritage includes several Mayflower passengers, a Jewish German emigrant, and a native American ancestor. Alexandra married at New York City, 28 October 1995, **Prince Alexandre Egon von Furstenberg**, born New York City, 25 January 1970. Her sister, **Marie-Chantal Miller,** married in London, 1 July 1995, **Paul, Crown Prince of Greece, Duke of Sparta**, born Tatoi, 20 May 1967, son of Constantine II, king of the Hellenes from the death of his father until he was forced into exile 13 December 1967, and of his consort, Anne-Marie, Princess of Denmark. Prince Alexandre's mother is fashion designer Diane von Furstenberg, now married to Barry Diller, the media executive responsible for the creation of Fox Broadcasting. Alexandre's great-grandmother was American **Jane Ann Campbell**, Princess di San Faustino. Prince Alexandre's grandfather was Prince Tassilo von Furstenberg whose second wife was American oil heiress and arts patron **Cecil "Titi" Blaffer Hudson** (1919 – 2006) whose father, Robert Lee Blaffer, was a founder of Humble Oil (now Exxon) and whose mother, Sarah, was a daughter of William T. Campbell, founder of Texaco.

Among the guests at Titi's 1975 Paris wedding to Prince Tassilo was Princess Grace, formerly Grace Kelly, and her husband Prince Rainier, who was a cousin of the groom through their Baden grandmothers. Although Alexandra and Alexandre have two children, their marriage was plagued with rumors of separation and they were divorced in 2003. The Millers' other sister, Pia, is married to Christopher Getty, a grandson of billionaire Paul Getty by his third of five wives, Adolphine Hemle.

Nancy Ann Miller, born 9 September 1907, in Seattle, Washington, was a daughter of Alaska gold prospector John Miller and amateur pianist Jennie Schaefer Miller. Her father went to Alaska in 1898 seeking gold and extracted more than $1 million from his Miller Gulch strike, near Valdez, before dying in 1917. Nancy spent much of her childhood in Alaska where she was said to be "a tomboy among the children of the camp." Her grandmother said of her, "Many a time she was saved from an early death by being pulled out by the heels from the creeks of the neighborhood." Later returning to Seattle, she was educated in public schools and at the University of Washington where she studied Oriental civilization and was a member of a sorority. Her Swiss grandmother, Mrs. Louis Schaefer, insisted that she spend her summers abroad and Nancy was visiting Switzerland with her grandparents when she met her future husband, H. H. Maharaja Sir Tukoji Rao III Holkar, at Le Kursall Casino in Lausanne. He was so infatuated with her that he followed her to France and then to the U.S. where he met her extended family at Salt Lake City and asked her grandfather for permission to marry.

H. H. Maharaja Sir Tukoji Rao III Holkar, 13th Maharaja of Indore, on a 1913 official visit to London.

Nancy sailed with her grandmother on the *S. S. Genoa*, arriving at Bombay on 26 December 1927. There the American consul was waiting to warn her not to marry her fiance', whose family was notorious. Holkar's father had abdicated as Maharaja of Indore in his son's favor on 31 January 1903 when Nancy's fiance' became maharaja at the age of twelve. The son, in turn, was forced to abdicate in favor of his only son, Yeshwant (by his first wife), on 26 February 1926, due to his involvement in a scandal concerning the murder of a protector of his favorite "nautch" dancing girl, Mumtaz Begum (who was slashed in the face), in what became known as the "Malabar Hill murder." The dancer was saved only because four passing British officers came to her rescue using the only tools at their disposal, their golf clubs. It was she who identified the attackers as employees of the maharaja. She apparently had a baby by the maharaja but the infant girl was taken from her and killed by a nurse. Three of her Malabar Hill attackers were later executed and four deported. The maharaja's only choices were to abdicate or be tried for his involvement in the murder. Nancy's husband was allowed to retain most of his immense wealth and continued to be called "maharaja" even though his son had succeeded him. His annual allowance of £50,000 was equivalent to the combined income of the kings of Denmark, Norway, and Bulgaria.

While his subjects did not hold him at fault for the murder he had ordered, they were initially appalled that he would make a Caucasian woman their maharani. The junior of his two other wives went on a prolonged hunger strike in an attempt to prevent the marriage. Prior to the wedding, in an elaborate ceremony witnessed by ten

Nancy Miller, seated on the left, with her mother, sister, and grandparents.

thousand subjects, Nancy was first admitted to the Dhangar caste, then adopted by Princess Tarabai, who in turn gave her to be adopted by Colonel Lambhate, an official of the groom's household, so that he could give her in marriage. The next day, all warnings to the contrary, Nancy married at Bar Wada's Daryava Palace in the presence of one thousand guests (followed by a banquet for ten thousand) on 17 March 1928, **H. H. Sir Tukoji Rao III Holkar XIII Bahadur, 13th Maharaja of Indore,** born 26 November 1890, died Paris, 21 May 1978. Some American clerics attacked Nancy for her conversion, with one publicly calling her "a traitor to all religions." She became a Hindu prior to the ceremony, learned to ride elephants, and wore a diamond ring on her nose and a red caste-mark on her forehead. She was given the name and style "Her Highness Maharani Shrimant Akhand Soubhagyavati Sharmishtha Bai Sahiba" (or "Sharmistha Devi" in the shortened form). Nancy's husband gave her two diamond earrings known as the "Indore Pears" of forty-seven and forty-six carats, today valued at more than $4 million. It was said that the maharaja could sink his arms up to the elbows in his chest of diamonds and jewels. Immediately after the wedding the groom was sued by one of his former mistresses who claimed that she and their daughter had been imprisoned for eleven years against their will.

The Holkars were a prominent Maratha family who ruled first as rajas then as maharajas in central India as part of the Maratha Confederacy until 1818 and then as an independent princely state of British India until the 1947 independence. They ruled over more than one million subjects in an area of ten thousand square miles. Their assets were said to exceed $70 million and their palaces were attended by more than two hundred servants (he turned over all but three palaces to his son at his abdication). Nancy's husband's son, Yeshwant, was only seventeen at the time of his father's abdication and reigned under a council of regency until coming of age in 1930. He eventually signed the instrument of accession to the dominion of India in 1947 and merged his state into the Madhya Bharat Union the next year.

Nancy and her husband lived at the magnificent Lal Bagh Palace where they raised their four daughters and her husband's daughter, Manorama, who died of tuberculosis in Nancy's arms at the age of twenty in 1936. Nancy had four daughters of her own (*Time* magazine noted the 1929 birth of the eldest as "a girl-child of swarthy skin, jet black hair and beady brown eyes" and declared that the maharaja was disappointed not to have a son but rushed home from playing baccarat at Cannes nonetheless), Sharada, Seeta, Sumitra, and Sushila. Sumitra married a son of the maharaja of Patiala and had a daughter. Seeta married Vijayendra Ghatge of the Kagal royal family, feudal rulers of Kolhapur, and had a son who was an actor and a daughter who was killed in an Air India bombing in 1983. Nancy was said to be popular in her role as wife and mother and was "held in high respect ... for the simplicity of her ways."

Things were not as easy at Cap Ferrat where the couple spent much of their time at their villa. It was said that half of Riviera society received her warmly as a maharani while the other half shunned her as unbefitting their company. Nancy struggled to learn Hindi, excelled at tennis and classical piano, and her husband became so adept at bridge that he was called "The Indore Sport." The couple also had a lavish home outside Paris that was said to "make the members of the old French nobility who are his neighbors look like paupers." Nancy was a mentor to her step-son's second American wife, "Fay" (see separate entry under **Marguerite Lawler**), not only helping to ease her into her role as wife of the maharaja but also to deal with her husband's serious drug addiction. Nancy's husband spent his last days bedridden while she played piano to soothe him. She served as an excellent hostess to their family and frequent guests and was devastated at the death of one of their granddaughters in an Air India bombing. When her husband died on 27 May 1978, Nancy gave up Lal Bagh palace and moved into a smaller one, Sukh Niwas. She became a strong supporter of the preservation of Indore's historic resources and was frequently visted by her larger family.

Although Nancy made elaborate plans to be cremated and a modest marker placed near her husband's cenotaph, at her death in 1995 there were rumors that her daughter, Sharada, had poisoned her.

An autopsy was performed and there was never a proper mourning ceremony held for a woman who had so completely adopted her husband's native country. Her family continued to fight over their inheritance and their mother's possessions. Her step-son's daughter by his first wife, Princess Usha Devi, born in 1933, inherited the titles instead of her half-brother by an American mother. She had been declared heiress-apparent, in preference to her only brother, by special gazette of the government of India in 1950 and succeeded on the death of her father on 5 December 1961, an action that was confirmed by the president of India. She was later deprived of her rank, titles, and honours by the Indian government on 28 December 1971. She married Chandra Malhotra and their two sons were not in line for the Indore succession. Some sources call her half-brother the current maharaja but he has no succession rights as the son of an American mother.

Angela Mills, born New York City, 29 September 1863, died St. Augustine, Florida, 25 June 1956, was a daughter of Clark Wickham Mills and Julie Sophie Coleman Mills of Paterson, New Jersey. Angela first married in January of 1888 at New York City's prestigious Grace Church wealthy New Yorker Henry Mason Cutting, son of Lydia Mason Cutting and Heyward Cutting, whose family's fortune began in steamships and ferries. Henry's sister, Anne, married Baron Raoul de Vriere, Secretary of the Belgium legation in Washington. In 1887 Henry hired New York architect William Wright to build a hunting lodge in the Adirondack style at the confluence of the Matanzas River and Pellicer Creek in Flagler County, Florida, on a large estate

ARMS MAKE THE WOMAN

Bertha Krupp (1886 – 1957) was the world's wealthiest baby. As the daughter of Germany's "Cannon King" (the gun "Big Bertha" was named for her), she inherited a fortune of approximately $150 million while still a girl of sixteen and had absolute control of a town of more than two hundred thousand residents, fifty thousand of whom worked for her. When she married in 1906, the Emperor Wilhelm attended. The groom, who added the name of Krupp to his own, was Gustav von Bohlen und Halbach (1870 – 1950), formerly a gentleman-in-waiting at the Court of Baden and later a diplomat in Washington, Peking, and the Vatican. A wedding gift of $500,000 was distributed from the bride to her employees. The groom's father, Gustav George Halbach (1831 – 1890) was ennobled with the name von Bohlen und Halbach in a grant from the Grand Duke of Baden on 14 August 1871.

The groom's mother was the American-born Sophie Bohlen (1837 – 1915), whose father had been Dutch consul general in Philadelphia when she was born. Sophie's grandfather, Brigadier-General Henry Bohlen, emigrated to America where he made a fortune in the liquor business in Philadelphia. He recruited and led a regiment composed of Germans, the 75th Pennsylvania Infanty, who fought for the Northern army, and he was killed in action in 1862 (his great-nephew, Charles "Chip" Bohlen, 1904-1974, served as Russian translator to FDR at the Yalta conference and for President Truman at Potsdam; he was later U. S. ambassador to the Soviet Union, the Philippines, and France). Although General Bohlen was born in Bremen,

Germany, his American wife, Johanna Oswald, was born in New York. Gustav Krupp von Bohlen und Halbach was also chairman of the Reich Association of Industry. Because of his friendship with Hitler, his firm was offered facilities in eastern Europe and made extensive use of forced labor during the war. He was deemed too ill to stand trial at the International Military Tribunal and at the subsequent Krupp Trial held in Nuremberg in 1947. He died in 1950, having lived the remainder of his life in freedom. Gustav George Halbach's sister, Mathilde (1822 – 1848), born in Philadelphia, was the grandmother of Prince Bernhard zu Lippe, husband of Queen Juliana of the Netherlands. Their daughter is the current Queen Beatrix whose son, the Prince of Orange and great-great-grandson of two American women, will one day rule his country.

he called Cherokee Grove. There he hosted many friends from New York and Chicago who came to hunt and swim during the winters (the property included the first in-ground swimming pool in Florida). He died somewhat mysteriously in 1892 (perhaps on a boat en route to St. Augustine to be treated for a rattlesnake bite) and left his fortune and the property to his widow. In 1899 their youngest son, Henry, died of diphtheria in Liverpool on his way to Paris, and in 1926 their elder son, Heyward Cutting, was killed in an auto accident.

The widowed Angela then married stockbroker J. Lorimer Worden, whose father was the naval hero and Rear Admiral John L. Worden, commandant of the U. S. Naval Academy and commander of the *Monitor*. He greatly increased her inheritance but they were bitterly divorced after nineteen years of marriage. Worden then married in 1920 Mrs. Lounsberry Perry and disappeared at sea in 1938.

Angela married at the Russian Church in Paris, 30 July 1923, **Prince Boris Scherbatov,** born St. Petersburg, 25 December 1873, died New York City, 17 October 1949, whose family was ennobled in the ninth century. She became a member of the Orthodox Russian Church the day before their marriage. Attending the wedding were the Grand Duke and Grand Duchess Cyril and the Grand Duchess Marie. The groom's eldest brother was executed at Smolensk in 1921 while his next brother served as colonel and aide-de-camp to Grand Duke Nicholas. Six years after the Russian Revolution Prince Boris moved to Biarritz, then to New York City in 1945. He served for many years in the Russian imperial ministry of foreign affairs with posts in Vienna and Stockholm. After he and Angela were married

they renamed their Florida home Princess Place Preserve. She and her husband entertained exiled royalty there and in 1944 joined the Arts Club colony in St. Augustine, Florida. They also had a home in New York City where he died. In 1954 she sold the property to the Wadsworth family and the estate was eventually permanently protected by the state of Florida as Princess Place Preserve with an additional one thousand acres. Although she had children by her previous marriage, she had none with Prince Boris. Prince Boris' nephews, Prince Kyril and Prince Alexis, married respectively Americans **Adelaide Sedgwick** (whose first husband was Paris banker John Munroe) then **Lucile Forman,** and **Kathleen Comerford Whitehouse.**

Prudencienne Milmo, born Monterey, Mexico, 31 March 1872, died Monterey, 2 March 1958, was a daughter of Prudencia Vidaurri Milmo and Patrick Milmo (1824-1899, better known as Don Patricio Milmo, a native of County Sligo, Ireland) and granddaughter of Santiago Vidaurri (1809-1867). She married in New York City on 1 June 1896, **Prince Albrecht Stanislaw Radziwill,** born Poloneczka, 23 October 1868, died Mexico, 10 April 1927, son of Prince Mathias Radziwill and grandson of Prince Constantin Radziwill, Comte de Szydlowiec. The wedding took place at the Church of St. Francis Xavier, officiated by Archbishop Corrigan. The groom's brother served as best man and the *New York Times* made note of the fact that the bride was "a very dark brunette with rich complexion." Her grandfather, General Santiago Vidaurri, captured Monterey on 23 May 1855 and was installed as governor and military commander of Nuevo Leon. He then consolidated control of the neighboring states of Coahuila and Tampaulipas and attempted to establish "the Republic of Sierra Madre." He cooperated with U. S. and Texas officials in punishing Indians who raided the frontier. After annexing Coahuila on 19 February 1856, he formed the combined state of Nuevo Leon y Coahuila and controlled it as an independent fief. When Texas seceded from the U.S. in 1861 to join the Confederacy, a naval blockade closed all Texas ports and goods and supplies were diverted to Mexican ports controlled by Vidaurri.

When Napoleon III invaded Mexico and installed Emperor Maximilian on the throne, Vidaurri fled the advancing Benito Juarez and retreated to Texas. After a French army occupied Monterey, Vidaurri returned to Mexico and offered his services to the emperor. With the collapse of the empire in June of 1867, Vidaurri was executed as a traitor without benefit of a trial. Vidaurri's daughter, Prudencia, married a prominent Irish merchant, Patrick Milmo, who made his fortune from the border trade during the War. Milmo established his own family bank in Laredo, Texas, owned the Texas Mexico Railroad, and built a family compound on the Mesa de Cartujanos, a flat mountaintop spreading over forty thousand acres. Vidaurri and several Milmo family members are buried there in a quarried stone chapel modeled on one in Milmo's native Ireland.

The Milmo family still controls the surrounding ranchland. Prudencienne had one sister who married Eugene Kelly, son of the New York banker, and a brother, Patricio V. Milmo of San Antonio. Patricio V. Milmo's daughter, Laura, married media magnate Emilio Azcárraga Vidaurreta who began his empire by creating Mexico's first

Mattie Mitchell was able to overcome her father's reputation. She had more beauty than money.

television station. Prince Albrecht Radziwill served for a time as a diplomat in Washington, D.C. There were no children of the marriage. The 1.5 million-acre Milmo Ranch in Mexico was purchased in the late 1860s for $3.5 million by rancher Thomas Atlee Coleman.

Mattie Elizabeth Mitchell, born in Portland, Oregon, 28 August 1866, died in Paris, 20 February 1933, was a daughter of U. S. Senator John H. Mitchell of Oregon. He was born John Hipple in Pennsylvania but left his wife and children there and moved to

Oregon where he changed his name. In his first of three terms as U. S. Senator, his opponents tried to prevent his being seated, charging him with bigamy, desertion, and living under an assumed name. A senate committee decided against a full investigation. After his third term as U. S. Senator, he was convicted of land fraud for having received fees for expediting land claims of clients. He died 9 December 1905, while awaiting appeal of his conviction and sentence of imprisonment. Mattie met her future husband on the Riviera and they were engaged for several years. "This marriage is known to have been a love-match, as Miss Mitchell had no fortune whatever to offer as a dot," reported the newspapers at the time. She married in Paris on 11 February 1892, **Francois, 5th Duc de la Rochefoucauld, Duc de Liancourt, Prince de Marcillac, Duc d'Anville**, born 21 April 1853, died in Monaco, 24 February 1925. The religious ceremony was held at the Church of St. Clothilde in Paris and the bride (whose father was not present) was escorted into the church by the American ambassador, Whitelaw Reid. Guests included several Americans active in Paris society. After the wedding the bride's mother remained in Paris for two months as a guest of artist George P. A. Healy, who completed the bride's formal portrait just prior to the wedding.

In 1902 Mattie was sued by the Countess Spottiswood-Mackin

Above: U. S. Senator Mitchell was a bigamist, later convicted for land fraud. He died while awaiting his appeal.

Left: Mattie produced an heir but he died at the age of three.

(American-born **Sally Britton** of St. Louis). The duchess had leased a house from the countess but left it without paying because it was not adequately heated. The countess then filed a lien to attach the duchess's jewelry to satisfy the unpaid debt. The countess sued for libel and the duchess countersued for expenses and damages to her reputation. The court took five years to reach a divided decision that satisfied neither side. The la Rochefoucaulds had one child, the Duc de Liancourt, born 28 June 1905, who died of meningitis on 11 March 1909 after an illness of six weeks. The Duke de la

Rochefoucauld's younger brother succeeded as the 6th Duke and his line continues. Mattie was buried in the Vault of La Rochefoucauld Castle near Paris.

Beatrice Molyneaux born 14 February 1906, at New Orleans, Louisiana, married in Mexico, 26 November 1926, Antonio Aragona-Pignatelli-Cortes, **Prince of the Holy Roman Empire, 17th Duke of Monteleone, 16th Duke of Terranova, 18th Marquis of the Valley of Oaxaca, 15th Prince di Noia, Prince di Castelvetrano, 12th Prince di Valle, 15th Prince di Maida, 13th Duke di Bellosguardo, Duke di Laconia, 11th Duke di Girifalco, Duke d'Orta, 17th Marchese di Cerchiara, Marchese di Montesoro, Marchese d'Avola, Marchese della Favara, Marchese di Gioiosa, Marchese di Caronia, Count di Celano, Baron di Burgetto, Baron di Casteltermini, Baron di Menfi, Baron di Sant'Angelo Musciaro, Baron di Belice and Pietra Belice, Baron di Birribaida, Baron di Guastanella, Baron di Baccarasi,** a Grandee of Spain from 1938, born Naples, 18 December 1892, died 1 December 1958.

The origin of the Pignatelli Aragona Cortes branch of the family is linked to James I, King of Aragon 1208-1276. His direct descendant, Federico, 3rd King of Sicily (1250-1296), had a common law son, Orlando d'Aragona (born 1280) who became Viceroy of Sicily and was given the title of Signore (Lord) di Avola, later elevated to Marquess of Avola. Maria Concessa d'Aragona (around the year 1500), the only surviving descendant of Orlando d'Aragona, married Giovanni Tagliavia, first Marchese and later Duca di Terranova, who became (on the basis of Spanish law, i.e. the daughters transmitted titles and estates if there were no male heirs), Giovanni d'Aragona Tagliavia.

In 1648 Diego, a direct descendant of said Giovanni, married Stefania Cortes, the only surviving descendant of Hernan Cortes, the conqueror of Mexico, and thus became Diego d'Aragona Cortes Tagliavia. Diego and Stefania's daughter, Giovanna, married Ettore IV Pignatelli (1620-1674) who became Ettore Pignatelli Aragona Cortes. Beatrice and Prince Antonio had two children. He died in 1958 from injuries received after being hit by a motorcycle crossing the street in front of their palazzo in Rome. Their son, Giuseppe "Pepito," was born in Mexico in 1931 and succeeded his father. He married Maria Gallarati in 1959 but had no children and died in Rome in 1984 when the titles passed to a cousin, Nicolo, whose second wife was American **Mary Susan Morton.** Beatrice and Prince Antonio's daughter, Maria Gloria "Lola," married in 1946 the 2nd son of the 8th Earl of Jersey (as his second wife; they were divorced in 1971 and he died in 1980). They had one son and three daughters. The youngest, Lily, has a son by Prince Costantino Ruspoli di Poggio Suasa, a great-grandson of American **Josephine Mary Curtiss.**

(Mary) Elsie Moore, born Brooklyn, New York, 22 October 1889, died 21 December 1941, Greenwich, Connecticut, daughter of Mary Campbell "Kate" Moore and wealthy shipping broker and hardware manufacturer Charles Arthur Moore of New York City and Greenwich, Connecticut; married in Greenwich, Connecticut, 15 August 1907, Don Marino, Duke of Torlonia, **Duke of Poli, Duke of Guadagnola, and 4th Prince di Civitella-Cesi,** (who introduced the first motor car to Rome in 1892, causing havoc to fashionable carriages), born Poli,

Left: Spain's Queen Ena holding her daughters, including the elder, Beatrice. Right: Princess Beatrice in her later years. She was wed in the presence of more than fifty royals.

American **Gladys Deacon** after she rebuffed the marriage proposals of **Roffredo, 1st Prince Bassiano** (who married American **Marguerite Chapin**). Elsie Moore and Torlonia were separated in 1925 and divorced in 1928 when she returned to Connecticut and named an Italian noblewoman in her divorce suit. She renounced her Italian citizenship and again became an American citizen, but later reconciled with her husband to some degree and took her children back to Italy to be reared between the two countries. Her former husband died in 1933 and their son returned to Italy to claim his estate.

At one time the engagement of her daughter, Donna Christiana, was announced to John Jacob Astor III, but her mother termed the report "absurd." Despite the War, she spent the year of 1940 in Italy. Her son, Allesandro, 5th Prince di Civitella-Cesi (1911-1986) married in 1935 the Spanish Infanta Beatrice, daughter of King Alfonso XIII of Spain. The wedding took place in Rome with Beatrice wearing a six-metre train, a coronet of orange blossom (flown in that day from Valencia) holding her veil in place, in the presence of King Alfonso, the king and queen of Italy, some fifty-two princes of the royal blood, and more than four thousand visitors from Spain. After the ceremony, the young bride and groom were received by Pope Pius XI. Allesandro's fourth child married Paul-Annik Weiller (whose immensely wealthy father secured the Palazzo Torlonia for the family), whose daughter, Sibilla, married in 1994 Prince Guillaume of Luxembourg.

19 July 1861, died Rome, 5 March 1933, in whose villa Mussolini later lived. Her parents entertained lavishly at a home in Paris. One memoir of the era, Mrs. Hwfa Williams's *It Was Such Fun!,* paints an unflattering picture of Mrs. Moore's pretensions (when she died, one person said, "she left the world as she might have left the Ritz, with little tips for everyone") but is only complimentary about Elsie. The young couple first met in 1905 when she accompanied her parents to Venice. They were married two years later at the bride's home, Belle Haven, in Greenwich, Connecticut. Torlonia had been pursued by

Because Allesandro's grandchildren are descended from Queen Victoria through her granddaughter, Queen Ena of Spain, they are listed in line for the order of succession to the British throne (though they are barred from succession because they are Catholic). The Infanta Beatrice never lost her regal bearing and strictly observed protocol. When her daughters met the Duchess of Windsor, their mother forbade them to curtsey, forcing them to make a gesture somewhere between a curtsey and a wriggle in order to pass the scrutiny of both the Infanta and their cousin, the Duke of Windsor. Elsie's daughter, Donna Marina Torlonia (born 1916), married tennis star Francis Xavier Shields whose son, Francis Alexander Shields (born 1941) was the father of actress Brooke Shields (born 1965). The Torlonia family achieved fame when they successfully drained Lake Fucino, the Lacus Fucinus of the ancient Romans. Julius Caesar was the first to propose that the lake, which measured forty miles in circumference, be drained as it constantly overflowed its boundaries and flooded the surrounding towns. Emperor Claudius employed fifty thousand men for the task but did not succeed. The father of the 4th Duke, Elsie Moore's father-in-law, and his uncle employed French engineers and dug a tunnel through hundreds of feet of rock more than eight miles in length. The draining of the lake added more than 100,000 acres to Italy's cultivable land.

Elsie and her husband first attracted international attention in 1922 when he fought a sword duel with Count Filippo Lovatelli, a Roman sculptor. Their disagreement began at a charity ball under the direction of Mrs. Richard Washburn Child, wife of the American ambassador to Italy, concerning the price of a statue of the duchess carved by Lovatelli. The count was slightly wounded in the arm and Pope Pius XI immediately excommunicated the duke for his part in the duel. The duke was later reinstated in the Catholic Church when it was demonstrated that the count was the aggressor. The Torlonia family's claim to some of their titles was disputed by the Borghese family and the *Almanach de Gotha* sided with the Borgheses in several of those disputes. Elsie's husband was a great friend of Mussolini's and it was at his home, the Villa Torlonia, on the outskirts of Rome, that Mussolini's daughter, Edda, and Galeazzo Ciano, son of the Italian minister of communications, had their wedding breakfast. Mussolini then named his new son-in-law the foreign minister. Elsie's son, Prince Alessandro, arrived in the U. S. to see his ailing mother in November of 1941. Upon his departure on December 14 he was detained at Ellis Island by the FBI for twenty-four hours. Elsie died at her home at 375 Park Avenue in New York City at the age of fifty-three on 21 December 1941. Elsie Moore's sister, Bettine Moore, married William Taliaferro Close and they were the parents of actress Glenn Close, whose paternal grandfather had first been married to American cereal heiress Marjorie Meriwether Post.

Helen Stuyvesant Morton, born Newport, Rhode Island, August 1876, was a daughter of U. S. vice president (and New York governor) Levi P. Morton and Anna Livingston Street Morton. Helen's father had been U. S. minister to France. During the serious illness of President Harrison's wife, Mrs. Levi P. Morton served as official first lady of the United States. She and her husband contributed more

U. S. Vice President Levi Morton opposed his daughter's marriage but eventually reconciled with her after her divorce.

than $700,000 to the Cathedral of St. John the Divine in New York City. Their daughter, Helen, married in London, 4 October 1901 (divorced June 1904), **Paul Louis Boson, Comte de Perigord (and later) 6th Duc de Valencay, 5th Prince de Sagan, Duc de Dino,** born Paris, 20 July 1867, died Valencay, 9 May 1952, son of the 4th Duc de Talleyrand and 3rd Prince de Sagan, and younger brother of the Duc de Talleyrand who married American **Anna Gould.** Within a year of Helen's marriage to the Duc de Valencay, they were estranged when she "became dissatisfied with her noble French husband, came home to the protection of her father and mother. But her parents refused to take her back and she lived, another invalid, at Boulogne-sur-Seine" according to contemporary newspaper accounts. She obtained a divorce in 1904 and was completely reconciled with her parents.

The duke did not marry again for thirty-four years. Although married three times, he had no children. Before a notary in Paris, 10 May 1947, he adopted a son, Jean-Gustave, born 29 September 1929, who had earlier been recognized as a child of unknown parentage by his mother, Antoinette Morel, who became the duke's third wife in 1950 when the child was legitimized by the marriage and declared universal heir by the duke. In a legal petition of 1949, the duke's nephew, Helie, who eventually became 7th and last Duc de Talleyrand, 7th Duc de Dino, Duc de Sagan, challenged the legitimatization on the grounds that, at the time of Jean-Gustave's birth, his supposed parents had not yet met. On 26 March 1953 the court found that the recognition was fraudulent as the duke first met Antoinette at a dinner party in 1941 and Jean-Gustave was ordered to cease using the name Talleyrand-Perigord. The judgment was confirmed on appeal in 1955 and, while Jean-Gustave inherited the duke's sizable financial estate, he was prohibited from inheriting the titles which passed to the duke's nephew who died without children by his American wife, **Leila Emery.** Helen retook her full unmarried name and lived at 935 Park Avenue in New York City as well as at her father's estate, Ellerslie, at Rhinecliff-on-the Hudson, New York, designed by Richard Morris Hunt (who had already designed a ballroom for the Mortons' Newport mansion). She devoted herself to Catholic causes and built the Carmelite Monastery in Brooklyn in memory of her sister, Alice, who married Winthrop Rutherfurd after he had been engaged to marry **Consuelo Vanderbilt** before her mother forced her to marry the **9th Duke of Marlborough.**

After Alice's death, Winthrop married Lucy Mercer, mistress of President Franklin D. Roosevelt, who was with the president when he died in Warm Springs, Georgia. Helen Stuyvesant Morton died 6 September 1952, at her home in New York City. She had already given Ellerslie to the Roman Catholic Archdiocese to establish a boy's school. Helen was buried with her parents and sisters in the old Rhinebeck Cemetery.

Helene Moulton, born 3 September 1846, died 9 April 1918, was a daughter of Charles Frederick Moulton and Cesarine Metz Moulton. Her father was a cotton merchant in New York and acquired great wealth. He was a friend of Louis Napoleon and served as his host when the latter visited New York City. After Napoleon III became emperor of France, Charles and his family moved to Paris. Helene married in Paris, 4 November 1863, **Paul, Count von Hatzfeldt** (nephew of Francois who married American **Claire Huntington**), born 1867, son of Count Paul Hatzfeldt. He was for many years the German ambassador to the Court of St. James. They were divorced in 1874 but were reconciled and remarried at Baden-Baden, 7 October 1889. They had three children, Helene, Paul, and Marie. The father died in London, 22 November 1901, and Helene's son, Paul, born 1867, succeeded his uncle as the **2nd Prince von Hatzfeldt** in 1918. He married a granddaughter of American **Pauline Hoffmann**, Baroness von Stumm, and they in turn had only one son, Prince Francois, who was killed in action in World War II when the title became extinct, although the separate princely title of Hatzfeldt and Trachenberg passed to a cousin. The daughter, Helene, married Max, Prince zu Hohenlohe-Oehringen. Helene's brother, Charles Moulton, Jr., married soprano Lillie Greenough (a childhood friend of Jennie Jerome, wife of Lord Randolph Churchill and mother of Winston Churchill) who wrote her memoirs, *In the Courts of Memory,* 1858-1875, as Lillie de Hegermann-Lindencrone, wife of the Danish minister to the United States, whom she married after her first husband's death. Charles and Lillie had a daughter, **Lillie Suzanne Moulton,** who married **Count Frederik Raben-Levetzow** (1850 – 1933), foreign minister and chancellor at the Danish court of King Christian IX. Their daughter, Countess Lillie Raben-Levetzow, married American Lithgow Osborne, born 1892, private secretary to U.S. ambassador to Germany James W. Gerard during the early days of World War I. Osborne later served as U. S. ambassador to Norway.

Julia Mullock was born in Meansville, Pennsylvania, 18 March 1923, of Ukranian-American heritage. At the age of seventeen, after her father died from coalminer's asthma, her mother married a man from Brooklyn and the family moved there. In 1944 Julia joined the Navy for two years, later using her G.I. benefits to attend the Franklin School of Professional Arts in New York City. Julia began working for the I. M. Pei architectural firm but became dissatisfied with work and decided to move to Spain. She placed a notice on the office bulletin board for someone to sublet her apartment and a young Korean man in her office, eight years younger than she, responded by convincing her to stay. After learning her ancestry, he awkwardly employed several Russian words he had learned from his college roommates, charming her in the process. The young man was **His Imperial Highness Prince Lee Kyu,** born at Kitashirakawa Palace (now the Akasaka Prince Hotel) in Tokyo, 29 December 1931, son of Crown Prince Lee Un of Korea and of his wife, Crown Princess Pong-Ja, who was a daughter of the 2nd Prince Nashimoto and a descendant of Japan's Fushimi family (her first cousin was Empress Nagako of Japan, mother of the current Emperor Akihito). Prince Lee Kyu had an elder brother who was poisoned in infancy during a visit to Korea and, at Lee Kyu's birth, he became heir presumptive to the Korean throne. His uncle, His Imperial Majesty Yung-hui, crowned at Seoul in 1907, was the last emperor of Korea, having been made impotent (and barely escaping death) by the "coffee poisoning plot" believed to have been instigated by the Japanese in 1898.

At Yung-hui's death in 1926, his younger half-brother, Lee Un

Prince Lee Kyu, Korea's last crown prince, with his mother, a member of Japan's royal family.

(Julia's future father-in-law), was proclaimed "Grand Prince" and head of the Royal House of Choson that had ruled Korea since 1392. Prince Lee Kyu's mother, Japanese Princess Masako, was born at Tokyo, 10 November 1900, and after her marriage adopted the name Lee Pong-Ja and lived until 1989. Her marriage was arranged by the Japanese in an effort to annex Korea, a goal accomplished in 1910, eventually abolishing all Korean royal titles on 14 October 1947. Prince Lee Kyu, who had been rendered nation-less by the action, became an American citizen in 1959. He was educated at Center College in Danville, Kentucky, and received a masters degree in architecture from the Massachusetts Institute of Technology. He was an architect with I. M. Pei Associates in New York City, where he met his future wife, from 1960-64. They were married on 25 October 1958 at New York City's St. George's Catholic Church in a ceremony largely attended by Ukranian Americans. They relocated to Hawaii where Prince Lee Kyu assisted in overseeing the construction of the East-West Center. They lived near his parents with whom they took daily walks; it would

Julia Mullock Lee in later years.

Julia and her husband with the prince's mother.

be the happiest period of their marriage.

Prince Lee Kyu's father, Prince Lee Un, later lived in Japan and was offered the post of Korean ambassador to the Court of St. James in 1960 but declined due to ill health. On 22 November 1963 (the day of President John F. Kennedy's assassination) he was returning to Korea (on the first Japan Airlines jet to return there) at the express invitation of the new Korean president, Park Chung-Hee, when he suffered a massive stroke as his airplane was landing. He was immediately taken by ambulance to St. Mary's Catholic Hospital where he survived for seven years. Every day he was visited by his wife and their American-born daughter-in-law, Julia. She became a strong support to the older woman, particularly in her work with a school for the deaf and another for those afflicted with polio. Julia's father-in-law remained bedridden

and paralyzed for the remainder of his life, dying two days after his fiftieth wedding anniversary and, on 9 May 1970, was posthumously granted the rank of king eight days after his death. Prince Lee Kyu resumed honorary Korean nationality when they returned to live in Korea in 1964 where he and his American-born wife lived at the Nak Sun Je compound within the grounds of Chang Duk Royal Palace. Julia assisted her mother-in-law in working with many charities and began a dress-designing business operating from their quarters in the Royal Palace, hiring a deaf woman to sew for her and returning all profits to the handicapped. Employing her military status, she was allowed to shop on the U. S. military base and to send their adopted daughter, Eugenia Unsuk, to a Department of Defense school. She also worked at Catholic Relief Services, eventually becoming the only employee other than a priest.

Julia's husband succeeded as head of the Royal House of Korea at his father's death in 1970. He taught in universities and was a vice president of Trans Asia Engineering that eventually ended in bankruptcy. In the late 1970s he left for Japan but returned to Korea permanently in 1996. Under pressure from his family as his wife had not produced an heir, Prince Lee Kyu separated from Julia in 1974 and divorced her in 1982. She then moved out of the Royal Palace and divided her time between Korea and Hawaii, operating her dress design business from the Hyatt Hotel in Seoul, catering to such clients as Nancy Kissinger and Katharine Graham. She moved permanently to Hawaii in 1997 and, the next year, had a stroke from which she still suffers.

Left: Entrance to the queen's apartments at the royal palace in Seoul. Right: Julia's father-in-law, Crown Prince Lee Un.

Only after their divorce did Julia learn that her name had never been entered in the Choson Imperial family register for reasons that were never explained to her. Her husband never supported her or their daughter financially and last saw them in 1978, never again making contact. In April of 2003 she traveled to Korea in an effort to see her former husband one last time but she was not allowed access to him.

He suffered a nervous breakdown in 1980, lived intermittently with a Japanese astrologer, Mrs. Arita, and died alone of a heart attack on 16 July 2005 in his room at the Akasaka Palace Hotel in Tokyo, the fomer residence of his parents. Julia returned to Korea hoping to take part in the funeral ceremonies but was also denied that request. One year later, she again went to Korea for a ceremony marking the anniversary of his death but no one would take her to his gravesite in Namyangju. Eugenia Unsuk, their adopted daughter, was sent in 1975 to live with a missionary couple in Massachusetts where she was educated before marrying and moving to Hawaii near Julia. Julia Mullock Lee has been informed that she cannot be buried next to her husband and has requested that she be cremated and her ashes spread in the former family compound where she spent three decades in what she recalls as "a happy home."

There is disagreement as to which of several distant cousins might now be head of the Choson imperial family, although in 2005 the Yi Family Association designated Prince Yi Won, born in 1962 and educated at the New York Institute of Technology, as its head. He is a television producer and has served as a shipping manager with the Hyundai Corporation and General Manager of the Hyundai Home Shopping Company and is married with two sons.

Mae Murray, born as Marie Koenig, 10 May 1889, Portsmouth, Virginia, died at the Motion Picture Country Home in Woodland Hills, California, 23 March 1965. The "blonde vamp of the silver screen," and "the nation's Number One Glamour Girl," married first in 1908, W. N. Schwenker Jr., son of a millionaire. They divorced

Mae Murray in one of her more dramatic poses.

the next year and in 1916, Mae married the wealthy Jay O'Brien who was known as the Beau Brummel of Broadway. That marriage also lasted only a year and on 18 August 1918, she married the well-known movie director Robert Z. Leonard, in whose films she was a

Mae Murray with her husband, Prince David Mdivani. Considering what he did to her, perhaps the gun should have been aimed in another direction.

great success. They divorced on 26 May 1925, and on 28 June 1926, Mae married as her fourth husband, **Prince David Z. Mdivani,** one of the "Marrying Mdivanis" (see Louise Astor Van Alen), brother of Prince Alexis and Prince Serge. Rudolph Valentino and Pola Negri were their attendants at the marriage.

Mae Murray was the golden girl of Hollywood's most famous period. She rode to the studio in a Rolls-Royce cabriolet equipped with gold fittings and a sable lap robe. She once purchased a house for $50,000 cash because its seller played softly on the pipe organ while transacting business. She started her career as a dancer in a New York cabaret and got her first break in Irving Berlin's *Watch Your Step* with Vernon and Irene Vastle. When Irene became ill Mae stepped into her part and won instant celebrity. Ziegfeld then put her in his "Follies" where Hollywood pioneer Adolph Zukor offered her a film contract. Her most famous role came opposite John Gilbert in *The Merry Widow,* directed by Eric von Stroheim. During filming at the MGM lot, her demands became increasingly unreasonable and she once supposedly walked off the set calling von Stroheim a "dirty Hun."

Moviegoers were entranced by her waltzing and her "bee-stung" lips. After a string of successful and light movies, she amassed $3 million before retiring at the advent of talking pictures. Her husband, Price David Mdivani, took control of her career and badly advised her to leave her studio, MGM. In 1932 David's brother, Prince Serge Mdivani, who was then married to opera star Mary McCormic, and Prince David Mdivani and his wife, Mae Murray, capitalized $200,000

Mae Murray was left penniless on a bench in Central Park. She was later rescued in St. Louis and cared for by the Salvation Army before dying in a Los Angeles nursing home.

to found the Pacific Oil Company (almost all the money came from the two wives with the remainder from small investors). They struck oil in Venice, California, on land owned by Mae Murray, and opened the famous Venice oil fields. In June of 1933, both women were in the process of divorcing their husbands when the company records proved that the husbands had diverted substantial funds to their own accounts and falsified financial records. On 16 December 1933 David and Serge were indicted on fourteen counts of grand larceny by a grand jury. Their bonds of $10,000 each were immediately paid by their sister-in-law, Barbara Hutton (who quickly left the country with her husband, Prince Alexis Mdivani, who was implicated in the affair, before he could be served with legal papers) and trial set for January 1934.

Meanwhile, both women were pursuing their divorce suits and Mae Murray, testiying in Los Angeles Superior Court, stated that her husband had badly mistreated her, including "using both fists on me. He socked me and locked me in my room. On another occasion he broke into my dressing room and raped me." Her career over, Murray later testified that her husband had also broken her financially: "He took my stocks, bonds, and money. He left me penniless. I have no property, no income. Because of him I haven't been able to perform in a film for years." Her $3 million gone, she was evicted from a low-class tourist hotel in Manhattan for not paying her bill. "I packed an old hatbox with the things I needed to maintain myself and went to Central Park, where I stayed for three days and nights without a nickel to my name. I sat on a bench with my little hatbox. I walked out on my marriage with the clothes on my back." The divorce was granted on 11 February 1934 after a bitter custody battle over their son, Koran, who was born in February 1927. She lost the suit and the boy was reared by friends in upstate New York. He later took the name Daniel Michael Cunning and was an account executive for the First Albany Corporation in Troy, New York. He had two daughters, Pamela Ann Cunning and Cynthia Ann "Cece" Cunning, who married James B. Wilbur IV, whose great-grandfather, founder and president of the Chicago Royal Trust Company, was a benefactor of the University of Vermont.

In February 1964, Mae Murray was found wandering the streets of St. Louis, penniless, with no memory of how she arrived there. Only through a confirmation from theatrical circles in New York and Los Angeles was her identity confirmed and The Salvation Army paid her hotel bill of $13.20 and put her on a plane to Los Angeles. In later years, according to film historian Richard Griffith, "Her appearance eventually became an outlandish caricature of the superstar ... At charity balls, which she attended all the time, she would command the orchestra to play the theme tune from *The Merry Widow* and waltz to it solo..." She then lived, destitute, at the Motion Picture Country Home and suffered a stroke in August of 1964 and died the following March. A biography, *The Self Enchanted,* was written by Jane Ardmore in 1959. Many believe that Mae Murray was the model for Norma Desmond in Sunset Boulevard. David Mdivani met the French actress Arletty and fell madly in love with her. She became pregnant with his child but refused to carry the baby to full term having seen first-hand the fates of former Mdivani wives. David Mdivani continued to visit Arletty until her death. He married in Las Vegas on 18 September 1944 the American oil heiress **Virginia Sinclair** (see her separate entry). They had a son, David, and the father died in Los Angeles on 5 September 1984, outliving his former wife, Mae, by nineteen years.

Pola Negri, born as Apolonia Chalupec on 31 December 1894 (or 1897) in Lipno, Poland, became one of Hollywood's most famous silent film stars. When she was a child her father was arrested by the Russian army and sent to a Siberian gulag. As a result her mother moved to Warsaw where Pola was accepted into the Imperial Ballet. Her promising career was cut short by tuberculosis and, with the help of her mother's childhood friend, she was accepted into the Warsaw Imperial Academy of Dramatic Arts. She debuted as Hedwig in Ibsen's *The Wild Duck* and moved to the national theatre of Poland. World War I interrupted her rise and she and her mother were again cast into poverty. She resumed acting after the war and was discovered by film director Ernst Lubitsch with whom she made many successful movies in Germany. Adolf Hitler was so mesmerized by her that he personally countermanded an order forbidding her to work in Germany because she was supposedly partly Jewish (she later won a 10,000 franc judgment against a French newspaper which claimed that she had an affair with Hitler). Her film with Lubitsh, *Madame du Barry,* was released in the U.S. as *Passion* and it made them both immediate stars. They moved to Hollywood where she appeared in a string of successful movies and was known as a great rival to **Gloria Swanson,** who eventually married the **Marquis Le Bailly de la Falaise de la Coudraye** (1898-1972) (Swanson and Negri once had a cat fight with real cats). Negri married and divorced a Polish nobleman, Count Eugene Dambski. She became the mistress and fiancee' of Charlie Chaplin but broke her relationship with him in a verbal spat which was assiduously reported. As she later claimed, "A great deal has been

Pola Negri starred with Rudolph Valentino both on and off-screen. She brought his body back to Los Angeles from New York City at his death.

Left: Pola Negri was a popular star. Right: Valentino said of himself, "Women are not in love with me but with the picture of me on the screen. I am merely the canvas on which women paint their dreams."

her popularity began to wane. She was not forgiven when, in 1927, less than a year after Valentino's death, she married **Prince Serge Mdivani** (see Louise Van Alen and Mae Murray) and took him to live in her chateau in France. They divorced in a highly public proceeding at The Hague in November 1932 after she lost the bulk of her fortune, estimated in 1929 to be $5 million. She claimed that his mishandling of her financial affairs ultimately ruined her. Prince Serge then married wealthy opera singer Mary McCormic who was known as the "baby diva" and went through her money as well. Pola Negri returned to Europe for a while, then back to the U.S. to make her talking-picture debut in *A Woman Commands*. When it was not successful, she returned to Europe and remained there until the increasing Nazi domination caused her to leave in 1940 for the U.S. where she finally retired from films in 1964.

She lived for a while in one room in a small hotel in New York City and was forced to sell her jewels in order to survive. She then recovered some of her European property and moved to San Antonio,

written about my relationship with Charlie Chaplin. Unfortunately, much of it has been written by Mr. Chaplin. Still less fortunately, what he wrote was largely untrue. Rather than say he behaved in less than a gentlemanly fashion, I would prefer to excuse him on the grounds that all clowns live in a world of fantasy."

At the death of her former lover Rudolph Valentino, Negri rushed out of a film location to throw herself, heavily veiled in black and supported by bodyguards, onto Valentino's coffin. She brought his body back to Los Angeles from New York City with train stops along the way for his fans to pay homage. The public was unimpressed and

Texas, in 1957. She lived forgotten there with a female companion, Margaret West, until her death. She wrote *Memoirs of a Star* in 1970, but never regained her position or her money and suffered a brain tumor that she declined to have treated. She lived two additional years and died of pneumonia at San Antonio's Baptist Hospital, 2 August 1987, and was buried in Calvary Cemetery in Los Angeles. She left most of her estate, including rare prints of her early films, to St. Mary's University and her personal library to Trinity University, both in San Antonio.

Lida Eleanor Nicolls of Pittsburgh, born 28 July 1875, in Brownsville, Pennsylvania, was a daughter of John A. Nicolls and Lenora Thompson Nicolls and formerly the wife of Gerald Purcell Fitzgerald (by whom she had three sons and divorced in 1906 in Ireland). She married at Uniontown, Pennsylvania, 1 November 1911, **Victor, Prince von Thurn und Taxis,** born Ecska, 18 January 1876, died Vienna, 28 January 1928, grandson of the 6th reigning Prince von Thurn und Taxis. The first prince made his fortune as hereditary general postmaster of the German Empire, the Holy Roman Empire, the Netherlands and Burgundy, and was hereditary marshal of Hainault. Lida's marriage was not recognized as equal by the head of her husband's family. The wedding took place at the home of the bride's mother in Uniontown, Pennsylvania, performed by the Reverend William Spence in the presence of a few friends and family. She had $1 million from her mother's brother, Josiah Van Kirk Thompson (1854-1933), who controlled one-half of the undeveloped coal deposits in Pittsburgh. He owned 141,413 acres of coal fields in Pennsylvania

Lida Nicolls was given a substantial dowry by her mother's coal-magnate brother.

and West Virginia and in 1913 made $1 million in a single day, completely recouping the amount he had paid his second wife to secure a divorce. Thompson's businesses failed in 1915, but even then his aggregated holdings were valued at $65 million while his liabilities were $32 million.

Prince Victor and Lida lived in Budapest and Paris and she announced that she would never return to the United States. The groom's father, Prince Egon, became naturalized in Hungary before his marriage, thus rendering Prince Victor a Hungarian citizen. In February of 1914, a woman claiming to be the prior wife of Prince Victor and calling herself "Josephine, Princess Victor Thurn und Taxis," was in Westminster Police Court in London bringing legal action against James Henry Maur, then "residing in fashionable chambers in Oxford Street" according to the *New York Times.* Josephine claimed that she was born in Jacksonville, Florida, to wealthy parents who died when she was three and she was sent to a convent. At the age of fifteen, she stated in court, her guardian took her to Chicago where she was employed in a secretarial position. There she met

William W. A. Pike whom she described as "one of Chicago's richest men." Subsequently they exchanged private vows across a table in a restaurant and, according to her, they considered themselves to be married. Pike's family, however, refused to recognize the union as did the courts and her putative husband dropped her. She moved to New York City where she became an actress and appeared in 1907 in *The Gay White Way*. She insisted that, in a midnight ceremony at the office of a minister, she married Prince Victor who, according to her, proved to be a stay-at-home husband while she pawned various pieces of jewelry to support them. Supposedly the Prince left for Europe where she intended to follow until she learned that his family would not receive her. She subsequently became acquainted with James Henry Maur whom she met at a New Year's dinner in an elegant London restaurant. Josephine claimed that he was writing threatening letters to her under an assumed name in order to extort money by revealing her background. Maur was acquitted of the charges against him and, during the proceedings, Lida, Prince Victor's legitimate wife, went to London to protest the claims of Josephine and to document the fact that she was Prince Victor's lawful wife. She took the opportunity to assert that her name was Leonora and not Lida as news reports had indicated. She and the Prince had no children.

Although her marriage to Gerald Fitzgerald ended in 1906, litigation over the trust agreement he had created for her benefit and that of their three sons was not concluded until 1939, when the United States Supreme Court finally delivered an opinion concerning conflicting court jurisdictions in Princess Lida of Thurn & Taxis v. Thompson (305 U.S. 456, 1939). In 1949 she lost a suit seeking to annul the wedding of her son, John Purcell Fitzgerald, to a New York model, arguing that he was an alcoholic and unable to comprehend his actions at the time of the marriage. She also eventually sued her uncle who had provided her substantial dowry. Lida died on 6 December 1965.

Valerie Norrie, born New York City, 14 May 1903, died 18 March 1999, was a daughter of Ambrose Lanfear Norrie and Ethel Lynde Barbey Norrie, whose mother was Mary Lorillard, a daughter of tobacco magnate Pierre Lorillard III. Mary Lorillard Barbey's sisters were Helene, who married Count Herman de Pourtales (she was the first woman to compete in the modern Olympics), and Eva, who married Count Andre de Neuflize. Valerie Norrie's mother married as her second husband Count de Jumilhac. Valerie's cousins were Eleanor Lorillard Spencer (lady in waiting to Italy's Queen Margharita), who married the 7th Prince di Vicovaro Cenci; Maude Lorillard, who married the 3rd Baron Revelstoke; and Helen Seton who married the 4th Duke de Feltre. Valerie Norrie married in Paris, 21 July 1924, Joseph-Jean-Mathieu-Jérôme, **4th Duke of Pozzo di Borgo,** born Paris, 11 November 1890, died Paris, 12 May 1966. Her great-granddaughter, Valentine Pozzo di Borgo, born in 1984, is the closest friend of Charlotte Casiraghi, granddaughter of American-born Grace Kelly, Princess of Monaco, and daughter of Caroline, Princess Ernest of Hannover. Valerie's grandson's wife, Cecile, is currently the French ambassador to the Dominican Republic.

In 1198, one year before he died, Richard, Coeur de Lion, King

Valerie Norrie, the Duchess of Pozzo di Borgo, with her great-grandson.

of England, and Duke of Normandy established his headquarters in the castle of Dangu from which he held out against the king of France Philippe Auguste. The present castle of Dangu was built in 1896 by count Pozzo di Borgo with the stones of the castle of Montretout, previously owned by Madame de Pompadour, mistress of King Louis XV. The castle is still owned by the Pozzo di Borgo family, although their seat was in Corsica. Valerie's grandfather, Pierre Lorillard, consolidated the family-owned tobacco business that created and maintained a huge family fortune. Wags suggested that the family coat-of-arms should be "a cuspidor couchant with two cigars and a plug of tobacco rampant." Social diarist Philip Strong wrote that Lorillard "led people by the nose for the best part of a century and made his enormous fortune by giving them that to chew which they could not swallow." At Lorillard's death, Strong wrote, "How many cubic miles of smoke and gallons of colored saliva are embodied in the immense fortune that was his last week!" Alan Jay Lerner, the award-winning librettist for *Brigadoon* and *My Fair Lady,* married as his second of eight wives, Micheline Pozzo di Borgo and she was the mother of his son, Michael Alan Lerner.

Kathleen Norris, daughter of Dr. Frank Norris and Alice McCreevy Norris, born San Francisco, 16 July 1880, died San Francisco, 18 January 1966; first married to Gilbert Roberts Jr. After their divorce she married in San Francisco, 21 March 1961, as his second wife, **Prince Andrew Romanov,** born London, 21 January 1923, a great-grandson of Alexander III, Emperor of Russia. Prince Andrew was naturalized an American citizen 20 December 1954. By his first wife, Helen Dournev, he had a son, Prince Alexis, born in San Francisco in 1953, who married American **Zoetta Leisy.** Prince Andrew's second wife, Kathleen, was named for her grandmother, Kathleen Norris, author of eighty-two romantic novels that sold ten million copies (sixteen of her novels were made into Hollywood screenplays), as well as an ardent feminist and committed pacifist. The grandmother was also an advocate for prohibition and the abolition of capital punishment. Her first novel, *Mother,* was published in 1911 and her last, *Family Gathering,* in 1959. A 1922 novel, *Certain People of Importance,* was viewed as her best. She joined Charles Lindbergh in 1941 to address a rally in New York City to gain support against the use of U. S. Naval convoys for British war supplies. At her death in 1966 she left an estate of $1.2 million. Princess Andrew Romanov died at thirty-four, having had Prince Peter, born 1961, and Prince Andrew, born 1963. After her death her husband then married **Inez von Bachelin,** born Santa Monica, California, 11 October 1933.

Natalie "Lily" Oelrichs, daughter of Charles M. Oelrichs and Blanche de Loosey Oelrichs and widow of polo player Peter Martin, was born at Cheyenne, Wyoming, 12 October 1880, and died in San Francisco, 23 February 1931. Her father was a wealthy broker and social leader in Newport, Rhode Island, who was born in Baltimore and died at seventy-three in Newport in January of 1932. His grandfather had emigrated from Bremen, Germany, and married a daughter of American statesman Harrison Gray Otis. Charles's older brother was Hermann Oelrichs, head of Oelrichs & Co., American agents for the North German Lloyd Steamship Company. He died at sea in 1906. Natalie's parents lived in Newport for the last years of their lives where they were very socially prominent before their deaths only eleven months apart. Natalie married at Rostock, 14 April 1915, as his second wife, (his first was American **Elizabeth Pratt;** see her separate entry), **Duke Heinrich Borwin of Mecklenburg Schwerin,** born Venice, 16 December 1885, died Sarszentmihaly, Hungary, 3 November 1942, nephew of Friedrich Franz III, Grand Duke of Mecklenburg Schwerin, Prince de Wendin, and grandson of Friedrich Franz II, Grand Duke of Mecklenburg Schwerin.

Duke Heinrich Borwin made his first visit to San Francisco

Left: Lily Oelrichs was the second American wife of Duke Heinrich Borwin but that marriage also did not last.

Opposite page: Mrs. Charles Oelrichs and her daughter at fashionable Newport.

annulment and he married a third time. By Natalie's first marriage she had a son, Charles Oelrichs Martin, of San Francisco. She was reported to have inherited $5 million. Her will cut off her son completely "for lack of filial respect" and left her property in trust to her parents for life and afterwards to her sister, Mrs. Tweed, and Mrs. Tweed's children. Natalie Oelrich's cousin, **Elinor Douglas Wise** (Elinor's grandmother and Natalie's mother were sisters) married **Armand, Duc de Richelieu.** Natalie's great-nephew is society bandleader Peter Duchin, whose mother was Marjorie Oelrichs, credited by Cecil Beaton with having taken his heterosexual virginity. Duke Heinrich Borwin's uncle, Duke Heinrich Wladimir Albrecht Ernst, was created His Royal Highness Prince Hendrik of the Netherlands on 6 February 1901, the day before he married at The Hague Queen Wilhelmina of the Netherlands. Natalie, who continued to be styled

where he attended the Panama Pacific International Exposition and was a guest in the home of Natalie and her then-husband, Peter Martin. After her husband's death she and the duke were married and he worked for a short time as an automobile salesman in San Francisco. They returned to Germany where he wrote his memoirs, *High Highness, the Stoker.* Duke Heinrich's aunts were Alexandrine, queen of Denmark, and Crown Princess Cecilie of Prussia. Natalie and Duke Heinrich were divorced at Berlin, 4 June 1921, but there was no

incorrectly "Duchess of Mecklenburg" by the American newspapers after her divorce, pre-deceased her parents, dying 23 February 1931, at the age of fifty-one at the Hotel Richelieu in San Francisco where she had lived alone for the last year of her life. She had a sister, the openly bi-sexual Blanche, Mrs. Harrison Tweed of New York City, an actress, playwright, and author who was known by the pen name Michael Strange. She married actor John Barrymore and Leonard Thomas and was the mother of Diana Barrymore.

Betka Paine and her husband, Olo, Prince Sapieha-Kodenski. Betka's mother married the 7th Duke de Choiseul-Praslin five years before Betka's marriage.

Sarah Elisabeth "Betka" Paine, born Boston, 31 May 1895, died Nice, 17 September 1971, was one of three daughters of Charles Hamilton Paine (1853 – 1909) and Lucie Tate Paine. Her father's elder brother, William A. Paine, established the stock brokerage firm of Paine & Webber and Charles joined him there as a partner in 1881. William Paine also founded the highly profitable Copper Range Company in Michigan. The family controlled the Paine Webber firm until 1955 at the death of the last member of the family as its head. After Charles's marriage to Lucie Tate of Kentucky and the birth of their three daughters, Louise, Sarah, and Margaret, he retired from the firm and moved to Paris where the family lived in a palatial home in the Bois de Boulogne. They moved their furniture and art from Boston and continued collecting in France.

Louise married Captain Jacques de Sieges de Veynes, a French army officer who had been badly wounded in service. Margaret married Chevalier George de Spirlet of Belgium. Sarah Elisabeth Paine married in London, 15 March 1915, as his first wife, **Aleksander "Olo," Prince Sapieha-Kodenski,** born Oleszyce, 25 November 1888, died Nice, 16 December 1890, son of the 3rd Prince Sapieha-Kodenski (his elder brother succeeded their father as 4th Prince). They were married at Westminster Cathedral in London with the American ambassador, the Duke of Norfolk, Earl Lisburne, and Lord Mowbray attending.

After Sarah's father died in 1909, her mother, **Lucie Tate Paine** (see her separate entry), married the **7th Duke de Choiseul-Praslin** in 1910. The Sapieha-Kodenskis lived in Fountainbleau and had two sons, Leon and Charles, who both died in World War II. After

Sarah's death in 1972 her widower married second at Nice, 15 January 1976, Maria, Countess von Oppersdorff. His younger brother's great-granddaughter is married to the crown prince of Belgium and their daughter, Elisabeth, is the future queen of Belgium. The current head of the Sapieha-Kodenski family, Prince Michael, lived in the Belgian Congo until the 1960s, when he moved his family to Belgium after losing much of their property in the Congo. From his new home he was an active supporter of Solidarity in Poland and sent medical supplies there through the Caritas charity organization. He and his son and heir, Prince Alexander, encouraged Belgian investment in Poland after the change of government and purchased a large abandoned state farm where they employ many workers in the adjoining village and have converted the farmhouse into a hotel.

Prince Olo's uncle, Prince Adam, was named bishop of Krakow 1911, archbishop of Krakow in 1925, and was made a cardinal in 1946. In 1938 Archbishop Sapieha visited a school in Wadowice and was welcomed by its best orator, an eighteen-year-old Karol Wojtyla. The archbishop asked the impressive young man what he intended to do with his life and he answered that he planned to enter the theatre. The archbishop replied that it was a pity. The young man eventually became Pope John Paul II.

In 1995 the Paine Webber firm acquired Kidder & Peabody and by late 2000 the Paine Webber Group was the fourth largest private client firm in the United States. In 2003 it was purchased by the Swiss-based UBS Group and the 123-year-old name of Paine Webber was finally abandoned.

Myra "Daria" Abigail Pankhurst, born Cleveland, Ohio, 1859, died in Cannes, 26 June 1938, was a daughter of John Pankhurst, partner of Mark Hanna (1837-1904), a Cleveland industrialist who made his fortune in coal and iron and was later a powerful U. S. senator. At John Pankhurst's death in 1898 he had acquired a fortune as head of the Globe Iron Works in Cleveland. His daughter, Daria Pankhurst, first married Cleveland banker Herbert Wright by whom she had a daughter, Harriette. Daria divorced Wright and then married J. Huger Pratt. She was vacationing in France in 1900 when she played golf at the Dinard Club and was recruited for the U. S. Olympic team. In 1900, the first year in which women competed in the Olympics, she won a bronze medal in golf. Shortly thereafter she divorced her husband and eventually married in the Russian Church in Paris on 11 June 1913, **Prince Alexis Karageorgevich**, born 10 June 1859, died Paris, 15 February 1920, a former soldier in the Serbian army. The two witnesses to the ceremony were U. S. Ambassador Myron Herrick and Prince Arsen Karageorgevich, brother of King Peter of Serbia (the *New York Times* had mistakenly announced that he was to marry Daria). Prince Alexis was a grandson of Kara George, king of the Serbs, and a great-nephew of **Alexander I, Prince of Serbia,** so elected 15 September 1842, abdicated 3 January 1859. Alexander's son, **Peter I**, was elected king of Serbia on 15 June 1903, and proclaimed king of the Serbs, Croats, and Slovenes.

In 1899, Prince Alexis was said to be greatly interested in marrying Mabel Swift, daughter of the meat-packing family, but her father reportedly threatened to disinherit her if she married him. The

Left: Prince Alexis Karageorgevich, grandson of the king of the Serbs. Right: Writer Michael Arlen who once called himself, "every other inch a gentleman."

Committee from 1897 to 1925. He and his wife had three children—Atalanta, Daria, and Leonardo.

For the last ten years of her life, Princess Daria lived at the Villa Florentina in Cannes, where her granddaughter, Countess Atalanta Mercati, married the writer Michael Arlen in 1928. After Count Mercati and Harriette divorced, she married the Baron Emerich von Plugl, Austrian representative to the League of Nations, while Count Mercati, on 12 December 1926, in the private chapel at St. Cloud, married as his second wife Mrs. Leroy Newbold Edgar (Marie Manice) of New York City. Atalanta Mercati's husband, Michael Arlen, was born in Bulgaria as an Armenian named Dikran Kuyumjian, but changed his name in 1922 when he became a British citizen. He became known as a writer of worldly high society characters and was best-known for *The Green Hat.* Katherine Cornell starred in the New York theatre

International Herald Tribune opined, "A pretender to the Servian throne with a morganatic wife might add still further complications to the Balkan situation." Princess Daria was rumored to have said that the Karageorgeviches were created a royal family only because they had the most swine. Daria's daughter, Harriette Wright, married Count Alexander Mercati, Chamberlain to King Constantine of Greece and a childhood friend of the founder of the modern Olympic Games. Count Mercati served as a member of the International Olympic

production and it was later filmed twice in Hollywood with Greta Garbo and Constance Bennett. Tallulah Bankhead had the lead in the 1925 London production. D. H. Lawrence used Arlen as the model for Lady Chatterley's first lover, Michaelis. Arlen's recognition of social precedence reached its apogee in his *Farewell, These Charming People* in which Satan attends a swell dinner party: "'Young man,' said the Lord Chancellor severely, 'are you seriously implying that you are the Prince of Darkness?' 'We do not recognize that title,' cried Lady Surplice. 'It is not in Burke, Debrett, or the Almanach de Gotha.'" Another popular author of the era said that Arlen was "the only Armenian who never tried to sell me a carpet," while Arlen called himself, "every other inch a gentleman."

The Arlens' son, Michael J. Arlen, wrote a 1970 biography of his father called *Exiles.* The other Mercati sister, Daria Palmer, ran off briefly with Count Pali Palffy (husband of American **Dorothy Deacon,** formerly Princess Aba Radziwill) and died in a hotel in Geneva by setting fire to her bed, having fallen asleep, drunk, with a smoldering cigarette.

Evelyn "Eva" Florence Pardridge, born in Chicago, 21 January 1872, died 27 July 1944, was a daughter of Charles W. Pardridge (1844-1912) of Chicago. She married first on 14 November 1890, Samuel S. Clayton of Philadelphia. They had two children, Catherine and Paul, and were divorced. In 1898 she married **Prince Nicholas Engalitcheff** (1864 - 26 March 1935), then Russian vice consul at Chicago, who served with the Russian forces under General Brusiloff. He had come to the United States as a diplomat for Tsarist Russia and remained for the rest of his life.

In 1910 Evelyn's father, part owner of Hillman's Department Stores in Chicago, conveyed to Evelyn and her three siblings the Reliance Building in Chicago. At the same time he gave millions of dollars to various charities. Two years later he gave his children Chicago's Schiller Building, including the Garrick Theatre. The newspapers noted that the combined gifts gave Princess Engalitcheff a net worth of more than $1 million in her own right. She and Prince Nicholas were

In the center is Prince Nicholas Engalitcheff, a Russian diplomat who married two wealthy American wives.

divorced after eighteen years of marriage. Her suit claimed infidelity and named several correspondents, including Mrs. Jane Hathaway of a New York City hotel address. During the divorce proceedings Evelyn hired a bodyguard and made a public announcement that she

Eva Pardridge's father gave his children much of his wealth during his lifetime, making Eva wealthy in her own right. After divorcing Prince Nicholas she retook her maiden name.

was no longer responsible for her husband's debts. Prince Nicholas attempted to have the trial moved to Russia where he said many of his witnesses lived, but the initial divorce decree granted 23 February 1916 was made final in the New York Supreme Court. Eva retook her maiden name and announced her divorce with engraved cards. They had a son, Vladimir, who graduated from Brown University in 1922 and died the next year, possibly by suicide although it was reported as heart disease.

In December of 1916 Prince Nicholas Engalitcheff married a French woman, Melanie de Bertrand Lyteuil, who claimed to be immensely wealthy but was arrested for fraud stemming from purchases she made in Paris for which she never paid. In 1921 the Prince was reported to be living in New York City's Waldorf Hotel and was sued for non-payment of more than $2,400 owed to area garages. In court, when asked how much money he had, the Prince responded, "At the moment all I have is one dollar." He also declined to disclose the location of his wife but insisted that she had been with him at the hotel until recent weeks. He stated that his only means of support for the past eight months had been as a salesman for a Wall Street house that paid him $7.50 for every one hundred shares of stock he sold.

In 1933 he obtained an Enoch Arden decree dissolving their marriage and insisted that he presumed his wife was dead. The next year, on 5 November in the Russian Greek Orthodox Church in New York City, Prince Nicholas Engalitcheff married **Suzanne Bransford Emery Holmes Delitch** (see her separate entry). Eva Pardridge, formerly

Prince Nicholas Engalitcheff with Eva Pardridge, the first of his wealthy American wives.

young prince who was attached to the German Embassy. The War interrupted their courtship and she returned to America. The emperor of Germany was looking through the prince's photo album when he noticed a picture of a beautiful young woman and asked who she was. "That is the lady I love," he replied. "If I live through the War I intend to make her my wife." The emperor then gave his permission to visit America to ask for Amelie's hand in marriage on the condition that the emperor could keep the photograph. Amelie's father, a wealthy merchant and member of the Ohio legislature, stipulated that the couple must be married in Ohio. The prince traveled to Columbus, attended by officials from the German Embassy in Washington and Bishop McIlvaine officiated at the ceremony. Unlike many of her compatriots, she was not required to convert to Catholicism as the Lynars were Lutherans. May Amelie's only brother, Gus, was married to Emily Herron, sister of U. S. first lady

Princess Nicholas Engalitcheff, died 27 July 1944, at her suite at New York City's Hotel Carlyle, having never remarried. She was buried in Chicago's Oak Woods Cemetery.

May Amelie Parsons, born Columbus, Ohio, 14 June 1850, died Berlin, 8 October 1920, daughter of Amelia Withers Parsons and the Hon. George M. Parsons of Elmenhurst, Ohio, married at Columbus, Ohio, 16 May 1871, **Alexandre, 4th Prince zu Lynar,** born 17 September 1834, died Berlin, 3 November 1886. Amelie was visiting in Paris just before the outbreak of the Franco-Prussian War and there met the

Mrs. William Howard Taft, while another of the Parsons sisters, Marie, was married to William L. Breese, photographer and friend of architect Stanford White. Two Breese daughters, May Amelie's first cousins, married **Lord Willoughby de Eresby** (later **Earl of Ancaster**), and **Lord Robert Ines-Ker.**

After the Lynars' marriage the couple returned to Germany and lived at Lindenau Castle where she was allowed many favors by the king who granted her the style "Her Serene Highness." She died 8 October 1920 in Berlin and the properties in Ohio which had been

left her by her father—then valued at more than $1 million—were for a time denied her heirs because they were considered German-owned. Their suit to recover them was eventually successful. Their son, Count Ernst, succeeded his father as 5th Prince zu Lynar in 1886. Through a daughter are descended the current Prince Oettingen-Oettingen und Oettingen-Speilberg, Prince Fugger von Babenhausen, and Prince Hohenlohe-Bartenstein. Her grandson, then-Count Alexander zu Lynar-Redern, wrote in 1998, *Lost To The World,* the extraordinary tale of having buried the family silver, china, and crystal in a field near their home when the Russians were approaching. Fifty years later, he was allowed to reclaim the buried treasure—still in excellent condition even though the wooden crates had rotted away—but the family was never compensated for the loss of their extensive landholdings. His elder brother, who inherited the titles, had only daughters and Count Alexander succeeded as Prince Lynar at his brother's death in 2005. He has a son, Count Sebastian, who was born in Texas in 1981.

Elizabeth "Betsey" Patterson, born in Baltimore, Maryland, 6 February 1785, died in Baltimore, Maryland, 4 April 1879, was a daughter of William Patterson, an Irish immigrant who came to the United States before the Revolution and became the second wealthiest man in Maryland (after Charles Carroll of Carrollton, a signer of the Declaration of Independence, whose

May Parsons' father insisted that his daughter be married in her hometown. Her brother's sister-in-law was First Lady Mrs. William Howard Taft.

Betsey Patterson's legendary beauty lasted well into her later years when one observer said of her, "She simply did not age. It astonished everyone."

three Caton granddaughters married the 7th Duke of Leeds, the 8th Baron Stafford, and the 1st Marquess Wellesley, brother of the Great Duke of Wellington).   Betsey was a famous beauty painted in a three-face portrait by Gilbert Stuart. She met at a Baltimore party the youngest brother of Napoleon, **Jerome Bonaparte**, born at Ajaccio, 15 November 1784, died at Paris, 24 June 1860, who was a lieutenant in the French Navy fighting in the Carribbean. Born four months after his father's death, he was indulged by his mother and elder siblings and, as one biographer said of him, even as a boy he was the "spoilt brat he remained his entire life." To avoid capture by the British while in naval service he was forced to land in America, then traveled to Baltimore to visit a friend he met in the French Navy. Jerome was completely smitten with Betsey Patterson (a contemporary described her as having "a beauty which awakens desire and demands homage") and within two months they were engaged. Even though he spoke no English her French was excellent. President Thomas Jefferson wrote of the engagement to his Ambassador to France that the Pattersons were "in society with the first in the United States. These circumstances fix rank in a country where there are no hereditary titles."

William Patterson was a shrewd man. He insisted on a pre-nuptial contract that guaranteed his daughter one-third of her husband's estate if the marriage were annulled and also arranged for a Catholic wedding even though they were Protestant. The wedding took place on Christmas Eve 1803 in the Baltimore Cathedral, with the archbishop of Baltimore (then the highest-ranking Catholic official in the country) performing the ceremony. Jerome wore purple satin with diamond buckles while Betsey wore what one observer called "a mere suspicion of a dress." Although Jerome was underage, he had the written approval of his eldest brother, Joseph (later king of Spain), whose letter also mentioned their mother's blessing. Their brother Napoleon, although not yet emperor, already had dynastic designs for his siblings and was furious at the union. He had the marriage annulled by the French courts and immediately ordered his brother to return home without "the young person." By the time of the groom's return Napoleon was emperor. Jerome sailed to France with a pregnant Betsy but Napoleon had ordered that they were not to be allowed to land in continental Europe. Jerome, promising to set things right with his brother, disembarked for France and Betsey's ship set sail for Amsterdam where two French man-of-war ships denied her entry. The ship then sailed to England where within weeks she delivered a son, Jerome Napoleon Bonaparte, always called "Bo," born at Camberwell on 7 July 1805. Betsey wisely had the birth notarized and countersigned by both the Austrian and the Prussian ambassadors to England.

Jerome wrote to his wife asking her to be patient as he tried to appease his brother who referred to Betsey and her son only as "the Pattersons." The emperor appealed directly to Pope Pius VII for an annulment but the Vatican, noting the stature of the archbishop who performed the ceremony, refused to comply. It was the beginning of a breach that was to end with the emperor's excommunication and the pope's imprisonment. While Jerome was negotiating with his brother for his own titles and honors, he was writing to Betsey, "Be tranquil; thy husband will never abandon thee." Betsey refused Napoleon's offer of an annual pension of 60,000 francs if she would return to America and give up the name Bonaparte. Although she resisted enticing offers, her husband did not. He was named **Jérôme**,

Betsey's great-granddaughter, Louise Eugenie, Countess Moltke-Huitfeldt, who is the only member of Betsey's family to have present-day descendants.

Left: Charles Bonaparte, Betsey's grandson, was U. S. attorney general. Right: His brother, Jerome, personally escorted the Empress Eugenie to safety at the fall of the Second Empire.

Prince of France (with the designation of imperial highness) on 24 September 1806, **King of Westphalia,** 8 July 1807-26 October 1813, created **Prince von Montfort** by the King of Württemberg on 31 July 1816, and confirmed as Prince of France on 23 December 1852 (when his nephew regained the throne as Napoleon III).

Jerome's required concession was to give up Betsey and their son and to marry Princess Frederica Catherine, daughter of the King of Württemberg (of whom Napoleon said, "God created him to see how far human skin can be stretched"). Jerome wrote to his brother Lucien that he had made financial arrangements for his former wife and son, concluding, "your brother is unhappy but also say that he is not to blame." In 1808 he sent a letter to Betsey, who had returned to America, asking that their son be sent to him so that he could be reared "in a manner befitting his rank." When she refused, he sent a second letter offering her an annual income of 200,000 francs, a palatial home near his, and the title of "Princess of Smalkalden" (in Hesse-Nassau) for Betsey and "Prince of Smalkalden" for Bo. Her reply earned for her the respect of Napoleon when he learned of it: "I have no doubt Westphalia is a large kingdom, but it is not large enough for two queens." She was then negotiating directly with Napoleon for a permanent settlement and ended her letter to Jerome with the words, "I would prefer to be sheltered under the wings of an eagle to being suspended from the bill of a goose." When she threatened to marry a British diplomat, Napoleon made available to her a large income if she agreed not to proceed with the marriage.

Meanwhile Jerome was so dissolute and inept at running his kingdom that his sister-in-law, the Empress Josephine, on being told that each of Napoleon's brothers would succeed him in turn should no son be born to her, replied, "Ah, don't do the French the injustice of thinking they are so indifferent to their fate that they would accept a Prince like Jerome Bonaparte for their sovereign." Betsey had remained in Baltimore, which she loathed, and concentrated on seeking a brilliant future for her son. As the empire drew to a close, she arranged for the Maryland legislature in 1813 to grant her a divorce from her husband to prevent his seeking any of her American properties. The next year she was grievously insulted when Jerome and his second wife had a son and gave him Bo's exact name – Jerome Napoleon Bonaparte (later called "Plon-Plon."). Within months of Napoleon's final defeat at

Waterloo, she decided it was time for her long-awaited return to Europe (she left Bo in boarding school in Maryland where he became very close to his grandfather). She was particularly fond of England which she thought so great that "we must acknowledge that their monstrous vanity is excusable." Talleyrand was so impressed by her that he wrote, "If she were a queen, how gracefully she would reign." The son of the American minister to France wrote of Betsey's visit to Paris, "She is really beautiful and has a wonderful charm of manner. She is much sought after; her wit and beauty seem to open all doors to her."

Betsey's brother, Robert, had married Marianne Caton, a granddaughter of Charles Carroll of Carrollton. After his untimely death she was the mistress of the great Duke of Wellington until he tired of her and married her to his brother, the 1st Marquess of Wellesley. Thus were Napoleon and his nemesis related in a convoluted fashion through Betsey. Marianne's great fortune alleviated the Marquess's huge debts, but Betsey said of her, "She had however no success in France, where her not speaking the language was a considerable advantage to her, since it prevented her nonsense from being heard."

Napoleon's sister, Pauline, contacted Betsey through their mutual friend, the original John Jacob Astor, inviting them to visit her in Italy and even promising financial rewards for Bo. Betsey and Bo accepted but she wrote to her father, "a pretty woman of thirty-five is a bad object of calculations for nephews." Betsey was finally in her element in a daily round of balls, receptions, and dinners. She wrote to her father, who disapproved of her lifestyle, "I think it is quite as rational to go to balls and dinners as to get children, which people

Betsey Patterson was the first American woman to marry a future king. Her beauty and wit were legendary but her life was unhappy.

must do in Baltimore to kill time." In 1822 Betsey was visiting the Pitti Palace in Florence when she happened upon her ex-husband and his wife touring the pictures. He was startled and whispered to his queen, "That is my American wife." They neither spoke nor acknowledged one another nor did their paths ever cross again.

Bo went up to Harvard in 1824 and there was serious talk of marrying him to his first cousin, Charlotte, daughter of Joseph Bonaparte, formerly King of Spain who lived in New Jersey after the fall of the empire. Betsey continued looking for a suitable bride, writing to her father, "I am in hopes ... that if he cannot get a wife to support him, he will at least not get one for me to provide for." She was devastated, then, to learn while in Europe that her son had married a Baltimore girl, Susan May Williams. Betsey wrote to her father that she hoped there would be no children but, "as nothing happens which I desire, I do not flatter myself with an accomplishment of my wish on this subject." Betsey had little to do with her son for the remainder of her life but instead concentrated on increasing her wealth.

Her former husband lived on a short leash in the court of his father-in-law. When Jerome's wife died his pension from her was cancelled and he was forced to marry a wealthy widow, Marquesa Bartolini-Baldelli. She would not give him any money unless they first had sexual relations, and afterwards he would demand that his valet wash him from head to foot. Betsey had two grandsons born twenty-one years apart, Jerome and Charles, born in 1830 and in 1851, and they were as different in allegiances as possible. Jerome attended Harvard then graduated from West Point where his Commandant,

Robert E. Lee, wrote to his parents upon graduation that they could "take pleasure in comparing him to his princely relatives. Where worth makes the man and rank is but a stamp, his head can tower as lofty as the rest." Jerome left immediately for France where his first cousin had regained the throne as Napoleon III. Bo joined him there and the two were immediately invited to an audience with the new emperor who granted Bo French citizenship and recognized him and his son as members of the Bonaparte family (they pointedly refused an invitation from Bo's father, Jerome, to visit him). Bo's half-brother, Plon-Plon (of whom an Austrian archduke said he looked "like a worn-out basso from some obscure Italian opera house"), was furious at Bo's legitimization as he worried that his own rank in the order of succession would be affected. Young Jerome distinguished himself in military service for France and was decorated by three nations and three sovereigns for his bravery in battle, further infuriating his half-brother. In an effort to mollify both sides of the family, Napoleon III offered Bo the title "Duke of Sartene" and his son "Count of Sartene" if he would give up any rights to inheritance. Bo refused. A family council was called at which the American family members were granted the right to use the name "Bonaparte" but were denied any inheritance rights. Betsey's husband, the former King Jerome, died in 1860 making no mention of Bo in his will. From Baltimore Betsey's substantial fortune underwrote a costly legal challenge but the result was not successful.

Betsey retained her legendary beauty well into her sixties; as one biographer wrote of her, "She simply did not age. It astonished everyone. From a dynastic she became a physiological curiosity."

Bo died on 17 June 1870, dividing his estate between his two sons, Jerome and Charles. Betsey, who had more expectations of her younger grandson, Charles, bought out Jerome's share of his father's Baltimore home and estate and presented it to Charles. Young Jerome, still a distinguished soldier (he was to be called "Colonel" for the remainder of his life), personally escorted the Empress Eugenie to safety at the fall of the Second Empire then returned home to Baltimore. There he disappointed his grandmother by marrying on 7 September 1871 Mrs. Caroline LeRoy Edgar. Born an Appleton, she was a granddaughter of Daniel Webster but it was not the brilliant marriage envisioned by Betsey. The couple lived in Paris for six years before returning to Newport and to Beverly, Massachusetts, and had two children, Louise Eugenie and Jerome Napoleon. Betsey was still flourishing at the birth of her two great-grandchildren in 1873 and 1878. Her other grandson, Charles, never once visited Europe. He entered Harvard at the age of eighteen and graduated from its law school in 1874. He married at Newport in 1875 Ellen Channing Day, whose father owned the *Hartford Courant,* one of the area's leading newspapers. Charles's friend from Harvard, President Teddy Roosevelt, appointed him to the Board of Indian Commissioners where he did such a good job that Roosevelt named him Secretary of the Navy in 1905. After being assured that France would not object to having a Bonaparte in the U. S. Cabinet, Roosevelt appointed Charles U. S. Attorney General from 1906 to 1909. Among his accomplishments was issuing the order to establish the FBI. He had no children and died in 1921.

For the last eighteen years of her life, Betsey lived in a Baltimore boarding house where she expanded her fortune by saving far more than she spent. The *Baltimore Sun* said of her in 1873, "Though 88 years of age, Madame Bonaparte retains traces of a once wondrous beauty. Her complexion is still smooth and comparatively fair, while her peculiarly blue eyes are as yet undimmed." She reportedly lived her last years on nothing but milk and brandy, declaring, "Once I had everything but money. Now I have nothing but money." She died at the age of ninety-four on 4 April 1879 and is buried in Baltimore's Greenmount Cemetery where her gravestone reads, "After life's fitful fever she sleeps well." Her estate was valued in excess of $1.5 million at her death. Her only descendants live in Sweden and are from her great-granddaughter, Louise Eugenie (1873 – 1923), who married Count Adam Moltke-Huitfeldt. The current pretender to the Imperial Throne is a descendant of King Jerome's second marriage.

Jeanne Marie Beard Perkins, of Poughkeepsie, New York, was a daughter of Mary Beard Perkins and of lawyer and business executive Edward E. Perkins. He owned the Poughkeepsie newspapers and helped launch the political career of Franklin D. Roosevelt. Perkins was chairman of the Dutchess County, New York, Democratic Party from 1933 to 1944, and was a delegate to the National Democratic Convention from New York in 1912 and 1916. Jeanne married 15 June 1922, at St. Bartholomew's Chapel in Genoa, **Prince Fabrizio Colonna,** born Rome, 12 October 1893, died Rome, 12 June 1976, son of Prince Prospero Colonna, Prince of Sonnino, Duke of Rignano, who was a former mayor of Rome. The Colonnas are considered the most

The murder of multi-millionaire Sir Harry Oakes in the Bahamas was never solved.

important family in Rome, second only to the Gaetani di Sermonetas in antiquity. Pope Martin V (1417-1431) was a Colonna.

Jeanne's sister, **Olive Perkins,** had earlier married the **Marquis Stefano Antonio D'Amico** whom she met while he was attached to the Italian War Mission in the U.S. Colonna's father, Don Piero, governor of Rome, died 24 August 1939, and was a cousin of the Italian ambassador to the U.S., Don Ascanio Colonna. Prospero's wife, Maria Missimo, Duchess di Rignano e di Calcate, a title she had been permitted to bear since 1909, died at fifty-seven in 1916 at which time all three of her sons—Mario, born 1886, Piero, born 1891, and Fabrizio, born 1893—were fighting on the Isonzo front. Her titles passed to Fabrizio's eldest brother as Duke di Rignano. Fabrizio's next elder brother, Piero, married the Duchess del Garigliano and di San Cesareo (see **Grace King Connelly**), titles that passed to his son as Duke di Garigliano. Jeanne and Fabrizio had no children and she died in Rome in February of 1990. A Colonna cousin, Prince Marc Antonio Colonna, Duke of Paliano, was assistant to the Pontifical Throne and the highest lay dignitary in the Catholic Church.

Frances Kathryn Peters, born Los Angeles, California, 27 February 1905, daughter of James Abraham Peters and Mamie Teresa Morris Peters, married Phoenix, Arizona, 2 October 1936, **Prince Alexandre Galitzine,** born Moscow, 28 February 1908. He was artistic director for Universal Studios and was nominated for Academy Awards in 1943, 1953, 1962, and was a member of the Academy board in 1963. Their son, Prince Pierre, married American **Kathleen Page Pearsall** and had two children. Prince Alexandre's brother, **Prince Yuri "George" Galitzine,** born Moscow, 6 December 1916, died Los Angeles, California, 13 September 1963, was production director of Universal Studios and associate producer of the Walt Disney Company. He married in Los Angeles on 14 February 1942, **Carol Higgins,** born St. George, Texas, 29 January 1918, daughter of Charles Greenleaf Higgins and Jerusha Jackson Higgins. Their eldest son, Prince Alexandre, became an Orthodox priest and their other son and daughter married Americans. Alexandre and Georges were sons of Prince Alexandre and Lubov W. Gloebov of "the fourth line" of Galitzines.

The Galitzine brothers' work in movies acquainted them with the fashion photographer George Hoyningen-Huene, whom director George Cukor credited on such films as *A Star Is Born, Heller in Pink Tights,* and *Les Girls.* As a fashion photographer for *Vogue* and *Harper's Bazaar,* his subjects included Greta Garbo, his friend Katharine Hepburn, Ava Gardner, Marlene Dietrich, and Sophia Loren. He was a grandson of **Emily Lothrop,** daughter of George Van Ness Lothrop, who was U. S. ambassador to Russia at St. Petersburg and granddaughter of Gen. Oliver Strong of Rochester, New York, and of her husband, **Baron Barthold von Hoyningen Huene.** Emily was described as "a charming girl, very lively and full of spirit." Her husband was captain of the chevalier guards of the empress of Russia. A cousin of George Hoyningen-Huene was **Baron Ernst von Hoyningen-Huene,** who was one of the husbands of **Nancy Oakes** (1924 – 2005) and the father of her son. Nancy's father was multi-millionaire **Sir Harry Oakes,** 1st Baronet, who owned the largest goldmine in the western hemisphere. In 1943 at his home in Nassau, Bahamas, he was battered to death and his corpse partially incinerated and strewn with feathers. At the time the governor of the Bahamas was the **Duke of Windsor,** formerly King Edward VIII. He believed the local police were ill-equipped to solve the murder case and turned instead to two policemen he knew in the Miami police force. Within two days they arrested **Count Alfred de Marigny,** son-in-law of the murder victim, who had eloped with Nancy the day after she attained her majority (she almost died of surgeries necessitated by trench mouth contracted on their honeymoon in Mexico).

Sir Harry Oakes possessed a fortune of approximately $45 million (more than $500 million today) and the general opinion was that de Marigny had murdered him to obtain his daughter's inheritance. Nancy stood by her husband even though her mother was convinced of de Marigny's guilt. A jury acquitted him in less than two hours but added a stipulation that he be permanently deported from the island (he had angered the locals by his haughtiness, including his assertion that the Duke of Windsor was "a pimple on the arse of the Empire"). Nancy joined him in exile where their first stop was Cuba

to visit Ernest Hemingway.

The murder of Sir Harry Oakes was never solved, and Nancy continued her family's history of unhappiness. Her eldest brother, who inherited the baronetcy after their father's murder, was killed in an auto accident at thirty-nine. Another brother died of a drug overdose at twenty-eight. Their other sister was left in an irreversible coma by an auto accident. Even though her younger brother escaped the fate of his other siblings, once he inherited the baronetcy, disagreements with Nancy over the family fortune left them barely civil to one another for the rest of their lives. She had a son by von Hoyningen-Huene and married again after their divorce. When that marriage, too, ended in divorce, she reverted to the family name of her former husband and insisted on being addressed as "Baroness." As the *London Times* wrote in her obituary, "... since she drank more rum than was good for her, and could perhaps no longer distinguish between the truth and what she thought she remembered, [her comments] were of dubious value. They were always delivered with charm, however, especially if the recipient was a young man."

Virgilia Peterson, born New York City, 16 May 1904, was a daughter of Dr. and Mrs. Frederick Peterson of New York City and of Bridgewater, Connecticut. Virgilia was named for the gentle wife of Shakespeare's Coriolanus. Her father was a well-known psychiatrist who served as president of the American Neurological Association. She met Prince Paul Sapieha-Kodenski when, after two years at Vassar, she was a student at Grenoble University in France. They announced their engagement but her parents objected and the couple separated after two years. She was then married and divorced from Malcolm Ross of New York who, like his wife, was an author. She wrote of the experience, "However often marriage is dissolved, it remains indissoluble. Real divorce, the divorce of heart and nerve and fiber, does not exist, since there is no divorce from memory." She then went to Vienna to work on a novel and again met Prince Paul.

Virgilia married at London, 1 July 1933, **Paul, Prince Sapieha-Kodenski,** born Siedliska, 17 May 1900, died 1987, only son of Prince Paul Sapieha of Siedliska, Poland, and of Mathilde, Princess Windisch-Graetz. Prince Paul was a nephew of the archbishop of Krakow and a cousin of Prince Andre' Sapieha, commercial counselor of the Polish Embassy in Washington. His first cousin, Prince Alexander, married American **Elisabeth Hamilton Paine.** Dr. and Mrs. Peterson learned of their daughter's marriage to Prince Paul by a cablegram from London sent to Three Rivers Farm, their summer home in Connecticut. Prince and Princess Paul had a son and daughter before they were divorced and he died in 1987. Virgilia returned to the United States where she became known as a writer and critic. Her best-known work was *Polish Profile,* a memoir of her life in that country. She began moderating the popular television program *The Author Meets the Critic* in 1952. She married Gouverneur Paulding, senior editor of *The Reporter* magazine, in 1950 and he died only months before her death at her daughter's home in Sharon, Connecticut, in December of 1966. Virgilia once wrote in *A Matter of Life and Death,* 1961, "Words have their genealogy, their history, their economy, their literature, their art and music, as too they have their weddings and divorces,

their successes and defeats, their fevers, their undiagnosable ailments, their sudden deaths."

Romaine "Tootie" Dahlgren Pierce, born Biltmore, North Carolina, 17 July 1923, died New York City, 15 February 1975, was a daughter of Vinton Ulric Dahlgren Pierce and Margaret Knickerbocker Clark Pierce (later Mrs. Clark McIlwaine of Washington, D.C.). She first married on 23 May 1946, in New York City, William Simpson (a fact which, unfortunately, later caused her to be referred to as "Mrs. Simpson" by those who recalled the Duke of Windsor's American wife). They were divorced in 1948. She then married as his first wife, at the National Presbyterian Church in Washington, D.C., 4 February 1950, David Michael Mountbatten, **3rd Marquess of Milford Haven,** born 12 May 1919, died London, 14 April 1970, son of the 2nd Marquess of Milford Haven and of Countess Nadejda (Nada) de Torby, younger daughter of H.I.H. Grand Duke Mikhail Mikhailovitch of Russia, and grandson of Prince Louis of Battenberg (later created 1st Marquess of Milford Haven) and of Princess Victoria, who was a granddaughter of Queen Victoria of England. Romaine was a granddaughter of Admiral John Adolph Dahlgren, famous U. S. naval officer and inventor of the Dahlgren cannon (see **Maud Staples Ely-Goddard**). Her aunt was **Princess Charles Poniatowski** and her first cousin was the **Baroness de Overbeck.** Romaine paid for new teeth for her husband, who just missed being born a prince by two years, as the family's German titles were surrendered and lesser peerages assigned to them.

Romaine and the 3rd Marquess divorced in Mexico in 1954

and in London, 28 July 1960, without children; he had a son by his second marriage who succeeded his father in 1970 as the 4th Marquess when he was eight years old. The son's second wife, **Clare Steel,** is an American-born beauty and the mother of the current heir, the Earl of Medina. The marquess collapsed at Liverpool Street Station in London and died in the hospital, by that time out of favor with his cousins, the British royal family. The Battenbergs, traced to Duke Ydulf who flourished in the Benelux area in the sixth century, are among the most ancient houses in the West. They were forced by anti-German sentiment to change the family name in 1917 to Mountbatten, along with the British royal family's adoption of the name "Windsor," prompting their cousin, the German kaiser, to joke that he looked forward to seeing a production of *The Merry Wives of Saxe-Coburg*. Romaine married third, in New York City, 10 July 1964, James Busch Orthwein, president of D'Arcy, MacManus and Masius, a St. Louis-based advertising agency, and an heir to the Budweiser beer fortune. She died of cancer at fifty-two at Memorial Hospital in New York City, 15 February 1975.

Henrietta Guerard Pollitzer's mother was born a Guerard, a family of early Charleston, South Carolina, colonists, while her father was an Austrian Jew who came to South Carolina in the 1860s. Their children were raised in the Episcopal Church but their patrimony prevented entry into Charleston society. Henrietta dropped her last name in favor of her mother's maiden name. She met Edward V. Hartford, heir to the A & P fortune as well as an automobile inventor, on a ship from Palm Beach to New York. A & P was the first national

Grand Duke Michael was banished from Russia for marrying his wife, Countess von Torby, and thus escaped the executions of other members of his family.

Prince Louis of Battenberg was created the 1st Marquess of Milford Haven when the British royal family gave up their German titles. Right: Nada de Torby was Tootie Pierce's mother-in-law.

then King Cottage owned by Frederic Rhinelander King. Although her stock dividends totalled $1 million per year, she petitioned the court in 1926 to increase her son's trust allowance from $100,000 to $150,000, as "I do not believe that he should come into his inheritance with desires ungratified and wishes thwarted." In 1927, she purchased Seaverge, the Newport home of Commodore Elbridge Gerry, on five acres adjoining the ocean next door to Doris Duke's home, Rough Point.

She met Prince Guido Pignatelli when he made an appointment to ask her to purchase corporate bonds from the New York firm for whom he then worked. She married at St. Vincent's Church in Reno, Nevada, 25 April 1937, **Prince Guido Pignatelli,** (and eventual **Duke of Montecalvo, Marquess of Paglieta, Marquess of San Marco Locatola**), born at San Paolo, Belsito, 23 June 1900, died at Palermo, 5 February 1967, son of General Pompeo dei Duchi di Montecalvo and Princess Helene Pignatelli. Guido was created a prince ad personam by royal decree on 14 June 1941. After her marriage to Prince Guido, the European society magazine *Le Carnet Mondain* pictured her on the cover although the caption incorrectly stated that she was born at Hartford—there was no inconvenient mention of her former marriage. The couple left for a honeymoon boar-hunting in Czechoslovakia where they

grocery store chain, becoming number one in America by the 1930s when it operated 16,000 stores with annual sales of more than $1 billion. Henrietta and Hartford married in 1902 and had two children, including their son, Huntington Hartford, before her husband's death in 1922. The estate was left entirely to his wife but the fortune was in a generation-skipping trust to benefit her late father-in-law's grandchildren (Edward Hartford's two brothers were childless). Thus Henrietta controlled millions of dollars through her two children. Henrietta leased Chastellux, the Lorillard Spencer mansion in Newport, learned of legal actions filed by Prince Guido's American first wife, **Constance Wilcox Pignatelli** (whom he married 28 August 1925; she copyrighted *Egypt's Eyes,* a play she wrote as Princess Pignatelli, in 1924), daughter of George Augustus Wilcox and Mary Grenelle Wilcox, by whom he had a daughter, Marilena Pignatelli. At Guido's marriage to Henrietta, his Reno divorce from Constance was less than twenty-four hours old. Reno divorces were only in effect when both parties were represented and Constance was not. A trial was held in New York in 1938 where, on the stand, Constance testified of Guido's new wife, "All my friends called my attention to the fact that she was a grandmother. It annoyed me terribly." The judge found that the divorce was not legal in New York and Guido replied that it did not matter as he was a resident of Nevada and had no intention of returning to New York. He then received from the archbishop of Los Angeles a document stating that his marriage to Constance was annulled but a subsequent court in Florence, Italy, refused to accept the finding. Finally, in July of 1939, the Italian Court of Cassation ruled that his divorce from Constance was valid and an appeals court in Perugia upheld the decision.

In 1941 the couple brought a legal action against his cousin, Prince Ludovic Pignatelli (whose wife was American **Ruth Morgan Waters**), who was convicted of attempting to extort money from them by contesting Guido's right to the title. Prince Ludovic later died destitute in a New York City rooming house in 1956, having been critically injured when he hit his head in a fall. Henrietta and Prince Guido lived at Wando Plantation, her thirty-two-room plantation home and gardens designed by Olmsted, near Charleston, which was destroyed by fire in 1942, and in Washington, D.C., where he was attached to the diplomatic corps. She was diagnosed with leukemia and retired to Melody Farm, her home in Wyckoff, New Jersey, where she died on 3 July 1948, and was buried in Charleston's Magnolia Cemetery. Only months before her death she purchased the Joseph Manigault House in Charleston when it was being sold for back taxes and gave it to the Charleston Museum in memory of her mother. Her son received from her, separately from his large trust fund, more than $4 million in stocks as well as valuable property, while her widower was left $50,000 plus a living trust with an income of $10,000 per year—with the principal reverting to her son upon Guido's death. Her attorneys declared in court that "Her husband had virtually no property or income."

That amount was not sufficient for Prince Guido, and, four months after his wife's death, Prince Guido married in Reno, Nevada, 14 October 1948, then in Palermo, socialite **Barbara Eastman** of New York City, a descendant of Massachusetts colonists. Prince Guido's son by Barbara Eastman, Prince Paolo, born in Washington, D.C., in 1949, is the current 14th Duke of Montecalvo, 15th Marquess of Paglieta, and Marquess of San Marco Locatola. Married to Margery Baker since 1981, he has a daughter but no son or brother and there are no males cousins in his line.

Jamie Porter, born Greenwich, Connecticut, 27 June 1918, was a daughter of James Jackson Porter and Margaret Kelly Porter (later Mrs. John C. Hughes, Jr.). Jamie's father graduated from Harvard in 1914 and entered military service in World War I. Her paternal grandfather, William H. Porter, was a founding partner of Morgan Bank and of Bankers Trust, while her maternal great-grandfather was the founder of Chemical Bank. She was an only child and was born shortly before her father's death in France on 5 October 1918, while serving with the U. S. Army. At her birth she was rumored to be the richest baby in America.

Jamie married at Trinity Church in Lenox, Massachusetts, 22 July 1939, **Prince Andre' Gagarin,** born St. Petersburg, 23 November 1914, an officer in the U. S. Navy. The ceremony was performed by the bishop of the Brooklyn diocese of the Russian Orthodox Church and there were twenty-nine wedding attendants. Andre's father, Prince Serge, was imperial embassy consul at Constantinople. Prince Andre' graduated from Yale and was employed by the investment firm of Morgan Stanley & Company. The sons of Prince Andre' and Jamie Porter married Americans, while their daughter married the Marquess of Santa Lucia. Andre's brothers, Prince Sergei and Prince Peter, married respectively Americans **Frances Wickham** and **Nancy Tyner** (whose grandfather, John Hill, was one of the founders of McGraw-Hill Publishing Company of New York). The Gagarin family descends from Rurik, the founder of Russia in 867. Many present-day members of the family live in the United States. Prince Andre' Gagarin died 8 March 2002, and his widow lives in Connecticut.

Marian "Polly" Hubbard Powers, born in San Francisco, California, 12 February 1904, died in Capri, 17 July 1979, was one of three daughters of Frank Hubbard Powers (1864 – 1920) and Jane Gallatin

Powers (1868 – 1944). The other daughters were Grace Madeleine and Dorcas Jane, while their brother was (Albert) Gallatin. Her father was a Berkeley graduate who practiced law in San Francisco at the firm of Heller, Ehrman and Powers. He was also secretary of the Dabney Oil Company and an early developer of the electric industry in California. In 1902, with James M. Devendorf, he purchased all the unsold land in Carmel, eventually owning three quarters of the present town, and is credited with having founded Carmel-by-the-Sea. Polly's mother, Jane Gallatin Powers, was a daughter of Clemenza "Nemi" Rhodes Gallatin and of Albert Gallatin who made a fortune in the Sacramento gold rush. He rose from floor sweeper to president of the Huntington Hopkins Company, one of the largest hardware concerns on the west coast. He was an early partner of Collis Huntington and Mark Hopkins, who left the firm under his direction when they turned their attention to building the Central Pacific Railroad. The house where Jane Gallatin Powers grew up was built in 1877 and later became the California governor's mansion until Ronald Reagan's administration.

Jane studied art in Europe and eventually established the first art studio at Carmel in a barn built in 1864. In 1912 Jane fell in love with an artist (probably Wilhelm Heinrich Funk) and reportedly sailed with him to Europe, leaving her husband and children behind. After she returned, the affair was never mentioned again. It was assumed that she and her husband reconciled but, in 1914, her husband re-wrote his will, leaving his wife only a modest fixed income while the remainder of his fortune went to their children. In 1920 Frank H. Powers died

Polly Powers' father is credited with founding the town of Carmel-by-the-Sea in California. Although Polly's husband succeeded as the 4th Duke Dusmet de Smours, she had already died and never became duchess.

and his widow left for Europe, taking her three youngest children with her (Madeline had already married). Jane resumed painting and set up studios in Paris, Rome, and Capri. In September of 1925, her daughter Polly's engagement was announced in the *New York Times* by her maternal aunt, Mrs. Ernest Thompson Seton. Polly Powers married in Sorrento on 30 September 1925, **Don Marino Dusmet de Smours,** born Naples, 15 October 1896, died Capri, 14 February 1983, third son of the 1st Duke Dusmet de Smours (1853 – 1941). The young couple moved in 1926 to the Isle of Capri in the Gulf of Naples and eventually named their new home Villa Paradiso.

The ducal title was granted to Don Marino's father Luigi in 1896 and subsequently made hereditary with letters patent in 1925. In 1927 Polly's sister, Dorcas Jane, married Roberto Pennazzi-Ricci, an army officer, but died of fever less than two years later, leaving a daughter, Roberta. Jane, the mother of Polly and Dorcas, continued to live in Italy although the Depression drastically reduced her living allowance. Her son, Gallatin, had joined the U.S. Navy but was unable to locate his mother through any channels. Word reached Jane's eldest daughter, Madeleine, in San Francisco, that her mother needed a copy of her birth certificate to prove that she was Aryan. Without it, she was unable to obtain a rationing card for necessities. Madeline's son, Seth Ulman (Polly's nephew), was then a young medic with the U. S. Army and was in Rome the day it was liberated from the Nazis. He finally located his grandmother living near penury in faded elegance with little food and no resources. Shortly afterwards, Jane died and was buried in the "Foreigners" section of the Protestant

Cemetery at Rome (she, like Polly, was a Christian Scientist). Seth Ulman secured all his grandmother's paintings and left them in care of the American Embassy in Rome. After the War they were returned to California where they were found in 1980 in the basement of her eldest daughter's home in San Francisco. A 1983 retrospective of women artists included three of her works.

The eldest brother of Polly's husband, Don Fulco, succeeded their father as 2nd Duke and died in 1956 without a son. The next brother, Don Giovanni, succeeded as 3rd Duke and died unmarried in 1980. Don Marino then succeeded as the **4th Duke Dusmet de Smours** but Polly had died the previous year and never became duchess. She had two sons and the eldest, Don Luigi, succeeded his father as 5th Duke. Although the present duke's elder son, Don Thomas Marino, has only two daughters, the younger son, London surgeon Michael Eugene, has two sons born in 1988 and 1990. An uncle of the 1st Duke Dusmet de Smours, Melchiorre Dusmet (1818 – 1894) changed his name to Giuseppe Benedetto upon becoming a Benedictine monk. He was elected archbishop of Catania, Sicily, in 1867, and created a cardinal in 1889. The monastery at Catania was confiscated by the state soon after the founding of the kingdom of Italy. Giuseppe Benedetto was venerated by Pope Paul VI in 1965 and the announcement of his beatification was made by Pope John Paul II in 1981. His canonization is currently pending.

A first cousin of Polly Powers Dusmet was the writer Anya Seton (1904 – 1990), whose best-known historical romances were *Katherine* and *The Winthrop Woman*. Her father, Ernest Thompson Seton, was a founder of the Boy Scouts of America. A Dusmet cousin, Marchese Giacomo Dusmet, married American heiress **Edith Oliver** of Pittsburgh, a daughter of James Brown Oliver. Their daughter, Editta, married Don Filippo dei Duchi Lante della Rovere, son of American **Anita Allen** and grandson of American **Mathilde Davis** (see her separate entry).

Elizabeth Bleeker Tibbits Pratt of Kingston, New York, born Albany, New York, 27 January 1860, died Ponovich, Yugoslavia, November 1928, was a daughter of Brig. Gen. George Watson Pratt (who was killed at the Battle of Manassas) and Anna Attwood Tibbits Pratt, and granddaughter of U. S. Congressman Zaddock Pratt who owned the largest tannery business in the U. S. and was the founder of Prattsburg, New York. Her father was a cousin of railroad magnate Jay Gould. Elizabeth first married 21 April 1881, in New York City, **Count Amedee de Gasquet-James,** born 5 June 1846, in New Orleans, Louisiana, died 28 July 1903 in Dinard, France, who was a U. S. citizen. They had three daughters and a son. He died in Paris in 1903, leaving an estate of approximately $1.5 million which his will instructed was to be divided among his four children with their mother as executor. The will also stipulated that the corpus was to be placed in "one of the big trust companies." His widow filed suit in the U.S. in 1909 to have the will set aside on the grounds that he was not a resident of France where the will was filed and probated.

She had recently met **Duke Heinrich Borwin of Mecklenburg-Schwerin,** born Venice, 16 December 1885, son of Duke Frederic-Francois II and Princess Augustine of Reuss-Schleiz-Kostritz (Duke

Heinrich's first cousin, Cecilie, was then the crown princess of Germany). Elizabeth was fifty-three and he was twenty-six at the time—younger than several of her children. Because of his excessive spending habits, the duke had been placed by his family under a legal restraint by the German courts and a curator was required to approve all his decisions. Elizabeth and the duke traveled to Dover, England, and were married there at the Registry office on 15 June 1911. They returned immediately to France where a religious ceremony was performed. The U.S. court then found against her attempt to have her late husband's will set aside and her children, believing that she was spending funds on behalf of the duke, promptly filed an action against her for an accounting of their funds. Elizabeth's access to the money was then denied her.

A civil action was filed in France by the groom's family to annul her marriage to the duke as it had not been approved or sanctioned by his family or his legal curator. Her marriage to Duke Heinrich had already been declared unequal and it was then annulled by a tribunal in Mecklenburg-Schwerin. Elizabeth retook her maiden name and filed suit in England seeking to have the marriage recognized as it had taken place there. That court also found against her. Her children sought the return of more than a quarter million dollars she had already expended; the lower court found in their favor, the appellate court overturned the decision, and a higher court reinstated the original judgment on behalf of her children. In 1913, Elizabeth unsuccessfully sought a court order in France to force the sale of an automobile factory owned by her ex-husband, still contending that

Brigadier General George W. Pratt was killed at the Battle of Manassas. His father owned the largest tannery in the United States and founded Prattsburg, New York.

they had been legally married. Her suit was unsuccessful. Elizabeth then moved to Austria and became a citizen there. When her mother died, leaving her additional funds, the children also sought those in court, contending that their mother was now an "alien" under the terms of a 1918 law requiring the return of any assets owned by nationals in countries with which the U. S. was then at war.

Elizabeth's daughter, the Countess de la Mettrie, was decorated by France for her war work, while Elizabeth's son, Count George Pratt de Gasquet-James, was cited for valor as an army officer. Duke Heinrich Borwin's second wife, **Natalie Oelrichs,** was also an American. His uncle, Duke Heinrich Wladimir Albrecht Ernst, was created His Royal Highness Prince Hendrik of the Netherlands on 6 February 1901, the day before he married at The Hague Queen Wilhelmina of the Netherlands.

Anne Hollingsworth Price, born at Ellerslie Hall near Wilmington, Delaware, 25 August 1868, died Johannsdorf, 24 April 1945, was a daughter of Sarah Harlan Price and James Price, an original director of the Wilmington Insurance Company and president of the Wilmington & Susquehanna Railroad Company. She married in Dresden, 17 December 1890, **Friedrich Wilhelm, Prince von Ardeck,** born Offenback am Main, 2 November 1858, died Wilhelmshohe, 1 April, 1902, son of Wilhelm, Prince of Hesse-Philippsthal-Barchfeld and his first (morganatic) wife, Marie, Princess von Hanau and zu Horowitz, created Princess von Ardeck on 28 July 1876. His younger brother, Prince Chlodwig, succeeded their distant cousin as Landgrave of Hesse-Philippsthal in 1925. Prince Friedrich's brother, Prince Christian,

married American **Elizabeth Reid Rogers.** After Friedrich's death Anne married second at Mihalyi, Hungary, 4 February 1904, Joszi Dor de Jobahaza. The Ardeck family is now extinct in the male line. Anne's sister, **Mathilde Louise Price,** married in 1883 in Vienna **Baron Gabor Bornemisza de Kaszon,** and their great-granddaughter, Baroness Francesca Anne Thyssen-Bornemisza de Kaszon, in 1993 married Archduke Karl of Austria, eldest son and heir of Dr. Otto von Habsburg, head of the Austrian royal house. Their son will one day be head of the House of Hapsburg, claimant to the Austro-Hungarian Monarchy, and principal heir of the Holy Roman Empire. Another Price sister, **Sallie May Price,** married 22 October 1891 in Styria, **Maximilian, Baron Berg.** The fourth sister, **Margaret Plater Price,** married in 1882 in Baden, Germany, **Baron Edmund Wucherer von Haldenfield.**

Lillian Warren Price, daughter of Commodore Cicero Price of Troy, New York, was born in Mobile, Alabama, and died at her English home, Deepdene, on 11 January 1909. She first married wealthy New York merchant Louis Hammersley. She was a great beauty and was known for wearing white and covering the interior of her opera box in New York City in white orchids. After her husband's death, she changed the name by which she was called from "Lillian" to "Lily" because of the unfortunate popular line, "Lillian, rhymes with million," when she entered the marriage market. She married at New York's City Hall in a ceremony officiated by the mayor on 29 June 1888, George Charles Spencer-Churchill, **8th Duke of Marlborough,** born 13 May 1844, died 9 November 1892, the brother-in-law of

Left: When Lillian Price entered the marriage market, she changed her name to Lily because of the unfortunate sobriquet, "Lillian, rhymes with million." Right: Her money re-roofed Blenheim Palace where she was duchess.

energies into charitable works. Her substantial fortune paid to reroof Blenheim, add a magnificent pipe organ, and build a laboratory for the duke's amateur science experiments. He died suddenly from heart disease at Blenheim Palace on 9 November 1892.

Widowed a second time, Lillian married third on 30 April 1895, war hero Col. William Leslie de la Poer Beresford (1847 – 1900), third son of the 4th Marquess of Waterford. She was finally happy in this marriage and, by her third husband, the popular "Lord Bill," she had a son, William Warren de la Poer Beresford (1897-1919), at the age of forty-three. Having paid dearly for her ducal title, however, she continued to call herself (incorrectly) Lily, Duchess of Marlborough. Three years later she was a widow once again, when Lord Bill died of peritonitis at the end of 1900. Lily herself died of

American-born **Jennie Jerome** and later the father-in-law of **Consuelo Vanderbilt.** The marriage was largely arranged by Leonard Jerome, Jennie's father, who knew that the duke was in dire need of cash (he wrote to his wife, "I hope the marriage will come off as there is no doubt she has lots of tin"). It was not happy, however, as the duke was excluded from proper society because of his infamous divorce (his former wife even retreated to her earlier style as "Lady Blandford" to rid herself of the Marlborough name). He retreated to the arms of his mistress, Lady Colin Campbell, whose nude portrait by Whistler continued to hang over his bed. Lily consoled herself by throwing her

heart trouble at Deepdene on 11 January 1909, at the age of fifty-five. Her stepson, the 9th Duke of Marlborough, married **Consuelo Vanderbilt,** who wrote of Lily, "Mrs. Hammersley's...wealth had been freely spent installing central heating and electric light at Blenheim." Lily left a substantial fortune to her son who died unmarried at the age of twenty-one. Deepdene, the country estate where she lived and died, was leased from Lord Francis Hope, 8th Duke of Newcastle, owner of the Hope Diamond who had been married to American **May Yohé.** After Lily's death, it was leased to Almeric Paget, later **1st Baron Queenborough,** and his American wife, **Pauline Whitney.**

Katharine Quay, born Sewickley, Pennsylvania, died 1956, was one of four daughters of Jerome Anderson Quay of Sewickley, Pennsylvania, who served as U. S. Consul in Florence, Italy, and of Marion Pryde McKelvey Quay. Katharine's grandfather was U. S. Senator Matthew Stanley Quay who won the Congressional Medal of Honor for his heroics at the Battle of Fredericksburg. He was Pennsylvania state treasurer in 1886-1887, then chairman of the Republican National Committee in 1888; his success at fundraising was largely responsible for the election of Benjamin Harrison as president. Quay later said that the president would "never know how many Republicans were compelled to approach the gates of the penitentiary to make him president." Quay served in the U. S. Senate from Pennsylvania from 1887 until 1899 when he was defeated for re-election due to charges of corruption. He was then immediately appointed by the governor to fill the unexpired term but the senate refused to seat him. Quay was then re-elected in 1901 and served until his death in 1904.

The senator was proud of his native-American heritage and was known in the senate as a champion of the rights of American Indians.

In 1892, when President Harrison was seeking re-election, he told Senator Quay that God had gotten him elected. The senator replied, "Then let God re-elect you!" before storming out of the office. The senator's son, Jerome, was appointed U. S. Consul to Florence in the year after his father's death, having served as superintendent of the Pennsylvania State Reformatory. His daughter, Katharine, married in New York City, 14 October 1912, **Prince Napoleone Ruspoli** (of the 1st line), born in Rome, 24 November 1885, died in Rome, 9 November 1939, grandson of the 5th Prince Ruspoli and Prince di Cerviteri. There were no children. Katharine died at the Villa Ruspoli in Bagni di Lucca, Italy, in February of 1956, survived by her sisters, Miss Marion Pride Quay (who in 1900 wrote an interesting account of alligator hunting in Florida) of Bagni di Lucca and Miss Romayne Quay of Bridgewater, Connecticut. Another sister, Thetta Quay, was the wife of Robert Franks, private financial secretary to Andrew Carnegie as well as president of the Home Trust Company. He also served as one of the three original trustees of Carnegie's foundation. Prince Napoleone Ruspoli's uncle succeeded as head of the household and his line still holds the title.

Marie Jennings Reid, born at New Orleans's Jackson Square on 15 May 1870, was a daughter of Samuel Chester Reid Jr., and of Josephine Rowan Reid whose father, John Rowan Jr., was U. S. charge' d'affaires to the Two Sicilies in 1848. Marie's maternal grandfather, Judge John Rowan, was Kentucky's first U. S. senator. It was at his home, Federal Hill, near Bardstown, Kentucky, that his relative, Stephen Foster, wrote "My Old Kentucky Home." Marie was a paternal granddaughter of Capt. Samuel Chester Reid who commanded the privateer Brigadier General Armstrong in the War of 1812 and defeated the British frigates in the Battle of Fayal in the Azores (the U.S.S. Reid was named for him). It was Captain Reid who suggested in 1818 that the U. S. flag revert to thirteen stripes rather than adding a new one with each additional state in the union and that a new star instead be inserted for each new state. His wife sewed the first flag of that new design. His son, Marie's father, walked the halls of congress for years attempting to have his family reimbursed for the promised prize money from his father's capture of many vessels on the high seas. He was finally successful long after his father's death, although the sum did not make his family wealthy. His daughter, Marie, and her sister, Maud, were strict Catholics who attended the Georgetown Academy of Visitation in Washington, D.C.

There Marie met a young law student from Maine. She married on 21 September 1887, at St. Matthews Catholic Church in Washington, D.C., Col. Frederick Hale Parkhurst (1864-1921) of Bangor, Maine, who was elected governor of Maine in 1921 but died before taking office. As the Maine newspapers later wrote of her, "She originated the

Though not a great heiress, Marie Reid first married a future governor of Maine but was said to be "too large for a small town and away she went." She is pictured with her second husband, Prince Rospigliosi-Gioeni.

Marie Reid was never accepted by Rome society nor by her husband's family. The problem only intensified when she produced a male heir.

beauty secured many social invitations and she was entreated to remain for the winter season. She had known the Duke of Caracciola when he was assigned to Italy's embassy in Washington and he invited her to ride in Rome's Hunt Club. She was an expert rider in a country where women almost never rode. It was there that Prince Colonna introduced her to her next husband who asked upon seeing her on horseback, "Who is that magnificent woman?" She married at Lamporecchio 26 August 1901, Giusseppe, **4th Prince Rospigliosi-Gioeni, 10th Prince of the Holy Roman Empire, Prince di Castiglione, Duc di Zagarolo, Marchese di Giuliana,** born Rome, 25 October 1848, died at Stresa, 21 September 1913, who was twenty-one years older than she and had been considered a "confirmed bachelor." He was very wealthy and the head of a family that had given the church both Popes Clement IX and Clement X. It was said that many ambitious mothers with eligible daughters were crushed by the marriage.

Marie was shunned by her husband's family and an intense feud began between Marie and her sister-in-law (who refused to give up her apartment in the Rospigliosi palace as well as to surrender family jewels), wife of the next eldest son in the Rospigliosi family (captain of the Noble Guard at the Vatican), who fully intended for her own son to inherit the titles (the son was already twenty-four at the time of Marie's marriage). As the *New York Times* reported, "She bears the snubs of Roman society at least with outward philosophy." The problem intensified when Marie and her husband had a son, Girolamo, who was born in 1907 when his father was fifty-nine, thus supplanting his uncle and cousin as heir to the titles. The couple and their son lived at the

idea of wearing silver bells on her garters when she lived here, and as she tripped along the street they tinkled merrily. She was too large for a small town and away she went." Marie left her husband. They were divorced and the same newspaper said of her, "True granddaughter of the privateer she demanded plenty of sea room in which to navigate." By Parkhurst she had a son, Samuel Chester Reid Parkhurst (called "Reid"), and a daughter, Dorothy, who died at the age of sixteen.

Marie went to New York City for a while then to Rome where her

Rospigliosi Palace in Rome. Marie began protracted negotiations with the Catholic Church seeking to annul her first marriage, performed by Monsignor Chapelle who later became archbishop of New Orleans then apostolic delegate to Cuba and the Philippines.

Marie contended that she was not aware that her first husband was not baptized and that the marriage dispensation sought and approved by the priest was for a marriage between a Catholic and a non-Catholic. Because he was unbaptized, she contended that she had never been married in the eyes of the Church as the wrong dispensation had been granted. Believing that a religious dispensation would soon be issued, Marie and her second husband, Prince Rospigliosi, were married only in a civil ceremony and later sought a wedding fully sanctioned by the church. At one point the rumor circulated throughout Rome that Marie's former husband had died. Fearing that a second marriage would take place within the church, thus forcing the couple to be received, there was general rejoicing when it was learned that the former husband was not only alive but a member of the Maine legislature.

At one point, Marie loaned for display to a charity event in Rome a string of historic pearls together with a tasteful card reading, "Pearls of the Princess Rospigliosi." The committee changed the card to read "Pearls of the House of Rospigliosi" and Marie promptly withdrew them from display. Although a tribune of cardinals (led by Cardinal Marinelli, formerly papal delegate to the United States) found in favor of Marie in her efforts to annul her first marriage, the pope (heavily influenced by Rome society and by the Rospigliosi family)

overturned that decision and found that the first marriage was valid. Marie could therefore not be married to Prince Rospilgiosi in the eyes of the church. His Holiness also decreed that no further appeal would be entertained (although years later the marriage was finally recognized). Under civil law, however, their son was the rightful heir no matter what canon law dictated. When Marie's husband died in 1913, leaving her a substantial fortune, she seriously considered leaving Rome where she was certain to be ostracized. It was said, "nothing but cold stares and uplifted brows have greeted her in Rome." She had almost convinced her husband, before his death, to move to a villa on the Riviera but, as the *New York Times* reported, Prince Rospigliosi "was of the old stock that only half lived when away from the Eternal City."

In the year before her husband's death she gave a lengthy interview to the *New York Times* in which she contended that, as an American, she was entitled to a fair public hearing but that she had been the subject of public scorn and ridicule including a charge that she sought to have her son by her first marriage declared illegitimate by voiding her marriage to his father. "It is too bad to be one of those whom the sensational newspapers turn into 'copy.'" She also proclaimed that she was different from most American princesses because, "I did not purchase my title or obtain a bankrupt husband. Indeed, who was I here? A mere little frank American girl, without fortune." Her son, Girolamo, who succeeded his father as the 5th Prince Rospigliosi, proposed to Barbara Hutton immediately upon being introduced to her by the American-born Dorothy, Countess di Frasso. In fact,

The beautiful Amelie Rives was a best-selling author by the age of twenty-five. Her novel, *The Quick or the Dead?*, sold more than 300,000 copies and was considered risqué for its time.

Hutton complained to di Frasso that, once he started proposing, "He never stopped." Hutton declined, however, and Girolamo, who succeeded his father, married twice, including wealthy American **Marian Adair Snowden** (see her separate entry) but had no children. The titles passed to a son of his first cousin, Prince Giambattista (the same cousin whose mother had so opposed Marie), whose wife was American heiress **Ethel Bronson.** The new Prince Rospigliosi also in 1977 succeeded his cousin, Maria Giustiniani-Bandini, in the English title of 11th Earl of Newburgh.

Marie, formerly Princess Rospigliosi, died at Milan, Italy, 16 August 1930, having been shunned by society and widowed for seventeen years. In her 1912 interview with the *New York Times*, she opined, "I have seen some poor, poor dear little American girls buy a title – any American girl can buy a title of some sort, and I have seen them very badly treated." But, she concluded, "Mine has been a supremely happy marriage, and there was no reason for it to occur except that thereby two persons might become happy."

Amelie Louise Rives, born Richmond, Virginia, 23 August 1863, died Richmond, Virginia, 15 June 1945, was the daughter of Alfred Landon Rives (Chief of the Army Engineers for the Confederate States) and Sarah "Sadie" McMurdo Rives, granddaughter of the second Episcopal bishop of Virginia and a granddaughter of U.S. Senator William Cabell Rives, who was twice U. S. minister to France (1829-32 and 1849-53). He served in the U.S. Senate from 1835-1845 and was in the Confederate Congress during the War. Her father, who was born in Paris, was a godson of General Lafayette.

Left: Her first husband, Archie Chanler, was one of the "Astor orphans." He continued to support her financially even after her second marriage. Right: Amelie at her presentation to the Russian court in 1908.

Amelie, who was a goddaughter of Gen. Robert E. Lee, spent her childhood in Mobile and her summers at the family home in Virginia. She was privately tutored and had her first written article published in 1886 in the *Atlantic Monthly.* She made her debut at Newport in 1888 when a newspaper reporter wrote of her, "She has a great fashion of rolling her eyes in a manner that fascinated every man who met her. Her eyes were really wonderful, such great, deep eyes; and with that gold hair of hers and her fresh color and classic profile, she was quite stunning." Amelie was immediately pursued by and married at Castle Hill on 18 June 1888, John Armstrong "Archie" Chanler of New York City, a great-grandson of John Jacob Astor (Chanler's grandfather married as his second wife Medora Grymes whose niece and namesake, **Medora von Hoffmann,** married the **Marquis de Mores**), the eldest of the "Astor orphans." Amelie's sister-in-law called her a "dangerous goddess" after she caused the nervous breakdown of her husband's brother (whom she may have seduced). During the next three years Amelie and Archie lived in Europe and she studied art in Paris where she became addicted to morphine. Her husband added a phrase to the popular lexicon of the day when, after being confined to an insane asylum, he received word of his brother's marriage to a famous beauty of the day, who then took control of his fortune. Chanler immediately telegraphed his brother, "Who's looney now?" Their nephew, Ashley Chanler, married Infanta Maria of Portugal, granddaughter of Miguel, *de facto* king of Portugal from 1828–1834, and great-granddaughter of João VI, king of Portugal and the Algarves and emperor of Brazil (Infanta Maria's nephew, Duarte, is the current

Amelie was named for her literary aunt who was herself named for the first wife of King Louis Philippe while William Rives was minister to France. The aunt, her husband, and three of her four children died at sea when their ship went down en route to Paris. Amelie grew up in Mobile, Alabama, and at "Castle Hill," her family home near Cobham in Albemarle County, Virginia, built in 1764, where George Washington, Thomas Jefferson, and James Madison had all been entertained. In 1781 Amelie's great-grandmother, Mrs. Thomas Walker, delayed the British Colonel Tarleton and his troops so that she could secretly send word to prevent Thomas Jefferson from being arrested.

Prince Pierre Troubetskoy was introduced to Amelie Rives by Oscar Wilde who said that the two most attractive people at the party should meet one another.

head of the Portugese royal house and pretender to the throne).

In 1906 Archie Chanler claimed that his friend, the architect Stanford White, had tricked him into checking himself into the Bloomingdale insane asylum, "a madhouse for the rich," and he wrote about his experiences in a book entitled, *Four Years Behind the Bars of Bloomingdale,* or *The Bankruptcy Law in New York.* After his escape and resumption of his legal rights, Chanler legally changed his last name to Chaloner. Amelie divorced him in South Dakota (where she openly traveled with her future husband) in 1895 while he was hunting game in Africa. Amelie Rives was a successful novelist and friend of Oscar Wilde who sent to her in January of 1889 his fairy tales "written, not for children, but for childlike people from eighteen to eighty."

It was Wilde who introduced her to Prince Pierre Troubetskoy at a London party when he decided that the two most attractive people there should meet one another. Amelie Rives Chanler married on 18 February 1896, at "Castle Hill," **Prince Pierre Troubetskoy,** born Milan, Italy, 19 April 1864, son of Prince Pierre Troubetskoy and his second wife, American lyric singer **Ada Winans** (see her separate entry). Although he was not married, Prince Pierre previously had a daughter, Alexandra, in 1894, who in 1917 married Prince Sergei A. Timashev. Prince Pierre Troubetskoy and his two brothers were legitimated after their father finally obtained a divorce from his first wife in 1870 and married American Ada Winans, whom he had met when he was sent on a diplomatic mission to Florence. The senior Troubetskoys lived at Villa Ada on Lake Maggiore in Italy (Prince

Pierre's brother, Paul 1866-1938, was an accomplished sculptor whose many subjects included Mr. and Mrs. Willie K. Vanderbilt, Jr. in 1910). Prince Pierre painted portraits of Gladstone (in the National Gallery in Edinburgh and the National Portrait Gallery in London), the Marquess of Dufferin and Ava (in Town Hall, Dover, England), as well as several U. S. corporate executives after he moved to the U. S. in 1896.

Amelie was formally presented at the Russian Court in 1908. She and Prince Pierre lived at her family home, "Castle Hill," in Viriginia, where the servants called him "Mr. Prince." Her former husband continued to support them financially with an annual allowance and also paid her recurring bills for "nervous exhaustion" (he lived nearby in another crumbling mansion where he shot and killed the abusive husband of a woman who took refuge in his house).

Amelie wrote at least four volumes of fiction, numerous uncollected poems, and a verse drama, *Herod and Marianne,* in 1889. Her most popular novel, *The Quick or the Dead?*, written the year of her first marriage, sold an unprecedented 300,000 copies and was considered very risqué for its time. In 1908 Prince Pierre wrote a novel, *The Passer-By,* in which he satirized the thinly-disguised social leaders of New York and tried to explain the fascination for American women of old-world men such as himself. At the time he was quoted as saying that, "the American woman of society is simply starving for romance." He and his wife collaborated on a play, *Allegiance,* in 1918. In 1920 Amelie's play, *The Fear Market,* was filmed as a silent movie. Prince Pierre died on 25 August 1936, and Amelie was too weak and ill to attend his funeral when his body was carried by a farm wagon in a wooden coffin covered with pine boughs. Amelie followed him on 15 June 1945, having spent her last several years confined to bed. Her weight had declined to only eighty pounds although some said she kept her beauty till the end. There were no children. Amelie was buried at "Castle Hill" and is still said to haunt her former suite of rooms.

Surrender

by Amelie Rives

Take all of me,--I am thine own, heart, soul,

Brain, body--all; all that I am or dream

Is thine for ever; yea, though space should teem

With thy conditions, I'd fulfil the whole--

Were to fulfil them to be loved of thee.

Oh, love me!--were to love me but a way

To kill me--love me; so to die would be

To live for ever. Let me hear thee say

Once only, "Dear, I love thee"--then all life

Would be one sweet remembrance,--thou its king:

Nay, thou art that already, and the strife

Of twenty worlds could not uncrown thee. Bring,

O Time! my monarch to possess his throne,

Which is my heart and for himself alone.

Elizabeth Reid Rogers, born Jackson, Tennessee, 17 August 1893, died Cannes, 2 February 1957, was a daughter of Eunice Tomlin

Rogers and attorney Richard Reid Rogers, who was general counsel to the Isthmian Commission on the Panama Railroad and general counsel to the Interborough Rapid Transit Company of New York City. He was military governor of the Panama Canal Zone 1906-1907. His daughter married morganatically as his first wife at Berlin, 14 January 1915, **Prince Christian of Hesse-Phillippsthal-Barchfeld**, born 16 June 1887, died Geneva, Switzerland, 19 October 1971.

She was created by the Grand Duke of Hesse-and-by-Rhine the Baroness of Barchfeld, 14 January 1915, on her wedding day, then Princess of Hesse-Phillippsthal-Barchfeld on 14 November 1921, with the approval of the head of the family for their children to be accorded princes and princesses (in an act recorded by the government of Prussia on 23 June 1920). She was given away at her marriage by James W. Gerard, U. S. ambassador to Germany, who pointed out in his diary that the bride would not be allowed to share her husband's rank, explaining, "When Prince Christian and his wife go out to dinner in Berlin, he is given his rank at the table as a member of a royal house, but his wife is treated on a parity with the wives of all officers holding commissions of equal grade with her husband in the army. As her husband is a Lieutenant, she ranks merely as a Lieutenant's wife." Her rank improved dramatically when she was styled as Princess von Hesse several years after the marriage. Elizabeth and the prince lived in the Chateau de Rotenbourg in Paris.

Their children were Princess Elizabeth, Prince Richard Christian, Prince Waldemar (who married American **Ellen Hamilton**) and Princess Marie-Louise. They lived in Switzerland and the United States after the 1918 Revolution and, from 1925, in the Villa Mariposa in the California district of Cannes. At the time of her death, her son, Richard, lived in Mexico and son Waldemar lived in Texas with his Atlanta-born wife. Daughter Elizabeth married in 1949 Jacques Olivetti. Elizabeth, Princess of Hesse-Phillippsthal-Barchfeld, died at sixty-four in 1957 at her villa in Cannes to which both sons traveled for their mother's funeral. After his wife's death, Prince Christian married a Tasmanian and had another son, Prince Heinrich Christian. Prince Christian's elder brother, Prince Chlodwig, succeeded his distant cousin as Landgrave of Hesse-Philippsthal in 1925.

Helena Rubenstein, daughter of Horace Rubenstein and Augusta Silberfeld Rubenstein, was born at Krakow, Poland, on 25 December 1871. She briefly studied medicine in Switzerland and emigrated to Australia in 1902. Helena married first on 7 June 1908, in Sydney, American journalist Edward Morganbesser Titus, by whom she had two sons, Roy and Horace. In Australia she noted that the weather caused women's faces to appear rough and red. She opened a shop in Melbourne where she dispensed her own facial cream and taught women how to care for their skin. In 1908 her sister joined her and assumed management of the shop while Helena went to London with $100,000 to found what would become an international business. In 1911 at a London gallery opening of the sculptor Elie Nadelman, she purchased the entire exhibition to display in her international salons.

Helena and her first husband lived in Paris until World War I necessitated their move to the United States. She opened salons throughout the country and established the phenomenally successful

Helena Rubenstein made her own fortune offering women the promise of beauty. Her second husband was twenty-three years younger than she and held a dubious princely title.

title of his grandmother, born Princess Gourielli. Helena developed a line of male cosmetics in her new husband's name. Her company was enormously successful and she became extremely wealthy. She founded the Helena Rubenstein Pavilion of Contemporary Art in Tel Aviv where her collection of miniature rooms was housed. Salvador Dali painted her portrait in 1943 with her face superimposed upon the side of a cliff.

In 1953 she created the Helena Rubenstein Foundation, stating, "My fortune comes from women and should benefit them and their children, to better their quality of life." She contributed largely to health and medical research issues. In 1959 she went to Moscow as the official representative of the U. S. cosmetics industry at the National Exhibition. She died in New York City, 1 April 1965. Prince Artchil was president of the Georgian Association in

"Day of Beauty" in her shops. Helena and her husband divorced in 1937 and the next year in New York City she married **Prince Artchil Gourielli-Tchkonia** (sometimes spelled Courielli-Tchkonia), born Georgia, 18 February 1895, died New York City, 21 November 1955. Prince Artchil, who was twenty-three years younger than she, had a somewhat tenuous claim to the princely title; he was born a member of the untitled noble Tchkonia family of Guria and at some point took the

America from 1945 to 1947. He died 21 November 1955. Both Helena and Prince Artchil were buried in Mount Olivet Cemetery in Queens, New York, with his inscribed coat of arms, headed by a princely coronet, atop their graves.

Margaret Stuyvesant Rutherfurd, born New York City, 11 November 1892, died Paris, 10 February 1976, was a daughter of Lewis Morris Rutherfurd and his wife, Anne (daughter of Oliver Harriman). She was named for her aunt, the wife of U. S. diplomat Henry White, one of the signers of the Treaty of Versailles, and was called "Paqui" in her family as a diminutive of "Paquerette," a French daisy. Margaret's mother was the second Mrs. William K. Vanderbilt and thus step-mother of Consuelo, formerly Duchess of Marlborough. Margaret first married at her step-father's estate at Deauville, Normandy, in September, 1911, Ogden Livingston Mills, later secretary of the treasury, only son of Mr. and Mrs. Ogden Mills. They were divorced at Paris in May of 1920, and in October of 1922, she married **Sir Paul Dukes,** English author and lecturer, who had been knighted for his work as head of the British Secret Service in Russia. He was an avid proponent of Tantric which some described at the time as "spiritual sex." Margaret and her sister, Barbara Rutherfurd (Mrs. Cyril Hatch), were followers of a yoga cult led by "Dr. Pierre A. Bernard" (actually born Peter Coon, 1875-1955), usually referred to as "the Omnipotent Oom." He purchased an estate at Nyack, fifteen miles up the Hudson River from New York City, and established a commune that advocated free love and the worship of the Hindu goddesses of female energy. One of his largest financial supporters was Margaret's mother, Mrs. William K. Vanderbilt, who reportedly asked him to find husbands for her two daughters, both of whom were recently divorced. It was he who introduced Sir Paul Dukes, then a follower of yoga, to Margaret. They were married in an elaborate Tantric ceremony after being carried into the room in coffins (representing the death of their old lives).

After their wedding Margaret took to the New York stage, appearing

Margaret Rutherfurd was called "Paqui" by her family. She was a step-sister of Consuelo, Duchess of Marlborough, and married a succession of high-profile husbands.

Left: Prince Charles Murat, whom Paqui married twice. Right: Sir Paul Dukes, Paqui's second husband, was a British secret agent in Russia.

immediately begin buying an additional waterfront estate as well as adding substantial acreage to his compound. Barbara's new husband attempted to have her committed to an insane asylum in order to take control of her fortune but she and her sister both escaped their marriages with hasty divorces. Years later Oom was quoted as telling reporters who asked him about the million dollars he supposedly was given, "A million bucks! Out of the Vanderbilts! If I could do that I wouldn't be a mystic – I'd be a magician!"

Before Margaret's divorce from Sir Paul Dukes, there were persistent rumors that she was to marry Prince Charles Murat as soon as she was free to do so. Margaret married at the Church of St. Francois the Saviour in Paris on 9 July 1929, **Prince Charles Murat,** born Paris, 16 June 1892, died Mohammedia,

under her maiden name, Margaret Stuyvesant Rutherfurd. She studied dancing with the Diaghlieff troupe in London, Paris, and Monte Carlo. Her sister, Barbara, was married to the Omnipotent Oom's former partner in crime who was using a pseudonym to avoid the disclosure of his past. At the time, it was rumored that the pseudo-Doctor had received $400,000 from Margaret, $250,000 from Barbara, and another $400,000 from their mother for his services. One source insists that Mrs. Vanderbilt only loaned Oom $200,000 and was grateful to receive a $70,000 repayment. Whether true or false, he did

Morocco, 1973, third son of Prince Joachim Napoleon Murat, a direct descendant of the sister of Napoleon I. Margaret's witnesses included Jacques Balsan, husband of her step-sister, Consuelo Vanderbilt, while the groom's witnesses were his brother, Prince Joachim, and the Duke of Elchingen. They were divorced in 1939 and Margaret then married the artist Frederick Leybourne Sprague that November in Lynbrook, Long Island. After a final divorce, Margaret remarried Prince Charles Murat in New York City in 1945 and they lived on a nine-acre estate in Connecticut. He died in 1973 followed by Margaret in 1976.

Katherine "Kay" Linn Sage, born Watervliet, New York, 25 June 1898, died 7 January 1963, was a daughter of state senator Henry M. Sage of Albany, New York, president of his family's Sage Land and Improvement Company in Albany, which owned timber land in Michigan, Alabama, and California. His grandfather was a pioneering founder of Bay City, Michigan, and an early benefactor of Cornell University. The philanthropist Russell Sage was a member of their family. Their estate, Fernwood, is now a park owned by the village of Menands, New York. In 1923 she and her sister, Ann, toured Europe with their free-spirited mother and moved to Rapallo, Italy, to study art. She became a proficient artist and was particularly adept at painting portraits. She married on 31 March 1925 in Rome, **Don Ranieri Bourbon del Monte, 5th Prince of San Faustino,** whose mother was the American-born Jane Campbell. The service was held at the Church of San Tandrea, next to the Quirinal Palace, and was officiated by Cardinal Lega. It was said that "the entire body of Roman aristocracy" was present, along with the American ambassador, who escorted the bride down the aisle, and the staff of the American embassy. She later called the social world she entered as a young bride "a stagnant swamp." There were no children and the marriage was annulled on 18 June 1939, less than three weeks before he married American **Lydia Bodrero.**

Katherine Sage retook her maiden name and remained in Italy to pursue her interest in art. She became a close friend of the writer Andre Breton, artist Giorgio de Chirico, and other members of the surrealist school. Working as "Kay Sage," she became so accomplished that

Kay Sage turned her back on her former social world and became a committed surrealist artist.

Time magazine in 1950 called her "one of this country's most talented dream-scapists." She moved to Paris where she became associated with the Surrealist movement. In 1937 she began a relationship with artist Yves Tanguy (1900-1955) and they were married in Reno, Nevada, on 17 August 1940. After the war the couple moved to Woodbury, Connecticut, where both worked from their studio. They enjoyed a successful 1954 joint exhibition of their work at the Wadsworth Atheneum. Her husband died in 1955 and his widow's once-witty poetry then took on a decidedly dark edge. Sage spent much of her time defending the work of her late husband whom she called, "perhaps the only true Surrealist – almost like a medium." Her 1959 suicide attempt failed. Increasing blindness (several eye operations were unsuccessful) forced her to give up painting and she contented herself with producing several volumes of poetry. On 8 January 1963, just three days after Tanguy's birthday, Sage took her own life with a gun. A few months later, when the *New York Times'* art critic reviewed the spring galleries, he made only a passing reference to her, noting that "Kay Sage, a leading surrealist and widow of Yves Tanguy, died tragically on January 7th."

Adele Livingston Sampson, born New York City, 23 August 1841, died Paris, 13 August 1912, was a daughter of Adele Livingston Sampson and of Joseph Sampson, a wealthy Connecticut manufacturer and one of the founders of Chemical Bank. Adele was immensely wealthy and grew up in the family mansion at Broadway and Bond Street. Her first marriage, on 8 October 1862, to attorney Frederic William Stevens was remarked upon in New York society because of his lack of funds (the *New York Times* sniffed that as he was "a young lawyer with briefs yet to be won, and no hopes of family inheritance, his company was desired and sought for his excellent position, engaging qualities and handsome appearance and not for his possessions."). His bride, according to the same source, "while one of the great heiresses of the day was comparatively little known in society." The groom's mother was a daughter of Albert Gallatin, secretary of the U. S. treasury.

The new couple had four children and entertained lavishly, particularly after Adele's father died, leaving her almost all his vast fortune. They built a palatial home at the corner of 57th Street and Fifth Avenue where they imported an entire room from Ghent, Belgium, where it had been in use for more than a century. The house later became known as the residence of Secretary Whitney. Adele had been a student at the Prior School for Girls in Pelham Manor, New York, and maintained a love for the school for the rest of her life. When the owners sold its Bolton Priory, Adele purchased it in 1883 and gave it as a wedding present for her eldest daughter when she married Frederick H. Allen. It remained in the Allen family for many years. Adele spared no expense in building a Newport mansion, designed by

Adele Sampson was a great heiress of her day but was shunned by society when she left her husband and children for a titled Frenchman who was already married to an American wife.

McKim, Mead and White, where one ball in 1881 became famous for the pyramid of ice built in the dining room through which colored lights were trained during dinner.

The next year, however, Adele was quietly dropped from invitation

lists when it was learned that she had left her husband and children and traveled to France with the Marquis de Talleyrand-Perigord. He was the husband of Boston-born **Bessie Curtiss** and was considered "short and rather stout and decidedly ordinary-looking, and being moreover supposedly deeply in debt." It was learned that Adele had taken her two youngest daughters with her while leaving her son and eldest daughter with their father. The couple traveled throughout Europe making no effort to hide their relationship and it was said that Adele paid her lover's extensive debts. Paris society was shocked that the marquis would leave his wife and their daughter to join Adele. In 1885 Adele returned to New York City where it was rumored that she attempted to reconcile with her husband. She then traveled to Newport where she planned extensive renovations to her mansion until she learned that no one there would receive her. Bessie Curtiss had, meanwhile, divorced the marquis on 11 August 1886 (their daughter became the Princess Poggio Suasa).

Adele obtained an uncontested divorce and returned to France where, on 25 January 1887, at the American Church in Paris's rue de Berri, she married Maurice, formerly Marquis de Talleyrand-Perigord, but then the **4th Duke of Dino,** born 25 January 1843, third son of the Marquis de Talleyrand-Perigord. It was said at the time that he signed an agreement ensuring that she and her children would maintain complete control over her fortune. His father, in anticipation of inheriting the title of Duc de Sagan, bestowed upon his son his own title of Duc de Dino "in honor of his bride," the new duchess. He was the 4th holder of the title, born in 1843. Adele's dowry was

reported to be $3 million. The couple divorced in Paris, 3 April 1903, and had no children. The duke died in 1917.

Adele returned to her former married name and lived both in Pelham, New York, and in Paris, where she died. By her first husband, Adele's children included Frances Gallatin Stevens, who married Count Charles A. de Galliffet and then Count Maurice des Monstiers-Merinville of Paris, and Mabel Ledyard Stevens who married Count Micislas Orlowska of Paris. Frances's daughters, Marguerite de Galliffet, married Count Jehan de Jouffray-Gonsans, and Jacqueline de Galliffet married Count Gabriel de Mortemart. Mabel's daughters, Rose Orlowski, married Count Christian d'Anglau and Dorothee' married Count Alexandre Ledochowsk. Jacqueline de Galliffet de Mortemart's granddaughter, Letitia, married Cyril, Prince Wolkonsky. Adele's first husband, Frederic W. Stevens, surprised his friends and family by marrying his nurse, a Miss Seeley, in 1904. He was sixty-eight and his bride was thirty-five, although his family, who opposed the match, assured society that Miss Seeley "is reported to be of an excellent family." At Adele's death in 1912, her estate of more than $1 million was divided equally among her children. The title is now extinct, the last holder being the daughter of American-born **Anna Gould.**

Peggy Thompson Schulze, born New York City, 11 June 1921, daughter of Theodore Schulze and Margaret Thompson Schulze (later Mrs. Anthony J. Drexel Biddle), married as his first wife, at Paris, 14 October 1939, **Prince Alexander Hohenlohe-Schillingsfurst,** born Bern, 16 February 1918, died Delray Beach, Florida, 9 January 1984, son of

Peggy Schulze's mother, Margaret Thompson Schulze, who was Mrs. Anthony J. Drexel Biddle when this photograph was taken, was one of the wealthiest women in America.

Prince Alfred Hohenlohe-Schillingsfurst and his first wife, **Catherine Britton,** an American. She was often referred to as "Princess Peggy." Her mother, Margaret, was one of the wealthiest women in America. She was born in Helena, Montana, to Col. and Mrs. William Boyce Thompson, who built a fortune developing South African diamond mines and western U.S. copper mines. He accumulated many millions before he was forty and, in 1917, he was sent to Russia by President Wilson (under the guise of an appointment as lieutenant colonel in the American Red Cross) to ensure that the Russians would stay in the war and not negotiate a separate peace with Germany. He urged the U. S. recognition of the new Soviet Union and, when Washington delayed, he successfully wired J. P. Morgan for $1 million to support the provisional government. Thompson was an active philanthropist, treasurer of the national Republican Party, and was appointed by President Harding as U. S. envoy extraordinary to the centennial celebration of Peruvian independence. He sold stocks heavily after the Wall Street crash of 1929 and his net worth was reduced to $100 million. At his death in 1930 at their home in Yonkers, New York, Peggy and her mother shared Thompson's remaining $85 million estate. His greatest legacy was the Boyce Thompson Institute for Plant Research near Yonkers, New York, which eventually moved to the Ithaca campus of Cornell University. He also endowed the oldest and largest botanical garden in Arizona, which bears his name.

Thompson's daughter had first married New York banker Theodore M. Schulze, Peggy's father, and they divorced in 1931. In that year she married Anthony J. Drexel Biddle Jr., in a London registry office.

Biddle's diplomatic career began in 1935 as minister to Norway, then ambassador to Poland in 1937. They were in Warsaw when it was bombed by the Germans. The Biddles withdrew to London where he was named ambassador and minster to governments-in-exile. The Biddles divorced in 1945. She remained active in relief work during the War, writing *The Women of England* concerning her activities; royalties were given to the British War Relief. She died in Paris, 8 June 1956, at fifty-eight, having attended a gala performance of the opera the evening before in honor of King Paul and Queen Frederika of Greece. Her funeral in Paris was attended by the current and future supreme allied commanders in Europe as well as three premiers of France.

Peggy's son is the current heir to the titles. Prince Alexander and Peggy divorced and, in October of 1950, she married the singer Morton Downey. President and Mrs. Kennedy were the summer guests of Mr. and Mrs. Downey at Cape Cod in 1962. At the time Mr. Downey was president of the Coca-Cola Bottling Co. of New Haven, Connecticut. Her father's home, the Boyce Thompson estate overlooking the Hudson River in New York State, was given to Elizabeth Seton College by Mrs. Downey after she converted to Catholicism. By Prince Alexander, she had Princess Catherine and Prince Christian, both of whom married Americans and live in the U.S. Peggy's husband, Prince Alexander, married second, at Greenwich, Connecticut, in May of 1951, **Patricia "Honeychile" Wilder,** born Macon, Georgia, 8 September 1918, died New York City, 11 August 1995, a singer who frequently appeared on the Ed Sullivan Show. Mrs. Downey, the former Princess Peggy, died at forty-two

at her home at 640 Park Avenue, New York City, on 21 May 1965.

Laura Schwarz, born Los Angeles, California, 1 September 1883, was the wife of Robert A. Rowan who founded a construction company in Los Angeles in 1905. By the time of his death in 1918, its great financial success had transformed the skyline of Los Angeles. His widow married in Deauville, July 1924, as his second wife, **Domenico, 8th Prince Orsini, 10th Prince di Solofra, 9th Prince di Vallata, 6th Prince di Roccagorgo, Count de Muro,** born Rome, 7 November 1868, died Rome, 21 March 1947. She moved to Europe with her four children but required annual visits to her family in Pasadena, California, so that they would remain familiar with their American heritage. Domenico, Prince Orsini, returned to Italy from the U. S. shortly after the liberation of Rome. He held the office of prince assistant to the pontifical throne, the highest lay dignity of the Roman curia which is jointly held by the Orsini and Colonna families. At his death, his son, Prince Virgilio, was in the U. S. and immediately inherited his father's post at the Vatican. His children, including a son, were by his first wife. He died 21 March 1947, in Rome, at the age of seventy-nine with his wife, Laura, and his daughter, Isabella, at his side. Robert Rowan Jr., entered Oxford but returned to the States in 1931 at the death of his uncle, Duffy Schwarz, who had been president of Rowan and Company. The younger Rowan was an active art collector and became one of the best-known connoisseurs of modern art. He helped create the Pasadena Art Museum and was one of the founders of the Museum of Contemporary Art in Los Angeles. The majority of his priceless collection was left to Oakland's Mills

College Art Museum at his death in 1995.

Laura Schwarz Rowan, later Princess Orsini, had a daughter by her first marriage, Lorraine, who first married Robert McAdoo, then Thomas H. Shevlin, before marrying John Sherman Cooper at her mother's home in Pasadena. Cooper served for twenty years as a U. S. senator from Kentucky before being appointed as ambassador to India and to East Germany. As his wife, Lorraine Cooper became a well-known and influential hostess and was considered a great ally and partner of her husband. She was one of five women profiled in David Heymann's 2003 book, *The Georgetown Ladies' Social Club: Power, Passion, and Politics in the Nation's Capital.*

Rosalie Dorothea Selfridge, born Chicago, 10 September 1893, was a daughter of Rose Buckingham Selfridge and Harry Gordon Selfridge (1858 - 1947), founder of Selfridge's Department Stores. Selfridge started as a delivery boy, then clerked in a store until given a letter of introduction to the owners of Chicago's highly-successful Field-Leiter Company (Marshall Field's daughter would become Countess Beatty while Levi Leiter's daughters were the Marchioness of Curzon and the Countess of Suffolk and Berkshire). Selfridge began with a job in the basement storeroom and became so successful that he eventually rose to partner. He sold his interests in 1903 and indulged his taste for travel, eventually settling in London. There in 1909

Left: Department store founder Gordon Selfridge with his wife and daughter, Rosalie. Right: Prince and Princess Wiasemsky's daughter, Tatiana, always had Russian bodyguards.

he opened the highly successful department store bearing his name, where he was credited with the admonition, "The customer is always right." He was also the first to advertise the number of shopping days left until Christmas. In 1927 he bought out his largest rival and became the owner of one of the four largest store chains in the world, employing thirteen thousand people operating $50 million worth of stores throughout Britain. He eventually won the social acceptance he so craved and, in 1937, became a British citizen.

His daughter, Rosalie, married on 7 August 1918, in London, **Serge de Bolotoff, Prince Wiasemsky,** who was reportedly an advisor to filmmaker Alexander Korda. He was an aviation enthusiast who claimed to be the fifth person ever to fly in an airplane. The couple honeymooned in the south of France, then made their home in both

Left: Tatiana de Bolotoff-Wiasemsky would marry the son of a New Mexico silver mine owner. Right: Violette Selfridge married the aviator Viscount Jacques de Sibour.

London and in New York City. In 1921 Harry Gordon Selfridge purchased the lease of stately Lansdowne House in Berkeley Square and imported his aged mother to act as chatelaine, his wife having died in the tragic flu pandemic of 1918 (he also leased Highcliffe Castle near Bournemouth). It was at Lansdowne House that Lord Rosebery, then prime minister of England and the House's tenant, gave a great ball in honor of Queen Victoria's first jubilee, at which four sovereigns were present. Selfridge used the House to his advantage when his younger daughter, **Violette Selfridge,** born in Chicago on 2 June 1897, married on 19 February 1921 the aviator **Viscount Jacques de Sibour.** The ceremony was held at the Brompton Oratory and

Lansdowne House was opened for the reception that featured a large wedding cake topped with an exact replica of the groom's airplane.

In 1925 Rosalie's husband, Serge de Bolotoff, was accused by his detractors (including unnamed members of his own family) of having no right to bear the title of "prince." He attributed the charge to those who wished to cause political intrigue because of his efforts as chairman of the council of the Russian National Progressive Party. His wife added, "As my husband says, it is made for political ends." On 19 February 1926, Rosalie's youngest sister, **Beatrice Selfridge,** born 30 July 1901, married in London **Viscount Louis de Sibour,** eldest brother of her sister's husband, Jacques. The ceremony at St. James's Church, Spanish Place, attracted an impressive list of guests, including Princess Marie Louise, at least twenty peers, Prince and Princess Imeretinsky, and the French ambassador. The reception that followed at the bride's father's home, Lansdowne House, was the pinnacle of his social existence. At one time, his fortune was estimated at $40 million but he died in 1947 with only $6,176 in his estate. As the *New York Times* said at his death, Selfridge "spent a lifetime making up for the unkindliness of Providence, which brought him into this world in Ripon, Wisconsin, in the mid-nineteenth century, instead of in London when Elizabeth was queen."

Selfridge had well-publicized affairs with the famous Dolly sisters, who were Hungarian-born American actresses, and with decorator Syrie Maugham. He gambled heavily, gave lavish presents he could not afford, and was finally denied access to the store that bore his name, even though he had walked its floor three times every day while he was its head. He died a broken man living alone in a rooming house.

Rosalie and Prince Wiasemsky had a daughter, Tatiana Rosemary de Bolotoff-Wiasemsky, who married Craig Wheaton-Smith, and had a daughter and two sons. Tatiana's mother-in-law, Ernestine Wheaton-Smith, was the only child of Sir Ernest Craig, first (and last) baronet, who, from 1895 to 1911, owned and operated the Last Chance Mine in Mogollon, New Mexico, near Silver City before returning to England and a political career. Serge de Bolotoff, Prince Wiasemsky, died in London in 1955 and is buried at Putney Vale Cemetery, where he was joined by his wife, Rosalie, in 1978.

Conchita Sepulveda, born Mexico City, 2 May 1888, was a daughter of Ygnacio Sepulveda (born in Los Angeles, California 1842; died 1916), a Harvard-educated lawyer who served in the California assembly before his appointment as one of only two Los Angeles superior court judges, and of Erlinda de la Guerra. Sepulveda's family had been granted the lands of Santa Monica, California, at the end of the eighteenth century. Conchita was born in Mexico City where her father worked for the Wells Fargo Company and managed the business affairs of William Randolph Hearst. They were still living in Mexico during the 1911 revolution against Diaz, and her family knew many of the prominent Mexican leaders. Los Angeles's Sepulveda Boulevard is named for the family. Conchita married on 11 November 1916, Charles Henry Chapman, an Amherst graduate who was in the oil business in Los Angeles. They had at least one daughter, Conchita, and he died there, 7 May 1925. Conchita then married in Los Angeles, California, on 1 March

1929, **Prince Valerio Pignatelli di Cerchiara,** born 18 March 1886, died 6 February 1965, whose first wife, his cousin Maria-Gloria Aragona-Pignatelli-Cortes de Terranova, died after two years of marriage. Prince Valerio was decorated for heroism in World War I and in the War of Ethiopia. During World War II he was captured and imprisoned at Livorno. He wrote several historical books featuring a Pignatelli hero. Conchita was the society columnist for Hearst's *Los Angeles Examiner* for thirty years and knew Mussolini in Italy, Franco in Spain, and General MacArthur in Japan. She and Prince Valerio had a daughter, Stefanella, who married Joseph Werner of St. Louis. Conchita's marriage to Prince Valerio was annulled by the church, 24 January 1940, and he married in 1942 Maria (of the counts of Elia), whose father, Admiral Elia, invented the "Bollo" torpedo. Conchita died in Los Angeles, 6 July 1972, and was buried with her parents at the Santa Barbara mission.

Helen Seton, born New York City, 25 February 1893, died Noyal, 23 November 1983, was a daughter of Mr. and Mrs. Alfred Seton (Mary Lorillard Barbey) of New York City, granddaughter of Mr. and Mrs. Henry Barbey, and great-granddaughter of Pierre Lorillard, founder of Tuxedo Park, New York. She married in Paris's Seventh Ward City Hall on 21 October (civil) and at Paris's Church of St. Clotilde on 24 October (religious) 1933, **Auguste de Goyon, fourth Vicomte and Baron de Goyon and 4th Duc de Feltre,** born LaRoche-Goyon Castle, 17 July 1884, died Paris, 9 March 1957. He succeeded to his father's titles in 1930 and lived in Paris and at the Chateau de la Roche-Goyon at Cotes-du-Nord in Normandy. The founder of the Feltre line was a descendant of an Irish family who settled in France

Helen Seton was a Lorillard heiress who married the Duc de Feltre at the age of forty and produced an heir at forty-two. She is pictured here in 1915 shopping at a toy bazaar.

and was created Duc de Feltre by Napoleon in 1808. Upon his son's death in 1852, the title became extinct. The third Vicomte de Goyon, father of Auguste, was a Feltre descendant on his mother's side and had the title revived in his favor in 1864. Helen's Barbey aunts were the Baroness Andre' de Neuflize and the Countess de Jumilhac. Helen's son, Michel, succeeded his father as 5th Duc de Feltre and married in New York City as his first wife in 1965, American **Barbara Ann Baker,** born Milwaukee 1940, daughter of Paul W. Baker. They had a son and daughter (she was born in Kansas City) and divorced in 1978.

Theodora Mary Shonts, born in Washington, D.C., 21 March 1882, died in Paris, 19 October 1966, was a daughter of Amelia "Milla" Drake Shonts and of Theodore P. Shonts, president of the Clover Leaf Railroad, which acquired in 1907 the Chicago and Alton Railroad. He was also chairman of the Isthmian Canal Commission that built the Panama Canal. For the last twelve years of his life he was president of New York City's Interborough Rapid Transit Company and, at his death in 1919, all subways and trains in New York City were brought to a one-minute stop in his honor.

Theodora's maternal grandfather was General Francis M. Drake, fifteenth governor of Iowa where Drake University was named in his honor. Theodora and her sister, Marguerite, graduated from the fashionable Mount Vernon Seminary near Washington, D.C., and finished their education in Europe. In November of 1906 there was a Paris announcement of the engagement of Theodora Shonts to **Emmanuel, 9th Duke of Chaulnes and of Picquigny, Marquis**

of Dangeau, born in Paris, 10 April 1878, died in Paris, 23 April 1908. The would-be groom announced the engagement himself after his cousin's wife, the Duchess de Luynes, supposedly arranged the marriage. He was forced to repudiate the announcement when Theodora's father denied that his daughter was engaged.

There followed months of media speculation as the duke traveled to the U. S. to visit his purported fiancee' in Washington and to become acquainted with her father who continued to oppose the match even though Mrs. Shonts and her other daughter were said to be in its favor. Five months later, the young man's sister, the Duchess d'Uzes, came to plead her brother's case. The next month the young suitor came to stay with the Shonts family who again denied that a marriage would take place. In September he attempted to sail to Europe on the same ship as the Shonts family but his luggage made it aboard with his English valet while he somehow mistakenly traveled on a different ship.

In November of 1907, Mr. Shonts was finally convinced to allow his daughter to marry the duke when the groom agreed to waive any claim to a dowry, although that concession was generally disbelieved by the media who reflected the opinion of Paris society. The *New York Times* immediately stated that the future groom had a "much-encumbered estate" but was "the gayest of Parisian boulevardiers, and a spendthrift who has already run through two fortunes." His father died when the boy was only two, followed by his widow, the beautiful Princess Sophie Galitzine, who had brought her own family wealth to her marriage and only survived her husband by two years (their two

Theodora Shonts had to convince her father that she should marry a duke. In the end, she should have followed his advice.

young children were reared by their aunt, the Duchess de Luynes). The bride's mother enthused that the groom "thought America offered a splendid opportunity for self-development." She was of the opinion that, "When there is a great affection on the part of the woman and true love on the part of the man, much can be accomplished....I think affection can accomplish almost everything." Only a few society wags were quick to point out that the young duke had earlier been engaged to American heiress Eva Gebhard who reputedly paid some of the young man's bills (Eva married instead in 1917 the Baron Gourgaud). The duke returned to the United States in January of 1908 in preparation for the wedding and stayed in a Washington hotel while his fiancee' and her sister were guests of Mr. and Mrs. Richard R. Rogers, chairman of the Panama Canal Commission, whose own daughter, **Elizabeth Rogers,** would marry in 1915, **Prince Christian of Hesse-Phillippsthal-Barchfeld** and eventually become styled "Princess von Hesse."

Theodora Shonts finally married her duke in New York City at the Shonts home on East 35th Street on 15 February 1908, in a ceremony performed by the rector of St. Patrick's Cathedral. Several hundred guests were kept waiting when the elevator became lodged between floors. The bride's gown was designed by Worth of Paris and she wore a veil that had been ordered by Leopold, King of the Belgians, for the ill-fated Princess Stephanie when she married Rudolph, crown prince of Austria (who took his own life in 1889 in a double-suicide pact with his mistress). The impressive guest list included President and Mrs. Roosevelt, Vice President and Mrs. Fairbanks,

Top: Mr. and Mrs. Theodore Shonts are in the center. The man without a hat is the 9th Duke of Manchester, husband of American heiress Helena Zimmerman.

Bottom: Theodore Shonts was responsible for building the Panama Canal.

Theodora Shonts and friend at the Cedarhurst Cup horse show.

the Speaker of the House, several ambassadors, the chief justice and other Supreme Court justices, generals, cabinet members (including Attorney General Charles Bonaparte, great-nephew of Napoleon I), and many well-recognized figures of society. Every dress and flower arrangement was reported in detail and the guest list was provided to eager members of the media. On the night before the wedding Mr. Shonts took several of his foreign guests on a private railcar to visit Niagara Falls. After the wedding ceremony the couple left on an extended honeymoon beginning in Mobile, Alabama, where the Shonts family owned a home, and continued to Palm Beach. They announced their plans to sail for Europe in the spring and to live on both continents. Society leader Frederick Townsend Martin took the opportunity to entertain at a tea and musicale the groom's sister, the Duchess d'Uzes, whom he had known well in Paris, and introduced her to one hundred of New York society's finest members.

Within five weeks of the well-publicized wedding, a Paris tailor sued the groom for non-payment of bills owed to him since 1901. Only two weeks later, on April 12, the young couple made its Paris debut at the Opera where society leaders openly strained to catch a glimpse of this new American import. It seemed that Theodora, the young Duchess, had finally reached the prize that had so long eluded her. Two weeks later, it was all over. On April 24 the groom died in what was generally believed to be a morphine overdose although it was reported as a heart attack. He had long been a morphine addict and was said to have gone on a particularly excessive binge just before his wedding trip. An autopsy was conveniently waived. The bride's father had only that morning received letters from his daughter assuring him of her happiness. Mr. Shonts had recently arranged for his son-in-law to be named European agent for both the Erie Railroad and Wells-Fargo.

While the bereaved young widow retired to the family's country seat consoled by the Duchess de la Rochefoucauld (the American-born **Mattie Mitchell**), newspapers immediately revived stories of the dissipation of the Chaulnes family. The *Times* recounted that the young duke's mother "died miserably in a garret at Bellevue after a prolonged and senationsal dispute with the austere Duchesse de Chevreuse over the possession of her children." Having already pointed out that the young duke "had been financially embarrassed before his wedding with the American heiress," the newspaper then insisted that, while the duke's many creditors were elated at his marriage, they then learned that "under a regime of separation of property, his personal fortune has not been augmented." Finally, they hoped that the young widow's title, "which has weighed so heavily on certain women of the younger branches of the Luynes, may be lightened for her." Their restraint, however, did not prevent their printing that the young duke's body was found with "bottles containing cocaine, ether, and morphine." The widow's family immediately joined her in France where her father insisted that his son-in-law had died of a heart malady and that he had "feared for his daughter's reason for a time." If Theodora thought that she could leave her husand's family behind,

she was mistaken, for she learned a short time after his death that she was pregnant. Their son, Emmanuel, was born 16 November 1908, seven months after his father's death, and immediately succeeded as the 10th Duke of Chaulnes and of Picquigny.

In 1911, Theodora's father wrote to her and to her sister a poignant letter of rebuke chronicling the slights he had endured from his wife and his daughters. He insisted that Theodora's marriage to the duke had been at her mother's insistence and that a similar marriage to a titled husband had been planned for the other daughter, Marguerite, until he intervened. She married instead diplomat Rutherfurd Bingham, son of General Theodore Bingham, a close friend of President Theodore Roosevelt, who wrote in 1908 as New York City's Police Commissioner that, "Hebrews accounted for one-quarter of the city's population, but one-half of it's crime rate...not astonishing given the character of these people." Shonts' letter to his daughters charged that their mother's influence had instilled in them "her perverted ideas of life and have breathed the atmosphere of deceit and hypocricy she everywhere created." He insisted that the final insult was receiving a letter from their mother threatening to publish love letters from him to his mistress, Amanda Thomas, if he did not pay his wife $7,000. Shonts reiterated, however, that he loved both his daughters and wanted to welcome them back into his life, but insisted, "Your mother can get a separation—a divorce—anything she wants. I can never respect her again."

Three weeks before her father's 1919 death, the Duchesse de Chaulnes, who had been visiting her parents in New York City, sailed to France with her son in the belief that her father's health had improved. His will created a firestorm when it was discovered that he had left his wife only $5,000 and a portrait of herself painted by Prince Troubetskoy (husband of American **Amelie Rives**), while his mistress, Amanda Thomas, received everything else, including a valuable three-hundred-acre farm in Bucks County, Pennsylvania, which they had often visted together. Within weeks, Shonts' widow was dispossessed from her Park Avenue apartment when she could not pay rent. She was scheduled to be evicted on Christmas Eve but her daughter, the duchess, announced publicly that she would fight for her mother's rights and would ensure that her mother's rent was paid. Mrs. Shonts stated that her only asset was the $5,000 life insurance proceeds she expected to inherit from her husband's estate. His will specified that, should she contest his wishes, even that amount would be forfeited. Instead she brought a one million dollar alienation of affection suit against Amanda Thomas and sought a court injunction to prevent the woman from realizing any assets of the estate. Although her daughter the Duchess de Chaulnes made a court appearance on her mother's behalf, the courts eventually found against the widow after an earlier decision in her favor.

By the time all litigation was ended, the estate was in debt for more than a half million dollars. It was disclosed publicly that, since 1902, Shonts had paid his wife and each of his two daughters $93,000 per year, later reduced to $45,000 annually. In 1917 he paid a bill of $135,000 for jewelry they purchased in Paris. His mistress, Amanda Thomas, was found to be a respectable woman separated from her husband. She lived in the same apartment building as Shonts and had "been kind" to him in his last illness. She was twenty years his junior and the mother of a son, Herbert, to whom Shonts left the jewelry given to him by the boy's mother. To his grandson, the Duke of Chaulnes, Shonts left his star sapphire pin while his pearl studs were to go to the yet-to-be-born first son of his other daughter, Marguerite. Mrs. Shonts died at a Washington sanitarium in 1933 and was discovered to be insolvent. She was returned to her native Iowa for burial.

Theodora, Duchess de Chaulnes, retreated into obscurity after her father's death. As late as 1915 she was prominently photographed, along with her young son the duke, accompanying her sister and the American-born **Helena Zimmerman**, Duchess of Manchester, at the Homestead in Hot Springs, Virginia. In 1922 she was attached to the retinue of American Mrs. C. P. Wichfeld, heiresss to the Swift meat-packing fortune, when she arrived in London from Paris with eighty pieces of luggage or boxes and was fined one thousand pounds for unpaid duties. Theodora, Duchess de Chaulnes and Picquigny, died in Paris in 1966 having never re-married. Her son never married and, according to a family member, he was unable to have children. At his death in 1980, his titles reverted to his cousin, the Duke de Luynes.

Helen Karr Simpson, born 22 February 1895, daughter of Dr. Elmer E. Simpson and Clara Seacrist Simpson of Chicago, graduated from Vassar in 1918 as an honor student and member of Phi Beta Kappa. She did her graduate work at the University of California the next year and in 1920 spent a year in the Canadian Rockies. While she was a student at Vassar she met **Prince Ladislas Radziwill** of Poland and they later became engaged. They were to be married in Chicago but the prince became very ill and Helen traveled to London where he was hospitalized. On 10 January 1923 they were married while he lay in a hospital bed with pneumonia and the prince died three hours later. The princess then returned to Chicago where she made her home and spent much of her time during the next two years traveling.

On 13 September 1924 she and her brother, Stanley B. Simpson, were in Kineo, Maine, walking about two miles from their hotel in search of a valuable diamond ring she had lost on Mount Kineo, when she fell more than one hundred feet from a cliff on the north slope of Mount Kineo and was killed. Her body was caught in the trees on the face of the cliff and had to be lowered several hundred feet to Moosehead Lake before it could be brought back to the village by boat. Evidently she lost her footing when some earth gave way under her feet at a point where the rock rises almost perpendicularly more than seven hundred feet. Her body was taken to Boston where a solemn high mass of requiem was celebrated at St. James's Roman Catholic Church on 17 September. The mass was celebrated by the Reverend Robert E. Lee, who was at Mount Kineo at the time the Princess met her death. The body was then placed aboard a train where fifteen members of her family accompanied her to Chicago for burial. (*There is no official record of this marriage.*)

Virginia Sinclair, born 1915, was a daughter of Elizabeth Sinclair and of Harry Sinclair (1876 – 1956), the founder of the Sinclair Oil Corporation and chairman of the board of Richfield Oil Corporation. From the time he founded Sinclair in 1916 before he was thirty-five until his retirement, the company's assets grew to more than $1.2 billion and its earnings topped $68 million. He was acquitted of the only criminal charge brought against him in the Teapot Dome oil scandals of the 1920s but served six-and-a-half months in jail in 1929 for contempt of court and contempt of the United States Senate. Secretary of the Interior Albert B. Fall was convicted of accepting a bribe from another oil operator and served one year in prison (popularizing the term, "the fall guy") while Edward Denby was forced to resign his position as Secretary of the Navy over the incident. Sinclair's directors unanimously gave their founder a vote of confidence as he left to begin his sentence. After Sinclair's release, his stockholders expressed their support of him and he continued the spectacular rise of his company. He was also an organizer of the early Federal Baseball League and a part-owner of the St. Louis Browns. He started a racing stable as a hobby and eventually won the Kentucky Derby in 1923.

The Sinclairs lived in a mansion at 2 East 79th Street in New York City. Virginia's mother, Elizabeth, was a concert pianist who became a patron of the Roman Catholic Church after her marriage and was honored by Pope Paul VI with the Cross Pro Ecclesia et Pontifice. Virginia Sinclair married at Las Vegas, Nevada, 18 September 1944, **Prince David Mdivani**, former husband of **Mae Murray**. Mdivani also had a long-standing relationship with the French actress Arletty, known as France's Garbo, best-known for her role in *Children of Paradise*.

Left: Brothers Serge (on the left) and David Mdivani. Their need for cash was real but their title wasn't.

Right: The Sinclair mansion in New York City.

Knowing more than enough about Mdivani's family, Arletty refused to carry his child to full term. David Mdivani and Virginia obtained their marriage license in Las Vegas and stated that he was forty-four and had been married before. She gave her address as Great Neck, Long Island, New York. The Rev. Frederick Lovett, pastor of the Las Vegas Baptist Church, performed the ceremony. The Mdivanis had a son, David. The 435-foot tanker merchant ship *S.S. Virginia Sinclair* was torpedoed in World War II on 10 March 1943 and seven of its crewmembers were killed. Prince David Mdivani died in Los Angeles on 4 September 1984.

Hazel Singer, born in Chicago, Ilinois, on 25 June 1882, died in Cannes on 8 May 1951, was a daughter of Charles J. Singer of Chicago, a wealthy broker and member of the Chicago Board of Trade as well as the influential Commercial Club. He began as a brokerage partner of Sid Kent and Benjamin "Old Hutch" Hutchinson, whose hard-driving bargaining in everything from pork bellies to wheat futures was well known in Chicago's early industrial days (the philanthropy of his son, Charles L. Hutchinson, president of the Corn Exchange National Bank in Chicago, later did much to erase the memory of his father's business practices). Charles J. Singer was Old Hutch's partner when their firm was able to corner the entire market on wheat futures. Singer later left the firm to become a partner at Schwartz, Dupee & Co., and was supposedly blackmailed in 1886 by an attorney who threatened to make public his part in the wheat scheme, although Singer denied he had actually paid any blackmail money. Singer's daughter, Hazel, married at the Romanian Church in Paris on 19 December 1901, **Prince John (Ioan) Ghyka** (1875 – 1922), son of Alexander Ghyka (1846 – 1902), who was at that time the Romanian minister to France (the father's two brothers were also accomplished diplomats). General Horace Porter, the American ambassador to France, and General Winslow were the bride's witnesses. Her two attendants were Marthe Leishman (who later married Count Louis de Gontaut-Biron) daughter of the then-U.

Left: Prince John Ghyka was a son of the Romanian minister to France. Right: The sultan of Turkey bestowed a decoration on Hazel Singer on her wedding day. She became a well-known hostess to royalty in the south of France.

S. minister to Turkey (and later ambassador to Italy and Germany) and Miss Edith Clarke of New York City. Both the Turkish ambassador and the Austrian ambassador to France attended the ceremony and the sultan of Turkey bestowed a decoration on the bride in honor of the occasion. After a honeymoon the couple went to Romania where he was an officer in a Hussar regiment.

The Ghyka family descended from the Phanariots (from the Greek district of Phanar in Constantinople) who were employed by the early Turks as administrators. They eventually ruled over Moldavia

Natalie Barney was a well-known lover of, among others, Romaine Brooks, the American-born Winnaretta Singer, Princess de Polignac, as well as of Liane de Pougy, who was the wife of Prince George Ghyka.

and Wallachia from 1658 and received a princely title in 1673 in gratification for their alliance with the Habsburg dynasty. They were replaced when the Hohenzollern family united the Romanian provinces in 1859 but the Ghyka family retained their title and some of their lands. The Ghykas dug the first oil wells in their country. Queen Marie of Romania wrote of her friendship with the three Ghyka brothers, including John's father, who were all Romanian ministers at the same time, one in Berlin, one in Vienna, and one in Constantinople (Gregoire was married to a sister of Queen Natalie of Serbia). Queen Marie thought John's father, Alexander, "was the most witty of the three" and wrote that after his son's marriage to Hazel the son "had plenty of money to spend whilst his father was supposed to thrive on debts." Queen Marie also wrote of Romanian society that boasted so many Ghykas that a foreign visitor was introduced to numerous members and decided it must be an honorific of some kind. When he was introduced to a young member of the family, he exclaimed, "So young and already Ghyka!"

Hazel and Prince John had one daughter, Alexandra, who first married at the Romanian Church in Paris on 29 August 1922 the French millionaire industrialist Paul-Louis Weiller (1893 – 1993), who owned the Gnome et Rhone factory (by Weiller's second wife he had a son, Paul-Annik, who married Olimpia Torlonia, granddaughter of American **Elsie Moore** and of Spain's King Alfonso XIII, and they were the parents of Sibilla who married Prince Guillaume of Luxemborg). On 23 February 1924 Hazel Ghyka's granddaughter, Marie-Elisabeth Weiller, was born. The Weillers were divorced on

25 March 1931 and Alexandra's second and third husbands were Claude Raynal and Salvator de Arocha. Weiller purchased for his granddaughter, Pilar, Countess Jacques de la Beraudiere, the former London home of Margaret Thatcher in Flood Street. In 1942 Hazel's daughter, Alexandra, by then married to Claude Raynal, was deprived of her French nationality and relocated to Fallbrook, California. On 29 November 1951, her daughter by her first marriage, Marie-Elisabeth Weiller, married Pedro Irisarri, an architect of Spanish origin, who was a widower with two children.

Hazel, Princess John Ghyka, lived all the year round in the South of France where she received guests such as King Gustav V of Sweden, King Manoel of Portugal, and Grand Duke Dmitri of Russia, and played bridge with the Empress of Vietnam. Among her granddaughters was Claudine (daughter of Claude Raynal) who took her mother's maiden name of Ghyka and graduated from the University of Southern California in 1952. She married food writer Gerald Maurois, son of Andre' Maurois (1885 – 1967), the biographer, novelist, and member of the French Academy. Prince John Ghyka's first cousin, Prince George Ghyka (1884 – 1945), son of Gregoire, married in 1920 Liane de Pougy (1870 – 1950), the openly-bisexual author and courtesan whose most famous relationship was with the wealthy American lesbian Natalie Barney. Later in life she became a tertiary sister of the Order of St. Dominic. Another kinsman of Prince John Ghyka's was Prince Dimitrie Ghyka-Comanesti, who in October of 1925 married Valentina Bibesco (1903 – 1976), only child of the author Princess Marthe Bibesco (1886 – 1973). In a dazzling traditional ceremony, three consorts attended the wedding, creating a protocol puzzle—Queen Mother Sophia of Greece, Princess Consort Aspasia Manos of Greece, and Queen Marie of Yugoslavia (England's Queen Alexandra had attended her parents' high-profile society wedding in London). Valentina and her husband, Prince Dimitrie Ghyka-Comanesti, were released from Romanian custody after nearly nine years of arrest under the Communist regime. They joined her celebrated mother in England where she purchased a home for the couple, Tullimar, in Cornwall.

Isabelle Blanche Singer, born Paris, 27 March 1869, died Paris, 15 November 1896, was a daughter of Isaac Merritt Singer (1811 – 1875), inventor, actor, and founder of the Singer Sewing Machine Company, and of Isabella Eugenie Somerville Boyer Singer. Her mother, Isabella (1841-1904), was twenty-two when she married in New York City the fifty-two-year-old Isaac M. Singer. They were not recognized in society because of his numerous illegitimate children by several women (his total number of children eventually reached twenty-two), so moved to the Oldway Mansion in Paignton, England, on the Devon coast. They had six children: Sir Mortimer (high sheriff of Berkshire), Washington (high sheriff of Wiltshire), Paris (who tried to purchase Madison Square Garden as a dancing venue for his lover, the dancer Isadora Duncan, who had his child; the boy drowned in a freakish car accident that also took the life of his elder half-sister), Franklin (a yachtsman), Winnaretta, and Isabelle.

After Isaac M. Singer's death, his still-beautiful widow married a Belgian musician, Victor Reubsaet, Viscount d'Estemburgh, and

Left: The Singer Building in New York City where the Singer Sewing Machine Company continued to produce huge profits for its founder's large and unorthodox family. Right: An early advertisement for Singer's products.

1864, died Chantilly, 31 August 1912. At their marriage, New York City's *The World* wrote, "What the original cost of the Duke was does not appear, but it is evident already that French noblemen properly married, decorated, appointed, housed and fed are very costly commodities for an American heiress to deal in."

The duke was active as an athlete who participated in the first Algiers-Toulon motorboat race in which his was the only one of eleven entries not sunk in a storm. The first of his titles was French while the second was the only non-royal Danish dukedom. Their son, Louis, succeeded his father as the 4th Duke while their grandson, Count Edouard, married in Richmond, Virginia, 4 November 1950, **Caroline Triplett Taliaferro Scott,** daughter of Thomas Burch Scott Jr.,

with her share of Singer's $14 million estate (of four women by whom Singer had children, she was declared his legal widow) she was able to secure for her new husband the papal title of Duke of Camposelice. They lived in Paris where the new Duchess of Camposelice befriended the sculptor Bartholdi, who used her as the model for the Statue of Liberty. Her youngest daughter, Isabelle, married in Paris, 28 April 1888, **Elie, 3rd Duc Decazes and de Glücksbierg,** born Paris, 30 April

and Caroline Triplett Scott, of Richmond, Virginia (where she still keeps a home). The only daughter of Isabelle and the duke was Marguerite, who became famous as the writer Daisy Fellowes (1890 – 1962). She first married in 1910 Prince Jean de Broglie who died in 1918. Daisy was a novelist, poet, and fashion icon, and was the best-known proponent of the work of fashion designer Elsa Schiaparelli. She was largely raised by her mother's lesbian sister, Winnaretta,

The writer Daisy Fellowes, Isabelle's daughter, was a chief proponent of the fashion designer Elsa Schiaparelli.

Princess Edmond de Polignac. Daisy supposedly caught her first husband in bed with their chauffeur. He died of influenza while serving with the French army in Algeria although some reports insisted that he committed suicide as a result of his wife's discovery of his sexual preference.

They had three daughters: Emmeline, Countess de Casteja (whose mother-in-law was the American heiress **Katherine Garrison**); novelist Isabelle (who married the Marquis de La Moussaye); and Jacqueline. Daisy once said of her three daughters, "The eldest is like her father, only more masculine. The second is like me, only without the guts. And the last is by some horrible little man called Lischmann." Daisy married as her second husband in 1919 the Hon. Reginald Fellowes, a grandson of the 7th Duke of Marlborough, who had a brief affair with **Consuelo Vanderbilt,** wife of his cousin, the 9th Duke. Among Daisy Fellowes's lovers was Duff Cooper, the British ambassador to France. She once informed one of her lovers that she had contracted a venereal disease by calling him on the telephone. When he answered, she said, "I have something to tell you." He then heard three claps of her hands, "Clap, clap, clap." Her sexual appetite was as legendary

as it was varied. She once asked a woman to come to her home to participate sexually in "unspeakably sadistic things." She and another woman opened the door and the visitor was immediately "beaten to a pulp and left in disarray." Only then did they discover that their visitor had come from a shop to fit Daisy for a hat. When the correct woman arrived Daisy and her friend were too exhausted to receive her.

The eldest grandson of Isabelle Singer and her husband was the 5th Duke Decazes, who married Solange du Temple de Rougemont, whose American mother was **Edith Devereaux Clapp.** When their son, Louis Frederic, succeeds as the 6th Duke, he will thus have two bloodlines through American wives. Isabelle was not happy in her marriage with the duke. French society would not receive her because of her father's notoriety and, when the Duke of Orleans was married, she was barred from attending by the Court of Vienna although her husband was present. Isabelle committed suicide in 1896. Her sister, **Winnaretta Singer,** married first, **Prince Louis Scey de Montbeliard,** and second, **Prince Edmond de Polignac.**

Winnaretta Eugenie Singer, born Yonkers, New York, 8 January 1865, died London, 26 November 1943, was a daughter of Isaac Merritt Singer (founder of the Singer Sewing Machine Company; see her sister **Isabelle Singer**) and Isabelle Eugenie Somerville Boyer Singer. She was married on 27 July 1887 at the age of twenty-two, chiefly to escape her step-father's designs on her fortune, to Prince Louis Scey de Montbeliard (although his title was questionable as he was the third son of the Marquis de Scey de Brun so technically

243

Left: Winnaretta was a generous patron of the arts and the source of important commissions of new musical compositions. Right: A younger Winnaretta in the garden with her mother.

Barney, Colette, Romaine Brooks, and she had a long relationship with Violet Trefusis, daughter of Edward VII's favorite mistress, Alice Keppel. Winnie was introduced by a mutual friend, Robert de Montesquiou, to **Prince Edmond de Polignac,** born Paris, 19 April 1834, died Paris, 8 August 1901, youngest son of the 3rd Duke de Polignac. His father was minister of state in the Restoration government of King Charles X and condemned to prison after the July Revolution of 1830. Edmond's mother had liberal rights to visit her husband in prison and Edmond was the youngest child of their union. In 1836 the father was allowed to leave prison if he became a permanent exile, and he and his family moved to Bavaria, where he was granted the rank of prince by the king in 1838. As a young man, Edmond returned to Paris, where he studied music and became a composer of note. He entered a composition contest for a

he was only a count). On their wedding night she climbed atop a wardrobe and struck him with an umbrella when he attempted to consummate their union. Five years later the marriage was still unconsummated and was annulled by the Vatican on 1 February 1892. Winnaretta began to have open sexual relationships with women, although her fortune and her title, which she retained, prevented her from social ostracism. Among her most famous lovers were Natalie

new opera in 1867 and ranked fifth behind Massenet but ahead of Bizet. When he met de Montesquiou, who was twenty-one years his junior, in 1875 he was immediately smitten by the handsome young man. De Polignac was also homosexual and had little money, so his friend's suggestion of a *marriage blanc* with Winnie was one which suited each party. They were married at the Chapelle des Carmes in Paris on 15 December 1893. What de Montesquiou had not counted on was that the couple would become devoted to one another, even if not sexually, to the exclusion of the younger man. The couple became well-known patrons of the arts and appeared together at the 1898 premiere of Faure's *Pelleas et Melisande,* which was dedicated to Winnie. They purchased the Palace de Montecuccoli on the Grand Canal in Venice where they were hosts to a celebrated artistic salon. Edmond died on 8 August 1901 and was buried in the Singer family crypt in England. Winnie's brother, Paris, was the father of Isadora Duncan's child. Duncan wrote of Winnaretta, "She had a handsome face, somewhat marred by a too heavy and protruding lower jaw and a masterful chin. It might have been the face of a Roman emperor, except that an expression of cold aloofness protected the otherwise voluptuous promise of her eyes and features." Duncan thought that her aloof manner was "really a mask to hide, in spite of her princely position, a condition of extreme and sensitive shyness." *Opera News* wrote authoritatively of Winnie, "She was the most princely patron of music since the Counts Esterhazy. Masterpieces by Stravinsky, Satie, and Faure' were composed because of her; she rescued the Diaghilev Ballet from bankruptcy and helped install it in Monte Carlo; she gave Marcel Proust access to the dukes and duchesses of the Faubourg Saint-Germain, thus providing him with raw material for his novel; she gave several paintings to the Louvre, including Manet's controversial nude *Olympia.*" A more profane assessment is Virginia Woolf's comment, "to look at [her] you'd never think she ravished half the virgins in Paris." Similarly, Harold Nicolson said of Winnie, "I have seldom seen a woman sit so firmly. There

Winnaretta is in the center surrounded by friends. At top left in a light suit is her husband, Prince Edmond, while Marcel Proust is in the top center with mustache.

was determination in every line of her bum." Winnie established the Foundation Singer-Polignac, still one of the largest in France, in support of the arts. Winnie's brother, Paris, had a daughter whom he named Winnaretta in honor of his sister. She married Sir Reginald Leeds in 1926. Prince Edmond's brother, Prince Camille de Polignac, volunteered and served as a brigadier general in the Confederate Army where he was attached to the Army of the Tennessee. In Winnie's brief memoirs, she wrote, "I think that originality differs entirely from eccentricity, and I could never see any novelty in any works that combine the dullest and most antiquated technique... thank God, there is no hard and fast rule about the beauty of a Work of

Art." Opinions may differ as to her physical attractions, but Princess Edmond de Polignac, who inspired and gave birth to so many artistic accomplishments, was her own best creation as a work of art. She died in London at the age of seventy-eight on 26 November 1943.

Marian Adair Snowden, born Indianapolis, Indiana, 22 April 1912, was a daughter of Mrs. Walter S. Davidson and her former husband, oil prospector James H. Snowden, who was an early investor in Standard Oil. They lived in New York City, Southampton, and Newport, Rhode Island, where Marion and her younger sister, **Janet Elizabeth Snowden,** enjoyed a high social profile. Their summer home at Southampton, "Heathermere," was robbed of approximately $100,000 of jewels after a "fashionable tableau" was presented there in 1927. They had an eighty-foot yacht, the Sea Horse, which partially burned in 1929 while docked at the Sag Harbor Club. James H. Snowden died in 1931, leaving an estate of approximately $4 million to his two daughters and one son, as well as to his current wife (their mother had another son, Walter S. Davidson Jr., by her second husband).

Only months later, Marian Snowden eloped and married in Rome on 27 November 1931, Girolamo, **7th Prince Rospigliosi-Gioeni, Prince of the Holy Roman Empire, 2nd Prince di Castiglione, 7th Duc di Zagarolo, 2nd Marchese di Giuliana, Count di Chiusa, Baron di Miraglia and di Valcorrente,** born Rome, 27 August 1907, died Marshall's Creek, Pennsylvania, 28 September 1959. They met four months earlier while she was touring Europe. The ceremony was performed at Maccarese in the village church on an estate formerly owned by the groom. His mother was American **Marie Parkhurst,** whose protracted litigation with the Catholic Church was unsuccessful in validating her marriage but civil law allowed her son to inherit his father's titles. The newlyweds honeymooned in Europe and planned to live at the Rospigliosi Palace in Rome even though it was, at the time, leased to the American ambassador. Two months after their wedding the couple sailed from Naples for the U.S, where her mother asked port officials to deny entry to the prince, claiming that he was heavily in debt and relying upon his wife's inheritance to pay his creditors. The Commissioner of Immigration instructed his employees that there were no legal grounds to deny entry to the couple. They took advantage of their visit to have a second marriage ceremony performed by a judge in New York City on 10 February 1932. The princess's next visit to the United States, in 1933, was made without the prince and she responded to reporter's questions by insisting there was no marriage rift although she did admit that they had mounting debts.

In August of 1933, Prince Rospigliosi arrived in the United States accompanied by his cousin, **Don Francesco Caravita, Prince di Sirignano** of Naples, who was an amateur racecar driver. Within twenty-four hours, he had introduced his cousin to **Janet Elizabeth Snowden,** his sister-in-law, and they were immediately married on 17 August 1933 in the offices of the deputy city clerk in New York City without her mother's knowledge or approval. She was nineteen and he was twenty-four and their only witnesses were her sister and brother-in-law, Prince Rospigliosi. Five days later, the bride sought an annulment, claiming that she had known her husband for only a day when they married and had been convinced that he had great wealth and would be providing her a monthly allowance of $300. The initial annulment was granted but was later overturned on appeal in December of that year. Even though the prince did not contest the application, the appellate court found that public policy dictated that the "sacred institution of marriage" should be upheld and that the couple knew what they were doing when they entered into their union. Janet immediately left to join her mother and took advantage of the occasion to announce that she was heading to Hollywood to become a motion picture actress.

Meanwhile Prince Rospigliosi was named vice president of a New York City liquor firm while his debts continued to mount. He and his wife admitted in 1934 (the same year his mother was killed in an auto accident in Naples and his wife was seriously injured in a taxi accident in New York City) to a judgment against them in Italy totaling more than $72,000 and that creditors sought to have one-tenth of her trust income attached to pay the debt. That same year Janet Snowden flew to Mexico to have her earlier marriage to her wayward prince legally ended so that she could wed William Sherman Gill, a former bit actor and newspaper reporter who had been married to early screen actresses Evelyn Farriss and Rene Adoree. They immediately wed in June of 1934 in Ensenada, Mexico. In September of 1935 Marian flew to Reno to seek a divorce from Prince Rospigliosi. When she learned that she would have to establish residency, she then flew to Mexico where she could obtain a divorce in three days. Having successfully ended her marriage, Marian returned to New York City where on

28 May 1936 in Jersey City, New Jersey, she married Louis F. Reed Jr. of Orange, New Jersey (his earlier wife had been Marie Hartford Hoffman, daughter of a wealthy A&P executive, whom he married in 1931 and divorced four years later). Her brother and the groom's brother were both present. The couple then sailed for Bermuda, accompanied by the groom's mother and her new husband, Walter Hoving, president of Lord & Taylor (and later chairman of Tiffany & Company), whom she married the day after her son's wedding.

Eleven months later Marian divorced Reed to marry again. This time the groom was Bradley S. Dresser, son of oil operator Carl K. Dresser and of Mrs. Henry H. Rogers, widow of Col. H. H. Rogers Jr., who was the son of an immensely wealthy Standard Oil pioneer and creator of the Virginia Railroad. Col. Rogers's sister was Cara, Baroness Fairhaven, while his daughter by a previous wife was the beautiful **Millicent Rogers**, who married **Ludwig, Count von Salm-Hoogstraeten.** Again, Marian's marriage ended in a Reno divorce one year later. In 1938 Prince Rospigliosi was involved in a hit-and-run auto accident in New York City while then living at the Hotel Weylin.

On 1 June 1943, Janet Snowden Gill, formerly (albeit briefly) Princess di Sirignano, plunged to her death from the window of her sixteenth-floor apartment at the Savoy-Plaza Hotel in New York City. She was twenty-nine and had three children. According to her husband, he was home on leave from the army visiting his wife. They had packed to travel to Washington when each decided to take a nap in separate rooms. When he awoke, she was gone and a window was open. Gill was on the telephone, evidently trying to reach members of her family to learn where she was, when police arrived at their apartment having found her body below. Although no note was found, police determined that she had either committed suicide or fallen accidentally. Only after her funeral did her mother, brother, and sister convince police to reopen the case. Her body was exhumed and an autopsy performed to determine whether she had been poisoned. The tests were negative and police confirmed their earlier conclusion. At the inquest, however, it was disclosed that Janet planned to marry an unnamed army lieutenant to whom she had written explicit love letters. She had informed her husband of her intent to divorce him and was only in their apartment to discuss custody terms for their three children. Her husband insisted that, on the night of their meeting, he effected a reconciliation and his wife agreed to cancel her divorce plans. Also disclosed at the inquest was the fact that Janet's mother had opposed her daughter's marriage to Gill and had never met him in their ten years of marriage. The autopsy concluded that Janet was alive when she left the apartment window. No charges were filed.

Girolamo, Prince Rospigliosi, formerly the husband of Marian Snowden, married second, in Palm Beach, Florida, 17 June 1946, Jenny Elizabeth Angell, born Norway, 23 November 1907. They lived in Miami Beach and he died near Monroe, Pennsylvania, 28 September 1959. He had no children by either marriage and the titles passed to the son of his first cousin, Giambattista, and his American wife, **Ethel Bronson.**

Eleanor Lorillard Spencer, born New York City, 7 February 1851, died Rome, 6 May 1915, was a daughter of Lorillard and Sarah Griswold Spencer. The very social Spencer family came to America in 1633. Her brother, Lorillard, was president and publisher of *The Illustrated American.* He owned a famous mansion in Newport, "Chastellux," on Halidon Hill, which was later leased by Mrs. Edward Hartford before she became Princess Guido Pignatelli. Eleanor was a granddaughter of Pierre Lorillard, the immensely wealthy tobacco manufacturer for whom the term "millionaire" was first coined for his obituary. Her first cousin was the never-married philanthropist Catherine Lorillard Wolfe, one of the original subscribers to the Metropolitan Museum of Art. Eleanor and her siblings were largely reared in Paris where her family moved in 1867 when she was an impressionable sixteen-year old. She married in Paris on 25 June 1870, **Virginio, 7th Prince di Vicovaro Cenci, Marchese di Rocca Priora, Baron Romano,** born Rome, 16 August 1840, died Lyon, 6 November 1909. His family became well-known because of the public execution in 1598 of Beatrice Cenci, her brother Giacomo, and their mother, Lucrezia, who murdered the father, Francesco Cenci, after his repeated abuse of them, culminating in incest with his daughter, Beatrice. She became a heroine to the lower classes of Rome and was said to return each year on the night before the anniversary of her execution carrying her severed head. The tale inspired writers such as Shelley, Stendahl, and Dumas.

Prince and Princess di Vicovaro Cenci had only a daughter, Princess Beatrice, Marchesa di Rocca-Priora, who was born in Florence in

1877. She lived in Paris and did not marry and the line became extinct in the principal line. Although their daughter was granted the title of marchesa in her own right, a cousin of her father became the 8th Prince di Vicovaro Cenci. Eleanor's reclusive brother, Charles Griswold Spencer, died in Paris in 1906, leaving an estate of more than $2 million. One will left his estate equally to Eleanor and their two brothers, William and Lorillard Jr. (who was married to Madeleine Astor's sister, Katherine), while another left everything to Eleanor. Her attorneys argued that the second will should be honored because it was written in France where Charles was a resident. A lower court agreed but on appeal the decision was reversed when no evidence could be presented that Charles no longer considered himself an American. In fact, his mental capacity was called into question when it was revealed that, in 1895, he telegraphed an announcement of his own death from Paris and later sent another telegram to his brother Lorillard Jr., instructing the brother to commit suicide. The case was not finally terminated until 1908 in a verdict the *New York Times* termed, "a decision which reads like an epitomized version of an Alexander Dumas story, instead of a musty old law decision."

Eleanor's husband died in November of 1909 leaving her, according to the same source, "a magnificent estate in Paris and a country place in Switzerland." She served as lady-in-waiting to Queen Margharita of Italy and died in Rome in May of 1915. When her brother, bibliophile William A. Spencer, died on the Titanic in 1912, leaving an estate of more than $4 million (his wife and their maid were rescued), he left his sister a bequest of $50,000. When Eleanor died, her estate of more than $1 million was left largely to her daughter with strict instructions to her executors "particularly guarding her concerning the persons who surround her." A large bequest also went to the Policlinico, Rome's largest hospital. There is still in Italy an Eleanor Lorillard Spencer Cenci Foundation that grants funds to deserving organizations. Eleanor's daughter, Princess Beatrice, left almost all her fortune to the *Istituto Pasteur-Fondazione Cenci Bolognetti,* a non-profit institution established in 1956 at the University of Rome devoted to scientific research connected with the Institut Pasteur in Paris and the University of Rome.

A Cenci cousin, Prince Alessandro (1888 – 1966), married American **Felicité Oglesby** (1879-1954), daughter of three-time Illinois Governor Richard J. Oglesby, who was a close friend of Abraham Lincoln.

Elizabeth Helen Sperry, daughter of Caroline Elizabeth Barker Sperry and Simon Willard Sperry, founder of the Sperry Flour Mills in Stockton, California, was born in Stockton, California, on 10 June 1872, and died at Les Bories in August of 1911. She married in Paris, 6 October 1894, **Prince Andre' Poniatowski,** (and later) **3rd Prince di Monte Rotondo,** born Paris, 25 January 1864, died Les Bories, 3 August 1954. They were married in Stockton and spent most of their time in San Francisco, where their three sons were born. *Cosmopolitan* magazine wrote in 1899, "The princess has the full enjoyment of her title with all its honors and accessories, yet she lives in her own country, among her own people." Elizabeth's sister, Ethel Sperry Crocker (Mrs. William H. Crocker, whose husband was a son of Charles Crocker), was the mother of Ethel Mary Crocker,

Prince Poniatowski was first engaged to Maud Burke who was to re-create herself as Emerald, Lady Cunard. Elizabeth Sperry and her husband spent much of their time in San Francisco where their sons were born.

who married **Count Andre' de Limur** of Paris.

Prince Andre' Poniatowski considered himself to be Italian but his lineage was Polish. His grandfather was created Prince Poniatowski by the emperor of Austria in 1850 after his birth was legitimized in 1847 - the same year that the grand duke of Tuscany created him Prince di Monte Rotondo. He was master of the horse to Emperor Napoleon III and was descended from the old Lombardy Counts of Tarelli, who emigrated to Poland in 1569. One of his ancestors, Stanislaus Poniatowski, was elected king of Poland in 1767. Andre's father inherited the princely title in 1873 and Andre' inherited in turn in 1906 at the death of his elder brother (who was married to American **Maude Goddard**). Prince Andre's mother was Louise le Hon, the illegitimate daughter of the Duc de Morny, who was himself the illegitimate son of Auguste, Count de Flauhaut, by Queen Hortense of Holland. Andre' was in the mining business in San Francisco.

The couple later lived in Paris and at the Casa Speranza near Mougins in the Alps. Elizabeth and Andre's son, Stanislaus, born in Paris in 1895, succeeded his father as Prince di Monte Rotondo in 1954. Their second son, Carl Casimir, born in San Francisco 1897, married Anne de Riquet, Countess de Caraman-Chimay, who was a niece of the 4th Prince de Chimay and his wife, **Clara Ward** of Detroit (Carl's son, Prince Michel, served as French minister of the interior under Giscard d'Estaing). Their third son, Prince Marie-Andre', born at San Francisco 1899, married at Paris, 27 December 1919, **Frances Lawrance,** born at Bayshore, Long Island, 22 July 1901.

Before Prince Andre' married Elizabeth Sperry, his engagement to **Maud Burke** of San Francisco had been announced. Maud was a ward of real-estate titan Horace Carpentier, who provided her dowry. Her open relationship with playwright George Moore necessitated a marriage after she was rejected by Prince Andre', and Maud quickly married Sir Bache Cunard, 3rd Baronet. She changed her first name to Emerald and became a famous hostess in London. After championing the cause of fellow American **Wallis Simpson** with the Prince of Wales, at Edward VIII's abdication Emerald complained, "How *could* he do this to me?"

One grandson of Prince Andre' and Elizabeth Sperry, **Prince Edmond Poniatowski,** married at New York City on 1 May 1952, as his first wife, **Anne Darwin Goodrich,** born Adams County, Virginia, 10 October 1925, died 1977.

Laura Macdonald Stallo, born Cincinnati, 15 August 1890, died Palm Beach, 30 October 1972, was a daughter of Edmund K. Stallo, attorney of Cincinnati, and Laura Macdonald Stallo, and granddaughter of oil millionaire Alexander Macdonald, vice president of the Standard Oil Company, and of Eugene and Helena Zimmerman Stallo. Edmund Stallo's father, John, a native of Germany, came to the U. S. in 1839 and in 1885-89 was minister to Italy under President Cleveland. Laura's grandfather, Alexander Macdonald, amassed a huge fortune in Standard Oil. He and his wife reared their granddaughters when Laura Macdonald Stallo died at a young age. Many of their holidays were spent at their grandparents' palatial home, Dalvay By the Sea, on Prince Edward Island, Canada. When the grandfather died, he left $15 million to his two granddaughters, who were then sixteen and

Laura and Helen Stallo were reared by their grandparents whose fortune was from Standard Oil. Much of their time was spent, pictured here, on Prince Edward Island at Dalvay By The Sea.

seventeen. Their fortunes were left to the care of their father, who so badly mismanaged their funds that eventually there was little left. Laura married at Paris, 30 June 1914, **Francesco, Prince Rospigliosi,** born Rome, 8 July 1880, died Rome, 19 May 1943, son of Prince Camilo, who was a brother of **Marie Parkhurst's** husband, Prince Giuseppe. His brothers, Prince Giambattista, Prince Ludovico, and Prince Clemente, married Americans **Ethel Julia Bronson, Mildred Haseltine,** and **Claire Weil.**

Edmund and Laura Stallo, the parents of Laura and Helen. The mother died young and the father badly mismanaged the fortune the girls inherited from their maternal grandfather.

1912 and seven years later he married Mrs. Clarissa Cook of Salt Lake City. Laura and Helen's father mismanaged their Macdonald fortune to such a degree that it was dissipated during his lifetime. In February of 1940, at the request of Stallo's third wife, he was committed to a state rest home near San Francisco where he lived in poverty before dying at eighty-six on 16 March 1947. He was buried at Spring Grove Cemetery in Cincinnati. Laura's sister, **Helen MacDonald Stallo,** married **Prince Michel Murat.**

Helen Macdonald Stallo, born Cincinnati, 4 September 1892, daughter of Edmund K. Stallo, attorney of Cincinnati, and Laura Macdonald Stallo, and granddaughter of oil millionaire Alexander Macdonald, vice president of the Standard Oil Company, married at Paris, 6 February 1913,

Laura later became the hostess of the Ambassador Hotel in New York and lived in Palm Beach. She had two daughters who both married New Yorkers. Laura's cousin was **Helena Zimmerman,** daughter of Eugene Zimmerman of Cincinnati, who married in 1900 the **9th Duke of Manchester** of England and later married the 10th Earl of Kintore. Laura and her sister, Helen, were considered great beauties. Their father, Edward K. Stallo, married second, after their mother's death, in 1904, May Harrington Hanna, former wife of Dan. R. Hanna, son of U. S. Senator Mark Hanna of Ohio. They were divorced in

Prince Michel Murat, born Alexandrov, 7 February 1887, died Paris, 8 June 1941, son of Prince Louis Napoleon, and grandson of American **Caroline Fraser** and Lucien, 3rd Prince Murat. She had one daughter, who married writer Jean Paul Frank, then journalist Ferdinand Aubergenois of Paris (whose son is actor Rene' Aubergenois). In 1924, Prince Michel was forced to leave Paris to avoid his tailor's bill of more than eleven thousand francs. Helen and Prince Michel divorced in Paris, 7 November 1928, and she died in Paris, 1 April 1932. Her sister, **Laura,** married **Prince Francesco Rospigliosi.**

Prince Michel Murat married as his second wife another American, **Isabelle Macmillan.**

Gladys Virginia Steuart, born 18 July 1891, died 19 November 1947, was a daughter of John Henry Steuart (1831 – 1892), U. S. consul at Antwerp, and Mary Virginia Ramsay Harding Steuart (1891 – 1947, later Mrs. de Strale d'Ekna), whose father was a Virginia millionaire. Gladys met at the Austro-Hungarian Embassy in Paris in 1912 and married at St. Joseph's Roman Catholic Church in Geneva, 29 July 1914, Count Gyula/Julius Apponyi de Nagy-Apponyi (1873 – 1924), son of **Count Ludwig Apponyi,** grand marshal of the court of his imperial and royal apostolic majesty of Hungary. Gladys' sisters, Muriel and Fanny, married respectively Count Seherr Thoss and Count Laszlo Karolyi. Gladys and Gyula Apponyis' daughter, **Countess Geraldine Apponyi,** was born in Budapest, Hungary, on 6 August 1915. When the Austro-Hungarian Empire collapsed, the family fled to Switzerland but returned to Hungary in 1921.

At the death of Count Apponyi on 27 May 1924, his widow took her three daughters, Geraldine, Virginia (who later married Count de Baghy de Szechen), and Gyula, to live near her widowed mother in Menton in the South of France. There Gladys married a French Army officer, Gontrand Girault, by whom she had more children, Guy, Sylviane, and Patricia Girault. Her Apponyi in-laws insisted that her children by the first marriage be returned to Hungary where they were enrolled at the Sacred Heart boarding school in Pressbaum near Vienna. The young and beautiful Geraldine's grandfather's fortune had been depleted and she accepted work as a shorthand

Geraldine Apponyi became the first half-American queen when she married King Zog of Albania.

typist. She then sold postcards at the Budapest National Museum where one of her uncles was director. A photo of the then-seventeen-year-old Geraldine, taken while leaving a ball at the Karolyi Palace in Budapest, was given several years later to a sister of King Zog of the Albanians, who introduced the young woman to the king in December of 1937. He asked for her hand almost immediately and Geraldine, who became known as the "White Rose of Hungary," was raised to

Left: King Zog was originally prime minister and president before declaring himself King of the Albanians in 1928.

Right: Prior to her marriage Geraldine was raised to royal status as Princess Geraldine of Albania.

royal status as Princess Geraldine of Albania. On April 27, 1938, in Tirana, Albania, Geraldine married the king, who was twenty years her senior, in a civil ceremony witnessed by Count Ciano, Mussolini's envoy. She was Roman Catholic and he was Muslim and promised to build for her a Catholic chapel in their royal palace.

King Zog I, Skanderbeg III of Albania (born Ahmet Zogolli, his name was later changed to Ahmet Zogu, born 8 October 1895), was king of Albania from 1928 to 1939. He was previously prime minister of Albania between 1922 and 1924 and president of Albania between 1925 and 1928. At twenty-two, Geraldine was the second-youngest queen in the world (after Egypt's Queen Farida). The couple drove to their honeymoon in a scarlet open-top, Mercedes Benz, which was a present from Adolf Hitler (Hungary's Regent Horthy sent a phaeton and four Lipizzaner stallions). Geraldine's marriage made her mother, Gladys, the first American-born mother of a queen. Geraldine's only child, her son, Leka I, was born at the royal palace in Tirana, Albania, on 5 April 1939. Although Geraldine retained her Catholic faith, her son was Muslim and a godson of King Faisal of Saudi Arabia. King Zog's rule was cut short with the invasion of Albania by fascist Italy in April 1939 and the family fled the country into exile only two days after the birth of their son. The puppet government passed the throne to Italy's King Victor Emanuel III. From 1946, Geraldine and Zog lived in Greece, Turkey, England, Egypt (where they lived until King Farouk was toppled in 1952), the United States (at Knollwood, their estate on Long Island), France, Rhodesia, Spain, and finally South Africa. Their son, Leka I, is the current claimant to the Albanian throne. When he married an Australian, Susan Cullen-Ward (1941 – 2004), Queen Elizabeth II sent a telegram of congratulations. They have a son, Crown Prince Leka, who was born in South Africa in 1982 (his maternity ward was supposedly declared temporary Albanian territory for one hour so that he would be born in Albania).

King Zog died in Hauts-de-Seine, France, on 9 April 1961. It was said that he had survived fifty-five assassination attempts. Queen Geraldine, the first half-American queen, died in Albania on 22 October 2002, where she had been invited to return by forty members of Parliament that same year. Their son's activities have ensured that he will never assume his father's throne. For years he was an arms dealer (sometimes referred to as "Rambo of the Balkans") for which he was arrested in Thailand. In 1999 he was arrested in South Africa and his diplomatic privileges revoked when police found more than seventy weapons with 14,000 rounds of ammunition in his home. When his airplane landed in Gabon for refueling, troops who had been hired by the Albanian government to arrest him surrounded the plane. He appeared in the door with a rocket launcher and his would-be attackers fled. He re-entered Albania for the first time in 1993, greeted by five hundred supporters, under a passport issued by the royal court-in-exile. Although the government refused to acknowledge the passport (which listed his occupation as "king") he was allowed to visit, declaring that he would renounce the passport if a referendum on the monarchy failed.

Leka returned again in 1997 when two thousand supporters greeted him and his weeping mother. The promised monarchy referendum was held and only one-third of voters favored its restoration (Leka made accusations of voter fraud but they were largely disproven). He organized an armed insurrection and was sentenced in absentia to three years imprisonment for sedition, a conviction that was pardoned in 2002 when he re-entered the country to live. That same year, he attempted to bring almost ninety pieces of arms, including hand grenades and rocket launchers, into Albania. His son, the crown prince, now lives in Tirana.

Frances Simpson Stevens, born Chicago, 1894, died 1976, was a daughter of Mrs. Arthur O. Probst and her former husband, Mr. Stevens. At the Dana Hall school she was an accomplished equestrian, played forward on the hockey team, and mastered the French language. She then left for Madrid where she studied with the artist Robert Henri who encouraged her to enter an oil painting in the 1913 Armory show in New York City. It received no notice or acclaim but there she met Mabel Dodge who encouraged her to study in Italy and arranged for her to stay with a friend in Florence. She became one of the earliest proponents of the Futurist school and was expected to give up her career when she became engaged to the **Marchesse Salminbeni.** Instead she broke the engagement and returned to the U.S. at the outbreak of World War I and became active with the artists in Alfred Stieglitz's gallery, eventually having her first one-woman show in 1916. Her work was categorized as "machinery in motion, war and the bigger things in life rather than the human figure." Perhaps drawn to his family's fight against Bolshevism, Frances married in the marriage chapel of the municipal building in New York City, 19 April 1919 as his second wife, **Prince Dimitri Galitzine** (of the 3rd line), born at Archangelsk, 11 March 1882, died Nice, 5 December 1928. His father, Prince Nikolai, who died at St. Petersburg, 2 July 1925, was governor general of Moscow and the last prime minister of the Russian Empire. Prince Dimitri's first wife, whom he married in 1908, Nina Vladimirovna Bockmann, was killed by Bolsheviks on 19 February 1918. They had no children.

Frances and Prince Dimitri met when he was attached to the Russian Embassy at Washington, D.C., and attended a dinner in New York City in honor of the Russian ambassador where Frances Stevens, then a Red Cross worker, was also a guest. She organized and directed at the Hotel des Artistes in New York City a Red Cross Auxiliary and was later decorated by the Italian government for her work. The prince was twelve years her senior. Immediately after the wedding they left for California and Japan on the way to Vladivostok, where he had a naval command (he had been a prisoner in the Russo-Japanese War). The couple expressed a desire to return to Siberia, where she would nurse the sick and wounded, to join the fight against Bolshevism. His family's financial loss at the fall of Nicholas II was said to be $20 million.

Frances was assumed to be homosexual and, perhaps unsurprisingly, there were no children of the marriage. Frances was a respected artist and the only American directly associated with the Italian futurists. A 1917 magazine article (*Every Week,* 2 April 1917) said of her, "Fresh from a discreet New England boarding-school, fate plunged Frances Stevens into Italy just as the Futurists there published their fiery manifesto. Instantly Miss Stevens learned how to say 'No more slavery to Nature – a running horse has not four legs but twenty' in Italian, allied herself with the revolutionists, and earned the distinction of having Brussel sprouts and other things thrown at her work by the enraged Academicians." Some of her work appeared in the 1915-16 **Rogue** with writings by Gertrude Stein.

In 1923 she returned to the U.S. to regain her American citizenship, telling reporters that her husband was then enrolled in a school funded by Mrs. W. K. Vanderbilt Sr., "for destitute Russian noblemen and noblewomen" in Paris learning to be a carpenter while his father was preparing to be a cobbler. She assured them that her husband was making good kitchen tables and chairs although "when he shows them to me he still expresses an aristocratic disdain." Overall, however, she was greatly in favor of the school, telling the *New York Times,* "I believe everybody should work ... I am much prouder of my father-in-law when I know he is making an honest living mending and making shoes and carrying potatoes on his back... than I was when he had everything and knew nothing of the intimate trials and suffering of humanity." As for her husband, she insisted that, "I love him and propose to stick by him. But he has his lesson to learn, the lesson of the 'middle way.'"

She expressed admiration for Mussolini and, while she was pleased that a law had been passed in 1922 to allow women such as she to retain their U. S. citizenship when marrying a foreigner, she thought that the law should be retroactive and allow her to have that right automatically. Finally, she was of the view that "Bolshevism has many fine principles but the trouble is that the people in Russia are too ignorant to carry them out." The princess then left for her suite at the Plaza Hotel.

In 1925 she announced her plans to settle in England and race her impressive stable of twenty-two horses. She also said that she had made a bid for the cinema rights for the opening of the new racecourse at Bournemouth but submitted her offer too late to be accepted. It was then her intention to give up painting in favor of the camera. Her husband died in 1928. In 1961 Frances was admitted to the Mendocino State Hospital in California where she became a ward of the state and lived in various nursing homes. She was said to be working on her memoirs but the manuscript was never found. She died on 18 July 1976 at the age of eighty-two and had no next-of-kin nor any record of an estate. A 1994 article, "In Search of Frances Simpson Stevens," was published in *Art in America* magazine. She is remembered, if at all, for a single painting in the Arenberg collection at the Philadelphia Museum of Art.

Anita Rhinelander Stewart, daughter of William Rhinelander Stewart and Annie Armstrong Stewart, was born at Elberon, New Jersey, on 7 August 1886, and died at Newport, Rhode Island, on 15 September 1977. Her father, although trained as an attorney, managed several trusts established by his old and socially prominent family. Mrs. Stewart's sister was Mrs. Anthony J. Drexel, whose daughter later married the 14th Earl of Winchilsea and Nottingham. The Stewarts were divorced in 1906 and she married a few months later James Henry "Silent" Smith who had unexpectedly inherited $50 million from an unmarried uncle, becoming overnight one of the wealthiest men in America. Silent Smith was then more than fifty, had never been married, and lived in a modest apartment while working as a stockbroker. After his inheritance he was immediately taken up by the very social Mrs. Stuyvesant Fish. After he married Annie Armstrong Stewart he settled $1 million on her beautiful daughter, Anita, as she entered the marriage market (Anita's mother would add another $1 million at her daughter's wedding). Smith bought the palatial New York residence of the late William C. Whitney at the corner of Sixty-eighth Street and Fifth Avenue, opposite Central Park. The $2 million purchase price was considered a bargain. Annie Armstrong Stewart preferred a high social profile to her first husband's fondness for quiet evenings at home and she soon became one of Silent Smith's favorite hostesses. Within a month of her divorce she and Anita sailed

Left: Anita Stewart held most of the cards in her marriage negotiations and played them well. Right: Prince Miguel de Braganza, whose father was usually referred to as "the pretender to the Portuguese throne."

who was married to a baronet, Sir George Cooper, was left $3 million. Anita met in Paris in April of 1909 Prince Miguel de Braganza, whose father, the Duke of Braganza (usually referred to as the pretender to the Portugese throne), was a son of the de facto King of Portugal from 1828-1834 and a grandson of Joao VI, king of Portugal and emperor of Brazil. Miguel's family lived in exile in Austria where Emperor Franz Joseph was generous to them. Only three months after their meeting, the engagement of Anita Stewart to Prince Miguel was announced at a concert dance in London where her mother had leased the Berkeley Square home of the Duchess of Somerset. From his summer home in Bar Harbour the bride's father declined to comment about his daughter's engagement. At first it was announced that the marriage would be morganatic but Anita

for Scotland where Annie married Silent Smith. The Smiths then took a world cruise honeymoon on the Drexel yacht, accompanied by Anita as well as the Duke and Duchess of Manchester (she was the American-born **Helena Zimmerman**). The groom, who had been married only months, died of a heart attack in Kyoto, Japan, on 27 March 1907. Although he was required to leave the bulk of his estate to two nephews, his widow received what was reported to be as low as $3 million and as high as $30 million, while her daughter, Anita, was given an additional half-million trust fund. Silent Smith's sister,

refused to accept anything less than a title of princess. On September 6th the generous Austrian emperor, Franz Joseph, announced that he had created Anita a princess in her own right. The *New York Times* wrote, "It seems easier than we thought for an emperor to transform a plain American Miss into a Princess, when no principality goes with the title and no pecuniary endowment. Miss Stewart is buying her own principality, and is expected to endow rather than be endowed." Then it was learned that the groom was to renounce his inheritance rights as Portugal's then-king was unmarried as was his heir, his uncle the Duke of Oporto (who in 1917 would marry American **Nevada Stoody**). Again Anita refused to consent to the marriage on those terms. So, on the eve of the marriage, Anita's mother paid all the groom's substantial gambling debts in exchange for his not renouncing his succession rights and for Anita's refusal to convert to the Catholic faith. The groom's father then created his son the Duke of Vizeu. After all the necessary negotiations, Anita Rhinelander Stewart married at a small Catholic church near Tulloch Castle (which her mother had leased for the season) outside Dingwall, Scotland, on 15 September 1909, **Prince Miguel de Braganza, Duke of Vizeu** (ad personam by his father 1909), born Reichenau, 22 September 1878, died New York City, 21 February 1923. Anita was given away by her brother, who wore the Stewart tartan and the event was a high-profile social gathering for the American expatriate community, including the Bradley Martins, who attended with a house full of guests (including their daughter, the Countess of Craven) from their nearby shooting estate. A

Anita Stewart refused to accept a morganatic marriage and was created by Austrian Emperor Franz Joseph as "Princess de Braganza" in her own right.

Catholic bishop, who said daily mass for the visiting king and queen of Spain when they were visiting in the area, pronounced the pope's personal blessing at the end of the ceremony. The first stop on their honeymoon was to visit the generous Franz Joseph in Austria, where Anita was formally presented to court. While they were away, creditors searched the prince's home in an effort to confiscate anything that could be sold to settle his considerable debts. At the time it was reported that one-fifth of the dowry was to be committed to creditors.

Anita had a daughter and two sons but the marriage was not happy. At the outbreak of war Prince Miguel joined the kaiser's army. Anita sailed with her children for New York City, where she was met at the pier by her father whom she had not seen in eleven years (at his death he would leave the largest portion of an estate worth more than $2 million to Anita). A revolution in Portugal in 1910 ended that country's monarchy and its king fled to England. In 1920 Prince Miguel, Duke of Vizeu, renounced his claims to the Portugese throne one week before his elderly father renounced his own rights in favor of his third son, Dom Duarte. Although Prince Miguel's renouncement was supposedly a retroactive one that included his children, there has always been a question whether he could renounce his children's rights. His American descendants have wisely never pressed the claim and have lived productive lives free of any royal intrigue. Dom Duarte's son is the current Duke of Braganza and pretender to the Portugese throne.

After the war Prince Miguel joined his family in America, where he became an insurance salesman in the firm of his brother-in-law in 1922.

The next year Prince Miguel died of influenza at the age of forty-four. In 1926 Anita renounced her titles and regained her American citizenship. She opened a photographic studio in New York City and remained friendly with her husband's family, announcing in 1934 the engagement of her sister-in-law, Princess Maria Antonia, to Ashley Chanler, nephew of the first husband of Amelie Rives, Princess Troubetskoy.

Anita married second, on 2 April 1946 (the same year in which her only daughter committed suicide), Lewis Gouverneur Morris of Newport, Rhode Island, scion of several early American colonial families. He had served five months in prison in 1921 as a result of the financial failure of his brokerage firm. He died in 1967. Anita's mother married in 1915 a man who was younger than Anita, Jean H. E. St. Cyr, whose much older wife had died four months earlier, leaving him $1 million. At one time it was alleged that he had been born Jack Thompson and was a bellboy before adopting a French name in order to enter society.

When Anita's mother died in 1925 at El Cerrito, her California home, her estate was said to be $40 million and her young husband received one-third interest. At the time of her death it was disclosed that Prince Alexander von Thurn und Taxis, a cousin of Prince Miguel de Braganza, received almost one-quarter of a million dollars from the estate as payment for an outstanding debt. In 1914 Anita had assigned her future interest in that portion of her mother's estate to satisfy a court-ordered judgment for her husband's substantial debt to his cousin. Anita, formerly Duchess de Vizeu, died on 15 September 1977 at her home in Newport, Rhode Island. She was ninety-one and died on the sixtieth anniversary of her wedding to Prince Miguel de Braganza.

Nonnie May "Nancy" Stewart, born Zanesville, Ohio, 20 January 1878 (although she used the year 1883 on her tombstone), died London, 29 August 1923, was a daughter of William Charles Stewart and Mary Lavina Holden Stewart, whose father was mayor of Zanesville, Ohio. She married her first husband, railroad contractor George Ely Worthington, in 1894. She divorced him in 1897 (he died unmarried in 1950) and four days later married William B. Leeds, Sr., "the tinplate king." His wedding gift to her was a mansion on New York City's Fifth Avenue. In 1904 they purchased the Frederick Vanderbilt mansion in Newport, Rhode Island, where they entertained lavishly. They had a son, William Jr., whose father died in Paris, 23 June 1908, leaving his widow $40 million. The wealthy young widow moved to Europe where there were constant reports of her engagement to a string of suitors including Prince Louis Bonaparte.

After a long engagement she converted to the Greek Orthodox Church and married in the Russian Chapel at Vevey, Switzerland, as his first wife, 1 January 1920, **Prince Christopher of Greece,** born Pavlovsk, 10 August 1888, died Athens, 21 January 1940, youngest child of Prince Wilhelm of Denmark, who assumed the throne of Greece as King George I of the Hellenes on 31 October 1863, and of his wife, Grand Duchess Olga of Russia. King George I was assassinated

Dowager Queen Olga of Greece, born a grand duchess of Russia, stands between her youngest son and his wife at their wedding.

Left: From left, Prince Andrew (father-in-law of Queen Elizabeth II), with his brothers Prince Nicholas and King Constantine. Right: Their youngest brother, Prince Christopher, wed American Nancy Stewart Leeds.

the parents of the current Duke of Edinburgh, were forced to leave Greece in 1922, Nancy was their chief means of financial support. She was famous for her hospitality to friends and acquaintances and was known to remove a piece of expensive jewelry when it was admired and give it away. Nancy Leeds' son by her second marriage, William B. Leeds Jr., married in 1921 Prince Christopher's niece, **Grand Duchess Xenia,** daughter of Grand Duke George and Princess Marie of Greece and Denmark, and great-granddaughter of Tsar Nicholas I of Russia. The younger Leeds and his wife had one child, Nancy, before divorcing, and Grand Duchess Xenia married another American, Herman Jud, but they had no children. Her granddaughter recalled that Nancy was "so very sweet to everyone. She was very placid, always exquisitely dressed, coiffed, and bejewelled." The godmother of Nancy's son was Alva Vanderbilt Belmont (mother of Consuelo, Duchess of Marlborough), while the godmother of Nancy's granddaughter was Queen Mother Helen of Rumania. Nancy was ill the last few years of her life with rectal cancer and her family believed that her Greek doctors hastened her demise with too many useless operations. She died with her husband, her mother-in-law (Dowager Queen Olga), her son, and her daughter-in-law at her bedside. The *New York Times* wrote in her obituary that Nancy was "the only American who ever became and remained an officially recognized princess of the royal blood, accepted on full equality as a member of a reigning European

in 1913 and his eldest son succeeded as King Constantine I. Prince Christopher's three nephews each succeeded to the Greek throne as George II, Alexander, and Paul, as did Paul's son as Constantine II. Nancy Stewart's millions helped re-establish George II on the throne and he rewarded her by creating her Princess Anastasia of Greece in her own right, the first American woman to receive such an honor. She was said to have given more than $1 milllion to the Greek forces fighting the Greco-Turkish war. After her marriage she continued funding many charitable organizations, relief camps, and hospitals in Greece. When Prince and Princess Andrew of Greece,

Nancy Stewart's vast fortune helped restore and maintain the monarchy in her husband's country. She was widely-known as a generous and reliable friend.

family." At her death her jewels alone were sold for $4 million. One diarist of the era recalls commenting on the size of the Grand Duchess Cyril's pearls when young Princess Ileana, daughter of Romania's Queen Marie, looked up and said, "Oh, they're not nearly as big as Auntie Nancy's!" While married to Prince Christopher Nancy leased Spencer House in London and completely recovered all the wall coverings which were in shreds; she also installed bathrooms. She used crowned monograms on all her linens, handbags (encrusted in diamonds) and umbrellas. As her granddaughter recalled, "Crowns were everywhere and why not, I suppose, as she earned it ... but Uncle Christo was devoted to her and very undone when she died." Prince Christopher's second wife was Francoise, Princess d'Orleans, daughter of the Duc de Guise, who became head of the Orléanist line upon the death of his cousin Philippe Duc d'Orléans in 1926. Prince Christopher and his second wife had a son, author Prince Michael of Greece, whose first cousin is Prince Philip, Duke of Edinburgh, consort of Queen Elizabeth II.

Nevada Hayes Stoody was born 21 October 1885 (some sources say as early as 1870 which seems more likely) in Ohio, the second child of Jacob Walter Stoody (1846-1922) and Nancy Miranda McNeel Stoody (1848-1922), who married in 1867. She died 11 January 1941. Her origins were never clear, but she came from a small town in Ohio to New York City before 1906. Her first husband, Lee Agnew, was New York representative of the old **Record-Herald.** They were divorced in Manhattan and he later invented a device for delivering folded newspapers from presses - an invention that made

him very wealthy. When he died 31 January 1924, he left her the excess income from his estate over that which was necessary for the support of their son, Lee Albert Agnew Jr. The excess was substantial. A day after her divorce from Lee Agnew Sr., in 1906, she married William Henry Chapman who was then in his seventies. When he left her more than $8 million at his death one year later, the newspapers dubbed her "the $10 million widow." She immediately went to Europe where it was reported that those vying for her hand included Lord Falconer (later the 10th Earl of Kintore who married American heiress **Helen Zimmerman,** formerly Duchess of Manchester), Count A. F. Chereff-Spiritovitch (a younger officer in the army of the Tsar), Prince Mohammed Ali Hassan, and Count Aubert de Sonies who came from Paris to New York on the same ship with the widow. While the count was in the lobby of the St. Regis Hotel waiting to present flowers and

Nevada Hayes Stoody styled herself as "the Crown Princess of Portugal," a far more flattering title than her earlier one, "the $10 million widow."

a proposal of marriage, she departed by a rear exit with Philip Van Valkenburgh, a prominent member of an old New York family.

They were married in Connecticut on 23 November 1909 and were divorced after a short time amid protracted legal battles; she finally settled $200,000 upon him in 1910. She immediately left for Europe where the press continued to report those seeking her hand in marriage. Nevada married morganatically in Rome, 26 September and in Madrid, 23 November 1917, **Don Alfonso of Portugal, Prince of Braganza, Duke of Oporto,** born Ajuda, 1 July 1865, died Naples, 21 February 1920, son of King Luis I. He forfeited his inheritance rights to the throne by his marriage and his financial allowance from the royal family was cut. Nevada styled herself as the crown princess of Portugal. Her husband was the uncle of King Manuel of Portugal and only brother of King Manuel's father, the murdered King Carlos. King Victor Emanuel, a cousin of the Duke of Oporto, gave him asylum in the royal palace in Naples and a reported allowance of $10,000 per year. The Duke of Oporto died in Naples in 1920 having fled there after the Portugese Revolution. After the death of the king of Portugal, Nevada petitioned the republican government – to no avail - to grant her all the royal family's funds as she considered herself its senior member. She sailed to the U. S. in 1921 to have made a silver casket on a bronze base (weighing half a ton) in which to convey her late husband's body from Naples to Lisbon. There it would be displayed in the Pantheon before the Duke of Oporto was buried next to his murdered brother, the late king. In 1935 the Duchess of Oporto traveled on the *Ile de France* to New York where she reported that, having spent two months in Germany, she was "greatly impressed by Adolf Hitler." She jealously guarded what she perceived as her rights as crown princess and once, on a trans-Atlantic cruise which also included the Grand Duchess Marie of Russia, to ensure that she be seated on the captain's right at dinner rather than the grand duchess, she entered the dining room ahead of all other guests to take her seat. She died 11 January 1941, in Tampa, Florida, at St. Joseph's Hospital after an illness of ten days. She had spent the winter in Tampa for the preceding ten years. She left a son, David Agnew, of New York, and four sisters.

Lucie Grundy Tate, born 27 April 1868, in Liberty, Kentucky, daughter of William P. and Louise Rose Tate of Stanford, Kentucky, first married 20 January 1892, Charles Hamilton Paine (1853 – 1909) of Boston. He was a partner with his brother in the banking firm of Paine, Webber & Company and retired early with his fortune. The Paines moved with their three daughters, Louise, Sarah, and Margaret, to Paris and lived in a magnificent home next to the Bois de Boulogne. Louise married the heavily-decorated soldier, Capt. Jacques de Sieges de Veynes; Sarah "Betka" married **Prince Aleksander Sapieha** (see her separate entry); and Margaret married Chevalier George de Spinet. After Charles H. Paine's death in 1909, his widow married in London on 29 November 1910 as his second wife, **Marie Jean Baptiste Gaston, Duc de Praslin** (whose mother was American-born **Marie Elizabeth Forbes**), born Ryde, Isle of Wight, 13 November 1876, died Marseille, 8 September 1937.

Soon after their marriage the duchess was in a Tours court having charged a self-styled "Count d'Aulby de Gatlgny" with attempting to blackmail her with compromising love letters she had written to him. She begged the court to spare her from the humiliation of hearing them read aloud but the judge would not comply with her request. The "count" was eventually convicted and sentenced to thirty days in jail but his American-born wife was spared any sentence for her part in the extortion plot. The duke and duchess divorced in 1922 and the titles were inherited by his younger brother, making their American-born mother, Marie Elizabeth Forbes, the dowager-duchess, the mother of two dukes.

Dorothy Cadwell Taylor, born Watervliet, New York, 13 February 1888, daughter of leather-goods manufacturer Bertrand LeRoy Taylor and Nellie Cadwell Taylor, was known for her black hair, blue eyes, and seductive figure. She married in 1912 British aviation pioneer Claude Grahame-White, who organized Britain's first airmail service (he landed a plane on the White House lawn during their courtship and invited President Taft for a flight). He was the only man to hold the three most coveted flying gold medals and the first Briton to hold an internationally-recognized pilot's license. They divorced 17 December 1916, in London, just after Dorothy inherited between ten and fifteen million dollars of her father's $50 million estate (her brother, who was a governor of the New York Stock Exchange, received the remainder).

When Dorothy was thirty-four, she married on 29 June 1923, at New York City, **Count Carlo di Frasso,** born 22 January 1876, younger son of **Ernesto, 7th Prince di Frasso, Prince di San Vito, Prince di Crucoli. Count Carlo,** who was twelve years older than Dorothy, had earlier married at London, 23 April 1906, **Georgina Wilde,** born St. Louis, Misourri, 14 December 1885, step-daughter of Henry Siegel, and they divorced 18 February 1921.

Although Carlo was from a distinguished Roman family, he had no money. He was a deputy in the Italian Parliament and served as master of the Oriolo Fox Hounds in Rome. When Count Carlo arrived in New York City for their marriage, he told waiting journalists that Mussolini was both loved and feared in Italy but that the entire country was behind him "because of his leading Italy out of chaos."

He added that the king of Italy had great admiration for Mussolini. The newly-married Dorothy rode side-saddle next to Italian cavalry officers and spent more than $1 million to restore Villa Madama, the count's sixteenth-century family home, designed by Raphael and built by Pope Clement VII, nephew of Lorenzo de Medici, in the early 1520s. In its restored glory, she often hosted seated dinners for two hundred guests. Biographer Jeffrey Meyers reported that Barbara Hutton wrote of life there that "it was hard to tell whether the Countess threw one party that lasted all summer or a series of weekend parties that lasted all week. Guests just came and went as if the Villa Madama were a Grand Hotel."

Dorothy also purchased homes in London, New York, and Beverly Hills. A reporter once asked Dorothy to describe paradise, and she replied, "The English writer Max Beerbohm said that Paradise to him was a four-post bed in a field of poppy and mandragora. I say it depends who's between the sheets." She and her husband were very open about their affairs and her lovers included the writer Ben Hecht, actor Cary Grant (to whom she introduced one of his wives, heiress Barbara Hutton), and mobster Bugsy Siegel. Actor Gary Cooper arrived at the Villa Madama as a houseguest in 1931 and they began a torrid affair during which she was credited with imbuing him with the polish and elegance for which he became known. She purchased a new wardrobe for him and taught him to dress with style. When Cooper departed the Villa Madama to return to Hollywood, Dorothy gave a spectacular party for him that included Crown Prince Umberto of Italy, England's Duke of York (later King George VI),

Dorothy di Frasso was caricatured as "the Countess de Lago" in the play and movie, *The Women*. She had the money and panache to entertain lavishly at the Villa Madama.

the Earl and Countess of Portarlington, and Prince Christopher of Greece, widower of the fabulously-wealthy American **Nancy Leeds.** Another guest was Barbara Hutton to whom Dorothy had, as a favor to Barbara's aunt Marjorie Post Hutton, introduced to her as Barbara's escort for the evening, **Prince Girolamo Rospigliosi.** Rospigliosi, who had no funds to maintain his seventeen homes, began proposing to Hutton the moment he met her "and never stopped" according to her. Hutton was more impressed by Gary Cooper and Prince Girolamo contented himself by marrying American **Marian Adair Snowden** a few months later.

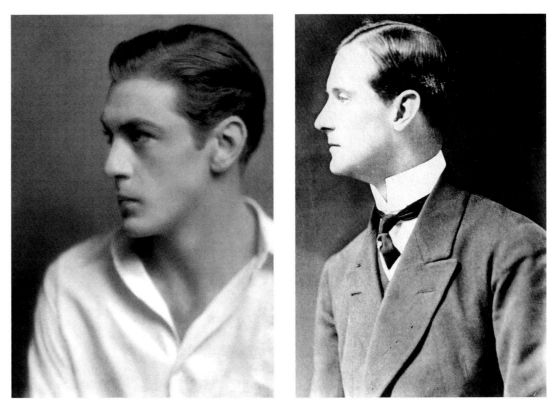

When Cooper returned to Hollywood, Dorothy di Frasso followed him and they scandalized the film community for several

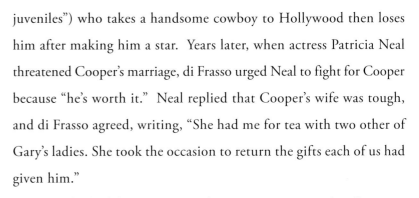

Left: Dorothy was credited with teaching handsome actor Gary Cooper the style he portrayed onscreen. Right: Dorothy's husband, Count Carlo di Frasso, ignored his wife's affairs while she did the same of his.

months. Cooper's lifestyle began to tell on him and friends noticed that he was losing weight. His work began to be affected and his doctor prescribed rest. At the time, actress Tallulah Bankhead attended a party and was asked why Cooper had not yet arrived. She replied, "He's probably worn to a frasso." Cooper's relationship with Dorothy was satirized in Claire Boothe's 1937 play, *The Women,* in which Dorothy became "Countess de Lago," "a silly, amiable middle-aged woman" (a wag had referred to her as "a mature connoisseur of Hollywood juveniles") who takes a handsome cowboy to Hollywood then loses him after making him a star. Years later, when actress Patricia Neal threatened Cooper's marriage, di Frasso urged Neal to fight for Cooper because "he's worth it." Neal replied that Cooper's wife was tough, and di Frasso agreed, writing, "She had me for tea with two other of Gary's ladies. She took the occasion to return the gifts each of us had given him."

Dorothy had designer Howard Darn create a special Rolls-Royce

Phantom II for her in 1933 which was known as "the Countess." She gave a party in 1935 at which Clark Gable met his future love, Carole Lombard. Guests were instructed to wear white and Lombard arrived wearing a white nightgown, in a white ambulance, from which she was carried into the house on a white cot by three interns in white uniform. Lombard later gave the ambulance to Gable and he drove it for two years. Dorothy di Frasso became so well-known to readers of society columns that George Kaufman and Moss Hart included a reference to her in their play, *The Man Who Came to Dinner.*

After her infatuation with Gary Cooper waned when he married, she met the gangster Bugsy Siegel at the Santa Anita racetrack and they began a stormy affair. Helen Hayes later wrote, "After the romance with Gary broke up she had a fling with a gangster in Palm Springs, Bugsy Siegel. That doesn't reflect much style and taste, does it?" Dorothy's relationship with Seigel made her the target of the FBI who followed and documented her every move for a time. One official 1941 FBI communique' reported her as living in "a pretentious villa at Acapulco, Mexico" and claimed that she was "notorious for her nymphomaniac propensities, lecherous parties, and publicity seeking." The FBI also claimed that she was an agent for Italy's Mussolini and that she "may be financed by Mexican Government to draw Hollywood film stars to Mexico City." At Barbara Hutton's request, Dorothy called the crown prince of Italy to seek an official pardon for Barbara's cousin, Jimmy Donahue, who had been arrested for petty fraud and was in an Italian prison. According to the FBI document, the king of Italy effected Donahue's release and Hutton paid a $17,000 fine. When

Barbara Hutton and Cary Grant stayed at a hotel in Mexico City just before their marriage, their room was bugged by the FBI because of their relationship with Dorothy di Frasso. The agency recorded Hutton's telephone conversations with Baron Gottfried von Cramm in Germany, a former Davis Cup tennis champion who had been arrested for homosexual activities (he would become Hutton's sixth husband in 1955).

In a 1991 movie, *Bugsy,* starring Warren Beatty and Annette Bening, actress Bebe Neuwirth portrayed di Frasso. Cary Grant referred to Dorothy di Frasso in his autobiography as "a friend whose rare ability to laugh at herself so often dispelled my own gloom." He fondly recalled that "her palatial Villa Madama in Rome was the scene of indescribably lavish parties. The Villa Madama, the classic site of so many Hubert Robert paintings, was taken over by Mussolini's Fascisti government for Hitler's use during the war. In light of events to come, it was Dorothy's haunting grief that she didn't arrange to leave a time bomb in the place before departing to live in America," (it was leased to the Italian Ministry for Foreign Affairs in 1937 and sold to the Italian state in 1941).

In 1954 Dorothy spent a week visiting Marlene Dietrich in Las Vegas. On her return by train to Los Angeles, she was discovered by one of her party, the actor Clifton Webb, dead in her seat. She was dressed in fur and a $50,000 diamond necklace. Her death occurred on 4 January 1954. Cary Grant later wrote, "It was my unhappy mission to accompany her body to New York for the funeral and a gathering of those who, like myself, would miss her amusing presence and the loyalty of her friendship." There were no children of either of her marriages and her husband's nephew is the current Prince di Frasso.

Emily Stuart Taylor, born New York City, 5 May 1888, died 27 January 1974, was a daughter of Civil War veteran Colonel Stuart Taylor. She was first married to Ernest A. Wiltsee, a California mining engineer. He wrote several books about his mining experiences in California, Mexico, South America, and South Africa. They divorced in 1921 and the marriage was annulled in February 1923 at St.-Siege. She and her husband had a son, Stuart de Rapalie Wiltsee, who graduated from Yale, then joined the Paris brokerage firm of H. Hertz & Company. In 1929 he died at the age of twenty-one, having suffered for nineteen days of blood poisoning due to carbuncles on his lip. Prior to his death his mother married at Paris's Church of St. Honore d'Eylau on 16 April 1923, Don Carlo, **2nd Prince di Bitetto,** born Naples 16 December 1891, eldest son of the 1st Prince di Bitetto, aide-de-camp to the king of Italy who awarded the princely title 1 February 1891. The U. S. ambassador, Myron T. Herrick, gave away the bride and the Italian ambassador was the groom's witness.

The prince's father was a second son of the Cito Filomarino family who also held the titles of Prince della Rocca d'Aspro, Marchese di Torrecuso, Duca di Perdifumo, Prince Mesagne, Marchese di Paupisi e Torrepalazzo, di Capurso, di St. Chirico, di Ceglie et Carbonara, Conte di Castello and Barone di Finoccieto. In 1931 Don Carlo succeeded his father who had been, as Rear Admiral Prince Luigi Filomarino of Bitetto, commander of the third battle division of the Royal Italian Navy. Don Carlo and Emily lived in Rome and Paris

Emily Taylor as drawn by Helleu while she was Princess di Bitetto.

Mabel Taylor's marriage to Chlodwig, Prince zu Hohenlohe-Waldenburg-Schillingsfurst was unhappy. They divorced and the marriage was annulled in 1943.

and had no children. Don Carlo had a younger brother, Don Mario, born 1893, who was a member of the Italian royal court. The titles passed to a cousin. Emily's cousin, U. S. Senator Claiborne Pell of Rhode Island, announced her death in 1974. His father had been one of Emily's witnesses at her marriage to the prince.

Mabel Taylor, born Philadelphia, Pennsylvania, 9 November 1886, was a daughter of neurologist Dr. J. Madison Taylor and of Emily Drayton Taylor. Her father was a noted physician at Harvard Medical School and was among the first in the medical community to advocate for therapeutic massage as well as hypnotism. Mabel's mother, Emily Drayton Taylor, was an accomplished artist and one of the founders of the American Society of Miniature Painters. President and Mrs. McKinley were among those whose portraits she painted. In 1924 she went to Belgium to paint a minature of Cardinal Mercier and received a special prize from the Pennsylvania Academy of Arts for it. Her other honors included a gold medal at the Earl's Gallery in London in 1900.

Mabel first married Gifford Cochran whose father paid Eugene O'Neill $30,000 for the rights to produce the 1933 movie *Emperor Jones,* starring Paul Robeson. He also adapted Weill's *Threepenny Opera* and *Mack the Knife* for the stage. After their divorce, she married at Olmutz, 21 September 1927, as his first wife, **Chlodwig, Prince zu Hohenlohe-Waldenburg-Schillingsfurst, von Ratibor und Corvey,** born Alt-Aussee 30 July 1897, died Munich 3 May 1968, son of Prince Mauritz. His grandfather, Prince Chlodwig, was imperial chancellor 1894-1900. Prince Chlodwig's great-grandfather, Prince Victor I, in 1840 renounced his rights to the Schillingsfurst titles and was created Duke von Ratibor and Prince von Corvey in Prussia. Mabel and Prince Chlodwig divorced in Palm Beach and the marriage was annulled at Augsburg, 1 February 1943. Prince Chlodwig had only a daughter by his second marriage, and the current heir to the Hohenlohe-Schillingsfurst title had an American mother, **Peggy Thompson Schulze.** Mabel chaired the women's division for the Salvation Army annual maintenance appeal during its 1947 and 1948 drives.

Mabel Taylor married third, on 11 May 1950, in Labelle, Florida, foxhunter James Cameron Clark, heir to the Coats & Clark thread fortune. His former wife had been Lady Irene Pratt Cubitt, daughter of the 4th Marquess Camden (and granddaughter of the 6th Duke of Marlborough), and his next wife was Marion Taylor Gibson, former daughter-in-law of artist Charles Dana Gibson. Mabel and her last husband lived in Palm Beach where she died in January of 1967, survived by her husband, a daughter, two sons, grandchildren and great-grandchildren.

Natividad Mercedes Terry, a daughter of wealthy sugar plantation owner Antonio Terry y Dorticos and Grace Maria Dalton Secor Terry, was born in New York City, 25 September 1882, and died in Paris, 23 December 1960. Her grandfather was Don Tomas Terry y Adan (1806 – 1886), a native of Venezuela who became the wealthiest man in Cuba (some accord him the title of the first billionaire in the Americas) where he emigrated in 1830 and developed the town of Cienfuegos. He married on 31 October 1837 in Cienfuegos, Teresa Dorticos y Leys and they had eight children, including a daughter,

Natividad Terry's grandfather was the wealthiest man in Cuba. Her granddaughter, Anne, married Valery Giscard d'Estaing and was first lady of France.

Natividad "Natalia," who married the diplomat Alberto Blanc who was created a baron by King Vittorio Emmanuele in 1893. Blanc served in Washington as the first ambassador of the united Italy before becoming ambassador to Spain and then to the Ottoman Empire.

Another child of Don Tomas Terry was Antonio, who was the father of Natividad Mercedes.

When Don Tomas died his children built in his memory the palatial theatre in Cienfuegos bearing his name. Natividad Mercedes Terry married in Paris, on 7 July 1902, **Prince Guy Faucigny-Lucigne and Coligny,** born Belle-Isle-en-Terre, 12 January 1876, died Paris, 7 July 1914, son of the 2nd Prince de Faucigny-Lucigne and Coligny, Prince de Cystria, and of Charlotte, Countess d'Issoudun, who was an illegitimate daughter of Charles, Duc de Berry. His brother, Ferdinand, succeeded their father as 3rd Prince de Lucigne. They had three daughters and one son. The son, Jean-Louis, first married "Baba," Baroness von Erlanger, and he frequently hosted Elizabeth, the Queen Mother, on her visits to France. One of the Faucigny-Lucigne daughters, Princess Aymone, married Francois, Count Sauvage de Brantes, who died in a concentration camp at Mauthausen in 1944. His daughter, Anne Aymone Sauvage de Brantes, married Valery Giscard d'Estaing and was first lady of France from 1974-1981.

After Prince Guy's death, Natividad married at Paris, 12 July 1918, Jean Iswolsky, whose father, Alexander, was the Russian ambassador to France, and whose maternal grandfather, Count Toll, was the Russian ambassador to Germany. Natividad's first cousin, **Nathalie Terry** (1877 – 1962, daughter of Don Francisco), married Count **Stanislaus de Castellane** (1875 – 1959), younger brother of Count Boniface de Castellane, who married American heiress **Anna Gould.** Nathalie eventually inherited the historic Chateau de Rochecotte that had belonged to her husband's grandmother, the Duchesse de Dino. Nathalie in turn left the chateau to her brother, Emilio Terry y Sanchez, a celebrated architect and interior designer, who decorated the Monaco apartment of American-born Princess Grace of Monaco. Emilio Terry, whose unfinished portrait was painted by Salvador Dali in 1930, observed, "A room without a cornice is like a man without a collar."

Allene Tew, daughter of Charles Henry Tew of Jamesville, New York, and Janet Smith Tew, was born at Jamesville, New York, 7 July 1876, and died in Paris, 1 May 1955. She first married Theodore Hostetter of Pittsburgh (by whom she had two children, Theodore Jr. and Greta, who married Glenn Stewart) who died in New York City, 3 August 1902. She married second at New York City, 27 December 1904, Morton Colton Nichols and they divorced and she resumed the name Hostetter. She married third at London, 5 December 1912, Anson Wood Burchard, chairman of the board of the International General Electric Co. and vice chairman of the board of General Electric Co., who died 22 January 1927, at a luncheon party at the home of Mortimer Schiff in New York City. Burchard was one of the foremost electrical engineers in the country. His and Allene's home, at the corner of 69th Street and Park Avenue, was purchased in 1925 from Mrs. Henry P. Davison and had been assessed two years earlier at $530,000.

The widowed Allene then married in Paris, 10 April 1929, as his second wife (his first had been Viktoria, Princess of Prussia, by whom he had a son and daughter) **Prince Heinrich XXXIII** of Reuss (of the younger line), born 26 July 1879, died Stonsdorf, 15 November

Left: Prince Heinrich XXXIII of Reuss. Right: At his wedding to Allene (he is without hat) with his brother, Prince Heinrich XXXII, as his best man.

Alexandra of Russia. He was in the diplomatic service at the German embassy in Paris, having served in Japan and Austria. They married at the Mairie' of the 7th Arrondissement in the morning, then after the civil ceremony, Dean Beekman officiated at a religious ceremony at the bride's home at 33 rue Bardet de Jouy. Those attending included the German ambassador and the groom's brothers, Prince Henry XXXII and Prince Henry XXXIV. The bride was given in marriage by Captain Steele, naval attache' of the embassy in Paris. After a honeymoon they traveled to England and from there sailed on the *Mauretania* for New York. After their arrival, educational leaders gave a luncheon at the Princeton Club for Prince Henry XXXIII to discuss the exchange of undergraduate engineering students between

1942, son of Prince Heinrich VII, German ambassador in Vienna, and Princess Marie Alexandrine. He was a member of one of the oldest reigning houses of Europe and was a descendant of Emperor Henry VI of the Holy Roman Empire. The House of Reuss reigned for many centuries until the revolution of 1918. With each century the numbering of the sons, all named Henry, began again. The groom held a doctorate of philosophy from a German university and served as an officer in the 2nd Dragoon Guard, the regiment of the Empress

Germany and America. Allene held a luncheon in New York City at which she announced her contribution of $300,000 to Stevens Institute of Technology in memory of her late husband, Anson Wood Burchard, who was a graduate of Stevens.

Prince Henry and Allene were divorced at Paris 31 October 1935. She married fifth at Geneva, 4 March 1936, **Paul, Count Kotzebue,** who died at Paris 13 September 1966. He was an Estonian of Russian origin whose great-uncle, Ernest Kotzebue, was Russian ambassador in Washington in 1895. By a decree of the Grand Duke Kirill dated 11 January 1934, Paul von Kotzebue was authorized to bear his great-uncle's title of count. They purchased, in 1940, Vincent Astor's Newport villa, Beechwood, and entertained there often. Prince Heinrich XXXIII of Reuss was secretary of the German embassy and died at Stonsdorf, 15 November 1942. Allene, Countess Paul de Kotzebue, lived at 740 Park Avenue in New York City, and died at seventy-nine at her villa in Cap-d'Ail on the French Riviera in May of 1955, where she had spent the winter with her last husband. Her will was filed in probate court in Newport, Rhode Island, 25 May 1955, and her estate was estimated at $15 million. By her direction the estate was divided into thirds with one part to Stevens Institute of Technology in memory of her third husband, Anson Wood Burchard, one part to her widower, Count Paul de Kotzebue, and the last to her friend Kathryn Cohue of New York. Her niece, **Lucy Tew,** married in 1938 **Prince Georges Dadiani,** with Nikolai Kotzebue serving as best man. From a corpus of more than $13 million, the Allene Reuss Trust in New York City annually distributes more than a half-million dollars in grants to organizations usually benefiting the visually-impaired.

Lucy Tew, born New York City, 8 August 1912, daughter of Eleanor Scott Tew and William H. Tew of New York City, married on 8 January 1938 in the Greek Orthodox Cathdral of New York City, **Prince Georges Dadiani,** born at Tiflis, 3 February 1912, son of Prince Nicholas Dadiani and Princess Maria Tsereteli. Lucy was a niece of **Allene Tew,** the second wife of Prince Heinrich XXXIII of Reuss (of the younger line). A personal representative of the archbishop

of the Greek Orthodox Church presided over the marriage ceremony and the best man was Nikolai Kotzebue of the family of the bride's uncle. The couple lived in Paris and had no children. He died in Paris, 15 October 1985, followed by her death in Paris in 1989 and they are buried at Leuville-sur-Orge, Essonne. The last head of the Dadiani house (descended from the dukes of Mingrelia) was H.S.H. Prince Nikolaoz Dadiani (whose father was the Russian candidate for the throne of Bulgaria). He served as gentleman of the bedchamber to the emperor of Russia and died in a Bolshevik Prison Hospital in March 1919. The line is now extinct in the male line. One of Prince Georges Dadiani's cousins, Princess Salome' Dadiani, married in Paris in 1868, Prince Achille Murat, whose American mother was **Caroline Fraser.**

Anne Huntington Tracy, born 21 May 1890, was a daughter of Charles Edward Tracy and Jenny Bigelow Tracy and a niece of Mrs. J. Pierpont Morgan (Fanny Tracy). Her grandfather, John Bigelow, was President Lincoln's ambassador to France and ambassador to Germany. Anne married 11 September 1926 in the Highland Falls, New York, Episcopal Church **Prince Simon Constantine Sidamon-Eristoff,** born 6 February 1891, died 10 October 1919. The service was conducted in both the Orthodox and Episcopal rites. He was born in Tiflis, Georgia, and graduated from the Cadet School and later from the Grand Duke Michael Artillery School in St. Petersburg. During WWI he served with Russia's 1st Artillery Brigade in actions against Austria-Hungary and German forces. In 1918, when Georgia declared its independence, he joined the Army of the Georgia Republic as a

Anne Tracy at her marriage to Prince Simon Sidamon-Eristoff. Prince Simon studied at Johns Hopkins University and became a successful engineer.

colonel. He was made chief of staff of the infantry division, responsible for defending the Black Sea front against the Communists. When that movement collapsed, he left Georgia aboard an American destroyer and landed in Constantinople. He came to New York City in 1921, accompanied by two cousins. They were assisted after their arrival by Normon O. Whitehouse, who in 1920 had married their cousin, Princess Tamara Bagration Moukhransky. Whitehouse had been part of an American Peace Delegation to the Caucasus in 1919 when he met his future wife. Prince Simon studied engineering at Johns Hopkins University and became a vice president and director of Quinn Engineering Company, and died at Stonihurst, his wife's family estate in Highland Falls, New York, 13 September 1964. By Anne Tracy he had a son, Constantine, born 1930 (who married Anne Phipps, granddaughter of steel industrialist Henry Phipps), and a daughter, Anne, born in 1931. By a previous marriage to a cousin, Princess Tamara Sidamon-Eristoff, he had a daughter, Mrs. Zurab (Irene) Abdusheli. His funeral service was held at the Russian Orthodox Church of Christ the Savior in New York City. Prince Simon's second cousin, Princess Xenia, married Charles K. Moser, U. S. Consul in Tiflis, Georgia. Another cousin, Prince Dmitri Sidamon-Eristoff, married Nicole Chavane, daughter of Mrs. Donald B. Adams of Hastings-on-Hudson, New York. Anne Tracy's cousin, **Lucy Tracy Lee,** daughter of William P. Lee of New York City, married in 1883 the **2nd Baron Grimthorpe** of England, and died immediately after giving birth to her son, who eventually succeeded in 1917 as the 3rd Baron Grimthorpe.

Cecilia Ulman, born New York City, 6 July 1863, died Paris, 9 April 1927, was the wife of Ferdinand Blumenthal, the senior member of the firm of F. Blumenthal & Co., leather merchants, who came to the U. S. from his native Frankfurt-am-Main around 1875. He established a New York City office of his family business that had been founded in 1715, and opened factories in Wilmington, Delaware, which were incorporated into his firm. He retired early and had a home at 19 Spruce St., New York City, and at 34 Avenue du Bois de Boulogne in Paris, which was referred to as a "showplace" containing "a famous collection of art." He was a well-known collector of antiques and his Paris home was filled with paintings of the Barbizon school, including a number of Corots. He was made a chevalier of the Legion of Honor for his interest in French arts. Blumenthal died 20 October 1914 on board the steamship Patria on his way from Naples to New York City, leaving two sons by Cecilia, William and Cecil. She then married as his second wife at Paris's Church of St. Pierre du Groscallou (where she was escorted down the aisle by the American ambassador, William G. Sharp) on 14 November 1917, Louis, **2nd Duc de Montmorency, Count de Perigord,** born Paris, 22 March 1867, son of 1st Duc de Montmorency, prominent figure at the court of Napoleon III, who was a son of the 3rd Duc de Valencay of the Princes de Sagan and Dukes de Talleyrand-Perigord. He succeeded his father 26 March 1915. His first wife had been a daughter of the Duc de Rohan. The duke was forty-eight at the time of his second marriage and had no children by Cecila. After Cecilia's death in 1927 he married again, in 1950, at the age of eighty-three and died the next year at Paris, 26 September 1951, and the line is now extinct.

After her marriage to the Duc de Montmorency, wags in Paris referred to the former Mrs. Blumenthal as the "Duchess of Montmorenthal." In May of 1919, Cecilia's brother, J. Stevens Ulman of New York City, one of the first prominent Jewish members of society, announced the engagement of his nephew, "Cecil Charles Blunt," who was a vice president of F. Blumenthal Co. The bride

Cecila Ulman's granddaughter, Countess Laetitia Pecci-Blunt, formerly Princess of Venosa, with her great-nephew, Prince Gregorio Boncompagni-Ludovisi.

was Donna Anna Laetitia Pecci (1885 – 1971), only daughter of Count and Countess Camillo Pecci of Rome (Pecci was a nephew of Pope Leo XIII, as his father was the pope's younger brother). The two were married in 1919 and adopted the name "Pecci-Blunt" after Cecil was created a count by his wife's great-uncle, the pope. She became a great patron of the arts and owned an art gallery that featured the work of new and emerging artists. The world premiere of Ned Rorem's War Scenes took place on 23 March 1955, at a private concert in the Countess Pecci-Blunt's Roman palazzo. Many of the Blumenthal paintings were inherited by Count Cecil Pecci-Blunt and three Corots and one Delacroix are now in the collection of the National Gallery of Art in Washington, D.C. The Pecci-Blunts had a daughter, Laetitia, who married Prince Don Alberto, **Prince of Venosa** (of the Boncompagni Ludovisi family). Both she and her father, Count Pecci-Blunt, retained their U. S. citizenship.

Count Pecci-Blunt met a younger man, Cecil Everley, who was then serving behind the counter at the London department store, Lillywhite. He was formerly a footman to the 7th Earl of Beauchamp, who was publicly disgraced in 1931 for homosexual offenses (King George V is reported to have said at the time, "I thought men like that shot themselves."). Count Pecci-Blunt and Everley began an intimate relationship and the count gave him a house in California and another, *La Rondine,* on Cap d'Ail, in the south of France. Everley, who was known as good-looking but boring, once asked society hostess Daisy Fellowes, after her sale of the *Sister Anne,* "Do you miss your yacht?" (purchased with the substantial fortune inherited from her American grandmother, Isabelle Singer, Duchess Decazes) to which she replied, "Do you miss your tray?" Cecil Beaton's diary referred to Cecil Everley as "a rather pathetic and silly chorus boy sissy." Everley began painting in California in 1953 and his works eventually were in the collections of the Aga Khan, Princess Grace and Princess Caroline of Monaco, Greta Garbo, Greer Garson, and Estee' Lauder. Count Cecil Pecci-Blunt divided his time between his life with his wife and children and that of his life with Cecil Everley. His long-suffering wife was referred to as "La Reine des Deux Ceciles."

Louise Astor Van Alen, born New York City, 10 May 1910, died Santa Barbara, California, 30 December 1997, was a daughter of James Laurens Van Alen and Margaret L. Post Van Alen, and granddaughter of James J. Van Alen (U. S. ambassador to Italy in 1893) and Emily Astor Van Alen (who was a daughter of William and Caroline Schermerhorn Astor, universally referred to as "the" Mrs. Astor who created the "400"). Louise married first in May of 1931, **Prince Alexis Mdivani,** born 1905, and married second, his brother, **Prince Serge Mdivani,** born 1903. Alexis was part of an ambitious and clever family known as the "Marrying Mdivanis," with five children who had far more charm than money. The princely title was not real. In fact, their father, Zakharias, said that he was the only person ever to inherit a title from his children when their mother, in seeking refugee documents, registered herself at the police station as "Princess Mdivani" after fleeing from Russia. Alexis's sister, Roussie, married the Spanish painter, Jose' Maria Sert, who was famous for his Waldorf Astoria murals, and she was the mastermind behind her brothers' marriages. Their other sister, Nina, married Dennis Conan-Doyle, son of the creator of *Sherlock Holmes* (she eventually controlled the estate of Sir Arthur Conan-Doyle, married her husband's secretary, and died a drug addict).

Alexis Mdivani had been in love with the beautiful Silvia de Rivas but he was considered unsuitable for her and she married Count

Louise Astor Van Alen with her second husband, Prince Serge Mdivani, brother of her first husband. He died on the polo field after being kicked in the head by a pony.

Henri de Castellane. He then courted Louise Van Alen and, after they were engaged, he began to pursue Woolworth heiress Barbara Hutton, who was a childhood friend of Louise Van Alen. Louise's mother strongly opposed their marriage. Once Alexis and Louise were married and she provided a substantial living allowance, his pursuit of Hutton became public and they were seen together in Biarritz only two months after his marriage to Van Alen. One of Hutton's biographers, C. David Heymann, recounts Prince Alexis's joy at his new-found wealth. "Alice-Leone Moats, living in Paris at this time, wrote: 'He had to show each new thing off, and before a polo match at Bagatelle, he dragged his friend Chico Kilvert to the stable so that she could see his ponies. The horse blankets were adorned with closed crowns about the size of a witch's cauldron. Chico, doing her best to keep a straight face, asked, 'Aren't the crowns a bit small?' That worried him. 'Do you really think so?' he replied."

Louise and Prince Alexis divorced at Gravenhage in November of 1932 and, five months before Barbara Hutton reached her majority, she married Prince Alexis. Because he was a French citizen and the marriage took place in Paris, Alexis would have been entitled to all Hutton's vast wealth had her father not insisted upon a pre-nuptial contract that awarded Alexis an outright $1 million, plus an annual allowance of $50,000 for life. Alexis's brother, Prince Serge Mdivani, had first married silent film star Pola Negri. When her career began to decline, he married wealthy opera singer Mary McCormic, who immediately regretted her decision and divorced him. **Prince Serge Mdivani** then married at Palm Beach, 8 February 1936, Louise Van Alen, his former

sister-in-law, before dying on the polo field after being kicked in the head by a pony on 15 March 1936, near Delray Beach, Florida. Their other brother, Prince David, married Mae Murray, a wealthy movie star, and left her with neither money nor career. Only five months after Barbara Hutton married Prince Alexis, Serge and David were charged with theft, embezzlement, and larceny and Alexis was implicated in the charges. Hutton paid all the bills for them and took her new husband out of the country so he could not be served with legal papers.

Louise's final husband, whom she married 19 August 1947, and with whom she lived in Santa Barbara, California, was Alexander Saunderson, born 5 September 1917. He was captured by the Germans at Dunkirk and spent five years as a prisoner of war. He inherited from his father Castle Saunders in County Cavan, Ireland, and was a half-brother of Demeter Larisch of Greenwich, Connecticut, formerly Demeter Graf Larisch von Moennich, who died in 1959. Louise's cousin, **Margaret Astor Drayton**, daughter of William Backhouse Astor Drayton and Helen Fargo Squiers Drayton, married **Curt, Count von Haugwitz-Hardenberg-Reventlow.**

Consuelo Vanderbilt, born 2 March 1877, was a daughter of William K. Vanderbilt (a grandson of Commodore Vanderbilt, founder of the family fortune) and of Alva Smith Vanderbilt of New York City and Newport. She was named for her godmother, Alva's childhood friend **Consuelo Yznaga** (see her separate entry), whose brother Fernando was married to Alva's sister. In the year before little Consuelo's birth, her godmother married Viscount Mandeville who would succeed his father as 8th Duke of Manchester. From an early

Consuelo Vanderbilt was one of the greatest heiresses of her day. Her socially ambitious mother forced her to marry the 9th Duke of Marlborough.

age Alva's socially ambitious mother groomed her for a career as a princess or duchess. As Consuelo wrote of her mother in her memoirs, "it was her wish to produce me as a finished specimen framed in a perfect setting." Governesses taught all her lessons and she was privately administered the entrance examinations for Oxford and Cambridge, both of which she easily passed. She was also forced to wear an iron brace to improve her posture. When she made her debut in Paris, she was favorably referred to as "la belle Mlle. Vanderbilt au long cou" for her long and elegant neck. Consuelo had fallen in love with a young and handsome friend of the family, Winthrop Rutherfurd, but her mother would not hear of the union. They were kept apart and even his letters to her were confiscated. American-born Minnie Stevens Paget arranged for Consuelo's first introduction to the young 9th Duke of Marlborough. His father had died in 1892 having spent the money of his second wife, American heiress **Lily Price Hammersley** (see her separate entry) and the son was badly in need of financing. Alva and Consuelo attended a dinner at Blenheim Palace and invited the young duke to visit

the **9th Duke of Marlborough, Marquess of Blandford, Earl of Sunderland, Earl of Marlborough, Baron Spencer, Baron Churchill, Prince of Mellenberg** (of the Holy Roman Empire) and **Prince of Mindelheim** (in Swabia) (although the Marlborough name is best known for the brilliant military career of the 1st Duke culminating in his victory at Blenheim, the Emperor Leopold created him Prince of the Holy Roman Empire in 1704 and, the next year, the emperor's son and successor, Joseph, created him Prince of Mindelheim). The couple became close to King Edward VII and often entertained him at Blenheim. The playwright Sir James Barrie wrote of her, "I would stand all day in the street to see Consuelo Marlborough get into her carriage." Though the couple had two sons ("the heir and the spare"), the marriage was unhappy and they separated in 1906 and divorced in 1920. The next

Consuelo produced two sons, "the heir and the spare," in a marriage estimated to have cost her family at least $15 million dollars.

them in Newport. With all Newport society waiting impatiently the expected marriage proposal was duly made and accepted before the attorneys went to work on an extremely lucrative wedding contract that gave the duke $2.5 million outright (with a guaranteed annual yield of 4 percent), a new town house in London, plus major repairs to Blenheim Palace, all of which totaled $15 million. Consuelo arrived late to her own wedding, her eyes red and swollen by tears covered by a veil. In the biggest social event of the year, Consuelo Vanderbilt married at New York City's St. Thomas' Church on 6 November 1895

year the duke married American **Gladys Deacon** (sister of Princess "Aba" Radziwill; see her separate entry) who had been his mistress for several years. Gladys was also a close personal friend of Consuelo and there are differing opinions of whether the Duchess was unaware of her husband's relationship or whether she may have known and approved of his choice of her successor. Consuelo then married a French aviator, Jacques Balsan, after her finally-contrite mother helped her secure a 1926 Papal annulment of her first marriage by admitting that she had forced Consuelo to marry the duke. Consuelo wrote

Left: Consuelo was happy in her second marriage to aviator Jacques Balsan. Right: The 9th Duke of Marlborough married another American who had been a close friend to him and to his wife.

her memoirs, *The Glitter and the Gold,* in 1952 and, at her death at the age of eighty-seven on 6 December 1964, she was buried in the Churchill family plot in accordance with her wishes. The current duke is her grandson.

Rosalie Van Zandt, born New York City, 28 December 1833, died Florence, Italy, 8 July 1914, was a daughter of Thomas Van Zandt and Louisa Julia Underhill Van Zandt, and a granddaughter of Wynant Van Zandt and Maria Underhill Van Zandt. Her grandfather was an early settler and developer of the area known as Douglas Hill in the Queens borough of New York City. The mansion he built there in 1819 still exists as the Douglaston Club, and he donated the land and funds to establish Zion Episcopal Church. Rosalie first married on 15 February 1853, in New York City, Dr. Joseph Karrick Riggs, a son of Elisha Riggs, founder and president of Riggs National Bank in Washington. The bank was chosen in 1844 as the sole federal depository in Washington and, in the following year, financed the invention of the telegraph by Samuel Morse. In 1847 Riggs Bank lent the federal government $16 million to finance the Mexican War.

Rosalie and Joseph Riggs had four children, two of whom survived childhood. Their son, stockbroker Karrick Van Zandt Riggs, married in 1884 Pauline Drouillard Oothout whose daughter, Pauline Drouillard Riggs (1886-1942), married Robert B. Noyes and contributed several paintings, including Gilbert Stuart portraits, to the National Gallery of Art and the Metropolitan Museum of Art, in memory of Elisha Riggs. Dr. Joseph K. Riggs received his medical education in the United States but moved with his family to France in 1866. When the Franco-Prussian War began in 1870, he joined the American Ambulance Service and served throughout the siege. Clara Barton traveled to Strasborg, France, during the Franco-Prussian War. She enlisted as a volunteer and learned firsthand about the Red Cross Movement, founded in Geneva, Switzerland, in 1863. The American Ambulance Service, a forerunner of the American Red Cross Motor

Left: Medora von Hoffmann was uniquely suited to the Wild West. She was said to be almost as good a shot as her husband (right), the Marquis de Mores.

woman to marry into the Ruspoli family. Prince Paolo had first married **Florence Frances York** (1838-1874), by whom he had three daughters, Elena, Leopolda, and Laura, but had no children by his second marriage. Prince Paolo's younger brother, Prince Emanuele, was created the 1st Prince di Poggio Suasa in 1886 and married as his third wife in 1885 American **Josephine Curtiss.**

Medora Marie von Hoffmann, born Staten Island, New York, 1857, died Cannes, 3 March 1921, was a daughter of Athenais Grymes von Hoffman and Louis A. von Hoffmann, a New York banker and one of the founders of the Knickerbocker Club. She married on 15 February 1882, Antoine-Amedee, **Marquis de Mores and de Monte-Maggiore,** born Paris, 15 June 1858, died Africa 1896, eldest son of Don Richard, Duke of Vallombrosa and of l'Asinara, Count

of San-Giorgio, Baron of Tiesi, Tissi, Ossi and Usini. Although her father was usually referred to in New York society as "Baron von Hoffmann," (including his obituary), his title was not recognized by the *Almanach de Gotha*. Medora's maternal grandparents were Susanna Bosque Grymes (third wife and widow of William C. C. Claiborne, first American governor of Louisiana) and John Randolph Grymes, United States attorney for Louisiana and personal counsel to

Corps and Ambulance Service, flew a flag throughout the Siege of Paris during the Franco-Prussian War and a Riggs descendant donated the flag to the American Red Cross in 1947.

After Dr. Riggs's death in Paris on 22 February 1883, his widow, Rosalie, married in Paris, 11 April 1888, **Prince Paolo Ruspoli**, born 10 January 1835, died 28 April 1913, grandson of the 3rd Prince di Cerveteri. According to the *New York Times*, she was the fifth American

Andrew Jackson during the Battle of New Orleans, who resigned his post to represent the pirate Jean Lafitte. Medora was named for her maternal aunt, who was the second wife of Samuel Ward, acclaimed Washington lobbyist, whose first wife was Emily Astor, daughter of William Backhouse Astor (Ward's sister, Julia Ward Howe, wrote "The Battle Hymn of the Republic").

In the early 1880s, de Mores decided to make his fortune in the American West. He settled in the Dakotas territory at the junction of the Little Missouri River and the Northern Pacific Railroad. He named his new town "Medora" for his wife and immediately began establishing himself in the cattle business, making use of his father-in-law's capital. In June of 1883, the marquis and a companion were accosted by three cowboys who reportedly threatened their lives. De Mores killed one of them and was tried three times for the murder – each trial with a different judge. His faithful wife moved into his jail cell and shared confinement with him while he was acquitted on each occasion. The marquis began butchering two hundred cows per day and shipping beef in newly-refrigerated boxcars to Chicago. He amassed 26,000 acres and built a twenty-six-room mansion later called "The Chateau de Mores." In his small town of Medora, he built a brickyard, stores, a saloon, a hotel, a newspaper, and even a Catholic Church. In 1883, the same year in which de Mores tackled the Dakotas territory, Teddy Roosevelt arrived to shoot buffalo. Struck by the success of the young marquis, Roosevelt bought 450 head of cattle and went into the same business. De Mores soon wrote a letter to Roosevelt, accusing him of undercutting the marquis on a deal

and Roosevelt took the letter as a challenge to a duel. The two were able to settle the matter amicably and Roosevelt eventually returned to New York having lost his entire investment.

In 1885, while on a business trip to New York City, de Mores was informed that he must return to the Dakotas to be tried once again for the cowboy's death. In reply to a *New York Times* reporter's questions about the trial, he insisted, "I have plenty of money for defense, but not a dollar for blackmail." Although the marquis was acquitted again, his business ventures repeatedly failed. His New York investors had approved a credit line of $7,000 and were astounded when they were presented with invoices for $50,000. By the end of 1887, the marquis admitted defeat and his land, said to be worth $175,000, was sold at auction for $71,000, including ten acres on the Kansas River within the limits of Kansas City. The marquis announced that he was abandoning his failed businesses to go tiger hunting in India. The *New York Times*, referring to Medora as "a handsome wife, as courageous, even, as he is himself, and scarcely a whit behind him in hunting accomplishments," announced that she would accompany her husband, continuing, "She has been through the savagest parts of our Western country, galloping into dangers galore ... The rifle is a toy in her hands, and buffalo and grizzlies and wild deer have gone down in regiments for her bullet's sake." The *Times'* final verdict on the marquis's abandonment of western life was that he "has given up being a rich man. The experience didn't seem to suit him exactly. He started in well four or five times, but somehow each time he managed to get over the troublesomeness of it." The newspaper's conservative estimate was that he and his investors had lost $1.5 million.

After the de Mores's sojourn in India, the family moved to France, where the marquis became involved in politics and was a participant in several duels. He became virulently anti-Semitic and blamed Jews for most of his business losses. In 1896 he was murdered in North Africa by his escort of Tuareg tribesmen while crossing the Sahara where he was trying to join the French and Arabs in the Khalifa's holy war against the Jews and the English. In 1903, Medora returned to the Dakotas and was interviewed by a local newspaper. She explained, "I want my children to see the place where we lived so long... I loved Medora, I love it still, and it will be very dear to my memory. I will not let Medora die until after I do. I can't tell just what I will do, but I must see the old ranch." She lived until March of 1921 and died at the palatial Villa Vallombrosa at Cannes.

The couple had three children, Athenais, Louis (who succeeded his grandfather as **Duke of Vallombrosa** and **Duke of l'Asinara** but never married), and Paul. The fully-restored Chateau de Mores is now part of a 128-acre park operated by the state of North Dakota. In 1903, President Teddy Roosevelt revisted Medora where, as he described it, "the entire population of the Bad Lands down to the smallest baby had gathered to meet me." He visited once again in retirement in 1911. Medora's sister, **Pauline von Hoffmann,** married the immensely wealthy German industrialist **Baron Ferdinand von Stumm,** who was ennobled by Wilhelm II in 1888 and authorized to add "Halberg" to his last name. His family owned the Neunkirchen Iron and Steelworks. Ferdinand served as imperial ambassador to Madrid from 1887 to 1892, and entertained the kaiser at von Stumm's Castle Rauischholzhausen where the baron died in 1925. One of von Stumm's paintings, a de Goya portrait of Don Antonio Noriega, now hangs in the National Gallery in Washington. The von Stumms' daughter, Maria, married Prince Paul Hatzfeldt, son of American **Helen Moulton.**

Elizabeth Ashfield Walker, born Washington, D.C., 11 May 1896, died Monaco, 17 November 1976, daughter of William Henry Walker and Grace Atlee Husted Walker, married in Monaco (as his second wife) on 27 June 1963, **Victor, Prince de Polignac,** born London, 17 June 1899, died 4 November 1998, nephew of **Prince Edmond de Polignac** who married American **Winnaretta Singer.** Prince Victor was a son of **Prince Camille Armand de Polignac** (1832–1913), whose father was Charles X's minister, and of his wealthy wife, Margaret Elizabeth Knight. Prince Camille served as a brigadier general and division general for the Confederacy during the American Civil War (where he was called "The Lafayette of the South"). He volunteered for Confederate service and was a lieutenant colonel on the staff of Beauregard at Shiloh and Corinth. He then was promoted to brigadier general and served on Taylor's staff in Mississippi before being given his own command in the Red River campaign at Mansfield. As a major general, Prince Camille traveled to France to seek his country's support for the Confederacy and was there when the war ended. He remained in France and eventually served in the Franco-Prussian war before dying in Paris in 1913 as the last surviving major general of the Confederacy. His son, Prince Victor, had no children by either wife.

Helena "Ella" Holbrook Walker, born Detroit, 17 January 1875, died Bellagio, 22 June 1957, was a daughter of Franklin Hiram Walker of Detroit. Ella's father was a multimillionaire liquor distiller who inherited the Hiram Walker Distilling Company from his father. Her grandfather moved to Michigan from New England and began a

Victor, Prince de Polignac, pictured here with his mother, was the son of "the Lafayette of the South," who was the Confederacy's last-surviving major general.

grocery business. After successfully distilling his own cider, in 1856 he purchased property in Ontario on the Canadian side of the river where he built his distillery. His success threatened U. S. distillers and congress legislated that he designate his whiskey as having been produced in Canada, thus the birth of "Canadian Club." In the 1880s, Walker moved his family back to Detroit and built both a short railway and a ferry service to connect his Walkerville distillery to Detroit. Ella married first at Detroit, 15 June 1897, **Manfred, Count Matushcka, Baron von Toppolczan and Apaetgen,** of a prominent Silesian family; he was an officer in the former kaiser's bodyguard. They divorced at Berlin, 20 October 1925, and she had the marriage annulled (she adopted his niece, Countess Huberta Matuschka).

She then married at Versailles, 6 December 1930, socialite James Hazen Hyde, whose American former wife, **Marthe Leishman, Countess de Gontaut-Biron,** was the sister of **Nancy, Duchess of Croy.** Their father was the U. S. ambassador to Germany. Ella and Hyde divorced at Paris 26 May 1932 and she married as his second wife at Vrana 18 October 1932, **Prince Alexander von Thurn & Taxis** and (from 1923) **1st Prince della Torre e Tasso, 1st Duca di Castel Duino** (1881-1937), favorite son of the famous Princess Marie von Thurn & Taxis, friend of Rainer Maria Rilke. Ella's marriage to Prince Alexander was not recognized by the prince's family and he had no children by her (although his grandson, **Prince Ludwig,** married American **Frances Goodyear**). She reigned over a sixteenth-century villa at Bellagio overlooking three arms of Lake Como and the Alps, crowned by the ruins of a medieval fortress. She died at her Villa Serbelloni on the shores of Lake Como near Bellagio, Italy. She left $2 million plus her villa at Bellagio to the Rockefeller Foundation and the remainder of her estate, more than $8 million, was left to Frau Huberta von Scheon, the niece of her first husband, whom Ella adopted. Prince Alexander died 17 June 1916, in Detroit. The 2nd Prince della Torre e Tasso married as her second husband Princess Eugenie, daughter of George I, king of the Hellenes, and his queen, Grand Duchess Olga of Russia. Princess Eugenie's nephew is Prince Philip, Duke of Edinburgh.

Clara Ward, born Detroit, Michigan, 17 June 1873, died Padua, 9 December 1916, was a daughter of Captain Eber Brock Ward and his second wife, Catherine Lyons Ward. Manufacturer Eber Ward of Detroit, called "The King of the Lakes," was reportedly the wealthiest man in Michigan. At his death in 1875, his property alone in Michigan was valued at more than $3 million and he served as the first president of the American Iron and Steel Association. He was largely responsible for having developed shipping lines across the Great Lakes and later built rolling mills in seven cities near Chicago, Detroit, and Milwaukee. Clara met in Nice and was married by the papal nuncio at Paris, 20 May 1890, Joseph de Riquet, **19th Prince de Chimay, Prince de Caraman,** born Paris, 4 July 1858 (he was fifteen years her senior) died Chimay, 25 July 1937, of a Franco-Belgian house. She was given a marriage settlement of $2.5 million by the estate of her father. Prince Joseph was a member of the chamber of representatives in Belgium.

Clara was supposedly bored by life in the little village of Chimay

Clara Ward's antics were constantly reported in the newspapers of her day. Her first marriage bored her but made her a princess. Right: Clara pictured in full *pose plastique,* with flesh-colored body suit and slave bracelets.

having never married. The father remarried in 1920 a French woman and had another son, Prince Joseph, born 1921, who succeeded his father as 20th Prince but renounced his titles upon becoming an American citizen when the titles passed to his next brother, Elie. Clara's husband's grandson is the current 22nd Prince de Chimay, Prince de Caraman.

Clara remarried in 1898 Rigo Janczi, a Hungarian violinist who referred to himself as a Gypsy prince. They became Hungary's beautiful couple in 1905, sometimes requiring police protection from the crowds who surrounded them. He told of their meeting by insisting that "the night I saw her first she turned from King Leopold to smile at me. Ten days later, like two gypsies, we stole from her palace in the dead of night" when he took her to his mother's hut in the mountains. To that mother Clara gave a pearl necklace with a diamond clasp that hung on a nail by the fire. Supposedly Clara

and was even reported to have thrown gold coins from the battlement of her castle to watch the villagers fight for them. He and Clara were divorced 19 January/20 June 1897 (annulled at St. Siege 28 June 1911,) and she "enjoyed a gay and scandalous career which gossips compared to that of Lola Montez" according to the *New York Times.* They had a daughter, Countess Marie, born 1891, who married in 1918 Georges Albert Leon Decocq, and a son, Joseph, who would have succeeded his father but he died in 1920 at the age of twenty-five,

then bought the mountain on which the hut sat and gave it to her new mother-in-law. They moved to Egypt and for her new husband she "built me a white marble palace on the Nile. An Italian architect designed the stables for the sixteen jet-black Arabian horses she bought for me. ... She bought a menagerie of baby elephants, lions and tigers to amuse me. She gave me my $5,000 violin and caskets of jewels. Her allowance of $500 a month for me has not failed once since she started it twenty years ago." By the time he wrote that account Clara and Rigo had divorced and she pursued other loves.

As Cornelia Otis Skinner wrote of Paris in *Elegant Wits and Grand Horizontals,* "The midnight resort par excellence for the Horizontals was, of course, Maxim's....Few society ladies would have dared to be seen within the art nouveau interior of that naughty place, with some emancipated exceptions such as Princesse Caraman-Chimay, née Clara Ward from Detroit, Michigan, who eventually ran away with the violinist Rigo and appeared at the Folies Bergères in pink tights and a series of 'Plastic Poses.'" Clara was painted by Toulouse-Lautrec in *A Princely Idyl, Clara Ward,* now at the Cleveland Museum of Art. After her 1911 divorce, another American woman, Mrs. Casper E. Emerson Jr., left her husband for Rigo and he played the violin in the Little Hungary Restaurant, a small tea room opened by his new wife, before dying near destitution in 1927. Rigo was buried in the National Vaudeville Association plot at Kensico Cemetery in Westchester County, New York. On a visit to Paris, Clara deserted Rigo for a Spaniard. In the end, she married an Italian named Peppino Ricciardi who was a stationmaster on the Vesuvian Railway. She sued him for divorce in 1910 after the court's unsuccessful attempts to bring about their reconciliation.

In 1915 her mother, Catherine Lyons Ward Morrow, died, leaving Clara only $1,000 of her own $1 million estate. Clara, formerly Princess de Chimay, died at her villa in Padua, 9 December 1916. Her estate of $1.2 million was divided into trust funds and left to her son, Joseph, her daughter, Marie, and her last husband (with the corpus reverting to her children at his death), and a small bequest to

Clara's second husband, Rigo Janczi, with whom "like two gypsies, we stole from her palace in the dead of night."

a cousin in Chicago. There was a rumor that she died a pauper with nothing left except a few jewels, but the American consul at Venice stated publicly that Clara "was in possession of a very large income and lived in a manner befitting its possessor. At the time of her death she occupied the best suite at the Hotel Stella d'Oro. During her sickness she had the assistance of expert physicians, and everything that money and medical science could do in her last illness was done. Her funeral was elaborate and costly." Prince Joseph's brother, **Prince Alexandre,** married American **Mathilde Lowenguth.**

(Bessie) Wallis Warfield was born at Blue Ridge Summit, Pennsylvania, on 19 June 1896, a daughter of Teackle Wallis Warfield and Alice Montague Warfield. Her father died when she was small and she was reared in genteel poverty in Baltimore, Maryland. On 8 November 1916 she married Navy pilot Earl Winfield Spencer, Jr. When he was posted to the Far East, Wallis remained behind and supposedly continued her affair with an Argentinian diplomat. She joined her husband in 1924 but they separated the following year and divorced in 1927. On 21 July 1928, Wallis married Ernest A. Simpson, who was a former Coldstream Guard. During their marriage she was introduced to the Prince of Wales and eventually replaced his two successive mistresses, Freda Dudley Ward and the American Thelma, Viscountess Furness (twin sister of the senior Gloria Vanderbilt). The famously-beautiful Margaret, Duchess of Argyll, described Wallis after their meeting as "quite a plain woman with a noticeably square jaw, and not particularly amusing." The Prince of Wales's father, King George V, died on 20 January 1936 and the son

Edward, Prince of Wales (later King Edward VIII and the Duke of Windsor), with his parents, King George V and Queen Mary.

his marriage to a divorcee and the governments of the various British dominions were also decidedly against the marriage. Wallis was granted a divorce from her second husband on 27 October amid growing knowledge of her relationship with the king (information denied most British subjects as it was kept out of the newspapers). Amid growing controversy Wallis fled to France where she stayed with her American friends Katherine and Herman Rogers. On December 7, Wallis read a statement to the media prepared by the king's assistant, announcing her willingness to give up the king for the sake of his country. He would not hear of it, however, and on 10 December 1936 signed a document of abdication in the presence of his three brothers. That day, as H. R. H. the Prince Edward, he made his historic radio broadcast announcing that he could not rule without "the woman I love." He had been king for 325 days. He left for Austria to stay with Baron Eugen de Rothschild and his American-born wife, Kitty (originally Catherine Wolff of Philadelphia), so that Wallis's final divorce would not be compromised. On 8 March 1937 the new king, George VI (formerly Duke of York) created his elder brother Duke of Windsor and granted him the style Royal Highness. But, in a snub that was never forgiven, the style was for him only and was not to be extended to his wife. The former king and the woman he loved were reunited on 4 May 1937 at the Château de Candé in France, owned by the wealthy Paris-born American citizen Charles Bedaux who was later found to be a Nazi sympathizer. With no member of the British royal family present, on 3 June 1937 (the birthday of his late father the king) they were married at the Château de Candé with Americans

The Duke and Duchess of Windsor. Although she was not entitled to be called a "Royal Highness" he insisted that their staff and close friends do so.

ascended to the throne as **Edward VIII, King of Great Britain and Ireland, Emperor of India,** born at White Lodge, Richmond Park, Surrey, on 23 January 1894, died at Paris, 28 May 1972. The following day he watched the announcement of his accession from a window at St. James's Palace with the still-married Wallis at his side. The king's position as Supreme Governor of the Church of England precluded

Katherine and Herman Rogers as two of four attendants. The couple lived in France and made a particularly controversial visit to Adolf Hitler at which he was reported to have said that Wallis "would have made a good queen." The king refused to believe that there would not be a useful position for him in his country's service but, other than a period as governor of the Bahamas, he and his wife spent the following decades in a constant schedule of parties, benefits, and café society. She was admired for her sense of style and was frequently listed among the world's best-dressed women. Lady Diana Cooper said that people "sharpened up" when she came into a room because of her wit. The duke was said to enjoy her dominance of him and made no objection to her public belittling of him on several occasions. The British royal family refused to receive the duchess until 1965 although the Queen visited the duke twice in the London Clinic that year and he occasionally met members of his family with his wife. There was also a more public reception at the unveiling of the Queen Mary memorial in 1967. Queen Elizabeth, whose father had unexpectedly ascended the throne at the abdication of his brother, went to visit the Windsors during a state visit to Paris ten days before his death. The Duke of Windsor died of cancer on 28 May 1972 and his then-senile wife was invited to stay at Buckingham Palace for his funeral service. The duchess spent her last years under the malevolent control of her attorney, Maitre Suzanne Blum, who virtually locked her in her house and cut off her contact with friends and acquaintances. She finally died in Paris on 24 April 1986 and is buried with the duke behind the royal mausoleum at Frogmore. Some of the proceeds from the sale of her extensive estate, including a famous jewelry collection, were directed by Maitre Blum to the Pasteur Institute in Paris, although the duchess had never expressed any interest in its work.

Ruth Morgan Waters, born at Atlantic City, New Jersey, 5 May 1893, was a daughter of George Jason Waters and Bertha Wolnes Waters (who was a granddaughter of former Mayor Fox of Philadelphia). Ruth's father was head of the Ambassador chain of hotels and her aunt was the Marquise Meyronnet de St. Marc. Ruth married in New York City, 4 May 1915, **Prince Ludovico Pignatelli d'Aragon, 26th Count di Fuentes,** born Biarritz, 21 January 1878, died 1956, formerly secretary of the Spanish legation at Washington, son of Prince Luigi and of Emily Cavendish of the Dukes of Devonshire. The couple met at Nice, France, and renewed their acquaintance at Narragansett Pier. Before the prince knew Ruth, he arrived in New York City in 1911 and was driving an automobile that overturned in Central Park, pinning him beneath it. He suffered six broken ribs and deep gashes on his forehead and face that left permanent scars.

He returned to France the next year where cable reports stated that he had shot himself in desperation after being "jilted" by an American girl to whom he had announced his engagement. She was Mary L. Duke, daughter of multimillionaire Benjamin N. Duke and a first cousin of heiress Doris Duke. He had earlier announced his engagement to Helen Hilton but that marriage also never took place. He returned to the U. S. soon after and was detained at Ellis Island while an investigation into his connection with a gambling house took place. It was said at the time that he had been

Prince Ludovico Pignatelli-d'Aragon openly pursued several heiresses before marrying Ruth Waters. After their divorce he was indicted for blackmail and died in a rooming house where he lived in obscurity for the last seventeen years of his life.

expelled from France.

He and Ruth eloped and their marriage was performed at the Church of St. Ignatius Loyola at 84th St. and Park Avenue in New York City. At the time it was reported that the prince's relationship with Ruth had elicited a duel. None of the bride's family had been informed of the wedding and the couple was met with a "round scolding" when they went immediately to the bride's parents' home in New York City. Only that morning Mr. Waters had denied that any engagement had taken place between the two. As the bride was twenty-two and the groom thirty-seven, there was nothing legally which could be done so her parents decided to forgive the couple and accept the marriage. They left for a honeymoon at Hot Springs, Virginia, then returned to a home they purchased in Merrick, Long Island. Within three months of their marriage the groom filed a petition for bankruptcy. His chief creditors were the widow of a man who was killed in a 1914 auto accident in which the prince was driving, and the two passengers in the other car, who also had outstanding judgments against the prince. The prince sued the Sun newspapers in 1922 for their account of his having left the employ of his father-in-law's hotels but the judge ruled in favor of the publisher.

The couple had a son, Ludovic, who was born on Long Island and lived only one month. Later, they lived at Cap Ferrat and had a daughter, Isabelle, born 1923. In 1932 the prince sued his wife, seeking not only custody of their daughter but also asking that Ruth be deprived of the use of the title of princess. The court granted custody to Ruth but stripped her of her title. Two years later the prince sailed to America seeking to overturn the custody decision but was unsuccessful. Ruth returned to her maiden name and, in 1941, Prince Ludovico was indicted by a federal grand jury in New York City for his attempt to blackmail Princess Guido Pignatelli, formerly **Henrietta Hartford,** mother of the A & P heir Huntington Hartford. He had attempted to disprove his cousin's use of the princely Pignatelli title and thus deprive Henrietta's right to be styled as a princess.

Isabelle, the daughter of Ruth and her former husband, succeeded to her father's titles as 27th Countess of Fuentes and 8th Duchess of Solferino. In 1943 she was serving in the Women's Emergency Corps at the Navy recruiting station in Beverly Hills when her engagement was announced to a soldier, John F. O'Shaughnessy. In 1956 Prince Ludovico was critically injured when he fell and hit his head in a west-side rooming house in New York City where he had lived for the past seventeen years. His landlady stated that she was unaware that her tenant was a prince but the Spanish Embassy, where he had once worked, confirmed his identity. The Welfare Department asked for assistance in finding any relatives.

Margaret "Peggy" Carrington Watson, daughter of Garrett F. Watson and Ann Wendenburg Watson, was born in Richmond, Virginia, 12 February 1899, and died at Bayonne, 27 December 1993. She graduated from the Eastman School for Girls in Washington, D.C., where one of her classmates was a daughter of Baron von Hengelmueller, the Austrian-Hungarian minister to Washington and dean of its diplomatic corps. On one occasion the ambassador and Booker T. Washington were both visiting President Theodore Roosevelt at approximately the same time. Hengelmueller finished first and took the overcoat he thought was his. As he walked down the White House drive wearing the overcoat, he placed his hands in its pocket to retrieve his gloves and found instead a rabbit's foot, or, as it was reported at the time, "just the left hind foot of a graveyard rabbit, killed in the dark of the moon." The *Detroit Journal* reported, "The Austrian Ambassador may have made off with Booker T. Washington's coat at the White House, but he'd have a bad time trying to fill his shoes."

Hengenmueller's daughter eventually married in 1923 as his second wife the eldest son of the 3rd Baron Brougham and Vaux (had he lived twenty days longer he would have succeeded his father in the title) and she and Peggy remained life-long friends. Peggy and her family later lived in Newport, Rhode Island, where a contemporary remembers her as a "townie" – not a member of the summer colony. In fact, he believes that her mother ran a boarding house. Supposedly, her maternal grandmother was Baroness Marie von Ketteler of Stuttgart, whose mother was the Countess von Schwerin. A cousin was the Baron Freidrich von Ketteler, German minister to China, whose assassination incited the Boxer Rebellion (his wife was American **Matilda Ledyard**).

The Count of Paris, head of the French royal family, recounted that Peggy and her future husband, Prince Charles-Philippe, met in a bar in Tangier after his parents sent him to Morocco as a result of his heavy drinking. According to the count, he was so drunk when he met Peggy that he collapsed and, as she could not carry him, she had

to bring him home in a wheelbarrow she found nearby. The Count of Paris became fond of Peggy, eventually asserting that, "She was a bit 'piquée' [gently mad], but he was too. And they matched perfectly." After their meeting, Peggy went to Paris to stay with her childhood friend, Mrs. Brougham, and then to London, where she was a guest of Princess Marie Louise de Bourbon, her future sister-in-law. Peggy was then stricken with acute appendicitis and was taken to hospital for an immediate operation. Still showing the effects of her recent illness, Peggy married at London on 14 April in the Covent Garden Registry Office, **Prince Charles-Philippe, the Duc de Nemours,** (and from 1931, also) **Duc de Vendome and d'Alencon,** born Neuilly-sur-Seine, 4 April 1905, died Neuilly-sur-Seine, 10 March 1970, a great-grandson of King Louis Philippe of France who was ousted in the revolution of 1848 (Charles-Philippe's great-aunt was the Empress Elisabeth of Austria). There were only three witnesses and Peggy's parents were informed by telegram after the ceremony had taken place. His parents had opposed the match and attempted to have the Vatican refuse to grant a dispensation for marrying a non-Catholic. The difference in their age (she was six years older than the groom) was also a subject of conversation. The prince's mother had earlier denied that there were plans for her son to marry the American. Even though his family insisted that Peggy would not enjoy the title of

Prince Charles-Philippe and his wealthy and autocratic mother, the Duchess de Vendome. He was already Duc de Nemours and would become Duc de Vendome and d'Alcenon. He and his American wife had no children.

duchess as his family had not given consent to the marriage, several highly-placed members of the French aristocracy disputed that claim, insisting that, "It is curious that while so many spurious titles are going around unchallenged, a real one should be questioned when one happens upon it."

Perhaps in an effort to silence any opposition, the couple wed again in a Paris civil cermony on 26 September 1928, followed later that day by a religious ceremony in a Catholic church. Prince Charles-Philippe was the third child but only son of the Duc de Vendome and d'Alencon. The Almanach de Gotha noted that the marriage was not recognized by the royal house of France. His mother was a sister of King Albert of the Belgians and his father was known as "the sporting Duke" because of his ability with a pistol or rifle. At the time of his father's death less than three years after his son's marriage, the Duc de Nemours was reported to be sheep farming in Rabat, Morocco. His mother, who was a well-known shot, in the autumn of 1907 "added to her popularity by bringing down a ferocious stag that was reported to have killed a woman." She endeared herself to the public by refusing to leave the scene of the Charity Bazaar fire in Paris in 1897 in which she helped to rescue many persons who were overcome by smoke. She inherited one-third of the large fortune of her father, the count of Flanders. Eight months after Peggy's marriage, her sister-in-law, Princess Marie Louise, married in London as her second husband (her first marriage was annulled) a wealthy American, **Walter Kingsland**, born New York City, 23 April 1888, died 20 July 1961, grandson of a former mayor of New York City.

Peggy and her husband had no children and, according to one friend who knew her in her last years, "She was a bit strange by the end." She organized in Paris sales of her possessions in 1971 and again in 1989. Peggy was a frequent topic of conversation within the French royal family. She wanted her pet dogs to be buried in the family vaults at Dreux but the Count of Paris would not consent. He did agree to have her buried with her husband and her parents-in-law in the royal vaults. Peggy's funeral was held at Sainte-Eugénie church in Biarritz on 29 December 1993, followed by a funeral and interment in the royal chapel of Dreux, on 30 December 1993, when she was laid to rest beside her husband.

(Ethel) Margaret Whigham, born at Newton Mearns, Renfrewshire, Scotland, 1 December 1912, died in a nursing home at Pimlico, England, 25 July 1993, was the only child of George Hay Whigham and Helen Hannay Whigham. When she was only three weeks old she moved to the United States where her millionaire father was chairman of the Celanese Corporation of Britain, America, and Canada. After graduating from the fashionable Miss Hewitt's School in New York City, she returned to London where she was debutante of the year. After a relationship with Prince Aly Khan, the future husband of American **Rita Hayworth,** her engagement was announced to the 7th Earl of Warwick but that wedding did not take place. Margaret married on 21 February 1933 at London's Brompton Oratory the wealthy American golfer Charles Sweeny (1909 – 1993), son of Robert and Teresa Hanaway Sweeny. He introduced the Duke of Windsor to the game of golf and established the first of the RAF's American Eagle

Squadrons. Margaret Sweeny became so well-known that even Cole Porter included her in his lyrics for "You're the Top!" In 1943 she was visiting her doctor when she fell forty feet down an elevator shaft and was seriously injured. As a result, she lost all sense of taste and smell and, according to some sources, her sexual appetite became voracious.

She and Sweeny were divorced in 1947 and she married as his third wife on 22 March 1951, Ian Douglas, **11th Duke of Argyll, Marquess of Kintyre and Lorne, Earl of Argyll, Earl of Campbell and Cowall,** born 18 June 1903, died Edinburgh, 7 April 1973, whose American mother was **Aimee Suzanne Lawrence,** daughter of John Lawrence of New York. The duke's first wife was a daughter of the 1st Lord Beaverbrook. Their only child, Lady Jeanne (1908-1988), first married the author Norman Mailer and then John S. Cram, a descendant of Jay Gould, father of Anna Gould, Princess de Sagan. The 11th Duke of Argyll's second wife, American **Louise Hollingsworth Morris Clews,** was a grand-niece of President Madison and a daughter of Henry Clews who was appointed by U. S. treasury secretary Chase to sell bonds to keep the Union troops supplied for the Civil War. Afterwards he organized his own financial company and President Grant appointed him the agent of sale for U. S. bonds to foreign markets. Clews declined nominations as secretary of the treasury, mayor of New York, and collector for the port of New York.

Left: Margaret Whigham, Duchess of Argyll, was so famous that Cole Porter included her in the lyrics of a song. Right: With her daughter, the Duchess of Rutland.

By Louise the duke had two sons, including his heir who succeeded as 12th Duke. In a scandalous divorce suit in 1963 (the same year as the Profumo scandal that almost brought down the British government), the duke accused his third wife, Margaret Whigham, of having committed adultery with a list of eighty-eight men, including three royals and two government ministers. At the trial, he introduced photographs of her, nude except for a triple strand of pearls, performing fellatio on a nude man (whose head was cut out of the photo) while another man masturbated in the background. The most common guesses as to the men's identity were the actor Douglas Fairbanks Jr., and minister of defense Duncan Sandys, the son-in-law of Prime Minister Winston Churchill. In granting the divorce, the judge found that the duchess had engaged in "disgusting sexual activities" and that she was "a completely promiscuous woman whose sexual appetite could only be satisfied with a number of men." She published her memoirs, *Forget Not,* in 1975 with no mention of the headless lover. It is now established that there were two men – Fairbanks and Sandys – and that one of the two took the photographs while the other was engaging in sex with the duchess. At the time, the only Polaroid camera – still in experiemental stages – belonged to the ministry of defense and was thus available to Sandys. Fairbanks's handwriting on the photographs later confirmed him as the other man.

The 11th Duke of Argyll's fourth wife, whom he married 15 June 1963, was **Mathilda Coster Mortimer,** daughter of Stanley Mortimer, born in Geneva of American parents on 20 August 1925, died at the American Hospital in Paris on 6 June 1997, by whom he had a daughter, Elspeth, who lived less than a week. The 11th Duke's grandson, Torquhil, born in 1968, is the current (13th) Duke and has a son, born in 2004, who is his heir, the Marquess of Lorne. He has kept on display at Inverary Castle a portrait of his American grandmother, **Louise Clews.** Margaret Whigham had two children by her first husband, American Charles Sweeny—Frances born in 1937 and Brian born in 1940. In 1958 Frances married as his second wife the **10th Duke of Rutland** and from that time both mother and daughter were duchesses. Frances's husband died in 1999 and her son, David, is now the 11th Duke of Rutland. In her autobiography, Margaret wrote, "I had wealth, I had good looks. As a young woman I had been constantly photographed, written about, flattered, admired,

included in the Ten Best-Dressed Women in the World list, and mentioned by Cole Porter in the words of his hit song, 'You're the Top.' The top was what I was supposed to be. I had become a duchess and mistress of an historic castle. My daughter had married a duke. Life was apparently roses all the way."

In her last days the duchess admitted paying guests to tour her home and, after a fall, she moved into a hotel where she was unable to pay her bill. Having finally gone through all her inheritance, she was moved to a charity ward of a nursing home in Pimlico where she died at the age of eighty. She was buried in Surrey with her first husband.

Susan Whittier, born 18 June 1874, died 4 December 1934, was a daughter of Elizabeth Chadwick Whittier and her husband, General Charles Whittier, who died suddenly on the *SS Mauretania* in the Atlantic on 14 May 1908. He was appointed in 1898 a lieutenant colonel in the volunteer army. He later became interested in railroads in the Orient and was appointed president of the American-China Development Company, which owned and operated the Hankow-Canton Railroad. In 1905, with J. Pierpont Morgan, he negotiated the sale of the railroad to the Chinese government for $6.7 million. One of his daughters was Mrs. Ernest Iselin of New York, while his other daughter, Susan, married in 1894 **Prince Serge Belosselsky-Belozersky** (1867-1951), one-time Cossack general and aide de camp to the last Russian tsar (as well as to Grand Dukes Vladimir and Alexander). Susan was a famous beauty in St. Petersburg and spoke fluent Russian. A young Grand Duke Dmitri Romanov became infatuated with her

Top: Susan Whittier spoke fluent Russian.   Bottom: Susan's husband was aide-de-camp to the last tsar and was frequently with the royal family, all of whom were executed.   Susan's son also married an American heiress.

and was banished from Russia for four months as a result.

At the time of the Revolution she and her husband escaped with their two sons and lived near Tonbridge in Kent where she died. He died 21 April 1951 while living in a tiny flat over a shop in Tonbridge, England, where he referred to his existence as "the life of a cabbage." They had two sons, Serge and Andre, the second of whom became head of the incoming news section of the BBC and died a bachelor in London at the age of fifty-one in 1961. In 1946 the senior Serge visited his son Serge at his home at 79 East 79th St., in New York City. After Serge's death in 1951, the junior Serge shipped many of their possessions to Castle Hill, his home in Massachusetts. The Belosselsky-Belozersky Palace, about two miles from the center of St. Petersburg, now houses the Municipal Cultural Center. Serge, a son of Susan and the senior Serge, also married an American heiress, **Florence Crane** (see her separate entry), of the Chicago plumbing manufacturing family.

Elaine Daniels Willcox, born Denver, Colorado, 22 June 1906, died 17 November 1973, was a daughter of Charles MacAllister Willcox, president of the Daniels and Fisher Stores in Denver, and a granddaughter of U. S. General Orlando B. Willcox. She studied at the Wolcott School in Denver and later in Lausanne, Switzerland. She also attended the Sorbonne in Paris as well as Columbia University in New York City and was officially presented to the British court in 1923. She married in New York City, 30 September 1927, as his second wife, **Balthasar Gyalma, Prince Odescalchi,** born Szkiczo, 12 January 1884, died 14 July 1957, grandson of the 5th Prince

Elaine Willcox and her husband, Balthasar, Prince Odescalchi. He became a U. S. citizen and they lived in Denver.

diplomatic service as a young man. Prince Gyalma's first wife, Dorothea, was a daughter of the British M. P. Henry Labouchere. Dorothea's first husband, Marquis Carlo Rudini, committed suicide. She then married Prince Gyalma in 1915 but the marriage was annulled. In her third marriage she became the well-known Roman hostess Princess Dora Ruspoli, who died in 1944 when she was visiting her ill chauffeur in a poor area of the city and fell through a trapdoor in an unlighted hallway, dying instantly from a crushed skull. Prince Gyalma and his second wife, Elaine Willcox, divided their residences between Palm Beach, Denver, and Cuernavaca, Mexico. Gyalma became a U. S. citizen immediately after World War II, died of cancer in New York City, and was buried in Denver. Their son, Prince Carlo, was born in 1928 and killed in a mountain-climbing accident in 1946, and a daughter,

Odeschalchi and 5th Duke of Sirmio. Gyalma was a member of the Hungarian branch of the ancient Italian family that traced its lineage to the Enrico Erba, vicar of the Holy Roman Empire, in Milan in 1165. He was descended from Livio Odescalchi, a nephew of Pope Innocent XI, who was created a prince of the Holy Roman Empire in the seventeenth century. Beethoven dedicated three of his piano concerti to the Odescalchi family and his 5th, "the Emperor," was dedicated to his student, Princess Odescalchi.

Gyalma was born in Hungary and served in the Austro-Hungarian

Princess Flaminia, was born in 1933. Elaine died of cancer and multiple sclerosis in Denver on 17 November 1973, and was buried in the Willcox plot in Denver along with her husband and son.

Thelma Jeanne Williams, born Nashville, Tennessee, 15 November 1930, a daughter of Richard Williams and Josephine Owens Williams, died 5 June 1988 at the Rutland Regional Medical Center, Rutland, Vermont. She married as his second wife 20 December 1960 (civil) at Saint Maur-sur-Loir, Eure-et-Loire, France, and at the Romanian Church (religious) at Paris, **Prince Carol Mircea of Hohenzollern,**

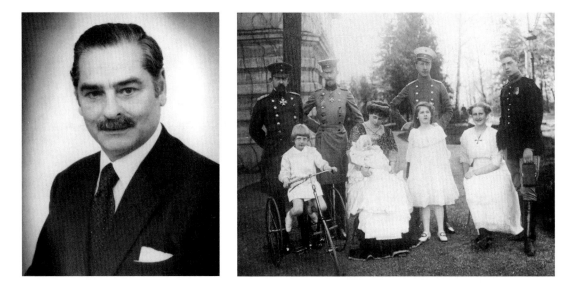

Left: Prince Carol Mircea of Hohenzollern was legally given the right to his name and title but was not allowed to succeed his father, King Carol II of Romania.   Right: The Romanian royal family into which Thelma Williams married.

born Bucharest, 9 January 1920, died London, 27 January 2006, son of Carol II, later king of Romania, and his first wife, Jeanne "Zizi" Lambrino, whom he married secretly when he was crown prince. They had one son, Alexander, born 1 September 1961 in Dorset, England, and were divorced in 1977. By his first wife, opera singer Helene Nazavitzeni (who sang under the name "Lena Pastor"), Prince Carol Mircea had a son Paul Lambrino (or) von Hohenzollern, who married in Bucharest, 15 September 1995, **Lia Georgia Triff,** born Great Lakes, Illinois, 23 February 1949. Prince Carol Mircea was considered to be "oversexed" and one obituary of him noted that "anatomical descriptions, when overheard, were mistaken for descriptions of the Eiffel Tower."

His legal rights to his name and title were upheld in a court action in Paris, although he was not allowed to succeed his father. Because his father did not approve of his marriage, Carol Mircea had no succession rights, although he was legally declared in 1955 to be legitimate even though he was born after his parents' annulment. He and his mother never again saw Carol Mircea after their forced divorce and, when Zizi died in 1953 in a charity ward in Paris on 11 March 1953, her son cabled his father for funds to bury her but there was no reply. Carol Mircea's younger half-brother, Prince Michael, is the current pretender to the throne of Romania. Prince Carol Mircea's mother, Zizi Lambrino, sued her former husband in 1926 to recognize their son and to provide substantial financial support for them both. She introduced as evidence love letters he wrote to her even after their marriage was annulled at the insistence of her husband's parents. Carol was served legal papers in his Paris hotel seeking ten thousand francs. Carol also refused to appear when his son sought admission to an elite French boarding school.

Prince Carol Mircea's grandparents, King Ferdinand and the ever-dramatic Queen Marie (a favored granddaughter of England's Queen Victoria), brilliantly steered their country through years of turmoil and war and were justifiably loved and appreciated by their subjects. Their success with their sons, however, was limited at best.

Prince Carol Mircea's father, Carol II, king of Romania, renounced his rights 28 December 1925 but reneged on the renunciation and was proclaimed king 8 June 1930, then abdicated again on 6 September 1940. As king he was particularly vindictive to his mother, who refused to recognize his first marriage as he had married without his parents' consent or knowledge in Odessa, 31 August 1918 (annulled 1919), Joanna Marie Valentina "Zizi" Lambrino, born Roman, Romania, 3 October 1898. Carol II married second at Athens 10 March 1921 (divorced 1928), Helen, princess of Greece and Denmark, born Athens, 3 May 1896, died Lausanne, 28 November 1982. Carol II married third at Rio de Janeiro, 3 June 1947, Elena Lupescu, born Hertza, Moldavia, 15 September 1899, died Estoril, 29 June 1977.

King Carol II's brother, Prince Nicholas, was disowned by his parents and even his family name was taken from him. Two of their sisters, Elisabeth and Marie, were queens of Greece and Yugoslavia, while their other sister, Princess Ileana, became a nun and is buried in the cemetery of the Monastery of the Transfiguration in Ellwood City, Pennsylvania. Alexander Hohenzollern, the son of Thelma Williams and Prince Carol Mircea, had no contact with his Rumanian family who refused to acknowledge him. In March of 2004 he was crossing a road during a snowstorm in Aspen, Colorado, when he was struck by an oncoming SUV. Both his legs were broken and he suffered extensive internal injuries. He was airlifted to a regional medical center for the first of several surgeries. At the time he worked as a ski pro in the children's division at the Buttermilk Ski and Snowboard School in Aspen and, the year before, he had been officially certified as a hang-glider in Aspen. At the time of the accident, his employer solicited funds from friends and associates in order to pay mounting medical bills. Prince Carol Mircea, his father, married once more and died in 2006.

Catherine Daingerfield Willis, born 17 August 1803 at Willis Hall, near Fredericksburg, Spotsylvania County, Virginia, was a daughter of the swashbuckling but financially reckless Colonel Byrd C. Willis and was a great-grand-niece of George Washington. As a young woman she married Atchison Gray. Less than twelve months after their marriage he died, followed soon after by their infant. In about 1825 she moved with her parents, three brothers, and two sisters to Tallahassee, Florida. There she met Prince Achille Murat, nephew of Napoleon Bonaparte, who had been encouraged to relocate to the area by his friend, the Marquis de LaFayette. Catherine married at Tallahassee, Florida, 12 July 1826, **Achille, Prince Murat,** born Paris, 21 January 1801, died Jefferson County, Florida, 15 April 1847, eldest son of Joachim Murat, prince of the French Empire 1805, Grand Duke of Berg and Cleves 1806-08, king of Naples 1808-15, and of Queen Caroline Bonaparte, sister of Napoleon I. The couple went abroad and were entertained extensively. She was given a seat in Westminster Abbey for the 1831 coronation of William IV as king of England. Upon their return they developed their two thousand-acre plantation, Lipona (an anagram for Murat's princely title of Napoli) where Murat served as the first postmaster for the area.

After his marriage, Murat renounced his claim to the throne of Naples and became known as the Duke de Cleves. However, he preferred not to be called by his title and instructed his servants to address him as Colonel Murat. He died in 1847 leaving no children by his wife and one illegitimate daughter in Europe. Catherine inherited Lipona and, in 1854, she purchased Bellevue in neighboring Leon County, and that became her permanent home. She was intimately involved in the preservation of Mount Vernon, George Washington's home in Virginia, and chaired the state of Florida's fundraising drive for the effort, eventually achieving the highest per capita amount raised by any of the thirty contributing states. During the war years she led local soldiers aid societies and sewing circles to clothe the Southern troops.

In early 1866, her late husband's cousin, who had ascended the French throne as Napoleon III in 1849, recognized not only the losses she had incurred during the War but also the exemplary manner in which she had lived her life (unlike many Bonaparte relations). As a result, Catherine was granted a generous annuity by the new French government. Catherine died at Bellevue on 6 August 1867 and was buried with her husband in Florida. Prince Achille's brother, **Prince Lucien,** also married an American, **Caroline Fraser,** and from them descend many Murat family members, including **Prince Charles,** who married **Margaret Rutherfurd** and **Prince Michel,** who married both **Helena Stallo** and **Isabelle McMillin,** as well as Prince Pierre who married in 1934 Princess Isabelle d'Orleans, daughter of the Duc de Guise, head of the Orleanist line of the French royal house.

Ada Winans, born approximately 1831, died 1917, was a daughter of Anthony van Arsdale Winans (1797–1849) and a Mrs. Jay who was not his wife. He was a grocer and merchant in New York City with a store on Front Street that burned in the great fire of 1835. Ada was a lyric soprano who went to Italy to study music. There she met the diplomat **Prince Peter Troubetskoy,** born in Tulcin, 22 August 1822, died 28 August 1892. He had been appointed governor of Smolensk and of Orel in 1844 and was later sent on a diplomatic mission (which included supervision of the Russian Church) to Florence, Italy, where he met Ada Winans. He was already married to Princess Varvara Troubetsaya by whom he had three daughters, Tatiana, Elena, and Maria. After leaving his wife and children to live openly with Ada, he was never able to return to Russia.

Prince Peter and Ada Winans lived at Villa Ada at Ghiffa on Lake Maggiore in Italy. He was an accomplished botanist and established an important garden on the grounds of their estate. In 1870 Prince Peter obtained a divorce from his first wife and then married Ada. At that time they obtained legitimation for the birth of their three sons, artist Prince Peter born in 1864 (who married American **Amelie Rives;** see her separate entry), Prince Paul born in 1866 (who would become a famous sculptor), and Prince Eugene in 1867. In 1884 financial reverses forced Prince Peter to sell Villa Ada. He later left Ada and their sons and retired with his then-mistress, Marianna Hahn, to Milan where their illegitimate son, Peter, was born in 1886. They then moved to Menton, France, where Ada's former husband died in 1892. Ada lived until 1917.

The Troubetskoys were descended from the Lithuanian grand duke Gedimin. In Russia, the family found itself under threat of extinction and, at the end of the seventeenth century, the last representative of the Russian branch of Troubetskoys asked their Polish relations to return to Russia. Two Troubetskoy brothers, Ivan Yurievich and Yuri Yurievich, returned and from them descend the Russian Troubetskoys, including Prince Peter. Ada and Prince Peter's second son, the sculptor Prince Paul, returned to Russia in 1898 where he befriended Leo Tolstoy whose portrait bust he sculpted. His most famous work was the equestrian monument to Tsar Alexander III, later displayed in the State Russian Museum. In 1900 Prince Paul won the Grand Prix at the Exposition Universalle in Paris.

Beatrice Winans, born Baltimore, 25 April 1884, was a daughter of Ross Revillon Winans and his second wife (who was also his first cousin), Neva Whistler, a half-sister of the artist James McNeil Whistler. Beatrice's great-grandfather was Ross Winans (1796-1877), a railroad engineer and inventor who was credited with having placed the first swivel trucks on four-wheel rail cars, allowing them to turn in a tight radius (an invention still in use today). His son, Thomas DeKay Winans (1820-1878), was sent to Russia (at the request of George W. Whistler whose daughter, Julia, married the senior Winans' son) to build the first railroad between St. Petersburg and Moscow. He was given $5 million for the five-year project, plus a maintenance contract that paid per rail car in use plus per mile traveled (a far more lucrative contract than the original one for construction). The payments increased so geometrically that the Russian government finally bought out the remaining terms for an additional $8 million.

Thomas Winans and his father devised the cigar-shaped hull for trans-Atlantic steamers. The son purchased an estate in Baltimore and built a mansion in Newport where he utilized waves to pump water to a reservoir on top of his villa. He also established a soup kitchen opposite his Baltimore home and fed as many as four thousand people daily during the War. Thomas's son (and Beatrice's father), Ross R. Winans, also built a mansion at Newport, next to his father's, called Bleak House, designed by Peabody and Stearns. It was destroyed by a tornado in 1938 but his sister's mansion next door, Shamrock Cliff, built in 1895, is still in existence. His Baltimore mansion was one of the first domestic commissions by the firm of McKim, Mead and White. Thomas Winans left an estate of more than $20 million at his death in 1878, allowing his son to live a life of leisure which included an acknowledged mistress, Alice O'Keefe, who unsuccessfully sued Ross R. Winans in 1883 for divorce, claiming that they had lived as husband and wife.

It was in the next year that his daughter, Beatrice, married on 24 June 1905 at the Church of Ste. Clotilde in Paris, **Prince Henri de Bearn et de Chalais, Count de Brassac et de l'empire Francais, Count and Prince de Bearn, Prince de Viana, Prince de Chalais, Marquis d'Excideuil, Count de Brassac and de Marsan**, and a Spanish grandee of the first class, born in Paris 3 May 1874, son of Laure-Henry-Gaston de Galard de Bearn and of Cecile-Charlotte-Marie de Talleyrand-Perigord, Princess de Chalais, from whom he inherited his princely titles. U. S. Ambassador McCormick and his wife attended the ceremony along with "many members of the old French aristocracy." The groom formerly was attached to the French embassy in Washington but at the time of the wedding was first secretary of the French legation at St. Petersburg. Beatrice's family maintained offices for their railroad and engineering empire in St. Petersburg, although the couple met in London where Beatrice and her parents (who married there) spent much of their time. Prince Helie de Sagan, husband of American-born **Anna Gould,** challenged Beatrice's husband to a duel, charging that he had no right to the Chalais title (although there was no claim that he was not the Prince de Bearn) but the duel never took place.

Beatrice had a daughter, Beatrice, and a son, Gaston, before dying at St. Petersburg 17 April 1907, six days after giving birth to her son. At her marriage, Beatrice's father gave her outright $300,000 in bonds. Shortly after marrying and before the birth of their children, she signed a will deeding the entire amount to her husband at her death. Her will would have allowed him to claim the entire amount but French law did not allow a parent to disregard children in a will. The prince agreed to accept $100,000 and leave the remainder in trust to his children but later sued the estate, claiming that the Maryland probate court, where the estate was filed, was unaware of his wife's original intent. In 1909 the Maryland court found in his favor and gave him the entire $300,000. In 1911 his creditors sued to attach the bonds as payment for his substantial debts. When the prince's father-in-law, Ross R. Winans, died in 1912, he left a $4 million estate with $500,000 bequeathed to his then-mistress, Dorothy Bateman of Newport, and no provision for his French grandchildren. Winans' other heirs then voluntarily surrendered $500,000 to go to the dis-inherited children in order to end a legal challenge brought

by the prince. The family is now extinct in the male line. Beatrice's daughter, Beatrice, married American John W. Freeman, whose mother was Princess Marie de Bourbon Braganza, a great-granddaughter of Francesco I, king of the Two Sicilies.

(Elinor) Douglas Wise, born 19 August 1890 in Annapolis, Maryland, died 1972, in Baltimore, was a daughter of Frederick May Wise and Lizzie Daniels Adams Wise, and a granddaughter of George Douglas Wise (1817-1881) and Laura May Wise of Baltimore, Maryland. She married in the Baltimore Cathedral with Cardinal Gibbons presiding on 8 February 1913, **Armand, 8th Duc de Richelieu and de Fronsac, Marquis de Jumilhac, Duc d'Aiguillon, Prince de Mortagne, Marquis de Pontcoulay, Comte de Carnac, Comte de Chinon,** born Paris, 21 December 1875, died at Doctor's Hospital in New York City on 30 May 1952. He was the son of the American **Princess Alice of Monaco** (Alice Heine) by her first husband and a great-great-nephew of the famous cardinal. According to a family member, Princess Alice "wanted her son, Armand, the 8th Duke, to marry at least a Serene Highness! He didn't follow her advice and went to Baltimore in 1913 from where he sent her a telegram announcing his Catholic marriage to Miss Douglas Wise, the penniless but handsome daughter of a distinguished Senator." Actually, Douglas's father was not a senator but he was a heavily-decorated Marine colonel who wrote his memoirs, *A Marine Tells It To You.* A graduate of the U. S. Naval Academy, he was on duty in China in command of the Monocasy when he died in 1901. His father, George Douglas Wise, was a member of congress and a great-uncle was governor

Douglas Wise and her husband, the 8th (and last) Duc de Richelieu. He was the only son of the American-born Alice, Princess of Monaco. Douglas studied voice under acclaimed opera singer Emma Eames.

died in 1952 and she died in Paris at the age of eighty-six on 28 August 1972. There were no children and the family is now extinct in the male line. Douglas's cousin, **Natalie Oelrichs** (Douglas's grandmother, Laura May, and Natalie's mother, Julia May, were sisters), married **Heinrich Borwin, Prince of Mecklenberg.** One of their cousins, Susan May Williams, married Jerome Napoleon Bonaparte whose mother was American-born Betsey Patterson. The 8th Duc de Richelieu's sister, Odile, married Count and Prince Gabriel de La Rochefoucauld (created in 1909 by the King of Bavaria). Odile's daughter, Anne, married John, Marquis de Amodio. They are deceased and both were the last of their family lines.

Mildred Lucile Withstandley, born 10 November 1899, at Brooklyn, New York, was a daughter of Josephine De Wyckoff Withstandley and of Victor D. Withstandley, who was metropolitan sales manager for National Distillers Products Corporation as well as vice chairman of the

of Virginia.

Douglas studied voice in France with the acclaimed American singer Emma Eames. She gave up the concert stage to marry and was considered a great beauty. In World War I she gave many concerts in the United States to raise funds for tubercular French soldiers and for her efforts she was decorated by the French government. She and the duke left France at the outbreak of World War II and she renounced her title and resumed her U. S. citizenship. The duke

Greater New York Fund. She first married M. L. Everett and in 1919 married Morris Roderick Volck whom she divorced in 1923. Mildred married at Prince's Row Register office in London as her third husband, 2 March 1932 (divorced 1937) as his first wife, **Michael, Prince Lichnowsky,** born Kuchelna, 9 December 1907, second son of the 6th Prince Lichnowsky who was the German ambassador to England at the outbreak of the First World War. At the time of their marriage, Michael was entitled to the courtesy title of prince

Prince Lichnowsky, Mildred's father-in-law, was the German ambassador to England at the outbreak of the First World War.

as the heir to his elder brother, Wilhelm, who had succeeded their father in 1928. Upon the birth of Wilhelm's son, the eventual 8th Prince Lichnowsky, in 1940, Michael was no longer eligible for the courtesy title and he was styled only a count.

Among the guests at Michael's marriage to Mildred were the Countess of Oxford and Asquith, Lady Furness, Princess George Imeritinsky, and the Austrian ambassador. After a wedding trip to Paris they lived in Berlin. The groom's father was the German ambassador to England 1912 – 1914 and was considered heavily pro-British. He argued that Germany's support of Austria would result in British support of Russia and France in a war defending Serbia against Austrian aggression. In 1916 he wrote a pamphlet entitled, *My Mission to London,* 1912-1914, in which he avowed that his efforts to maintain peace had not been supported by his government. It was published without his approval in January of 1918 and was the cause for his expulsion from the Prussian upper legislature. He spent the remainder of his life trying to explain his position. The British Foreign Minister, Sir Edward Grey, wrote, "Had Lichnowsky continued to be the trusted representative of his government, had they dealt frankly with him, and through him with us, after the murder of the Archduke, war might have been avoided."

The first Prince Lichnowsky was a great patron of Beethoven, who dedicated to him several piano sonatas. After Prince Michael's divorce from Mildred, he married again in 1953 and there were no children of either marriage. His nephew, the current 8th Prince, lives in Brazil with his family. Although Mildred was not married to the son of Germany's ambassador to England at the outbreak of World War I, at that crucial time the German ambassador to the United States, **Count Heinrich von Bernstorff,** was married to American **Jeanne Luckemeyer,** while the American ambassador to Germany, John Leishman, had a daughter, Nancy, who was married to the 13th Duke of Croy, then serving on the German front.

Mary Augusta "May" Yohé, born 6 April 1869 in Bethlehem, Pennsylvania, was the only child of an ironworker of German lineage, William W. Yohé, and his wife Lizzie Batcheller Yohe. She earned the nickname "Madcap May" in a life of light opera stardom, first appearing on the stage when she was ten years old. Friends who were of the opinion that she had talent sent her to Paris to study and she returned to the U. S. and began her career as a chorus girl in a Pittsburgh burlesque show. She made her operatic debut at the Temple Theatre in Philadelphia, receiving notice for the lower notes she was able to sing in her contralto voice, eventually earning the London appellation, "the girl with the foghorn voice." She first became nationally recognized singing the role of Prince Polydor von Prettywitz in *The Crystal Slipper* at the Chicago Opera House in the summer of 1887. One night as the curtain was rising the theatre manager learned that May had run away with a theatre producer. She was reached by pleading telegrams and returned to the theatre. She then eloped with a Mr. Shaw but they were arrested on a train bound for New York as he was already married.

In 1893 while appearing in New York City she aroused gossip because of her friendship with State Senator Walker of Corning. Looking for new worlds to conquer she toured in England and Australia before returning to settle in England. She was appearing there in *Little Christoper,* in which her rendition of "Honey, My Honey" supposedly

The long-suffering May Yohé enjoyed success as a singer after beginning as a chorus girl in burlesque. She may or may not have worn the Hope diamond onstage.

Left: A cigarette ad featured May in one of her featured roles. Right: The 8th Duke of Newcastle was supported by May but they divorced before he came into his title and she was never duchess.

created a furor, when she met the younger brother of the habitually-ill 7th Duke of Newcastle. On 27 November 1894 she married **Lord Francis Hope Pelham-Clinton-Hope, later the 8th Duke of Newcastle** (although May was never duchess). His father, the 6th Duke, was an inveterate gambler who was forced to leave the country in 1860 for failure to pay his gambling debts of almost a quarter million pounds. He married the wealthy heiress Henrietta Hope in 1861, although the wedding took place in Paris to prevent his creditors from having him arrested. The duke's father-in-law paid his debts and settled £50,000 per year on him but, by the terms of their agreement, the duke could never control the assets.

Among extensive estates in England and Ireland, Henrietta also brought to their marriage the famous Hope diamond, a blue-white gem of 44-1/2 carats, later said to have brought misfortune to its owners (a legend greatly enhanced by May). Lord Francis, May's husband, had adopted the additional name of "Hope" before his own to satisfy the 1884 will of his maternal grandmother and to inherit her estate three years later. Although Lord Francis' invalid brother, the 7th Duke, did much to regain the family finances, Lord Francis enjoyed an extravagant lifestyle reminiscent of their father's and quickly went through his inheritance. Lord Francis was declared bankrupt and his finances were not discharged until 1896 so May was forced to work to support him. She was a close friend of the Prince of Wales (later King Edward VII) who called her "Maysie." If she is to be believed, she, in turn, was afforded the familiarity to call him "Eddie."

The Newcastles strenuously opposed May's marriage to Lord Francis, who was even offered one million pounds by his brother if he would leave her. The couple moved to New York where May returned to the stage to support her husband. She was hired by Oscar Hammerstein for $1,500 a week to sing at his New York Theatre, and, not so incidentally, to wear the famous Hope Diamond (although her husband later maintained that she wore a replica while the original remained in a bank vault). A frequent visitor to their apartment was Captain Putnam Bradlee Strong, son of a former New York City mayor, William L. Strong. The Duke of Newcastle came to New York City in 1900 and was met at the pier by his brother. The duke convinced Lord Francis to return with him to England where he began divorce proceedings.

In 1901 May and Putnam Strong traveled together to the Orient. Upon their return Strong stole $300,000 of May's jewelry, pawned them, and left a note saying that he was so deeply in debt that he intended to take his own life. He had been seen almost daily at the races where his large bets never won (in this regard he was much like Lord Francis, whom one writer has described as "a fellow of abandoned habits whose genius for picking losers at Epsom and other race tracks was a legend in English sporting circles."). May publicly stated her intention to forgive Strong and take him back if only he would return. They traveled to Japan and were married there in Yokohama in 1902. In 1905 Putnam Strong was declared bankrupt, asserting in court that his only assets were the clothes he was wearing, valued at $50.

Meanwhile Lord Francis returned to England and, in 1902, sold the Hope diamond (with court approval) to pay his debts. He successfully sued his wife for divorce, naming Strong as the co-respondent. For a while he seriously pursued American **Gladys Deacon** (who eventually married the 9th Duke of Marlborough, formerly the husband of American **Consuelo Vanderbilt**) whose mother was being escorted throughout Rome by Lord Francis's brother-in-law, Prince Alfonso Doria Pamphili (husband of Lord Francis's sister, Lady Emily, even though Emily was still very much on the scene). In 1904, Lord Francis married Mrs. Olive Thompson Owen by whom he had a son (later the 9th Duke) and two daughters (one of whom worked briefly as a sales clerk in a Fifth Avenue department store). When Lord Francis' wife died in 1912, there was speculation that he would reconcile with May, whom he professed still to love, but that did not happen.

Instead, two years later, May married Captain John A. Smuts, a former officer in the British army and a cousin of the famous South African general. She was a nurse in Africa during the Boer War, then spent three years on a rubber plantation in the South Seas as a result of her friendship with the Sultan of Jahore. In 1919 she worked cleaning a Seattle shipyard office. May then operated a chicken ranch in California that failed, before returning to the stage once again. She earned enough in vaudeville to purchase a small farm and tea room in New Hampshire. When that venture also failed they lived near Boston where May worked as a WPA clerk for $16.50 per week. In 1920 she convinced a Hollywood producer to back an unsuccessful fifteen-episode serial called *The Hope Diamond Mystery,* followed the next year by her co-writing a movie called *The Mystery of the Hope Diamond.* She portrayed herself, and a young Boris Karloff was part of the cast. The film was also unsuccessful. In 1924, while they were living in a boarding house, Smuts was shot in the chest but insisted that he had been cleaning his gun when it accidentally discharged. The resulting publicity brought her briefly back to the vaudeville stage.

In the last year of her life May had to defend her honor against a lawsuit brought by a twenty-nine-year-old Hollywood actor named Robert E. Thomas. He insisted that he was May's son by her marriage to Putnam Strong and that he had been born in the last year of his parents' marriage in Portland, Oregon, where his mother had assumed an alias to prevent his birth from becoming known. The woman who adopted him at his birth testified on his behalf. Thomas sought a share in the $160,000 trust fund that Putnam Strong's mother had established for her son, as well as part of almost $500,000 Mrs. Strong left at her death. The judge found that his case had not been proven and he was denied any share in the Strong fortune. Madcap May died of a heart attack in Boston at the age of sixty-nine on 28 August 1938. Her husband, Captain Smuts, announced that she had only been ill for twenty-four hours.

Putnam Strong remarried and died at the age of seventy in 1945. The 7th Duke of Newcastle died childless in 1928 and was succeeded by May's former husband, Lord Francis, as 8th Duke. The 8th Duke, who had lost a leg to amputation after being shot in the foot in a hunting accident during his unmarried interval, died 22 April 1941 and was succeeded by his only son, the Earl of Lincoln, as 9th Duke who was first married to American **Jean Banks Gimbernat,** daughter of David Banks of New York City. They had no children (although he had two daughters by a second wife) and he died 4 November 1988. He was succeeded as 10th Duke by his third cousin, once removed, who was an entomologist at a Scottish Natural History museum. He held the title for less than two months before dying 25 December 1988 and the dukedom is extinct. A lesser title, the Earldom of Lincoln, passed to a kinsman at the age of seventy-five, who was gold miner, sheep-shearer, and welder in Australia.

The Hope diamond, which May Yohe referred to as "the blue stone that leaves its trail in red," was purchased by American publisher

Edward B. McLean for his wife, socialite Evalyn Walsh McLean. Her first-born son, Vinson, was killed in an automobile accident at the age of nine. Her husband ran away with another woman and spent much of her fortune. A chronic alcoholic, he died in a sanatorium. Their family newspaper, the *Washington Post,* went bankrupt and Evalyn was forced to sell some of her properties. Then, in 1946, Evalyn's daughter died of an overdose of sleeping pills at the age of twenty-five. The Hope diamond now resides in Washington's Smithsonian Institution.

(Maria) Consuelo Yznaga, born in 1858, was one of three daughters of Cuban-born planter Antonio Yznaga del Valle and his southern wife who was a childhood friend of Alva Smith Vanderbilt. Alva, of Mobile, Alabama, was to name her own daughter in honor of her godmother (Alva's sister married Consuelo's brother, Fernando). The family lived at Ravenswood Plantation at Lake St. John Concordia near Natchez, Mississippi, but left their Louisiana and Mississippi plantations after the war and relocated to New York City where the three pretty Catholic daughters were referred to as "the little Sisters of the Rich." Consuelo met at Saratoga Viscount Mandeville, heir to his father, the 7th Duke of Manchester. He was said to have fallen in love with her when she nursed him back to health during a severe case of typhoid. She married on 22 May 1876 George Montagu, later **8th Duke of Manchester.** In 1881 her younger sister, Natica, married Sir John Lister-Kaye, Baronet. Consuelo became an early mistress of Edward VII while he was still Prince of Wales and was reported to have taught him to play the banjo. Her husband was unconcerned

Consuelo Yznaga, Duchess of Manchester, was one of the earliest Anglo-American wives. Her god-daughter and namesake, Consuelo Vanderbilt, became Duchess of Marlborough. The first Consuelo did not approve of her son's marriage to an American heiress.

at their relationship as he continued an open affair with a music hall entertainer. He succeeded his father as Duke in 1890, the same year in which the son was declared bankrupt. Edith Wharton based her character "Conchita" in *The Buccaneers* on Consuelo. With little money left from her family, she was known to accept "favors" for introducing wealthy American girls to prospective titled husbands, but she was furious at her own son's choice of American Helena Zimmerman as a wife. Consuelo died in London on 20 November 1909. She was outlived for two years by her famously-beautiful German-born mother-in-law who was often referred to as the "Double Duchess" for having married as her second husband the 8th Duke of Devonshire whose mistress she had been while still married to the 7th Duke of Manchester. The male line of her family inherited the constant need for cash for which their title had long been known. Her son, the 9th Duke, once owed $5,000 for golf balls alone. He boasted, "Going bankrupt isn't so bad as it sounds. I remember my first bankruptcy. I was only 16 and went broke for a couple of thousand pounds." In 1935 he was in court yet again for the more serious charge of pawning family jewels his shrewd mother had wisely left in trust. He was sentenced to nine months in jail but an appeals court found that he "seems to have acted in good faith" and commuted the sentence. On leaving court the duke was declared bankrupt yet again. His son, the 10th Duke, invested the proceeds from selling the ancestral family home into a Kenyan plantation that went broke. The 10th Duke's eldest son, the 11th Duke, had no sons and was succeeded by his brother,

the 12th Duke, who achieved a level of notoriety unusual even for the Manchesters. He served in the Royal Marines before coming to the U. S. as an oilfield worker and ski instructor. His next stop was Australia where he was a crocodile wrestler and trouser salesman at a department store. He married the first of three wives there, had three children, and left just ahead of the bankruptcy court. He tried Canada without success before returning to England where in 1985 he was convicted of fraud for serving as the "front man" for forging U. S. bonds to secure London bank loans. The judge described him as "absurdly stupid and negligent," adding, "on a business scale of one to ten, the duke is one or less – and even that flatters him." Evidently freed by his idiocy, he avoided a prison term. The nadir of his business career, however, came in 1996 when he was extradited to the U. S. to enter prison resulting from his conviction of an attempt to swindle the National Hockey League's Tampa Bay Lightning of $34.5 million. He claimed at trial to be "56th in line for the British throne," to be a close school friend of the Prince of Wales, and to own a palatial family mansion in addition to $25 million in Weimar bonds purchased on behalf of Ethiopian Emperor Haile Selassie. Even his own attorney declared he was, "more of a dupe than a duke ... he's gullible, he's vain, he's foolish – and none of that is a crime." The duke was sentenced to two-and-a-half years in prison and entered solitary confinement in Virginia in June of that year. After his release, he returned to England and conducted wealthy Americans on tours at Stratford-upon-Avon before dying in 2002.

Helena Zimmerman, born in 1879, was the only child of Marietta Evans Zimmerman and Eugene Zimmerman of Cincinnati, a railroad president and major stockholder of Standard Oil. He was a native of Vicksburg, Mississippi, whose family had few resources so he volunteered for the Navy shortly after the outbreak of War when he was just sixteen. Afterwards he began in lumber and progressed to oil, becoming one of the founders of Standard Oil of Ohio and President of the Chesapeake and Nashville Railroad. In 1888 he convinced C. P. Huntington (step-father of **Claire Huntington** who married **Prince Francois Hatzfeldt**), to become his partner in building the Chesapeake and Ohio Bridge across the Ohio River into Cincinnati. The venture greatly increased their already-large fortunes. When the *New York Times* printed in 1892 its first national list of millionaires, Eugene Zimmerman was included. Helena's mother died when she was only two and she was privately tutored, finishing her academic career with French nuns at the Convent of the Assumption in Auteuil.

While visiting a spinster aunt in the spring of 1899, Helena met at a costume ball in the Brittany coast resort of Dinard the 9th Duke of Manchester, who had been a duke since the age of fifteen. Called "Kim" because of his secondary title, Lord Kimbolton, he was very fond of actresses and had been rumored to be engaged to the French actress Cleo de Merode. As one biographer has written of him, Kim was interested in two kinds of women, "actresses, who gave him

Helena Zimmerman, Duchess of Manchester, paid dearly for the right to her title and wore it proudly even after she divorced and remarried an earl.

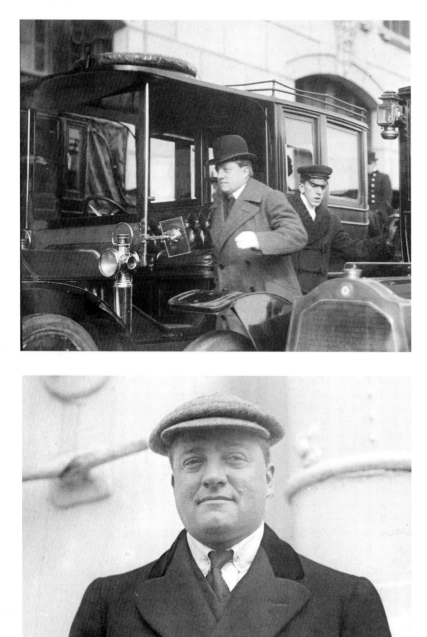

hopes of stardom, and heiresses, who gave him hopes of solvency." Two years before meeting Helena, Kim was so deeply in debt that, to stave off creditors, he announced his engagement to the American heiress May Goelet (she would marry the Duke of Roxburghe in 1903) even though he had not met her. Kim courted Helena but she left for New York City without a commitment. He followed her there and announced his intention to take to the stage as had his fellow insolvent peer the Earl of Yarmouth (later the the **Marquess of Hertford;** he would eventually marry the Pittsburgh coal heiress **Alice Thaw,** sister of the assassin of Stanford White, who seemed to be the only person who was not aware that her husband was homosexual).

Helena married 14 November 1900 William Montagu, **9th Duke of Manchester,** son of the 8th Duke and his American-born wife, **Consuelo Yznaga** (see her separate entry) who was the godmother of **Consuelo Vanderbilt,** Duchess of Marlborough. The groom was declared bankrupt just before his secret marriage to Helena. He worked as a newspaper reporter for the *New York Journal* while openly searching for a rich wife. Her father bought for them Kylemore Castle in Ireland where they hosted King Edward VII and Queen Alexandra in 1904. Their son succeeded his father in 1947 as 10th Duke of Manchester. Helena's great-grandson, born in 1962, is the current (13th) Duke of Manchester and has a son, Viscount Mandeville.

The 9th Duke of Manchester was accustomed to bankruptcy, a proclivity handed down to his successors. He briefly worked for the New York Journal while openly looking for a rich wife.

Helena and the duke divorced in 1931 and one month later he married in Greenwich, Connecticut, an English actress, Kathleen Dawes, but had no further children. Helena's cousins, **Laura and Helen Stallo,** married **Francesco, Prince Rospigliosi,** and **Prince Michel Murat.** In 1937 Helena married an old friend, Arthur George Keith, the **10th Earl of Kintore.** His father, the 9th Earl of Kintore, was governor and commander-in-chief of South Australia. Helena's last husband died in 1966 with no son and his sister, Ethel Sydney Keith (who died one day after her 100th birthday), succeeded to her father's titles. She was the widow of the 1st Viscount Stonehaven, cabinet minister and chairman of the Conservative Party (they had the distinction as husband and wife of having both sat in the House of Lords, although at different times), and their son changed his last name to Keith and succeeded to both his parents' titles. The current (14th) Earl of Kintore and Viscount Stonehaven is a son of an American mother, Mary Plum of Rumson, New Jersey, who died in 2006. Her husband, the 13th Earl, reportedly died by his own hand in 2004. Helena Zimmerman, formerly Duchess of Manchester and Countess of Kintore, died 15 December 1971 at the age of ninety-five at Keith Hall in Inverurie, Scotland, at the seat of the earls of Kintore.

> "It was a period when many of the daughters of America elected to marry and identify their lives with Europeans and notably Englishmen ... This period of social intercourse, this period of international relation is not likely to recur because Europe and its traditions no longer appeal with the same force and vigour to the American feminine mind as they did in the closing years of the Victorian era."
>
> – 9th Duke of Marlborough (who, like his father, married an American heiress)

> "And of course I can't put in a book what a beast Marlborough was."
>
> – Consuelo Balsan, formerly Duchess of Marlborough (speaking to Louis Auchincloss about writing her memoirs)

> "But the lowest note of infamy is reached by such a creature as this Marlborough, who proposing to divorce the woman when he at least cannot afford to throw any stone at her, nevertheless proposes to keep and live on the money she brought him, come my dear Sir ... surely you don't object to my considering the Duke of Marlborough a cad!"
>
> – U. S. President Theodore Roosevelt, writing to Whitelaw Reid, ambassador to the Court of St. James, on 27 November 1906.

INDEX

PHOTO ACKNOWLEDGEMENTS:

Sotheby's Picture Library – cover (Nancy Stewart, Princess Anastasia of Greece, painted by Boldini)

Library of Congress Prints & Photographs Division – 12 left, 14, 21, 22, 33, 44, 48, 50, 55, 58 left, 60, 61, 64, 69 right, 71, 74, 80, 82, 85 right, 87, 88, 100, 101, 103, 109, 113, 114, 115, 117, 118 top, 125, 137, 142, 146, 149, 156, 162, 164, 165, 167 left, 169, 171, 173, 179 left, 185, 188, 189, 190, 191, 194, 195, 202, 203, 208, 212, 213, 215, 216 left, 217, 220, 222 right, 226, 229 right, 231, 232, 233, 234, 238 right, 240, 242, 244 left, 250, 252, 254 left, 258, 259, 261, 262, 267, 268 right, 274 left, 281, 282, 283, 287, 290, 291, 294, 296, 300 bottom, 302 right, 307, 308, 310 right, 313, 315, 316

Helen Kirby - 15

Pierre-Frédérick, Duc d'Arenberg – 24

Barbara Calcagni Sallier de la Tour – 27

Cecil Stoughton/The John F. Kennedy Presidential Library and Museum, Boston – 28

The John F. Kennedy Presidential Library and Museum, Boston - 29

Courtesy of Cecil Beaton Studio Archive, Sotheby's – 30 left

Nina Auchincloss Straight – 30 top

Utah State Historical Society – 31

The Sterling and Francine Clark Art Institute, Williamstown, MA, USA – 37

Hugo Vickers – 38, 67, 167 right, 292

Harry Ransom Humanities Research Center, University of Texas at Austin – 41 top

Schuyler Chapin – 41 bottom

Duchess de Doudeauville – 42, 43

Tim Bauer - 47, 49

Princess Tatiana Belosselsky (Mrs. Adolfo Bezamat) – 53 top left, 300 top

Courtesy of Jekyll Island Museum – 53 top right

Dalmas, Marquis de Polignac – 57, 58 right

Duchess of Anjou and Segovia – 59

John Keffer – 63

Prince Boncompagni-Ludovisi – 69 left, 277

Mt. Washington Hotel – 76

Mrs. John G. W. Husted – 84

Office of Her Majesty Queen Noor – 91, 92

Alan Light – 98 top

The late Marquis d'Amodio, C.B.E. – 102

Andrew Alpern – 127

Darius Soudi – 131, 132

Princess Marie-Louise de Croy (Mrs. Frederick B. Adams) – 139, 140, 141

Princess von Isenburg – 143

Princess Anita Lobkowicz (Countess Charles de Cossé Brissac) – 145

Mrs. James A. de Peyster – 152

Count Bernadotte af Wisborg – 153

V&A Images/Victoria and Albert Museum – 159

Julia Mullock Lee – 172

Uniontown Public Library, Uniontown, PA – 180

Duke of Pozzo di Borgo – 182

Prince Sapieha-Kodenski – 186

Prince zu Lynar - 192

The Metropolitan Museum of Art, Purchase, Dodge Fund and funds from various donors, 2000 (2000.359); Photograph © The Metropolitan Museum of Art – 193

Erin Gafill – 206

Prince Serge Troubetskoy – 216 right

Barbara Hatch Spillman – 221, 222 left

Marquis de Galliffet – 224

Simon Wheaton-Smith – 228, 229 left

Countess Pilar de la Béraudière – 239

Dalvay by the Sea – 251

The late Nancy Leeds Wynkoop – 263

National Portrait Gallery, London – 264

Prince Carlo Cito Filomarino – 270

Heinrich IV, Prince Reuss – 274

Constantine Sidamon-Eristoff – 276

Madame Yevonde Archives - 298

Princess Flamina Odescalchi Kelly - 301

All other photographs from the author's collection or in the public domain.

The author wishes to express his sincere appreciation to the many family members and friends who provided photographs and information, some of whom desire to remain anonymous. In particular, he acknowledges the generosity of H.R.H. Prince Michael of Greece as well as the kindness and vital contributions of Hugo Vickers to whom he owes deepest gratitude.